Motivate Your Writing!

Motivate Your Writing!

STEPHEN P. KELNER Jr.

University Press of New England

HANOVER AND LONDON

Published by University Press of New England,
One Court Street, Lebanon, NH 03766

www.upne.com

PRINTED IN THE UNITED STATES OF AMERICA

5 4 3 2 1

LIBRARY OF CONGRESS CATALOGING-IN-PUBLICATION DATA

Kelner, Stephen P.
Motivate your writing! / Stephen P. Kelner, Jr.
    p.   cm.
Includes bibliographical references.
ISBN 1–58465–442–2 (cloth : alk. paper) — ISBN 1–58465–453–8 (pbk. : alk. paper)
1. Authorship. 2. Authorship—Psychological aspects I. Title.
PN147.K422 2005
808'.02 — dc22   2004028661

TO DAVID C. MCCLELLAND, WHO GOT ME STARTED,

AND

TONI L. P. KELNER, WHO GOT ME TO FINISH

CONTENTS

ACKNOWLEDGMENTS

A heck of a lot of people helped make this book possible. Though thanking everyone is well-nigh impossible to accomplish properly, I can but try.

First, I must thank my many contributors, who gave generously of their time, their thoughts, and their motives: Sarah Smith (with a special thank-you for past criticism rendered), Susan Oleksiw (a big editorial thank-you), as well as Marilyn Campbell, Carol Soret Cope, Phil Craig, Tony Fennelly, James Neal Harvey, Alexander Jablakow, Ellen Kushner, Margaret Press, Delia Sherman, David Alexander Smith, Patricia Sprinkle, Elizabeth Daniels Squire, Les Standiford, Kelly Tate . . . Go on out and buy their books. You'll find them (and a few of their myriad titles) described throughout these chapters. Indirectly, I thank *Writer's Digest* for their numerous articles quoting writers and how they do things, and Jon Winokur for his excellent little tome *Writers on Writing*.

Next, I must thank Professor David C. McClelland, my late mentor, who introduced me to the wonders of motivational psychology and guided me to a Ph.D. while never for a moment defining my direction for me. I took on a monstrous dissertation, and he let me, and I am the better for it. I refer to Nietzsche's famous words "That which does not kill me makes me stronger": McClelland pointed me toward my first career as well as encouraging me in my second and third careers.

My friends have offered support, readings, and occasional smart remarks: special thanks to Mike Luce, Dan Schaeffer, and Libby Shaw.

No acknowledgment would be complete without mentioning my family, who supported me directly and indirectly: my siblings, Bill, D'Arcy, Kathe, and Tamsin; my father, who taught me to enjoy craftsmanship; and my mother, who taught me to read before I was two and who instilled in me a genuine love of the written word. I have never suffered from "the watcher" to any significant degree, and I have her to thank for that.

A nod goes to my reputed ancestor Valerius Maximus, who assembled a book of quotations for writers and orators in A.D. 30 . Unknowingly I continued a family tradition!

Last and always, I must thank my wife, Toni L. P. Kelner: my best friend, favorite companion, lover, writer, critic, wit, and raconteur. She was the one who told me I had to write this book. Fair's fair. I helped her write hers.

INTRODUCTION Motivation and Writing— So What?

I can't understand why a person will take a year to write a novel when he can easily buy one for a few dollars.
FRED ALLEN, *Fred Allen His Life and Wit*

I am convinced that all writers are optimists whether they concede the point or not ... How otherwise could any human being sit down to a pile of blank sheets and decide to write, say two hundred thousand words on a given theme?
THOMAS COSTAIN, *Writers on Writing*

I write because I like to write.
PADDY CHAYEFSKY, *Writers Digest*

How often have you thought that you could write a book, if you could only make yourself do it? There are many stories to tell in this world, and with enough work you can tell them. And yet, you may have a fine prose style, a command of the language, and interesting stories, but you simply cannot begin writing. Or worse, if you do get started, you cannot finish. How do the professionals manage the mysterious writing process?

"A writer writes," says Harlan Ellison, who should know: he's won awards for speculative fiction, fantasy, mysteries, essays, and screenplays. He holds that there is no "secret" to writing, no mystery. He has written stories while sitting in storefronts to demystify and demythologize the process of writing. He writes daily in various genres and continues to win awards for it. He is also far from the first person to make that statement; Epictetus said, "If you wish to be a writer, write," around the year 110.

Isaac Asimov said he never set time aside to write without interruption, because he never had a choice; when he began to write seriously, he was working in his family's candy store. His family needed him to work, so he worked and wrote wherever he was. He wrote in crowded rooms and at the counter of the store, simply ignoring distractions. He had no privacy, so he wrote without it, and despite constant interruption. Almost five hundred books later, he showed no sign of stopping: "The one absolute requirement for me to write . . . is to be awake." He wrote the last installment of his autobiography in longhand on his deathbed.

So what of the rest of us, those who would like to write just one book, or story, or whatever? These people who can write in a store window or with constant interruption—they've got to be obsessive, right? They're the kind of people who wouldn't stop if they could. They are different, right? Abnormally gifted?

Yes and no, in that order. They are obsessed, in a sense, but they do not differ dramatically from anyone else, at least not where the ability to keep writing is concerned. Apart from practice, training, and checks from editors, the only difference between these people and you is that they feel *motivated to write*. Interruptions don't stop them, because their drive to write charges them up to retain their single focus, and they do not get distracted from the work at hand.

Being motivated means that on a deep emotional level you want something, enjoy doing it, and become frustrated if kept away from it. When you want to do something that strongly, you do it!

If you have enough interest in writing to read this, I would guess you have at least as much interest in reading. (If not, go right out and get a good book. There's lots of them.) If you have a real page-turner in your hand, how do you react when you have to stop reading? Violently? Do you think of the book all day, return to it anytime you can, and stay up late to finish it? That is a simple case of motivation in action: the emotional drive to continue. You can apply it to writing as well as to reading, and indeed to anything in life.

You can find a lot of material on motivation these days, from "subliminal tapes" to full-blown courses to sober tomes, most of it put together by earnest people who think they have the "One Sure Way to Success" (or con artists who shamelessly take your money, of course). This is not such a book. I will state with great confidence (though less earnestness, I hope) that there are many ways to achieve success in writing. This book will help you to define your personal pattern of motives, show you how your writing relates to it, identify your potential obstacles and sources of assistance, and, finally, enable you to adjust your writing to fit that pattern. In other words, you will identify what turns you on and explore how to use it. That allows your natural motivation to support your writing. The source of this knowledge is not my personal experience or a pet theory but the field of motivational psychology. This particular brand of psychology dates back to the 1930s, so it isn't a new idea. Research has continued steadily since that time, so we now have quite a body of knowledge.

I'm also tapping research done over the decades on creativity, the writing process, goal setting, obstacles, and other issues that can help or hinder your ability to write.

This scientific research on motivation has been applied to management, salesmanship, entrepreneurship, teaching, leadership, and other jobs quite successfully. This book discusses the scientific research from the writer's perspective and offers some practical suggestions for determining how you can apply these decades of research to writing your book (or short story, or essay, or whatever).

And just in case the idea of psycho-babble gives you the pip, let me reassure you. The research is no good if you can't understand it, so we'll take a look at some real people facing the problems of professional writing. I'll describe how real-life writers write, based on actual examples, and I'll also use a lot of quotations. Some have written or spoken about their craft in the past; some were interviewed and studied directly by me. They're good writers, and I'll rely on them to make some of my points for me.

But before we get going, I have two caveats:

Caveat #1: There is no easy approach (but you can do it).

Some people start with advantages; writing comes easier for some than for others. No matter what your natural gifts are, you must expend effort—perhaps an extensive effort. While I firmly believe that virtually anyone can write at some length if they really want to and that most people can even enjoy writing, the effort required may be more than you want to spend. This is not a "you can become a writer overnight" book. I don't believe you can become a writer overnight. On the other hand, don't expect boot camp or sweating blood in this book, either. (Though Red Smith said: "There's nothing to writing. All you do is sit down at a typewriter and open a vein.") Finally, don't expect to read a chapter of this book and write twenty thousand words (sixty printed pages) a day. Though if you do, please let me know so I can quote you on the cover of the next edition!

Caveat #2: Motivated writing does not equal good or salable writing.

Having motivation will enable you to write, but not necessarily to write competently. I make no judgments nor guarantees regarding your writing ability. I can only offer this: the more you practice, the better you will get—eventually.

Fantasist Ray Bradbury thought you should write a million words and then throw them out, because the first million are for practice. You might want to consider that a worst-case scenario. Please note that Bradbury also *sold* a good deal of his first million words. He wasn't being a snob; he based his statement on his own first million words, most of which he thought were pretty bad. He isn't alone in this thinking. He also knew that good writing and salable writing do not always overlap. There are good books that do not sell, and books that sell but are not good. The intent here is to get you to a point where you can get better and get sold, neither of which are possible if you don't write at all!

As Richard Bach put it: "A professional writer is an amateur who didn't quit." Lots of people write books on how to write well; I won't bother to share my opinions on the subject. Ask the experts. This book is about writing itself—motivating yourself to write, and finding ways to keep yourself writing.

So let's get on with it!

PART I: MOTIVATION
WHY PEOPLE DO WHAT THEY DO

"If you knew you would be poor as a church mouse all your life—if you knew you'd never have a line published—would you still go on writing—would you?" "Of course I would," said Emily disdainfully. *"Why, I have to write—I can't help it at times—I've just got to."*

LUCY MAUD MONTGOMERY, *Emily of New Moon*

Any writer is inevitably going to work with his own anxieties and desires. If the book is any good, it has got to have in it the fire of a personal unconscious mind.

IRIS MURDOCH, *Writers on Writing*

1 What is Motivation?

We are going to use a particular definition of "motivation" in this book, and it differs from the one in the dictionary. When we talk about "motives" here, we describe a very specific concept, developed through psychological research on tens of thousands of healthy, productive people. As a working definition, try this on for size:

> A motive is a recurrent concern for a general goal of which one
> may not be consciously aware; this concern drives, directs, orients,
> and energizes behavior, and can be seen in fantasy.
>
> DAVID McCLELLAND, *Human Motivation*

Let's turn this into English. A motive sits in the back of your head (metaphorically, not literally—let's not get into psychobiology here) and influences you. It isn't as specific as "I want to make money" or "I want to get published." It is something more general, such as "I find enjoyment in doing better" or "I feel emotion around being liked."

People show an infinite range of behaviors, so it may sound ludicrous when I say that only three motives can explain about 80 percent of human behavior overall. Nevertheless, it is true that for most people, a few basic drives explain most of their thinking and actions. That doesn't mean that people are simple, or psychology would be a lot easier to study. Furthermore, your actual behaviors and actions are not just based on these unconscious motives. They come out of what you value, what you have been taught, what you can do well, other characteristics of you as a person, and what is going on outside you.

For example, you may have a strong need to impress people. (This is known as the *influence* or *power motive,* and it will be discussed in more detail later.) Some can satisfy this need by public speaking—as a politician, or as an actor. But if you stutter, you are unlikely to want the opportunity to stutter in front of an audience. In fact, you may be highly motivated *not* to do so, since you might have a negative impact on an audience if you tripped over a word. Making a bad impression arouses strong emotion in you—fear, anger, whatever. This emotion pushes you away from public speaking. Instead, you may take up writing, hoping to impress people with your written words.

On the other hand, you may decide that you will not let stuttering get in the way of impressing an audience, because you value public speaking ability. Then your emotions (strongly wanting to be able to influence others through speaking) push you toward working to overcome this obstacle. Power motive drives the key actions in both of these cases, but in different directions. That's why we say that motives predict behaviors, not the other way around. Many behaviors can flow from the same motives.

However, motives may not predict consistent behaviors in the same person, let alone across people. Researchers have found that motives predict *patterns* of behavior, not specific decisions. That is why we talk about the general "concern for impact," which can be fulfilled by public speaking *and/or* wearing dramatic colors *and/or* coaching people *and/or* driving flashy cars *and/or* creative writing, etc. All of these things involve having an impact on people, in different ways. The exact behaviors you prefer come out of the unique person you are. So don't worry that psychologists can read your mind. They can't even read their own minds.

"...a recurrent concern..."

A motive is a *recurrent* concern because it does not go away. When your mind drifts, you are likely to fall into a pattern that is consistent with your motives. In other words, you think about what you like thinking about. (Think about it.) This does not apply at every moment of every day, but it applies frequently enough to constitute an ongoing trend for you. When you make a choice from equally important options, you are more likely to pick one that fits with your motives. When you enter a new situation, you are likely to see it in terms of your motives. In other words, when all else is equal, you go with your gut: what feels right.

If I examined all of your decisions over a year, I would probably find them tilting toward your strongest motive, because you would tend to go with that when you have a chance. For example, imagine yourself at the office. You can spend time crunching numbers, or you can go around and talk to people. You may wind up doing both every day, but which one do you do first? Which one do you stretch out, and which one do you postpone? The pattern of these things indicates your motives.

"...not be consciously aware..."

Because the motives are deeply buried, you may not consciously know yours; you just know that some things feel more enjoyable than others. Motives are essentially emotional in nature and (we psychologists think) come from older parts of the brain than your frontal lobes.* You probably would not put together the pattern of your motives from many individual enjoyable actions without concentrated and lengthy thought and self-analysis.

No, I'm not recommending years of expensive therapy (unless you feel you need it, of course). For our purposes, it is possible to identify at least some of your own motives with a little hard work and objectivity, using a few tried-and-true techniques. These techniques derive from another part of the definition above: motives can be seen in fantasy. But, you may ask, why should we care? Because motives influence your behavior.

"... drives, directs, orients, and energizes behavior ..."

People do what they want to do. That is the reason to look at motives. A motive is where you find excitement or pleasure. Therefore a motive will tend to *drive* behavior toward your motivated goal. It tends to *direct* your choices; if all else is equal, you do what you like. It *orients* a person toward possibilities; that is, you are more alert to signals that relate to something you like. Finally, it *energizes* you to go after something that emotionally satisfies you.

Motivated behavior is energized behavior: the kind of thing you leap toward rather than shy away from. Sustainable behavior, the kind of thing you want to do over and over again for years to come, arises primarily from motives. Pushing your motive button activates a source of renewable energy you can tap into again and again.

"... can be seen in fantasy."

Motivated subjects are fun to think about, so people's thoughts tend to drift their way. Daydreams, cherished dreams, and passing whims are likely to emerge from your motives. The method used most to tease out motives relies on this fact. You can try it out for yourself using materials included here.

Since the actions that satisfy motives feel so enjoyable, they are rewarding in and of themselves. Why do people work for hours, days, or weeks building a backyard deck or acting in local theater or writing? Not because someone pays them (well, not *just* because someone pays them) but because they enjoy it. If you *enjoy* it, you are more likely to do it.

That is the key to this book. First, to understand your own pattern of motives and what they mean; then to find ways to make the process of writing rewarding to you based on that information; finally to set up your environment and yourself to enable writing that feels rewarding. Other people suggest building regular habits to try to train yourself to write. That practice can help, but I sug-

---

* Some links have been identified to key neurotransmitters (norepinephrine, epinephrine, dopamine) that are largely controlled by the limbic system. You don't need to know this to take advantage of them, however.

gest that you focus on building enjoyment directly into the process of writing. Again, if the process becomes rewarding, you will be more likely to do it. Indeed, you may even *make* time to do it. Writers have sometimes referred to their vocation as an addiction—for good reason. Tennessee Williams said, "When I stop, the rest of the day is posthumous. I'm only really alive when I'm working." If writing is that rewarding all by itself, with no external reinforcement, what can stop you?

One more story of a highly motivated writer: Jane Austen, renowned for her lengthy and subtle novels of manners, was an extremely busy member of a Victorian household. She was never alone, and virtually never without work to do—even assuming that people at the time encouraged women to write professionally, which they certainly did not. She set a blank book on a sideboard, and every time she walked by, she wrote a few words. A phrase, perhaps a sentence, and no more. Every one of her books was written that way, a few words at a time.

Remember: If you are like most people, you don't have to be that motivated to write. Furthermore, you can motivate yourself despite obstacles.

One caution, however: I am not talking about magically inserting motivation that does not exist, I am talking about tapping that which you already have—and you certainly do have motives. The issue is to arouse motivation. Everyone has motivation, to different degrees, and in different forms.

A word on this subject from George Carlin: "What's all this stuff about motivation? I say, if you need motivation, you probably need more than motivation. You probably need chemical intervention or brain surgery. Actually, if you ask me, this country could do with a little *less* motivation. The people who are causing all the trouble seem highly motivated to me" (from *Brain Droppings*).

Just assume that you have the motivation—all you need is to aim it properly.

EXTRINSIC MOTIVATION

Sir, no man but a blockhead ever wrote except for money.
SAMUEL JOHNSON, *The Life of Samuel Johnson*

There are no retired writers. There are writers who have stopped selling . . . but they have not stopped writing.
WILLIAM A. P. WHITE ("ANTHONY BOUCHER"),
quoted by Heinlein in *Expanded Universe*

Motivation can be divided into two basic types: *intrinsic* motivation, the kind mostly discussed in this book, which includes both values and motives, and *extrinsic* motivation, the kind mostly discussed in this section. Extrinsic motivation comes from outside yourself; the most obvious kind is money. "Once I get paid for it," thinks the hopeful writer, "I will write all day long."

In fact, extrinsic motivation does not enable sustained effort. With rare exceptions, outside motivators end—and when they do, the motivation disappears too. The prop is gone. You can ruin perfectly good motivation that way. So take this as a warning now: you cannot depend solely upon external rewards to motivate your writing. (Of course, new writers don't have a choice in the matter!)

In one experiment comparing these two kinds of motivation, psychological researchers took people and asked them to work out puzzles, but they did not mention monetary rewards. They found that if you rewarded people monetarily afterward for something they thought they were doing only for fun (i.e., out of intrinsic, unconscious motives), they would lose interest or even reject the money! The characteristics of the task had changed. As gonzo journalist Hunter S. Thompson said in *The Great Shark Hunt*, "I've always considered writing the most hateful kind of work. Old whores don't do much giggling." His next sentence is telling: "Nothing is fun when you *have to do it*—over & over, again & again—or else you'll be evicted, and that gets old" (emphasis his). However, he made this statement in the middle of an essay describing a writing project he did enjoy, which he wrote on the side while covering a "very heavy" journalistic assignment that could have gotten him killed. The daily work was difficult, but the optional work was fun. But note that both were forms of writing! One he hated and procrastinated on; the other he loved, and he would work on it spontaneously at night, despite heavy demands in his daily life.

Remember: Don't rely on motivation outside yourself.
You cannot depend solely on external rewards
to motivate your writing.

Don't get me wrong. I do not recommend that you reject monetary recompense. Quite the contrary! How else can you keep time available for writing instead of "honest work?" I do recommend that you master the art of tapping your intrinsic motivation and try to keep that as your reason for writing, especially if you do not intend to live from the earnings of your publications right away. Money is the icing on the cake, not the cake itself. Therefore, I disagree with the learned Dr. Johnson. Robert Heinlein (the target of White's comment above) believed *consciously* that he wrote only to make a living, and when he made enough money to get by he would stop. He found that he was wrong.

When you have the intrinsic motive well established, as did Anthony

Boucher and Robert Heinlein, you will write. Selling what you write is a different issue.

As author William Wharton put it in *Writer's Digest*: "Don't write with sales or money in mind—it poisons the well at its source. If writing isn't a joy, don't do it. Life is short, death is long." Motivation from within goes with you wherever you go, while motivation from outside goes away from you. Of course, some people do write for survival, but not all writers, and it is not common enough for you to rely on being able to do it yourself. Science fiction writer Theodore Sturgeon had a desperate need to support himself and his family, but it did not break his writer's block. He had every extrinsic reason to keep writing but could not do so.

Even for those who say they write only as a job, why then did they select writing for that job? On some level, I am willing to bet that most of them like it, or at least feel addicted to it. It doesn't pay enough to be worth forcing yourself to do it. Stephen King has said that he would write even if they didn't pay him for it—which is not to say that he doesn't expect pay for his books now, just that he loves writing too much to stop just because they aren't paying him. In fact, when he announced his retirement from publishing (not writing), he said in a number of interviews that he fully intended to keep writing, because what else would he do between nine in the morning and four in the afternoon?

I'm going to be brutally honest here. As of this writing, the average advance for a first novel is $5,000 to $10,000. It does not matter whether you took a month to write your novel, or a year, or ten years; you are lucky to get more than that. That amount has not changed significantly in thirty years, as far as I can tell. Worse yet, the "midlist" of writers who can make a small or marginal living from writing have largely disappeared, at least in the United States. Only the rich and the poor remain. The former get the lion's share of promotion, support, advertisement, and movie deals; the latter get to pay their own way to conferences, call bookstores themselves, and hope that someone, anyone, comes to their signings. Stephen King can make millions, but take a look at how many books languish on bookstore shelves.

A typical successful novelist (and you better believe King is not typical) has written numerous novels, each of which stays in print for a limited time, contributes royalties for a while, and may come back into print again.

Even so, few novelists have a large enough audience, even with a lot of books in print, to sustain a career on writing income alone. Most people who make a regular living from writing do not write fiction; they are journalists who write for newspapers or magazines, technical writers who receive a salary for creating reference books, nonfiction writers who write texts, or very active self-marketers who sell stories to any market they can find, taking a single article and tinkering with it to suit a variety of markets, each time with a unique twist. This is not living in luxury. The brutal truth is that you cannot rely on extrinsic reinforcement because most writers simply don't get enough of it.

THE MOTIVES

*I write in order to attain that feeling of tension relieved and
function achieved which a cow enjoys on giving milk.*
H. L. MENCKEN, A Second Mencken Chrestomathy

As I noted above, there are three basic social motives that influence a large part of the behaviors we show. As with motivation itself, don't take the names too literally. Decades of psychological research and documentation have made their names official, but they are not necessarily the same as your own (or Mr. Webster's) definition. All are referred to as "needs," or, to avoid sounding needy, "motives." Everyone has all three, but typically not to the same degree. For educational purposes I might refer to those people who are relatively strong in one or another as they only have one motive, but all I'm doing is simplifying for clarity. In other words, there are no "achievement people" or "power people," there are only people with one motive that is relatively strong compared with their other motives.

The first (alphabetically) is the *Achievement motive*, or the *need for achievement*. People with a relatively strong or dominant Achievement motive get excitement and satisfaction out of doing better. This motive includes the desires for efficiency, improvement, meeting and bettering goals, and innovation, though a given person might not manifest all of the above. It sounds well suited for a writer sitting alone tapping keys, trying to meet internally set standards, but we shall see.

The second is the *Affiliation Motive*, or the *need for affiliation*. This is a concern for relationships: people with a relatively strong presence of this motive either strongly desire to be personally liked or have a concern for people in general, both positively (liking to do things for people) and negatively (cynically assuming that relationships never work out). This motive includes an enjoyment of social situations for their own sake, action to improve or establish a relationship, and anxiety about the disruption of a relationship. It suits the writing of certain kinds of stories and perhaps the other nonwriting tasks a writer must sometimes undertake (such as cocktail parties and dealing with fans).

The third is the *Power motive*, or the *need for power*. This motive is often seen (especially by English-speaking people) as negative or sinister, but in fact it is just a concern for having an impact on others. People with this motive particularly strong get excitement out of seeing others respond or change based on their influence. The Power Motive can help a writer understand how to write to an audience. Those high in this motive are not out to conquer the world but to impress it, influence it, or make a mark on it. It has nothing to do with morality but a lot to do with writing for others. If you prefer, call it the Influence Motive—a more accurate name.

These three motives define different patterns of life: meeting internal standards on your own, socializing with people in a friendly manner, and leaving a mark on people or the world at large. You may have any or all of these motives in profusion, but most people have one that is dominant enough that your *first* or *most common* thought is likely to match it. If you understand your motives, you can play to them, so to speak.

Motives act both as self-replenishing energy sources and enhancements for your perceptions. As Mencken noted above, a motive can drive you either to relieve built-up emotional tension or to meet goals ("function achieved," as he put it). Possessing a given motive to a significant degree will sensitize you to particular kinds of information, which in turn arouse energy: you look for what you like, and when you find it you get psyched. Past studies have shown that people high in Affiliation Motive, for example, are better at interpreting facial expressions than others and as a result are more alert to people's feelings about them. If you show people with high Affiliation Motive photographs of pairs of people, some of whom are romantically involved and some of whom are not, they will tend to correctly identify those in a relationship.

Those high in the need for power are adept at identifying (and often using) hierarchies, power structures, and influence opportunities, even those that are not explicit. If you show people with high Power Motive photographs of pairs of people, some of whom are boss and employee and some of whom are just random, the power people will be able to identify the boss-employee pairs fairly accurately.

The strongly achievement-motivated person looks to maximize efficiency or productivity by balancing moderate risk against moderate benefit. They are adept at assessing risks and find it natural to adjust their aim accordingly. They also try to improve their performance over time and tend to be constantly dissatisfied with it.

We know there are many more motives, but few of them make a major difference in daily life, and certainly not to writing. These three will act as our lens through which we observe writing.

2 Identifying Your Own Motives

The character of a man is known from his conversations.
MENANDER, *The Plays and Fragments*

*It is with trifles and when he is off guard that a man best
reveals his character.*
ARTHUR SCHOPENHAUER, *Counsels and Maxims*

In this chapter I introduce the themes in motivated thought. In other words, what do people strong in a given motive tend to think about? You can use these themes to think about what *you* think about, including why you do what you do. In the appendices you will find more formal exercises to identify motives that also rely on these themes, but if you are able to see these patterns of thoughts in many situations—your daydreams, writing, preferences—you will go a long way toward achieving an awareness of your motive pattern. These sets of "imagery," as they are called, describe the exact thoughts found in people relatively strong in a given motive. The next few chapters will look at how individual motives can manifest themselves in a given writer. Then we will spend some time delving into yours!

MOTIVE IMAGERY

To use this principle, you need practice in the technique of *content analysis*, also known as *thematic analysis*. One of the advantages of being adept at this technique is that it applies to many part of a writer's life, or indeed anyone's life. It is possible to code for motives in movies, books, speeches, even casual conversation. With somewhat more advanced knowledge you can even measure doodles.

The specific thoughts attached to the three main motives are listed below.

The Need for Achievement

The criteria for scoring the need for achievement derive from a *concern for excellence* or doing *better*. This priority can emerge in any of several ways:

- outperforming someone else who represents a standard of excellence;
- meeting or surpassing a self-imposed standard of excellence;
- accomplishing something new, unique, or innovative;
- long-term career planning.

The Need for Affiliation

The basic criteria for the need for affiliation have to do with a *concern around relationships*. That concern manifests, however, in three ways:

- **Positive.** Includes taking actions on another's behalf with no thought of recompense other than improving the relationship; feeling part of a greater whole (he was proud to be an American); and enjoying relationships.
- **Cynical.** Includes stories about hypocrisy (presenting yourself as better than you are); deception in a supposedly affiliative relationship (he was cheating on his wife).
- **Anxious.** Includes discussions of an interpersonal relationship; flow experience; negative reaction to separation.

The Need for Power

The criteria for scoring the need for power derive from a *concern for impact or influence on others*. There are, again, several ways in which this can emerge:

- Taking strong, powerful actions:
  - forceful actions that affect others;
  - unsolicited help, advice, or support;
  - attempts at controlling another through regulation of behavior or conditions of life, or through seeking information that would affect others;
  - attempts at influencing, persuading, or making a point with others for the purpose of convincing others to comply rather than to compromise;
  - attempts at impressing another or the world at large.
- Doing something that arouses strong positive or negative emotions in others.
- Concern with reputation or position, or with what others think of one's influence.

PRACTICE SCORING FOR MOTIVE IMAGERY

Below are three stories, each of which can be scored for one motive. See if you can decide which is scored for which. Answers follow.

1 The two young lovers sighed as they talked and walked together. They really enjoyed each others' company and hated the idea of parting this evening and going to their separate homes.
2 The two young lawyers laughed as they contemplated the surprise they were going to spring on the opposition lawyer the next day. They had a plan to get to the jury in a way that would knock him right off his feet.
3 The two young inventors grinned as they studied the plans. This might actually work! They had a shot at creating the first device of its kind, something that no one else had been able to do.

ANSWERS

1 Affiliation: The "lovers" "enjoying each others' company" "hated the idea of parting."
2 Power: "the surprise they were going to spring," "the opposition," "get to the jury," "knock him right off his feet."
3 Achievement: "inventors" "creating the first device of its kind," "something that no one else had been able to do."

The next few chapters contain depictions of writers with a single primary motive. You may see yourself in these depictions; you may have seen yourself already. You may also be inaccurate. Remember that these motives are unconscious, whereas your professed self-image is largely consciously created and strongly affected by the expectations of the world around you. Elsewhere in this book, you will find a method by which you can determine your own motives with a fair degree of accuracy. It will not be quite as precise as using formal motive assessment methods, but you can "reality check" your motives based on your actions and preferences as well.

As you read, try to assess how much each type resembles you. Do not be alarmed if more than one type seems to fit; you may just score high on more than one motive. Combinations of motives will be discussed later, and after that, what my research has found to be the typical motive profile of published writers. It helps to know what is available before focusing on one.

Remember that motives are *not* conscious. If you want to assess yourself accurately—a challenging job indeed without assistance—you have to distinguish between what you think is important and what you enjoy regardless of need. When you find yourself doing something you know you don't need to do and you don't know why, you may well be following a motive. (And yes, before you ask, Henry Murray identified the need for sex on his list of fifty motives. Don't look for it here.)

Here's what you can expect to see in the following sections on the three most important motives:

1 a detailed description of the motive in question;
2 the characteristics of effective feedback* for someone with that motive;
3 concrete suggestions to help those with this motive write more;
4 means of dealing with writer's block from the perspective of that motive.

---

* Throughout I refer to the word "feedback." Once limited to engineering and electronics, this word has entered the common domain as a description of performance information returned (fed back) to a person. Motives being energizing cycles, as it were, you can think of feedback as adding energy to the loop. One way to engage your motives is to feed the motive's specific desires—frequently.

3 The Achievement-Motivated Writer

As a rule reading fiction is as hard to me as trying to hit a tar-get by hurling feathers at it. I need resistance to cerebrate!
WILLIAM JAMES, Letters

If I could I would always work in silence and obscurity, and let my efforts be known by their results.
EMILY BRONTË, The Life of Charlotte Brontë

The writer must always find expression for something which has never yet been expressed, must master a new set of phe-nomena which has never yet been mastered.
EDMUND WILSON, "The Historical Interpretation of Literature"

Achievement-motivated people work alone happily. They reach for standards that may be known only to themselves, which they must meet or exceed. They enjoy coming up with new ways of doing things, and may spend some time considering the most efficient process to get the job done.

These people also need frequent feedback, to keep track of their progress toward their goals. Unfortunately, the nature of the writing business means that outside feedback is often not forthcoming. Even very successful writers may not be able to thrive on feedback that arrives weeks or months after the story was written. An occasional check is also not sufficient as feedback for daily writing.

What is appropriate feedback? It varies, but in general this kind of person will want frequent responses that are closely linked to the process that is being assessed. The person with a high need for Achievement wants to reach a goal but also wants to know how well he or she is doing along the way. Feedback—preferably positive and negative, in balance—provides a way to measure the progress toward a goal. If the feedback becomes more negativistic, then you must work a little harder; if the feedback leans toward the positive, then there is satisfaction from knowing that you are achieving your goal.

However, unrelentingly positive feedback arouses distrust in achievement-oriented people, or it deprives them of a sense of challenge. They are not engaged by easy tasks. If the feedback is unrelentingly negative, the challenge may appear too great, discouraging the effort. The achievement-motivated person thrives on the balance point: the moderate risk, the good chance of payoff that nonetheless takes some work.

William James's quote above refers to that sense of challenge—"resistance" is his word—which is needed to "cerebrate." It is interesting to note, in the light of James's quotation, that the achievement person frequently reads nonfiction, such as how-to books, or mysteries rather than other forms of fiction. That challenge must come one way or another—and the degree of challenge is not stable, either. Robert A. Heinlein wrote that he had to produce more and more words to get "that warm feeling" that writing provided him—eventually up to 250,000 words, which is nearly four short novels' worth. As he mastered longer and longer novels, he had to work harder to make the writing process difficult enough to be interesting to him.

Some achievement-motivated people reading this may have helpful spouses or friends around to give frequent, useful and detailed feedback on the content or progress of their writing. Others have readers (the more common sort, in my experience) who have a vocabulary composed entirely of "good," "I dunno," and "I don't understand it."

For our purposes, I assume that you belong to those surrounded by the latter group, and that you therefore need some helpful feedback, and that you are not yet at the point in your writing career where an editor or agent can help you instead. (Please note that "performance" might be as simple as length rather than quality—I'm not assuming that you are bad.) If you are high in the need for achievement, you will need some kind of feedback on your performance or progress that will encourage you from day to day.

So your challenge is to provide that *for yourself.*

CHARACTERISTICS OF ACHIEVEMENT FEEDBACK

There are several important characteristics that define useful feedback for the achievement-motivated person—not just any feedback will do. Your feedback mechanism must be:

1 Specific and consistent
2 Measurable
3 Applicable

Specific
Useful feedback must be quite specific in nature. A general note to yourself

is not really feedback: "I worked on writing today." How? Did you jot notes? Write an outline? Write prose? Unwind on the typewriter for a while? Make journal notes? Edit? Some activities are more useful than others as a measure of accomplishment. For solid feedback, you need to specify at least one type of measurement.

Don't limit yourself to only one type if more would help, but don't try to keep track of everything, either. It can get in your way if you spend more time accounting than writing. I would recommend that you select a consistent measure, and if you find you have easy breakpoints in your writing process (e.g., notes, outline, first draft, editing) then set a different specific measure for each interval. It is silly to count "words added" if you are editing down a manuscript and removing lots of prose, because you will be getting negative results (though you can count words subtracted too!), but it could be very helpful in the first draft, where generation is more important than refinement. As long as your measures are internally consistent, they will feel more reliable. You know when you are fooling yourself: don't give yourself the opportunity. Make your goals clear.

Measurable

This relates closely to being specific, but it is independent of it: you can be very specific without having a reliable measurement. "Number of paragraphs added," for example, is very specific but varies too widely for it to be of much use to people. The paragraphs of narration or of nonfictional exposition tend to be longer, while paragraphs of dialogue can be very short indeed. ("Oh?" "Yes.") Words, full lines, or full written pages are somewhat more reliable indicators.

Whatever you choose should be a reasonably clear, cleanly delineated ruler. A good ruler has reliable units of measure, which do not vary too much. If the divisions of your yardstick varied from half an inch to three inches apart, competent carpentry would be impossible. Make the measurement of your craft a little more precise.

Applicable

DAVID FROST: *How do you work? Do you get up early every day and write music?*

JIMI HENDRIX: *I try to get up every day.*
DAVID FROST INTERVIEW

Time spent sitting at the typewriter is a very consistent, reliable, and specific measure, but it is not terribly useful if you don't do anything there. Getting up early and writing music was not the way Jimi Hendrix worked. When keeping track of your progress, you should use an accounting to directly assess your writing or something directly related to it. It is not enough to focus on something around the writing.

An acquaintance of mine told me once that he was keeping track of the cups of coffee and cigarettes he had consumed while sitting in diners making notes for his book. After several years this person had yet to finish a chapter. You see, you can drink coffee and smoke without writing (and this person often did), so the association with writing produced simply lacked strength.

If you only drank coffee while writing (and drank at a steady pace), the "coffee ruler" might work better. Directly linking one addiction with another could get you into trouble, however; Freud found himself dependent on his cigars to think, even knowing he had developed cancer, and he had previously relied on cocaine to gain mental stimulation. Ideally, your writing productivity should not depend upon an external stimulus with negative consequences for your health. Despite the myths and legends, alcohol consumption is not obligatory to be a great writer.

The lesson here is that you must measure your writing reliably, or the feedback you get will not be helpful to you.

Concrete Suggestions

1 If you have a word processor with a word counting feature, use it every time you write. That way you can track your progress as measured by word count. If you are a "Beethovenian" writer, who edits and rewrites a great deal as you write, don't worry—just be aware that your goal may be more modest in the short term but more daring in the long term, assuming you don't edit later drafts as much. When you begin redlining a manuscript, count the number of lines of red or the approximate number of edits made or even pages marked up.

2 "Mozartian" writers, who generate highly readable first drafts fluently and who write at a fairly constant, steady speed, can time their writing. Rex Stout tracked the number of hours a day he spent writing so thoroughly that his biographer could identify exactly how much time he spent on each short story, novella, or novel. Stout would plot in his head and then move to the typewriter only when he had his story ready, so marking time there worked well for him. (I'll discuss Mozartian and Beethovian creators in more detail below.)

3 People who compose at the keyboard can keep track of their pages, or use a rough count of words, since word counts are more consistent for typewritten pages. Handwriters could use pages, an estimated word count, or even lines of script. Whatever you use, make it consistent, reliable, and really measurable. Even inches of text work fine, as long as you use a ruler to maintain accuracy. If you are a napkin-scribbler, either transfer your work to a regular sheet for measuring or figure out a way to count

napkins with some reliability. You could distinguish by size, for example, since that is fairly standardized, and then count large, medium, and small napkins filled with prose or at least verbal content. As you transfer to regular paper, you can count those sheets too. This may sound silly, but I know writers who write most of their early ideas on check stubs and receipts. If it works for you, use it.

4   If you have uninterrupted periods of time to spend writing solidly, you can count those.

5   Because productivity is also about good work, get a person to give you feedback. The new writer may find this tricky, since poor feedback can be worse than none at all. The achievement-oriented person craves feedback that will provide guidance as to the accuracy of movement toward the goal. A simple "that's good," or "I liked it" is not sufficient. Writers with an agent and/or an editor have a professional available to give feedback that may not be ideal but is at least well-informed. Whomever you may choose, make sure they have genuine interest in the work and will be both honest and balanced in their feedback. Some studies suggest that the "kiss to kick" ratio should be about four to one over time: four positive comments for each negative one. Be aware that if there is a particular issue that merits detailed discussion, this ratio isn't important. Go ahead and talk about it.

6   If you do things methodically (as many achievement-motivated people do), you can count things like "outline-points-turned-into-prose" or scene cards turned into actual scenes. Mystery writer Kelly Tate not only did that but kept two piles of scene cards: to be written, and already written. Moving cards from one pile to the other was "gratifying" to her (interview with author, 1994). Eliminating the pile (which could be four inches thick) was very satisfying indeed. I note also that the generation of scene cards enabled her to track herself in the early stages of her writing.

7   Do a combination. For jotted notes, count pages; for outlines, count major or minor categories, or both. If you want to get really sneaky, determine how many pages of outline translate into how many pages of prose for you, and multiply the pages of outline by that amount.

DEALING WITH WRITER'S BLOCK

What happens when you stall? For the achievement-motivated writer, there are ways to get the juices going. If you already have a fair amount of prose, just read it over and edit. I guarantee that the achievement-motivated writer will change *something*. Every change you make is a small step of improvement—that much closer to perfection.

I should warn you now, however—people high in this motive are rarely satisfied. The constant quest for improvement can drive you to rewrite over and over again. In a construct as complex as a book, there is no end to this kind of activity. You must exercise willpower and stop long enough to direct yourself to a different goal. As Paul Valery said: "A poem is never finished, only abandoned." (Or, as W. Arthur Rydee wrote: "A masterpiece requires two people—one to create it, and one to stand behind him with a club to hit him when it is finished.") As Washington Irving put it about his own books: "I scarcely look with full satisfaction upon any; for they do not seem what they might have been. I often wish that I could have twenty years more, to take them down from the shelf one by one, and write them over (*Writers on Writing*)."

Achievement-motivated people are always aiming at goals; as long as you have an interesting one in front of you all the time, you should be fine. Never let yourself get into a position of waiting for a response that could take months. That is obviously not useful feedback. I can suggest a number of strategies to cope with this, but the simplest is to start a new goal: begin your next book, start sending query letters to agents (assuming you don't have one) and publishers, start considering the marketing and map out places you would like to send copies. There are many possibilities around the external process of delivering your work to readers; it does not hurt to keep them in mind between writing bouts.

Some people may get so involved in the creative process alone that they never get to the point of actually selling their books. I again quote from Heinlein, whose fourth and fifth Laws of Writing proclaim: "You must put your work on the market" and "you must keep the work on the market until it is sold."

See, for example, figures 1 and 2. Where have you put your goals? Remember that they have very different results. How do you keep yourself going?

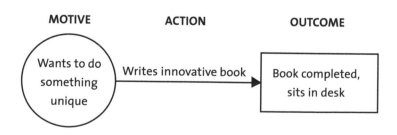

Figure 1. A way to write an unpublished book

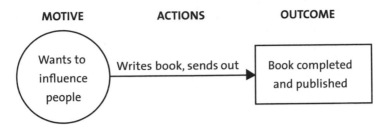

MOTIVE   **ACTIONS**   **OUTCOME**

Wants to influence people

Writes book, sends out

Book completed and published

Figure 2. A way to publish a book

Send copies to "reviewers"—family, friends, anyone who will read it. Even if they do nothing but find typos, they have contributed, and you will get some kind of feedback. While it is better to get information that improves the book in some noteworthy way, it is not absolutely essential in all cases. Simply getting content returned to you can be enough, in the sense that every "no" is that much closer to a "yes," as many sales people put it.

4 The Affiliation-Motivated Writer

When I was a ten-year-old book worm and used to kiss the dustjacket pictures of authors as if they were icons, it used to amaze me that these remote people could provoke me to love.
ERICA JONG, "The Craft of Poetry"

When I write, I aim in my mind not toward New York but toward a vague spot a little east of Kansas. I think of the books on library shelves, without their jackets, years old, and a countryish teen-aged boy finding them, and having them speak to him. The reviews, the stacks in Brentano's, are just hurdles to get over, to place the book on that shelf.
JOHN UPDIKE, Interview in *Writer's Digest*

We romantic writers are there to make people feel and not think.
BARBARA CARTLAND, *Writer's Digest*

These folks may have trouble shutting themselves into a room when there are people to see. To focus, these people need to consider how many others they can help with their book, or how much pleasure it will give them, or even how warmly they will be regarded (assuming they write books that make them appear likable).

Research has identified several types of affiliation that are concerned with relationships in different ways. Some people worry about whether others like them and work hard to become liked. They sometimes fail, because their anxiety about being liked leads them to overdo it. These people fear rejection and avoid conflict, because conflict is painful. This makes it difficult for these writers to face rejection or deal with an editor who might criticize them, so they must set up structures to carry them through the tough parts. One such structure might be a support system of people who give unconditional and unrestrained support to the act of writing, regardless of setbacks.

A well-designed writers' workshop can provide that support. These groups form to help members continue writing, and to give feedback as to their progress. (There is a section on what makes for a good workshop later.) Many workshops have associated rules or a charter, such as requiring that all members participate equally, in order to prevent abuse of the system by those who are unwilling to help critique—or by those who are unwilling to share their work but enjoy criticizing others. One group I know starts their first critique of any work with only positive feedback. In other words, the first session is always a cheering session to get past the uncertainty that plagues many people at an early stage of their work. This makes a lot of sense: some people try to write, conclude that their writing is bad, and then quit before really getting started. Their assessment may be absolutely correct at that time, but who said they cannot improve? In the first sessions of particular group, members may only say "I like this" and "I want to see more." This lays the groundwork of confidence for moving on.

The workshop—when done properly—fits the affiliation-oriented writer beautifully. By contrast, the achievement-oriented person may think at first that workshops are wonderful for the feedback opportunities, but in the long run putting up with the other people can frustrate them. All they want to do is go home and work alone, where they control the results. (Although they may find it satisfying to mark goals in terms of reading other people's work, that isn't our task here.) The primarily power-motivated person may like the idea of having an impact on all of those people but get absorbed in that (e.g., coaching others, convincing others of a point) instead of thinking about writing for an indirect or at least postponed impact of their own.

A supportive writing group can provide the uncritical friendliness these people crave (regardless of the actual assessment of the written material) and give them the security to feel comfortable trying to write. These folks will take the criticism happily as long as they feel they are liked personally by the critics— regardless of the reaction to the text. This may mean that they will not finish their writing task soon; they do not think in terms of goals like "finishing a book." They may in fact feel reluctant to finish a book associated strongly with positive, personal reinforcement.

The second type of affiliative person does not worry about people liking them; they simply enjoy doing things for people, and especially to benefit them. This sort can do things that help others without considering (or worrying about) the eventual outcome of the relationship. Satisfaction comes from a feeling of linkage to others, even in terms of just offering a benevolent action. Depending on the type of book you write, this motivation can fit well with a final endpoint of giving someone pleasure or helping them somehow. Self-help and inspirational books sometimes fall into this category.

The third type of affiliative person rejects the possibility of benevolent, mutually satisfying interaction. These people are cynical, and they may well write of rejection, deceit, and hypocrisy. However, they value others like themselves, especially the witty. The Oscar Wildes or James Thurbers of this world may exemplify this. These people can masterfully dissect the foibles of others and can be enormously entertaining, if a trifle unkind.

As is evident from my examples, I suspect that these people make fine satirists, commenting on the sad state of the world. Their motive in writing can be to make this sad state visible to others. In this they relate to power-motivated individuals as well. If they put up public lists of their goal accomplishments as feedback, rather than the number of words, they may prefer to post the number of "air strikes" against the target, keeping track of good lines that truly skewer the opponent. This somewhat nasty criterion can support satirical writing, journalism (especially the "new journalism" of Tom Wolfe, Hunter S. Thompson, and the like), and even scientific writing. There is a great satisfaction (for these people) in puncturing an inaccurate theory in public.

In any case, you should be alert to your feelings here. Delia Sherman, a fine fantasy writer, found she had a significant amount of Affiliation Motive and chose to join a writer's group that reinforced her; she found that the group helped her produce by satisfying this motive and (presumably) removing it as a concern.

CHARACTERISTICS OF AFFILIATIVE FEEDBACK

1 Friendly
2 Uncritical
3 Warm

Friendly

Affiliative feedback is essentially friendly in nature—you should feel happy with it and be confident that it is on your side. That does not mean it cannot be constructive criticism or even include negative assessments, but it does mean that it is delivered in a way that makes it clear that it was for you because you are a friend.

Uncritical

I do not mean by this that you should have no sense of improvement, but the baseline should be "I am good!" The achievement person values balanced negative and positive feedback, to assess the moderate risk that hovers between them. The affiliation-motivated person wants reassurance as to personal value. "Attaboys" or cheerleading are good, reinforcing choices for these people, who would really prefer being with somebody else to sitting in a room alone.

Warm

Emotion matters a lot to the affiliative person. If they feel warm, secure, and loved, they can produce far better than if they are insecure and lonely. Loneliness distracts many of us—for the affiliative, it may cripple their functioning. The comfortable affiliative writer can feel warm by thinking of the reading audience; early in a career I suspect it takes a more immediate presence. On the other hand, research has shown that affiliative people tend to write more letters to friends and loved ones.

Concrete Suggestions

1 Have someone in the room. This person need not be distracting but should be able to reassure you on demand. This will probably matter more in the early days; you will be able to get by without immediate affiliative feedback as your self-confidence grows. I have heard of writing workshops that actually do "writing camps," where members sit in a room together and write. "It keeps you honest," say participants. I think it keeps you happy as well.

2 Talk about your work with people. The writer's workshop can come in handy here, but not to impress people, as the power person would desire. Instead, it's an opportunity to get reassurance that *you can write*.

3 Find appropriate targets for your work. If you are aiming at a particular audience, take a sample from that audience (assuming one is available) and ask them to read your work regularly and comment on it. Hopefully most of the comments will be positive.

4 Write for a specific, real person. You need not actually send it to that person (though it helps), but write it with the same focus as a letter. Some books have actually been written that way. Tolkien, for example, wrote many stories in letters home to his sons. This allows you to think of the audience as real people you care for. The drawback of this is that you may write for their taste and not yours, but you can always rewrite—and some people find that more fun than writing new material.

5 You simply may not have this as an option, but I list it for the sake of completeness: if you have an audience demanding your work, an audience composed of intimates, the drive to write may well be enhanced. Charles L. Dodgson was just another Oxford mathematician until a trio of young girls demanded that he tell them stories, and then asked him to write them down. Thus was born Lewis Carroll—and *Alice in Wonderland*.

DEALING WITH WRITER'S BLOCK

In some ways, affiliative people are similar to those with a high need for power and influence (see the next section), in that they require another person to provide effective feedback. However, they require approval of themselves as people rather than a reaction to the book. An influence-motivated person might feel pleasure if someone has a violently negative reaction, because they want a strong impact, regardless of the direction. Not so the affiliative: they want to be considered good people, or they want to do something positive for another. To break writer's block may require hand-holding, or an enthusiastic person saying "Oooh! When can I read it?"

5 The Power-Motivated Writer

*If we had to say what writing is, we would define it essentially
as an act of courage.*

CYNTHIA OZICK

*You don't understand the humiliation of it—to be tricked out
of the single assumption that makes our existence viable—
that somebody is* watching...

TOM STOPPARD, *Rosencrantz and Guildenstern Are Dead*

*There is nothing more dreadful to an author than neglect,
compared with which reproach, hatred and opposition are
names of happiness.*

SAMUEL JOHNSON, *The Life of Samuel Johnson*

Ah, the glory of having a book before the world! This writer may dream of going
on talk shows, appearing on convention panels, or somehow changing people's
lives. A chief peril for this person is looking forward to having written a book
rather than actually writing—which is, after all, a solitary occupation, Harlan
Ellison's window-writing notwithstanding—or to short-cut the process and
just influence people directly, one at a time, instead of taking the time to write
a book first.

Your challenge: meet this need and feel that you make an impact. The impact
can even be on yourself. A primarily power-oriented person can get a charge out
of writing an emotionally arousing scene—after all, how do you know it
arouses people unless it arouses you? Thoughts about powerful scenes—scenes
that hit home and hit hard—come naturally to someone with this motive well
represented. Unfortunately, most works require linking content between powerful scenes, which may not hold the interest the same way.

How to feel that you have made an impact? Well, ideally, you should have an
actual person available. This reader will give you a sense of having had an
impact on a human being. This impact need not take place every session—

unlike with the primarily achievement-motivated person, the feedback can remain less constant or immediate—but it must be a reaction.

I write the big scenes first, that is, the scenes that carry the meaning of the book, the emotional experience.
JOYCE CARY, *Writer's Digest*

I have already alluded to some possibilities for impressing yourself: rereading sections, for example. If, in the middle of another part of your writing work you come up with a powerful idea, just jot it down. The temptation will be to hold off on your filler writing and get on with the hot scene. Save it instead, to motivate you to return to the keyboard. Set yourself the goal of accomplishing your current task in order to reward yourself with more exciting writing later. In the same way that some people complete jigsaw puzzles by going for a particular color or for the edges, you can go after certain kinds of scenes to propel yourself forward.

You can also display your work in various ways. Like the achievement person, you can count lines, words, or pages—but don't just write it down someplace hidden. Take a piece of paper and write it in HUGE characters. Post it on your wall—someplace reasonably public. Tell someone. Remember, the power-motivated person thrives on reactions. Putting the number up in public forces you to change it, or people will notice. In this way, you use the pressure of external people's impressions to drive your feelings—even if no one says a thing. If they do comment that your number has changed frequently (use different colors on successive signs for more contrast), then you have earned attention that will give you positive reinforcement.

Here I should put in a word for politeness. Nothing irritates people more than writers who prattle at length about their "work-in-progress," particularly those who quote their favorite lines in public places. ("I prefer dead writers because you don't run into them at parties," said Fran Lebowitz in a 1984 *Playboy* interview.) Such behavior will create an impact, all right, but not the one you might prefer. But there is nothing wrong with having a mysterious six-inch-tall number posted on your wall in a prominent position. If they ask you about it . . . well, that's their problem now.

While the achievement-dominated person gets motivation by the internal knowledge of visible progress, the mostly power-motivated person gets energy from knowing that someone knows about that visible progress; sometimes oneself is even enough.

To the power-motivated person that number on the wall might also be a threat—if someone comes by after a week and your number remains the same, she will wonder why, and you are going to have to tell her. Removing the number (to avoid that question) will have an impact, too. So you have, in effect, committed yourself to going on because you cannot bear to have someone know you have stopped. You must save face.

If you fear being "caught out" not changing that number, then I strongly recommend that you do not use this particular method. Fear does not provide a terribly good motivation for extended periods of writing. Enjoyment works much better here.

If you are writing a "useful" or "important" work, keep thinking about how many people you could affect, and how. Politicians with this motive tend to come from grass-roots movements, because they would rather know they have gotten one dollar from a million people than a million dollars from one person. They count the people they have influenced, no matter how little, not the dollar efficiency of fundraising. (Achievement-motivated politicians, by contrast, often get indicted for fundraising irregularities, since they find it easier to get their funds from a few rich people. Hey, it got Nixon.)

Make a list, if you like: how many people could read this book and gain from it? If you are writing a scientific work, how many colleagues do you have who might read it? Don't worry about whether they will—that will come after you finish the book.

In the course of writing *this* book I offered to make a presentation on the topic at hand for a mystery writers' conference. This kept me focused on what people would think of me and this book. It also guided the organization of my writing, and in my mental rehearsals of my presentation I determined which sentences flowed well, and which did not. I have spoken to writers' groups, conferences, and whatnot on numerous occasions, which kept my interest fresh, if only because I could continue to test the interest of my audience.

CHARACTERISTICS OF POWER FEEDBACK

1 Dramatic
2 Arouses strong emotion
3 Impactful

Dramatic

Good writing is supposed to evoke sensation in the reader—
not the fact that it's raining, but the feel of being rained
upon.

E. L. DOCTOROW, *Writers on Writing*

You are concerned with making a strong impression, or influencing people. Dramatic forms of feedback may influence you. For example: use bright colors on a progress form, or write a brief report that you mail to yourself, or announce it loudly somehow—even if only to yourself. If you do the latter, find a room with good acoustics and belt it out. Enjoy the resonance.

Arouses Strong Emotion

I write because I hate. A lot. Hard.

WILLIAM GASS, *"The Artist and Society"*

The power-oriented person tends to arouse emotions strongly in others, either positively or negatively. Emotion indicates a significant influence on a person, so people with this motive crave emotional impact. Arouse strong emotion in yourself, and you have given yourself a powerful form of feedback. Being dramatic can help; so can playing certain kinds of music that arouse you the right way. (Be careful—don't play Beethoven's Fifth Symphony if you are planning a quiet, professional document. They might clash.) If you need to stop occasionally and scroll through the entire document, or riffle pages, or howl at the moon, do it!

Impact

Give me a museum and I'll fill it.

PABLO PICASSO

Do something you will remember. Memorize the latest number, or write it on your palm, or post it in a really noticeable place—your door, for instance. That way you cannot miss it. If you get into the habit of seeing it in a particular place, then move it around or hang it at an angle. Surprise yourself. Pique your interest. People tend to get used to things—otherwise they would go bananas just keeping up with the world around them every day. You need to fight this tendency in order to trigger yourself.

Concrete Suggestions

1 Post progress dramatically. Colored writing will help—especially in red or some other bright color.
2 Make a stack of your latest manuscript sheets and place it someplace visible. (Use a copy or keep it someplace very safe as well as *visible*.)
3 If you are a Mozartian writer who writes from beginning to end without editing, post the last page you have written with a large, red page number marked on the page. Again, make sure it is visible. Your refrigerator door is a fine place, as long as the page stands out.

4 Announce your achievement to someone who will respond strongly—significant other, mother, friend—whomever will shout hooray sincerely. Faked or lukewarm responses won't do it. You might have to be sparing with this one, to avoid the "boy who cried wolf" syndrome. You may want to set a solid goal to be met first, to ensure a meaningfully dramatic statement. "I finished a sentence!" is not very impressive unless you write *very very slowly*. "I finished twenty pages!" or "two thousand words!" are more significant and meaningful. Be aware that the primarily power-motivated person tends to set unrealistic goals. If you choose not to announce until your book is half-finished, you may lose steam. Give yourself a moderate set of "rah-rah points." If you aren't sure what that might be, ask yourself how often you need reinforcement before flagging—or ask an achievement-oriented person. They usually set moderately risky goals spontaneously.

5 Have short-term and major-announcement points—little cheers and big cheers, as it were. If you write each night, you have no reason not to take pleasure in your accomplishment each night, but don't get out of hand until you have justified your pleasure.

DEALING WITH WRITER'S BLOCK

What happens when you stall? For the power-motivated writer, as for the achievement-motivated writer, the reason may be because the process of writing is no longer associated with the motive. In other words, it isn't fun. For a person high in the need for power, this could take several forms. First, the writer may not have a feeling of having impact. At such times an audience becomes critical. Don't be afraid to ask friends and family to read your work; all they can say is no. If they do say no, you don't want them reading your work at that point anyway. Even if the person you want to read your stuff lives far away, go ahead and send them a package (with their permission, of course), or e-mail them your work. You'll have to do that eventually to sell your book, after all.

You may also have writer's block because you waited too long between writing sessions, and the work has gone cold. If you have enough material, read it from beginning to end and see what reaction it provokes. Where appropriate, try writing again, just to get words on paper. If your work is quite long—novel length, say—spend a couple of days reading. Keep your continuity, and start thinking about how to make a better impact again.

I described a prophylactic for the power-based writer's block above—don't write the powerful scenes out of order. Save them up for the slow times. It may be easier to get psyched up for an exciting scene.

If all else fails, write something completely different. Keep the association of writing and excitement.

In this example of the Power Motive influencing writing, Sarah Smith describes her book *The Moon Rock of Stars:*

> I thought I was losing my mind because I was on chapter 16 of 20 and I realized I was doing it wrong. I had to lose two characters. I couldn't figure out where it was going. I had no sense of being in control. I said "this is a good book to write for a second book. It kills you to lose control. You can write a book like the previous book you wrote." It was easy—except for things like plot and character! … This book—it really felt perverse. It felt like I was destroying myself—which in a sense I was. I wanted to get out of the sense that I had to write in this way and I had to succeed in this way to do what I was doing.

In this case Smith describes the sense of losing power through losing control of the work. For her, the loss of direction was disturbing, especially since the writing in this book was so different from the way she had learned to write. Writing it felt like a loss of identity. Losing power *and* identity is too much. As she put it, the book "felt perverse . . . I was destroying myself." Whereas an achievement-motivated person might have said "I wasn't up to the challenge," Smith felt she was "destroying" herself, a clearly power-related image. Fortunately, she recognized what was happening well enough to take appropriate action.

First, she identified that this was beyond her abilities at the moment. She did not attribute her failure to complete inability or stupidity (see the section on attributional style later in the book); she said "this is a good book to write for a second book." She knew she was stretching herself and realized that her present task ought to be to write something very different. It took her several months to write a twelve-page chapter, but she knew it was the right way to go. She already knew something that many newer writers do not: not every part of a book goes the same way, and not every writing effort works the same way. She had enough objectivity to realize that this book would take a different kind of approach, rather than letting the helplessness and lack of ability steer her away from writing entirely.

6 The Writer with Multiple Motives

Everyone has the obligation to ponder well his own specific
traits of character. He must also regulate them adequately
and not wonder whether someone else's traits might suit him
better. The more definitely his own a man's character is, the
better it fits him.

MARCUS TULLIUS CICERO

I once asked David McClelland, the guiding mind behind the field of motivational psychology, how he would describe a person who had all three motives relatively strongly. He said: "Confused."

The multiple-motive personality will enjoy a wide range of things and may shift from one choice to another based on which motive happens to have the upper hand at the time. Since these motives are unconscious, it is much harder to resolve contradictory desires than simply to make a choice—all you know is that you cannot decide. You may be highly motivated in general but unless you have a focus, you will bounce like a ping-pong ball instead of aiming and using all of that motivational energy.

John F. Kennedy was high in all three motives, and he was seen as dynamic, active, and bursting with energy despite his crippling back problems. The energy of your personality can project well beyond the limitations of your body. When they work together, multiple motives can give you a great deal of drive—you can shift gears when one motive is on the decline or adjust to a different situation that demands different thought patterns. Furthermore, they enlarge your sensory sensitivity to include a richer array of images. The flip side of that gift is that it also makes you more susceptible to distraction.

It should be possible to balance or interweave your motives effectively, but you may have to apply great force to do so. It helps to be aware—knowledge is power!—so that you can adjust your reward system to take all of your motives into account.

The important thing is to retain focus. If you can find ways of linking more than one motive, your chances of keeping your focus go up enormously. The job of writer has opportunities for all three motives, but how you indulge them will vary. J. D. Salinger, who rejects any kind of publicity and even the release of his image to the public, is unlikely to have a strongly externally-focused power motive, since he works hard to suppress a viable reward for it.

On the other hand, he might fear the temptation for a writer to get so involved with the social life—talk shows, parties, interviews, politics, and so on—that he ceases to actually *write*. (Remember, you do not judge a person's motives solely by his behaviors.) Truman Capote leaned in this direction and wrote too few books for a person of his talent. If Capote had isolated himself occasionally, he might have done more writing.

Science fiction and mystery authors have an option not available to many other authors: they can attend conventions. There is a science fiction convention (and usually more than one) on virtually any given weekend in the United States, and all of them delight in having a writer available to bring in more fans. However, some writers just go from convention to convention, enjoying the socialization—the affiliation, or the direct influence—so much that they never write again.

Conventions can be valuable in many ways: they provide access to fellow practitioners of the craft, they might inspire new ideas (satisfying Achievement Motive), they provide a source of positive, friendly reinforcement (which is appealing to Affiliation Motive), and they give opportunities to create a reputation and make an impact on readers, writers, and publishers (Power Motive). But if you have more than one motive pumping, make sure it is the right one for the purpose of writing and selling your work.

Motives are emotional, as noted above; you may find it hard to avoid doing something very satisfying in order to do something important. If you go into a situation with many choices, you need to sit down and think about what you need *before* you go. Otherwise you may run on "gut instinct," which (contrary to popular belief) may not be your best guide.

Now that you can see how differently motivated people may write, let's take a deeper look at *your* motives, using a simple method: finding out what you do for fun.

7 Discovering Motives Using Reality Testing

There is never a better measure of what a person is than what he does when he is absolutely free to choose.

WILLIAM M. BULGER, Boston Globe

The real character of a man is found out by his amusements.

SIR JOSHUA REYNOLDS

MOTIVE-RELATED BEHAVIORS

Since motives predict behaviors, you might expect that you can read someone by what they do. However, motives predict *patterns of* behaviors and *reasons for* behaviors more than they do specific actions.

You cannot judge a person by a given workday, for example, because much work is governed by the needs of the moment rather than personal enjoyment. Also, as I have noted before, there can be many motives driving the same behavior.

For example, salespeople often learn good people skills. But salespeople, especially in shorter-cycle sales, are often best driven by the Achievement Motive. A paradox? Not really. These people learn influencing behaviors to get to their truly enjoyable goal—the challenge of making a sale or beating a quota. The means are not the end where motives and behaviors are concerned.

Similarly, you cannot stereotype motivated behavior. I have frequently worked with people who complained about tyrannical behavior on the part of a manager and attribute it to power—they must be power-mad, a dictator. Upon investigation, however, these people often do not intend to crush their employees—what they do is focus completely on the goal, even if people are in the way, or zero in on such a high level of excellence that they have to interfere and coerce. This is the Achievement Motive in action. Power-motivated people are more likely to be aware of how other people are reacting.

In order to learn how to judge motives by behaviors instead of by stereotypes, you need to ask the following kinds of questions: What hobbies does a person enjoy? Which topic is she most passionate about? What ideals make her angry? Sad? Happy? After you've begun identifying a motive with a specific behavior for someone else, you're ready to look inward. I've provided a checklist of items that can be reasonably associated with one motive or another in the "Identifying Your Motives Worksheet."

IDENTIFYING YOUR MOTIVES WORKSHEET
STEPHEN P. KELNER JR.

The following sections have a variety of activities, which relate to one or more motives if done for enjoyment. Go down the list and check whichever ones you enjoy. If you want to add extra strength, you can put more than one check. At the end is a key to add up which support which motives.

HOBBIES

1 Handicraft ❑
2 Working on cars ❑
3 Being with family ❑
4 Being with friends ❑
5 Running committees ❑
6 Performing (acting, singing, dancing) ❑
7 Writing (!) ❑
8 Corresponding with family or friends ❑
9 Cooking for self ❑
10 Cooking for others ❑

HOT BUTTONS

1 Testing myself against targets, goals ❑
2 Meeting new potential friends ❑
3 Helping a friend ❑
4 Getting my point across to people ❑
5 Exploring politics ❑

TELEPHONE USE

1 Efficient, brisk, short (avoiding contact) ❑
2 Calling to get specific questions answered ❑
3 Friendly, calling to say hello, hard to get off phone ❑
4 Calling to connect with people ❑
5 Being called more than calling and distributing
   information ❑
6 Calling to gather general information ❑

---

7 Don't like calling; would rather fax, v-mail, or
   e-mail so I don't get into a conversation   ❏
8 Dislike calling because it feels cold and impersonal   ❏
9 Dislike calling because I can't see people's faces   ❏
10 Dislike calling because there are other ways to
   connect with more people at once   ❏

BOOKS READ FOR FUN

1 Instructions for techniques, skills   ❏
2 How-to, do-it-yourself   ❏
3 Mysteries (puzzles, "cozies")   ❏
4 Mysteries (hard-boiled, private-eye)   ❏
5 Mysteries (historical)   ❏
6 Romances   ❏
7 Stories with well-developed relationships   ❏
8 Biographies of leaders   ❏
9 Psychology   ❏
10 Theology   ❏
11 History   ❏
12 Stories with sexual content   ❏
13 Stories with violent content   ❏
14 Spy stories, thrillers   ❏
15 Science fiction ("hard")   ❏
16 Science fiction ("soft," "sociological")   ❏
17 Science fiction (military)   ❏
18 Fantasy (epics)   ❏

MY GREATEST SATISFACTION

1 Creating something new   ❏
2 Creating something of the highest quality, even if
   no one else sees it   ❏
3 Being with friends   ❏
4 Being with family   ❏
5 Having an impact on people   ❏

WHAT MAKES ME ANGRY?

1 Seeing things done badly or wrong   ❏
2 Seeing people hurt   ❏
3 Seeing people disenfranchised   ❏

WHAT MAKES ME SORROWFUL?

1 Lost opportunities for unique action ❏
2 Lost relationships ❏
3 Lost visibility ❏

SPORTS AND FUN

1 Golf (against handicap) ❏
2 Golf (with friends) ❏
3 Golf (competitive or betting) ❏
4 Bowling (against scores) ❏
5 Bowling (with friends or league) ❏
6 Bowling (competitive) ❏
7 Volleyball ❏
8 Basketball ❏
9 Baseball ❏
10 Softball ❏
11 Football ❏
12 Track and field ❏
13 Shotput ❏
14 High jump, long jump ❏
15 Professional or amateur competition (beating a record) ❏
16 Professional or amateur competition (beating other people) ❏
17 Soccer ❏
18 Rugby ❏
19 Water polo ❏
20 Horseback riding ❏
21 Hiking ❏
22 Kayaking ❏
23 Computer games (adventure) ❏
24 Computer games (cards, puzzles) ❏

	Achievement	Affiliation	Power
Hobbies	1, 2, 9	3, 4, 8	5, 6, 7, 10
Hot buttons	1	2, 3	4, 5
Telephone use	1, 2, 7	3, 4	5, 6, 9, 10
Books read for fun	1, 2, 3, 15	6, 7	4, 5, 8–14, 16–18
Greatest satisfaction	1, 2	3, 4	5
What makes me angry?	1	2	3
What make me sorrowful?	1	2	3
Sports and fun	1, 4, 12–15, 21, 24	2, 5, 7, 10	3, 6, 8, 9, 11, 16–19, 20, 22, 23

Please use this worksheet with caution. To illustrate the ways in which many motives can predict the same behavior, take three men playing golf together. One may be playing to improve his handicap (achievement), another may be playing because he enjoys the company (affiliation), and the third may be playing because he wants to influence his partners (power). That is why we do not use behaviors to *predict* motives, only to help validate them.

Now that you can see how differently motivated people may write, let's take a look at a range of actual published writers and their motives.

PART II: MOTIVATION
WHY PUBLISHED WRITERS DO
WHAT THEY DO

Art is a form of catharsis.
DOROTHY PARKER, *The Little Hours*

8 Motives, Readers, and Writers

The man who does not read good books has no advantage over the man who cannot read them.

MARK TWAIN

MOTIVES AND READING MATTER

Motives relate to many actions, preferences, and thoughts, including what you choose to read for fun. In brief, primarily achievement-motivated people like to read instructional nonfiction (how-to books) or mentally challenging stories (Agatha Christie, locked-room mysteries). Affiliative people like reading stories with well-developed characters (Jane Austen) or romantic stories (Barbara Cartland). Power-motivated people are interested in reading about what makes people tick (psychology, biographies of leaders) or in reading about impact or influence on others (hard-boiled mysteries, such as Raymond Chandler, or stories with aggression or political maneuvering, such as political thrillers).

Did you notice that that previous paragraph explains the constant battle between the "hard-boiled" (private eye) and "tea cozy" (Miss Marple) mysteries? Forget all of those arguments about which is more realistic, which is better written, or whatever. The real difference lies not on the intellectual level but the emotional. The typical private investigator deals with conflict, politics, direct aggression, alcohol, and manipulation—the negative side of the power motive. Well, you don't expect Mother Theresa to show up in a dark and gritty detective novel, do you? Though it could make for a really interesting story . . .

By contrast, the classic Agatha Christie novel emphasizes not the deeper feelings of or interactions among the characters but an intricate puzzle that you can work out as precisely as a chess problem. Often, obscure facts play a key role as well, either as the "gimmick," where everything hinges on knowing that pennies were made from steel in 1943, or as the opening of another world for the reader, as Tony Hillerman does with the Navajo. As mystery writer Aaron Elkins pointed out, you don't waste your time with mysteries because you learn something. This characterizes achievement-motivated thinking very well: improving your knowledge and challenging yourself.

Of course, a good cozy novel requires more emotional depth than a crossword puzzle, and a good hard-boiled novel needs more intellectual depth than Rock'em Sock'em Robots. But at one conference where I pointed this out, a woman came up to me and thanked me for explaining why she hated most mysteries. To her, characters just messed up the mystery. She adored Agatha Christie, but most modern cozies depend upon complex characterization, or even romantic relationships! Her comment immediately reminded me of Dorothy L. Sayers's dedication to *Busman's Honeymoon*: "It has been said, by myself and others, that a love-interest is only an intrusion upon a detective story. But to the characters involved, the detective-interest might well seem an irritating intrusion upon their love-story."

Sayers's broad and enduring popularity might well come from her understanding of this fact, for her books touch upon all three motives: the intricate puzzle (the railway tables in *Five Red Herrings*), the affiliative relationship (as above), and power and class relationships (*Gaudy Night, Whose Body?*). She has, literally, something for everybody. I could use her novels as an impromptu motivational test: which do you like the most? If you prefer *Five Red Herrings* to *Busman's Honeymoon*, I think I know why ...

Likewise, we can analyze the current crop of mystery fiction and see that more than one motive seem to emerge even within the classic divisions. Most modern cozies, as well as Sara Paretsky's V. I. Warshawski books, have an affiliative "hook" through family or friends that complements the puzzle aspect—and don't forget that the amateur usually competes with an official detective, which can be achievement (beat the standard) or power (beat the person—sometimes literally) or both, depending on how the competition is handled. People are complex, and the writer who forgets that is less likely to be successful.

In that case, what motive should the writer have? Originally, I expected that the motives of writers should reflect the motives of their readers—achievement-motivated writers would tend to write mysteries, affiliative writers would enjoy scripting romances, and power-motivated writers would create thrillers. If they bore any motive in common, it would probably be the achievement motive, since people with this motive as their strongest like to work alone, set goals, and get things done—all useful things for a writer. Make sense? I thought so.

Fortunately, science marches on despite the limitations of its practitioners: my hypothesis was dead wrong—at least for published writers.

THE RESEARCH

Over the years, a number of writers (around a couple of dozen) have kindly filled out Picture Story Exercises and answered my questions, or appeared on panels where they argued against each others' approaches under my moderation, and the results are quite striking.

I selected published writers because my purpose is to help others get to be published writers. In my experience, most would-be writers do not want to collect dirty paper by their desks; they want to have a real book in their hands and other people reading what they write. I share that feeling; after all, I am writing a book on this subject!

The writers cross various genres including primarily mystery, science fiction, and fantasy, with nonfiction such as true crime and textbooks and some oddballs here and there. They range from relatively new (one book) rookies to highly experienced award-winners with six-figure contracts. They include academics, technical professionals, journalists, advertisers, financial advisors, and physicists. They cover a lot of ground, but in retrospect, I cannot be surprised by what I found.

Remember the three motives? The convention in research is to display the motivational assessment in profile, after comparing the assessment to a research database or, in this case, a database of 80,000 people from around the world. In this way, we see not just a raw number; we see roughly how a writer compares with all of the people questioned. In other words, if a person's motive is at seventy-fifth percentile, it means that that person has a higher raw score than 75 percent of that huge group—better than 60,000 people, in fact.

The average results of my group of published writers appear in the graph below.

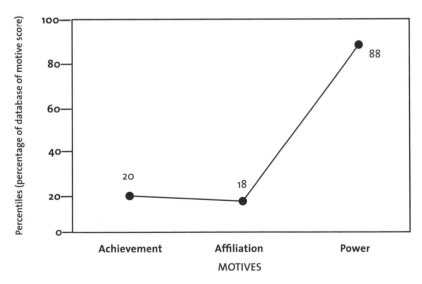

AVERAGE MOTIVE PROFILE OF PUBLISHED WRITERS

This means that the desire to influence drives published writers far more (on average) than the other two desires. These people want to know that others respond to them. Should this surprise us?

Remember, I said "published" writers. Why get published? To put your words before other people, of course. Philip R. Craig, author of a mystery series set in Martha's Vineyard, laughed when I told him his motive pattern, because he feels strongly that it is inappropriate to manifest your will over others—yet he is a mystery writer who wrote a novel focusing on the negative aspects of politics and being in a fishbowl. He still *sees* the power issues, but he warns against them. Sarah Smith, author of *A Citizen of the Country,* would rather die than tell someone they have to write their book a certain way, but she spends untold hours helping others, both as part of a writing workshop and by critiquing and coaching individuals on her own. The behaviors of seeing power relationships and coaching others relate to the Power Motive.

The achievement-motivated person can find happiness working alone and in isolation, as long as he or she gets feedback on progress toward goals and can constantly beat those goals over time. The affiliative person gets satisfaction from being with people and relating to them on a social or personal level. Only the power-motivated person gets enjoyment from seeing others respond to something he or she initiated. When a book appears on the shelves, people see it. When people read books, their thoughts change, and the author made that change happen. These writers need to know that somebody is there and has reacted to them.

Many writers are known as wits and raconteurs, which goes beyond their gifts for written language. With the desire to influence backing them up, they like to be in the limelight; if they are too shy or too slow to speak well in public, they may well hide so that no one knows what they look like.

One may easily mistake extroversion for the Power Motive. The extrovert certainly can be power-motivated, but the reverse is decidedly not true. J. D. Salinger may be fanatically protective of his privacy precisely because he understands what publicity means. An achievement-motivated person might not care, or notice, or even understand what it means to be in front of others until it is too late.

Hence the writer: impress thousands (even millions) of people even though you may be awkward, shy, or unattractive. Be impressive by proxy! Influence the world! Get people to think what you want them to think!

By now, you may be anxiously examining yourself, or writers that you know and love, for signs of incipient megalomania. You might think, little did I know of these monsters in our midst. And they seem so nice and retiring.

Take heart. Motives are where you find emotional satisfaction, but the thought does not equal the deed. As T. S. Eliot would put it, between the idea and the reality falls the Shadow. Who knows what evil lurks in the hearts of men? The Shadow—or more prosaically, our values.

Both Hitler and Mother Theresa demonstrated strong power motives;

Mother Theresa just managed to use her desire to influence in a rather more socialized manner, thanks to her conscious values. The uninhibited person with a high need for power may appear to be an egomaniac, manipulating others for personal gain. The inhibited, or socialized, Power Motive works for the betterment of a group—using influence to help everyone get along, for example.

Conscious values shape the way in which your motives emerge as behaviors. For example, thirty years ago American society generally did not accept the idea of women at the executive level of business. But a woman could be president of the parent-teacher association and no one would blink an eye. Both are leadership positions that are appealing to those with the Power Motive. One had society's approval, one did not; values made the difference. (A fuller description of values is in the next chapter.)

Unlike a person's motives, which stay relatively stable in adulthood, values can change rapidly in a person or in a society. Today female CEOs are more common. Likewise, while the simplest way to satisfy the Power Motive may be to hit something, how many people do that on a daily basis? Adults generally have a negative value on hitting someone to influence them.

As people grow into adulthood, they learn to channel the raw emotional energy of their motives into appropriate outlets. The key to this channeling is restraint. Freud thought that the primary purpose of society was to force people's instincts into socialized paths designed to serve society better. Why do we see "immediate gratification" as immature? Perhaps because adulthood implies the ability to postpone satisfaction to the appropriate time and place. We call those people who cannot do this immature, for good reason. We might not survive as a species—certainly not as a civilization—if we merely responded to our animal needs at whim.

We can measure the tendency to restrain motivational energy with an odd little measure derived from the the same exercise (the Picture Story Exercise, or PSE) that we used to track motives; it is called Activity Inhibition, or AI. This is a simple count of the number of times that the word "not" or the suffix "n't" appears in stories written to specific ambiguous pictures over roughly a half-hour period. A typical Picture Story Exercise averages about 450 words long. In an American population, the average adult has around 1.75 "nots"; having two or more means you are likely to be significantly restrained or socialized—significantly above the average, that is. Interestingly, the British need four or more to be considered socialized, which must say something about the respective cultures. In European countries speaking Romance languages (Spanish, French, Italian), even one "not" indicates AI. The AI measurement gives you an idea of how much you naturally tend to inhibit your motives. This can be useful to you in many ways, and it can be applied to any motive.

As a matter of course, I measured the AI of the writers in my database. The average was eighteen. Eighteen! *Nine times* the level of the typical well-socialized person in the United States. More than four times that of a socialized Brit!

I had never seen such numbers in my life. What did they mean? I suspect that the very act of putting thoughts to paper (instead of simply acting on them or speaking them) requires a high level of inhibition of motives. It is just plain harder to take a thought and write it down, let alone do so regularly and then edit it as well.

David McClelland captured it for me quite neatly: "When a typical person gets mad at you, he hits you. When a mystery writer gets mad at you, he takes a year to write a novel killing you off." How much more socialized can you get? My wife, Toni L. P. Kelner, bumped off her ex-boyfriend in her novel *Country Comes to Town* a mere fourteen years after she started dating me and eight after she married me. Now that's a mature expression of power!

BUT WHAT ABOUT ME?

You may now wonder, What if I lack the power motive? Am I doomed to fail as a writer?

Of course not. It just isn't as much fun—or you have to get your fun out of different parts of the process. Trouble is, if you get fun out of the process of writing and not the idea of being published, then you might collect a stack of unpublished books. If that's okay with you, then more power to you—that is, good luck. But most people want someone else to read their work.

How do you deal with a lack of motivation? One way is to provide yourself with a structure—that is, a means for your circumstances to force you to write, or send out letters, or whatever. Schedule your writing session in your book and treat it as a serious appointment. You can also use some of the pleasure-postponing devices mentioned elsewhere ("I can't do what I want until I finish 600 words").

Is it possible to sustain long works this way? Can one write, say, a hundred thousand words through will power and grit? Sure! But nobody said it was easy. Managing yourself becomes nearly a full-time job.

Another option is to try to hook your existing motive into your work, and that is the point of my discussion of reinforcers for each motive. I like this approach, though it takes a certain amount of refinement in your self-management. See below for more on this.

Another option is to give up, of course. Just find something else to do. On the other hand, I tend to think that having a dream helps you. Often the process of writing or being creative involves being blind to the realities around you, and I think this can be a strength. If you have read this far, you can probably write at least a little. Write short-shorts or something that only requires short bursts.

A fourth option is to change yourself. Not the easiest task, when you remember that people's motives have remained stable over ten-year periods. But it can be done.

9 Being Overmotivated

*Writing is a solitary occupation. Family, friends, and society
are the natural enemies of a writer He must be alone, uninterrupted, and slightly savage if he is to sustain and complete
an undertaking.*

LAWRENCE CLARK POWELL, *Books in My Baggage*

*An incurable itch for scribbling takes possession of many and
grows inveterate in their insane hearts.*

JUVENAL, *The Sixteen Satires*

I know what you're thinking: "What a problem to have! I'll deal with it when I
get there." That seems reasonable enough, but you may not realize what is happening until it is too late to moderate it. So let's look at what being overmoti-
vated means.

Remember that motives as we discuss them here are unconscious, emotional drives. That means that they do not necessarily work with your conscious
motives. They help shape your conscious actions, but they can also interfere
with your choices if they get out of control. I have seen an experienced,
confident adult unable to stop his hands trembling in a simple task because of
supercharged Achievement motivation.

You may get to a point where the drive to write begins overwhelming everything else, as Juvenal (a Roman satirist, apparently commenting on himself)
noted some centuries ago. You get distracted from other tasks when you could
be writing; you find other activities uninteresting or at least less interesting
than writing (troublesome when you are dealing with your significant other—
unless he or she also writes); and you may feel guilty when you are away from
the keyboard. For her first book, Kelly Tate set goals that were "too aggressive,"
and in her desire to meet those goals (achievement-driven, in this case), she
exhausted herself. She consistently met her goals—but at a cost to her health
and her daily functioning.

I said earlier that motivation can become an addiction—withdrawal symptoms and all. This is where the moderation of your motives comes in. You can make them work for you. The first step is to get your motives engaged, aroused, and firing up your writing. The second step is to make sure they do not run your life without your conscious, reasoned permission.

While the typical person will not get to the hand-trembling stage of motivation during the writing process, you may find that strong emotional engagement can interfere with your functioning. If you are particularly clumsy, or the words just aren't flowing the way you want, the backlog of emotional energy can become particularly frustrating. Ever fumble in a tense situation?

For example: you are out on a hot date. The pressure is on! You want to look cool, calm, and collected. As you put on your coat, you miss the sleeve. Grinning coolly, you realign your coat and slam your hand through swiftly, ripping the lining. The grin wavers, but you hold firm. You whip out your gloves without looking. As you smile in a dazzling manner, you struggle to put your left glove on your right hand. As your face reaches fire-engine red, you try harder, and things just get worse.

Why is this? That question was answered by two primate researchers named Robert Yerkes and John Dodson in the early twentieth century. They put food-deprived monkeys in a cage within reach of a short stick, which in turn was within reach of a longer stick, which in turn was within reach of a banana. To get the banana, the monkey had to get the short stick, use it to get the long stick, and use the long stick to get the banana. A well-fed monkey was disinterested in the whole process. Why bother, right? A somewhat hungry monkey could and would get the banana, thinking pretty hard for a monkey. But a *really* hungry monkey could not find a way to get the banana. Instead, he would grab the reachable stick, bang the bars with it, or even throw it at the banana. The hunger clouded his thinking.

Yerkes and Dodson had discovered something very important, one of the few things that psychologists dare to call a law—the Yerkes-Dodson Law, in fact: the relationship between motivation and performance is not a straight line—it is a bell curve. In other words, *moderate motivation leads to the best performance.* Neither excessive arousal nor underarousal will lead to successful outcomes. And so we return from monkeys to motivating writing.

In writing terms, you may have a brilliant idea, and you feel you must get it on paper before it fades. Perhaps time is short, putting on additional pressure. That is the moment when your right hand shifts over one key, and instead of "it was a dark and stormy night," you write "ot was a darl amd stpr,u mogjt." The process of back-spacing or deleting seems to take forever. You leap back onto the keyboard, and three words in you discover that the first is misspelled. And so forth. As motivational pressure increases beyond the balance point, your ability to function decreases.

So too much motivation can impair your life and your effectiveness. How do you take care of it? And is it possible?

Of course. In the research section below, I'll tell you what I found in published writers, who suffer just as much as anyone from *all* the various problems and obstacles described here, including overmotivation. Where do you think all of these descriptions came from, anyway?

When trying to handle overmotivation, think in terms of what tools you can bring to bear on it. Internal motivation is the problem here, not the solution (unlike most of the rest of this book), so we cannot use that. Other internal traits may assist you, including the ability to manage yourself or restrain and focus your motivation, but we will talk about that element later. The other major approach is to use things external to yourself. In other words, control your environment so that it helps you. Some of the clues given here around each motive can work both ways. A publicly posted word count, for example, can energize your power motive, but posting *both* your accomplishments *and* your goal can work to restrain you. Being held accountable to your goal can rein in your target somewhat.

We'll discuss all of these things in more detail later, but let's pick out one key thing: you can also try to get outside yourself and watch your own actions. At the extremes it should be easy: on your wedding anniversary, forget about writing and celebrate! What is tricky is when you have choices. That is, you have no special occasion that *forces* you to pay attention. Then you need to find a way to focus your attention. To judge this, I recommend that you consider your records of performance. If you have not written anything in a while, you should probably hit the desk. If you have been writing day and night, you can probably take a break safely enough.

Just remember that there is more to life than writing. (Really!) Once you get properly rolling, you can afford to stop. If you get severely sick, for example, don't worry about missing your daily (or weekly) dose. Get well instead, or substitute a minimal task—noting an idea or doing basic proofreading for half an hour—so that you can say you have done your writing for the day. Otherwise your motivation may take you past the point of being able to work.

On a larger scale, Kelly Tate found herself in a situation where she had to deal with a divorce, two kids, selling one house, buying another house, packing, and moving—and she found herself unable to write. So she gave herself a vacation. Rather than winding herself up tight and worrying about it, she said she would write nothing until September 1. (This was July, so she took off the rest of the summer.) By that time she had moved, largely unpacked, and was sending the kids off to school. The date also had personal significance from a lengthy schooling of her own: September is when you get back to work. So she did. She let herself relax instead of ruining herself. Note also that she did not just stop for an indefinite period; instead, she identified a specific interval to hold off on her writing. She controlled the interval. Not only that, but she made implicit assumptions: writing was the normal state, and her time off would be limited. She wasn't making it too easy on herself.

The same applies to important family events, vacations, and so on. Isaac Asimov wrote around five hundred books, it is true. But he also hated vacations and had been known to write on a beach. That's fine if you and your loved ones can stand it, but do be sure to *ask* them first. I have no desire to come between you and your family.

Remember, we are assuming too much motivation here. None of this applies if getting started is your problem. Giving yourself a vacation when you haven't been writing at all is not exactly a positive step (unless you're suffering a block from your motivational pressure, perhaps). The issue here is that being over-motivated can get in your way.

In the next section, we'll take a look at how you can manage yourself and your writing.

Remember: When the pressure is too high,
it becomes difficult to think. If you take on too many
tasks, the pressure will mount.

PART III: HOW WRITERS SEE THEMSELVES

Artists are meant to be madmen, to disturb and shock us.

ANNE RICE, The Seattle Times, 1990

An artist is a creature driven by demons. He don't know why they choose him and he's usually too busy to wonder why.

WILLIAM FAULKNER Writers at Work

The trade of authorship is a violent and indestructible obsession.

GEORGE SAND The Letters of George Sand

10 Where Writers Are Coming From

VALUES (AND MOTIVES)

Every asshole in the world wants to write.
JUDITH ROSSNER, *Writers on Writing*

Before we get further into the issues of motivation, we should discuss your values. Do you consider writing important? I don't mean that you must consider your prose to be deathless wisdom for the ages, just that you think it is important to you to keep doing it. If you are not convinced that writing has any meaning for you, quit now!

If, on the other hand, you are writing now and the very idea of quitting makes you snort with derision, then you value writing. The definition of a value (sometimes called a *self-attributed* motive, to distinguish it from the unconscious or *implicit* motive) is "something you consciously consider important." There are dramatic differences between values and implicit motives.

Motives are primitive emotional structures. It appears likely that you can find something like motives in nearly any mammal. Your typical dog can be happy about a relationship or upset when he can't influence you. Values, on the other hand, appear to be limited to those animals fortunate or unfortunate enough to have very complex thinking abilities: *homo sapiens sapiens*.

Values are cognitive in nature, meaning that they are conscious thoughts. They may go back a long way in your life, but at the core they can bend and change much more readily than motives. College students who refused to ever compromise with "The Establishment" have become lawyers and bankers; H. L. Mencken, the supposedly permanent bachelor and witty critic of marriage, changed his tune when he found the woman of his dreams. When people become parents, many new values appear as products of the equally new demands on them. Suddenly it becomes necessary to develop whole sets of tasks and rules, and your priorities shift dramatically.

There is nothing wrong with that. Things change, and the things you value can change with them. Values are adaptive structures—they allow you to roll with the punches and decide what is important for this time and this place. The values of a single twenty-year-old are very different from those of a married forty-year-old with children, and that is as it should be.

I'm not speaking on behalf of ethical relativism here; I'm talking about your priorities. As I write this, I have a three-week-old daughter in the room across the hall. Before she was born, I had a list of priorities; she has abruptly been inserted into the list, ahead of many other things. My core values have not changed, but their relative importance to my priorities has.

Both values and motives are kinds of motivation. My focus in this book is primarily on the deeper ones, because, as they are *not* as flexible, your life may flow better if you learn how to live with them. In addition, motives sustain behavior better than values—motives *provide* energy while values generally *expend* energy. Yet a strong-willed value can put the kibosh even on a strongly motive-based action.

A motive, being general and primitive in nature, gets no more specific than "I feel good knowing I have had an impact on others," or "I feel good when I have done something better." They are, after all, built into our brains to some extent—into the hardware, so to speak—which means they should be relatively simple. Values can be far more specific and complex, because they are formed above the level of basic brain biology—in the software. They *focus* the energy the right way.

If you wish to be a writer—or if you just wish to write—you should sit down and think about it. It does not matter what other people think of writing—only what you think. But if you cannot convince yourself that it matters to you, why should you bother to read this book, let alone make an effort to write?

Remember: Value your writing!
Your writing should be important to you.

If you have read this far, it seems likely that you do care to some degree. Take this chapter as a cautionary note. There are people who will pooh-pooh your efforts, ridicule your ambitions, and even criticize your writing. Avoid them. They're just jealous, because they don't think they could write themselves, or they have an exaggerated sense of the talent needed. Maybe they just don't like you. Why should anyone spend their time preventing you from doing something you want to do that hurts no one and may contribute something worthwhile? As my mother used to say about people who were rude to me: "Consider the source!" And get yourself away from it. You need to stay focused on your own values and no one else's.

Many writers had people who made fun of their ambition. Some of them grew up, got rich and famous, and got their revenge. Agatha Christie had an unhappy first marriage to a dashing R.A.F. officer, and a happy second marriage to an archeologist. Note how many mean, rotten characters in her books are dashing young officers, and how many nice archeologists there are. Many mystery writers of my acquaintance take the opportunity to bump off people they don't like in their books—suitably disguised, to be sure. You can satisfy your motivation in many ways!

The purpose of this book is to crank up your existing unconscious motivation so that it pushes you to write, and it is an easier task if you have some conscious values pulling from the other end. The types of motivation described here—the needs for achievement, affiliation, and power—can all be put in value terms as well; some people think it is important to meet and beat goals, for example, but they do not really get turned on by it. These people have the achievement value but not the Achievement Motive. Contrariwise, some enjoy having an impact on people (the Power Motive) but think it is bad or manipulative to try to influence others (a low power value).

If you can line up your values and motives, or even have them both tugging on the same task, you will have an enormous well of energy on which to draw, from both your heart and your head. Make it easy on yourself to write, because then your head will be saying "I think it is important for me to write" while your heart says "I enjoy writing."

Does this always work? No. Life is complicated. You may have equally important, mutually exclusive values. You may have immediate needs (like eating) that take over your longer-term desires. This happens to everyone, every day, and that is why it is useful to have both values and motives—one can pick up for the other at times.

But don't forget that one can block the other, too. "I want to have an impact and write" (motive), but "I should spend more time doing my bills" (value). Or: "It is important that I write tonight to stay on schedule" (value), but "I want to talk to a friend who is in town for a limited time" (motive). This is why I recommend that you ignore or avoid those who criticize your writing practices. They will create a new value in you, if you let them.

I do think that critics serve a highly valuable purpose in helping maintain standards of what writing should be, and no writer should assume total mastery of his or her craft. But for some people, criticism equals rejection. If you are a person who thinks that way, then stay away from critics, at least until you can develop a thicker skin.

Remember: Values are conscious thoughts, motives are emotional drivers. Try to link them where you can.

SELF-IMAGE AND SOCIAL ROLE: THINKING ABOUT YOURSELF AS A WRITER

The aim, if reached or not, makes great the life;
Try to be Shakespeare, leave the rest to fate.
ROBERT BROWNING, "Bishop Blougram"s Apology"

Motives are among our deepest and the most driving characteristics, shaping people's entire lives. However, that does not mean they cannot be shaped, diverted, redirected, or even thwarted. Your expectations of yourself or your role can influence even the power of these emotional drives.

If you see yourself as ineffectual, you are less likely to act, because after all, it won't work, right? Why take chances? If you see yourself as master of your own destiny, you may be willing to take more risks, because ultimately you believe it will work out, despite the many obstacles and opponents you may face.

In this section I want to trace where writers come from (who were they before they were writers?) and consider how they see themselves, what impact it has on them, good or bad, and then how you might see yourself. Finally, when you have accomplished something, do you see it as inevitably yours or as a happy accident? This, too, relates to how you see yourself and the fruits of your labors.

Here are the questions we will answer or discuss as we go:

- Where do writers come from?
- How do they see themselves? Does this view of themselves help?
- How do you see yourself?
- How do you attribute your successes and failures?

THE BACKGROUND OF WRITERS: WHERE DO THEY COME FROM?

When I read my first book, I started writing my first book.
I have never not been writing.
GORE VIDAL

Boozing does not necessarily have to go hand in hand with
being a writer, as seems to be the concept in America.
I therefore solemnly declare to all young men trying to
become writers that they do not actually have to become
drunkards first.
NELSON ALDRICH

Why did I write? what sin to me unknown
Dipt me in ink, my parents', or my own?
ALEXANDER POPE, "Epistle to Dr. Arbuthnot"

Where do writers come from? Most writers today do not start out as writers, because they cannot afford to unless they've had a large trust fund (like Larry Niven, who thanks a family member for just that in one book, because it enabled him to write, and to get rejected, and to learn for a solid year).

A study of good writers indicates that no single job is "required" as a prerequisite. In fact, you could argue the opposite (and some have): lots of "real world" experience strengthens your writing. All experience becomes grist for the writer's mill. Here are a few professions, followed by published writers who pursued them at some point in their lives, and sometimes at the same time, since writing isn't particularly well paid: Accountant, actor (Lauren Bacall wrote her own autobiography!), advertising professional, Aagent for MI-5, anthropologist, artist, astrophysicist, biologist, cartoonist, chicken farmer (Douglas Adams), chemists of all stripes, computer scientist, egyptologist, engineer, financial advisor, historian, jockey, journalist (okay, so this is sort of cheating), lawyer, librarian, magician (Houdini was not a gifted writer, but he published!), mathematician, medical doctor, mother, navy officer, neurologist, nurse, opthamalogist (Sir Arthur Conan Doyle—he didn't get a lot of patients, so he wrote instead), philologist, philosopher, priest (including Pope John Paul II, who wrote poetry), psychologist (yes, besides me), senator, speechwriter, stripper (former stripper, in Tony Fennelly's case), technical writer, therapist, veterinarian, and zoologist.

Almost any job can contribute to your ability to write; at the least, you will have experiences on which to draw. Jobs that require you to produce material on a regular basis (e.g., journalism, advertising) will blast you out of reliance on a muse, because if you cannot write to deadline, you are out of a job. This also builds up your self-image as being able to write on demand.

Some writers like a writing-related job, such as editing a magazine, because they stay attached to publishing; others like manual labor, because it has nothing to do with other people's writing and their minds are freed to think about their own.

Be what you are for your day job; it does not have to affect your writing, except in a positive way. Or, as one writer said when asked how long it took him to write his most recent book: "My entire life."

10 Assessing Self-Image

Why should a man who loves good painting, good wine, and
good food, living in a happy and well-deserved retirement,
suffer in the evening of life what all writers must suffer—in
Masefield's phrase 'The long despair of doing nothing well?'

GRAHAM GREENE

The act of writing puts you in confrontation with yourself,
which I think is why writers assiduously avoid writing. The
number of alcoholic writers makes a lot of sense because if
you're going to be face to face with yourself, maybe it's better
if you don't recognize that person.

FRAN LEBOWITZ

Writers, like everyone else, struggle with who they are. A writer who is unpublished wonders if he is really a writer; a stay-at-home parent questions priorities of kids versus writing and then wonders if she is really cut out to be a writer; someone who gets rejected thinks he is really no good as a writer at all.

Being published doesn't always help either. The paperback writer doesn't feel like a real author; the genre writer doesn't feel literary enough; the successful writer wants to be a bestseller; the bestseller wants to sell to Hollywood; the writer with dozens of movies produced from his books wants creative control or to be a director like Clive Barker.

Some people know they are writers, but some do not. Some, like Robert Heinlein or Kurt Vonnegut, stumble into it—the first because he was in ill health and needed money, and it seemed easy work (it was, for him), and the second because he had a personal story he had to get out but needed to learn how first. Some are obviously writers, but do not take either the profession or themselves seriously. And some want to be writers, work to be writers, and study to be writers, but always question whether they can really do it, even after they have a shelf-full of awards. And a few people think they are writers, then change their minds as they become better educated and realize how far they have to go.

Many stop there, but a few, like Robert Silverberg, take that acquired humility and use it to drive them to work all the harder. The same self-image can propel different people in different directions. In this section, I am hoping that I can help ensure that you always see yourself as a writer first. You may prefer to see yourself as a writer in training, but still—a writer first.

There is a literary conference on speculative fiction in Massachusetts, known as Readercon, that I have attended for years. For a while they had a panel called "Hacks vs. the Art Police." Some writers proudly proclaimed themselves to be hacks. They defined themselves as writers who did not obsess with literary attention but just kept writing books people wanted to read. Other people would take that label and use it to prod themselves. They turned the label of "hack" into a symbol of success. Remember that Shakespeare, Dickens, and Coleridge could all be considered hacks by some standards.

I have collected a number of words people have used to describe writers below. Not all are complimentary, but remember that most words can be used in more than one way. Ask yourself, "Which of these are me?" After that we can decide which might be helping you and which might not.

THE SELF-IMAGE SORT

Advocate	Impulsive
Amateur	Laborer
Artist	Lackadaisical
Avoidant	Literary
Catallyst	Missionary
Challenged	Obsessed
Comedian	Persistent
Craftsperson	Plugger
Creator	Popular
Dilettante	Professional
Disciplined	Reliable
Dogged	Sporadic
Doing a Job	Storyteller
Educator	Struggler
Entertainer	Success
Expert	Talented
Failure	Teacher
Gifted	Untalented
Growing	Wordsmith
Hack	Worker
Important	Writer

USING THE WRITER'S SELF-IMAGE SORT

1 Read the list completely and ask yourself, "What resembles me as a writer?"
2 Sort the list into two groups, "More like me as a writer" and "Less like me as a writer." They do not have to be the same size, but you should try to have at least fifteen words in each group.
3 Sort each of the two groups into two more groups, again "More like me" and "Less like me." This time, try to have at least seven in each group. You should now have four groups, each from seven to twenty words.
4 Take the topmost and bottommost groupings and decide on the top and bottom six items. Force yourself to choose, if necessary.
5 Compare the top six to the bottom six (the top 15 % compared to the bottom 15 %—okay, 14.3 %, really). What do you see?

This kind of thinking tool helps you to get a grip on a complex issue: how you see yourself. There are no "right" or "wrong" answers, only your answers. However, the comparison might help you to see what kind of person you think you are and what kind of person you think you are not.

Don't just do the "like me" list. You need contrast for the most revealing results. For example:

TOP SIX	BOTTOM SIX
Artist	Failure
Creator	Hack
Catalyst	Untalented
Growing	Amateur
Persistent	Literary
Wordsmith	Struggler

What kind of person does this sound like? Yes, it is a real person. Does this person sound confident? The kind of person you have to force away from the typewriter? Well, perhaps not entirely. This person sees him/herself as persistent and growing, but not necessarily obsessed or a craftsperson. This person might be susceptible to the "muse" myth or the "artistic temperament" myth that is described in Chapter 16.

Be alert to what you put in, and what you do not. This person considers him/herself talented and artistic but not literary. This could be an innovator, or it could be an eccentric who doesn't feel the need to see what others have done.

Don't treat this list as comprehensive; there may be more. If you find it hard to agree with any of these items, come up with your own. Identifying your self-image is very valuable to choosing your next steps. The next section discusses particular aspects of self-image that seem epidemic among writers I have studied; keep your short list in mind as we stroll through the minds of a few writers.

FOOLING THE WATCHER

LONGAVILLE: *I fear these stubborn lines lack power to move:*
O sweet Maria, empress of my love!
These numbers will I tear, and write in prose.
    WILLIAM SHAKESPEARE, *Love's Labour's Lost*, 4.3

Remember our earlier discussion of extrinsic versus intrinsic motivation? The expectations of others or yourself can inhibit your motives to write. At one literary conference I attended a panel titled "Fooling the Watcher." The entire panel of people—several award-winners among them, who had sold short stories, novels, and movies—discussed the difficulty of writing past or around their own internal critic, the voice of doubt. One member of this panel was so fearful of self-doubts that she wrote inside a trash can (that is, she put a pad inside a plastic bin) so as to avoid actually seeing the prose and thereby defeat the doubting voice within. Another panelist described turning down the brightness of the computer screen so she could not see the words. To my amazement, everyone on the panel and a number of people in the audience all nodded in agreement. "Yes, I understand that," they seemed to be saying. This is a common feeling. That panel helped propel this book as much as any other single experience I have had.

One way to defeat the watcher is to establish your own sense of self-worth; others, such as those above, simply found ways to avoid the watcher, unfortunately up to and including alcoholism and drug addiction.

Please note that the watcher is not a complete avatar of evil. This same panel agreed that sometimes you should invoke the editor and critic, or your work will never achieve competence. The question is when. If the critic emerges before you finish your first sentence, you may never reach the second, no matter how powerful your motivation.

In fact, a poor self-image can enlist motivation to *prevent* positive action. Take, for example, the Power Motive. It focuses on having an impact and sensitizes people to the reactions of others. A strong and positive self-image coupled with a strong Power Motive leads someone to face a crowd and say "What an opportunity to have an impact!" The same degree of Power Motive chained to a poor self-image will think "What an opportunity to embarrass myself!" One sees the positive potential for impact, the other sees the negative. The same applies for other motives: the Achievement Motive drives perfectionism and dissatisfaction with one's skill; the Affiliation Motive drives the fear of rejection by others. Who is right, the optimist or the pessimist?

Both are right. But the optimist will take an opportunity and possibly gain advantage out of it, whereas a pessimist might withdraw without ever having a chance to gain from it. If you do not believe you can write and publish, I guarantee you will not, because you will not bother to try. If you try, you may fail, but if you don't bet, you can't win.

That last sentence exemplifies a risk-assessment, and a value around one's best choice: "Better to have written and failed than never to have written at all." If you do not believe that, it will be very hard to write and do something with it, because it can undermine or even corrupt your own motives to try.

You may wonder why this feeling is so prevalent; I assure you that I can refer to the "watcher" in front of any group of five or more writers and easily half the heads will nod in agreement. I believe it is because the critical observer is an essential part of the creative self. Remember the "generate and select" mechanism of creativity? This is the selection section. Generativity without selectiveness produces gibberish. Note, for example, the many self-published cranks with theories about how Einstein was wrong (for example) or how medical science conspires to contaminate your body. Many such screeds show a lack of editing. So do "flames" on the Internet—writing that comes straight from the emotional center but does not stop at the mental editor on the way out. To balance both halves of your creativity requires a good deal of thoughtful effort.

Again, it is worth spending some time analyzing how you see yourself. To help you, let us discuss what I have seen in terms of self-expectation and self-image that affects the ability to perform.

"CAN I WRITE ON DEMAND?"

Writers who are overly concerned with the quality of their writing may refuse to finish, or edit over and over again. There are several reasons for this, primarily a lack of confidence in their own writing.

I used to take a long time with my writing, because I was afraid if I wrote quickly, it would not be good. I discovered when I had to write on demand that my prose did not change.

GEARY GRAVEL, Interview

I love deadlines. Deadlines are the only way I get anything done. I don't worry about the quality, because, hey, I didn't have time for that. I had a deadline.

ELLEN KUSHNER, Interview

These quotations refer to the quality of *letting go of criticism,* and some people cannot do so without an external source. Their own high standards and lack of confidence force them to rewrite until they are stopped.

The concept of a deadline, or indeed of any external demand, intimidates some writers. Several reasons apply here. First, a deadline is an *extrinsic* motivator. A deadline can establish in your mind the image that your writing belongs not to you but to someone else. Therefore it lacks fun—you are not writing for your own pleasure, but because it is just a job. Technical writers may not feel that way, because they always write on demand; likewise, reporters at least get personal credit for their work, which means it is theirs despite editing and deadlines. Nevertheless, if these professionals draw too clear a distinction between their personal writing and their work writing, the same effect may occur. Ideally, you can use deadlines to arouse your motivation rather than allowing them to delegate responsibility and ownership to someone else. With or without a deadline, your work ultimately belongs to you. Good goal setting creates an external motive that supports your own.

Another issue here is that the pressure of the blank page may inhibit starting the book at all. The expectations are too high even at the beginning. Some people find ways to give themselves permission to be bad. One writer I interviewed referred to his "zero draft" — the draft before the first draft. This writer, being a very meticulous and methodical person, felt he had to be meticulous even on his very first draft. He cites his use of this zero draft approach as very important for his writing.

12 The Imposter Syndrome: "Am I Really a Writer?"

I'm never going to be famous. My name will never be writ large on the roster of "Those Who Do Things." I don't do anything. Not one single thing. I used to bite my nails, but I don't even do that anymore.

DOROTHY PARKER, "The Little Hours"

The expectations of others also raise fears in a person about whether or not he or she is any good. "I'm just an impostor," he or she thinks. "Now they'll be sure to find out." Having others waiting on one's own work makes one feel inadequate to the task, because the threat of failure outweighs the promise of success. Failure is easy to imagine, since there are so many ways to fail. Anticipation of success requires a strong self-confidence, or at least an assurance born of experience.

The imposter syndrome has been written about elsewhere, including in this book (in the "Deadly Myths" chapter later on). But it merits some discussion here: in brief, it is the belief that you have fooled people into thinking you are good. In the course of observing a panel of writers who all suffered from this to some degree, an audience member asked, "How many awards, how many books does it take until you believe you are a writer?" One writer, Barry B. Longyear, just laughed. He had already won some of the highest awards offered in his genre and published over ten books, and he still suffered from it. One of his negative responses had been to drink, because drinking silenced the doubting voice. Motivation studies reveal that alcohol makes people feel strong and powerful—but at a price. This writer paid the price of alcoholism and rehabilitation: and ultimately, a decline in writing ability while intoxicated and an even greater inhibition while sober.

If you see yourself as an impostor, success will not magically change that.

of Terry Carr, an innovative editor who was then assembling a series of novels from new writers. He asked for a novel from Gibson, who wrote *Neuromancer*, the novel that set off the whole cyberpunk movement and coined the word "cyberspace." Eventually this led to the original short story becoming a movie. Frank Herbert took *Dune* to twenty-seven publishers. Richard Bach took *Jonathan Livingston Seagull* to over forty publishers. Whatever the intrinsic worth of each of these books and stories now, was it less when it was not yet published?

Remember that many people have material and few publishers have holes in their lineup. It takes time and effort to match the two up.

On the other hand, numerous writers have published one book, and no one says to these people, "Oh, you used to be a writer." No one worth listening to, at any rate. Remember *To Kill a Mockingbird*

3   **I have to write a story that someone (my mother, my friends, my colleagues, my roommate, my spouse) will want to read.** No, the only person who needs to read your story is you. Of course, you want others to read it (or you probably would not be a writer in the first place), but you cannot afford to be limited by one person's tastes. Nor can you be limited by the expectations or problems of those you happen to know. Why are they qualified to judge? Even if they bring some editorial discernment to the task, they may not like what you like. Their motives may well differ from yours. If you are just embarrassed by writing (say) a sexually explicit novel that your mother might read, then write under a pen name. Many others have, if only to disguise what they considered to be lesser works.

4   **I must do things (live my life) the way X does, or I am not really a writer.** If there are myriad ways just to write, how many more are the choices for living? There seems to be as much fiction about the creative process as there is created by that process, including statements such as "You must suffer for your art," or "Great writers are alcoholics and have terrible lives."

There are even myths about simply being a writer: "You should always carry business cards with your name on them, so you never miss an opportunity to sell yourself as a writer." No, I'm not kidding, that's a real piece of advice—but not from me. It applies more to freelancers who have published work under their belts and who wish to grab editors and the like on sight. "You should go to conventions and schmooze with everyone in sight." Contrast that with: "Writers can't go out and meet peo-

Instead, you will just think you have fooled everyone again, and when they find you out, your punishment will be that much greater for daring to win an award or publish so many books. Without a clear measurable standard that you will believe, no outside success will ever make you "good enough." In some ways Hemingway succumbed to his own expectations of himself to be a "real man." When in his old age he suffered physical disability and apparently felt he could no longer "be a man," he committed suicide. We are our own worst taskmasters, and only we can change that.

Sometimes something as strong as therapy or psychoactive chemicals is needed, but what is ultimately required is a change of self-image. Writers often hold several false assumptions and compulsions, especially (though by no means entirely) those in genres where they can hear from their fans, such as mystery and science fiction. Here are a few:

1   **I must write another book/article/story/etc.** False. Some people have one book in them. There is nothing wrong with that, especially if it is a good book. I'd guess most people want to avoid the situation described in a They Might Be Giants song: "I've got just two songs in me, and I just wrote the third." Nobody requires you to write except you. If you have a contract, that's a different matter, of course, but the principle still applies. Just because someone else wants you to write a book does not mean you want to write a book. I leave to you the moral struggles about taking money to produce a book you do not wish to write. For many professional writers, the work involved in writing a book they do not wish to write is much preferable to the work involved in being something other than a writer—"honest work," as some describe it. It happens to many people. The good news is that with enough practice you can write a decent work even if it feels like pulling teeth all the way. Joe Haldeman describes one book that sounded like fun when he contracted for it and turned out to be agonizing. When he finished, he was surprised to note that it was actually pretty good.

2   **I must continue publishing to be a writer.** Not so! A writer writes—no more, no less. Publishing is susceptible to the vicissitudes of the market, the whims of editors and agents, the presence of money to spend on authors, and so on. Sometimes the best writing cannot get published for years because it goes beyond the current state of the art. William Gibson, now recognized as a fine writer and the originator (if not the only practitioner) of the "cyberpunk" subgenre of science fiction, shopped around his first short story in that genre, "Johnny Mnemonic," for *four* years. When the story finally sold, it attracted the attention

ple," "Writers must sit in their office and write for eight hours a day," or "You have to get to know the editors personally." Forget 'em all. There is no single pattern to successful writers' lives and conduct other than writing. Some habits may assist you in your writing career (e.g., delivering your manuscripts on time), but even then they are not obligatory to writing in the first place.

As for a few writers' lifestyles: Poe was nowhere near as unhappy or alcoholic as he was depicted to be—a personal enemy wrote the primary biography. Eugene O'Neill became a great writer after he quit drinking and wrote *Long Day's Journey into Night*. Isaac Asimov, one of the most prolific writers of our time, was a teetotaler; so is the multi-genre writer Harlan Ellison. Lots of writers are happy as clams, and no two are alike.

5   **I should listen to my fans/the critics/the reviewers/etc. and go with what they recommend.** Heinlein's Laws of Writing include "Never rewrite, except to editorial order." Good critics can help you improve your writing craft; bad ones or even mediocre ones may not understand what you are trying to do. There may be no particular demand for your voice, but if you want to write and publish, you must listen to yourself *first*. Don't let people automatically convince you of their opinions, even those you respect. If you believe they have a point, and that you have flaws in your technique (who doesn't?), then change your technique and keep going. My rule of thumb: the shorter and less specific the criticism, the less likely it is to be useful. Smart-ass dismissals are for the critic's benefit ("See how clever I am?"), not yours.

6   **I can only write in one genre effectively.** Let's look at the evidence. Harlan Ellison writes in the genres of speculative fiction, mainstream fiction, horror, fantasy, humor, erotica, opinion essays, movie reviews, and television reviews, and in the formats of short story, short essay, longer essays, screenplays, novella, and novel. Robert Graves wrote fiction (e.g., *I, Claudius*) to support his poetry, as did Mario Puzo (*The Godfather*). Edgar Allen Poe wrote newspaper stories, horror, science fiction, psychological thrillers, poetry, humor, and essays. Shel Silverstein writes highly sentimental children's books (e.g., *The Giving Tree, The Missing Piece*), wicked parodies of children books (e.g., *Uncle Shelby's ABZ Book*), and highly explicit adult stories and cartoons for *Playboy*. Sarah Smith has written academic works, science fiction short stories, a mystery novel (*The Vanished Child*), a novel set in early 1900s Paris (*The Knowledge of Water*), technical writing, and a computer-moderated "interactive novel" called *King of Space*. Shakespeare wrote tragedies, comedies, and historical (what we would

now call "based on a true story") plays. The concept of a genre is a very recent one, started in the "pulp magazine" era of the twenties for the convenience of marketing books and magazines to a selected audience, not to reflect what writers actually do. Whole genres have been invented by a few writers who made them stand on their own. Stephen King has, almost single-handedly, made the horror genre distinct from fantasy and gothics, and even distinguished it from what horror used to be—Poe and Lovecraft, to name two noteworthy horror writers, differ sharply from King. If you enjoy writing in a genre, that's fine. Just don't assume you have to do so. In the heyday of the pulp magazines, the only way to survive as a writer was to churn out stories in whatever form would sell, so writers of pulp fiction wrote westerns, science fiction, mysteries, sports stories, whatever would bring them some cash.

However, don't assume that you should *not* write within a genre, either. Literary snobs tend to forget or overlook the fact that Dickens was a hack, Hemingway was a journalist, Faulkner wrote for Hollywood, and Shakespeare wrote to entertain the masses (using dirty puns and cheap humor). Thinking of yourself as writing in a ghetto does not do wonders for your confidence or self-assurance.

7 **I can only write in one length effectively.** Some people will say "you have to start out writing short stories before you move on to novels." Balderdash. Write whatever you want. The choice of length comes about through a combination of personal preference, the requirements of the story or essay, and the availability of a market. The novella is a fine and useful length that is almost impossible to get published, because it is too short for a separate book (in most cases, except for the occasional "double" books, once done by Ace Books and now by Tor Books), and most magazines don't like to fill up that much of their length with a single story, or only one per issue. So few people write *and publish* novellas. If you write only for fun, no problem. Similarly, the novel tends to be more effective economically than the short story, since it stays in print longer and generates more money over the long term, while an experienced writer does not expend that much more effort over a novel than over a good short story. On the other hand, the tight structure of a short story, while difficult for some, may be just what you need to get something finished properly. Some say that the short-short story is the most difficult form, but Fredric Brown was famous for writing dozens of them,

and Harlan Ellison has written virtually nothing else. I doubt that they refused to write "easier" stuff.

People also forget that each length had to be invented. The "novel" was invented only a few centuries ago. The fine distinctions noted by many magazines and awards (novel, novelette, novella, short story, short-short ...) came about much more recently.

8 **Only hardcover books are "real" books.** Most mystery, science fiction, and fantasy authors today started with "paperback originals" and moved on to hardcover deals. Sue Grafton, for example, with her alphabet series of mysteries (*A Is for Alibi, B Is for Burglar,* etc.) started in paperback, advanced to hardback in later books, then got her earlier books republished in hardback! Paperbacks are likely to get first-time fiction authors better sales and more readers, since people are more willing to invest in an unknown quantity in paperback than in hardcover. Nonfiction books are different, of course, because you can check qualifications. So are books with huge marketing budgets or a unique "hook," though these things might only distinguish their covers and size, not their quality.

9 **I'm not a real writer if I don't write full time.** Isaac Asimov, one of the most prolific writers of our time, did not go full time for ten years after he began publishing regularly. He finally did switch to full-time writing because he realized that his part-time writing paid as well as or better than his full-time university professorship, and full time writing would therefore pay more. On the other hand, some people are not cut out to write full time; most people cannot afford it. Either way, it bears no relation to the fact of writing or the role of writer.

10 **I have to write with a pen / typewriter / word processor to be truly creative.** A writer writes. Some use computers, some use fountain pens. They may even prefer their tools and perform better with them: Harry Turtledove writes in longhand, Eleanor Arnason uses only a Cross or Parker ballpoint pen, L. Ron Hubbard used a specially designed typewriter with single keys for "the" and "of," Gregory Maguire writes in notebooks, Spider Robinson uses an Apple Macintosh computer. Graham Greene said in the *International Herald Tribune* in 1977, "My two fingers on a typewriter have never connected with my brain. My hand on a pen does. A fountain pen, of course. Ball-point pens are only good for filling out forms on a plane." Nevertheless, do not confuse the tool with the process. It is an interesting historical note that

every time a new device was invented to make writing easier, some benighted "artist" would complain that it took the soul from writing. This has been recorded for the fountain pen (replacing the quill, for Pete's sake!), the typewriter, the electric typewriter, and the word processor. No doubt the first person to actually draw a story in mud bricks was criticized for removing the creativity of the spoken tale. Ignore these people. Use what you like, or what makes it easier for you. John Barth finds neatly typed first drafts "paralyzing," but Ralph Keyes finds the "elastic quality" of computers, where nothing is indelible, reassuring because "mistakes can be corrected, improvements made, material added." By the same token, you need not buy the tools these people use just because they like them. The fact that I simply adore my Apple Macintosh does not mean you have to give up your fountain pen. As Fran Lebowitz noted: "I don't write fast enough to require a word processor." Isaac Asimov, on the other hand, wrote too fast (and too cleanly) to require a word processor rather than a typewriter for anything shorter than a novel. These are the trappings, not the substance. (Although they may help to circumvent other obstacles; as one person put it, "If Dickens had had a word processor [instead of writing in longhand], a degree in English literature would take eight years instead of four.")

13 Attribution Theory

Ever tried. Ever failed. No matter. Try again. Fail again.
Fail better.

SAMUEL BECKETT, *Nohow On*

I have not failed. I've just found 10,000 ways that won't work."
THOMAS ALVA EDISON

Attribution theory is a body of psychological study devoted to people's attributions around their successes and failures. It has been linked to a variety of long-range impacts, not least of which is success in your job and in your life. For our purposes this is part of the feedback loop that begins with the completion or failure of a task. In other words, when you finish a book, why do you feel you managed to finish it? Is it due to your ability, dedication, and spunk? Or did you simply get lucky?

I am not referring to how people politely aver when praised, I'm talking about how you feel about your accomplishments or lack thereof. This can make a difference to your next accomplishment—or lack thereof.

IT'LL NEVER BE LIKE THIS AGAIN

I heard one writer talk about her fear of writing a second book. For her first book, she had nine wonderful months where she enjoyed writing. She stopped at one point and said, "This is too good to last." In this case she was correct: a week later, she lost her job, her home, and her time to write. It took two and a half years of hell (her phrase) to finish. Even though she won awards for that book, she was afraid to start again, lest it be as painful the second time. (Though I will note that she seemed pleased to be part of panels at conferences, which she enjoyed far more than the writing itself, which she had given up.)

This kind of reaction reminds me of the clinically depressed. One attribute of the depressed person is that they never think things are all that great, and, more importantly, that things will never get any better than this "not that great" state. Part of therapy for depressed people (when they are not so serious as to require medication) is to get them to remember that they have been happy before, and they have been depressed before, and they have come out of it. In other words, things change. You cannot assume that your whole life will be like any one small portion of it.

You may wonder where attribution theory comes in. Deciding that a single experience will happen all the time is an example of an attribution—in this case, that a failure is due to an enduring characteristic of the task itself. Clear differences in performance among people relate to their attributions. In brief, attributions fall into three dimensions: is the cause of the failure or success internal (me) or external (outside me); is the cause of the failure or success a temporary event or an enduring phenomenon; and is the cause of the failure or success a specific reason or a global one? The worst-case for most jobs is a failure attribution of internal/stable/global: I failed because I am no good at all. The attribution is internal (I am), stable (no good), and global (at all). Of course, if you are that bad, then there is nothing you can do about it, is there? Or at least that is what you might think.

Optimistic people do the opposite. "This time, in this place, it was not possible for me to succeed." In other words, it was time specific (this time), situation specific (this place), and external (it was not possible—it wasn't me). Some research I have participated in suggests that it may be appropriate to make an *internal*/temporary/specific attribution when the focus is in improvement. For example: "It wasn't my doing, but I'm responsible, and I'll fix it." Change is a normal part of our world. People grow, and alter, and the world alters as well. If you condemn yourself to a certain state, saying "that's just the way I am," you are not allowing yourself to get any better. In a business where you can spend years getting rejected, it helps to remember that editors don't reject you, they reject little pieces of paper with writing on them. George Scithers, the former editor of *Isaac Asimov's Science Fiction Magazine,* said that, so presumably he knows what he is talking about, especially since he helped a lot of good new writers get started.

In a case such as the writer described above, it is easy to assume that the next book will be the same as the first. But a moment's reflection will reveal that this is almost invariably not true. Presumably you will have developed your craft, so that things that were hard before will be easier now. It may also be that you pick a harder task, but getting past the first book often resolves a whole host of problems that will therefore not emerge in the second.

Many have written about the phenomenon of learned helplessness; a person deprived of effective action long enough loses belief in his or her own efficacy. Let's look at publishing a book the first time in this context. First, you write day and night, whenever you can, with very little outside support (unless you are lucky). People will cheerfully tell you that you have no chance and that you are wasting your time, or they will ask you if you are published yet, making you feel like a failure if you reveal that you are not.

Finally, you finish. You send out query letters and samples to agents and/or publishers. What happens? *Nada*. People you have never met send you criticism of your work, to which you cannot respond and that you cannot be sure is accurate. (One writer I saw on a panel brought an inch-thick stack of rejections for her first book, including these comments from two rejection letters for the *same* book: "characters not convincing" and "wonderful characters.") You are beset on all sides, and people who know you are trying will ask you if you are published yet, and if not, why not?

Then you sell. You get your pitiful advance (average $5,000 for the field *including* people like Stephen King), and your friends and coworkers assume you are filthy rich, because they think the average advance is $50,000. (Don't laugh—it's happened twice to my wife.) Then you have to start all over again, and maybe do your own marketing for the first book in the bargain, because otherwise you won't even earn back your advance.

This is an ideal setting for learned helplessness. The antidote is intrinsic motivation. You don't write to get that pitiful advance, you write because you want to write. You may write for yourself and no one else, but that is enough.

Writing is one of the few avocations that people do not allow you to pursue as an amateur. Many people are amateur painters, actors, even magicians—but when was the last time you heard of an amateur writer? If you dare to tell anyone you are a writer, their first question will invariably be "Are you published?" Or, even worse, "Where are you published?" It takes strong internal motivation to deal with this.

To hell with everyone else—if they don't understand, that's their problem, not yours. That is an example of external attribution for failure. Practice it: the editor had a bad day, the publisher is full of books, the market is bad, they have no taste. Just keep going. Every failure is that much closer to success. It works for sales people, it will work for you.

Remember: Don't blame yourself when there are plenty of other things to blame!

And one last word in this section before we get into specific motivational thoughts for the writing process: don't let anyone tell you their "one way" to write. There is one way—but it must be yours.

I am sure there are many other things you will hear about how to define yourself, who you are, and how you should do what you do. Just remember: *they don't apply to you*. Period. People will try to "help" you, out of the best of intentions, and only mess you up. Whatever works, works.

14 The Problem Solving Model:
Inside A Motivated Thinker

An artist is only an ordinary man with a greater potentiality—same stuff, same make up, only more force. And the strong driving force usually finds his weak spot, and he goes cranked, or goes under.

D. H. LAWRENCE, *The Letters of D. H. Lawrence*

We have discussed the core driver of the motive, but now it is time to talk about the elaborations around the motive: the subcategories. Motives do not manifest in a pure rush of emotion; they are filtered through your brain and come out in different kinds of thoughts, ranging from the "explicit need" statement ("I really want this relationship") to "instrumental action" (They worked day and night on their idea"). The pattern of thoughts that manifest around a motive is called the problem-solving model, because it relates to accomplishing a goal, and that's what motivation is about.

In the early days of motivational research, a very interesting experiment was done to discover what motives were about. The researchers studied the most basic motive of all: the need for food, otherwise known as hunger. They took sailors in the U.S. Navy and asked them to fill out a picture story exercise without telling them its true purpose: to discover how people thought who were hungry as opposed to those who were not. Some were fresh from the mess hall (the control condition), but some were at the end of a shift and anxious to eat. What did the hungry men write about when given ambiguous pictures? You might think food!

Not quite.

They thought about *getting to* food. From an evolutionary standpoint, you can imagine why that subtle difference is crucial to survival: someone who simply thinks of food when he gets hungry doesn't get fed. Someone who thinks about obtaining food does. That's why the model has only one category about visualizing the need and eight about getting to a goal or failing to do so.

THE PROBLEM-SOLVING MODEL IN EASY STAGES

Remember this diagram? I had different text in it before.

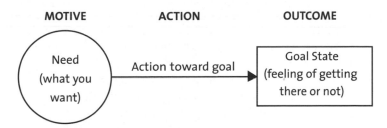

Figure 3. The problem-solving model: simple action

This is actually the problem-solving model at its simplest: motive (energizing thought or need), action, and result—accomplishing or failing the goal. The difference between the Achievement Motive and the Power Motive is *inside* the boxes: are you working toward an improvement goal, or toward influence on others?

However, if motivation is about *getting to* your goal, this simple model isn't enough. Successful people don't just think/act/receive. They do some other things, too.

One key element of effective problem-solving is *looking ahead*. Anticipating how hard it will be to achieve a goal, or how likely one is to succeed or fail, can have a big impact on what you choose to do. This is one of the reasons why achievement-motivated people don't often become writers: it's too much of a long shot! Achievement-motivated people tend to take moderate risks with a good chance of achieving a result. Power-motivated people, on the other hand, are anticipating the impact when they make it, so long shots just increase the impact from their perspective. Either way, anticipation is a critical element to motivated action.

So we add "anticipation" to the model, as a dotted line arcing over the action.

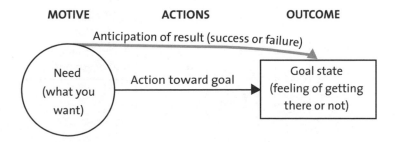

Figure 4. The problem-solving model: action plus anticipation

But, of course, all is not smooth when striving for a goal. You don't always have the option of seeing what will happen, and you don't always succeed in the action. There are obstacles or blocks to your success. In this model, we define two: *external* blocks, things outside you; and *internal* blocks, things yourself have. If you are trying to influence someone and they are never home, that is an external block. If you are trying to influence someone and you are incompetent at it, or even just hesitant, that is an internal block. Both can prevent you from success.

People aware of blocks are better able to circumvent them; so again, it is important to capture this thought in the model of motivation.

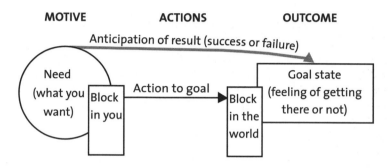

Figure 5. The problem-solving model: plus blocks

That covers almost everything. There is one other useful element to problem solving, and that is external assistance (like this book, or a writer's group). This is known, simply enough, as "help." This is (sometimes) how you get past those obstacles. And that is the entire problem-solving model!

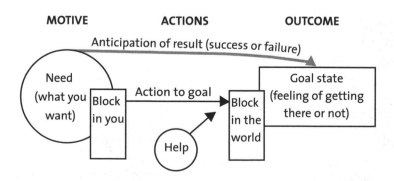

Figure 6. The complete problem-solving model

Remember that this model came from the study of numerous successfully motivated people, and it is a blueprint for thinking in a motivated way. We'll take parts of this for a lot of different uses, but to be clear, let's go through the subcategories again verbally, with a brief, writing-oriented description for each, sorted out by person, action, and result:

THE PERSON

Need: Explicit statement of the goal: "I really want to impress the critics with this one."

Block in the person: Obstacles to success in the actor: "I can't do it. I can't seem to finish a whole novel—I can't remember it all!"

Anticipation of success: Just what it sounds like: "I think I can pull this off. If I just write another thousand words, I'm done with this thing!"

Anticipation of failure: "I'm afraid I will fail. I'm afraid I can't end this book."

OUTSIDE THE PERSON

Instrumental activity: Action toward the goal: "I have worked day and night on this."

Block in the world: Obstacles to success in the world at large: "My printer is out of toner!"

Help: Outside assistance from another person: "My writers' workshop buddies all came over to help me with this section."

AROUND THE GOAL

Positive goal state: "I did it, and I feel fantastic!"

Negative goal state: "I'm really disappointed in myself for this."

This came from motivational research, but it describes exactly how to solve problems and accomplish goals. Most people don't show all of these all of the time. Here are a few examples of how people behave with only a few subcategories going strong:

- Instrumental action without anticipation or blocks: "Ready, fire, aim!" (or just "Fire!"). These people jump into action, but do not think about the ramifications.
- Anticipation of failure, block in the world: "Why bother?" These

people see all the reasons not to do something—writers are ill-paid, people steal your ideas, only a few people get published any given year—and as a result never begin anything.
- Need: These people know what they want but don't know how to begin to get it.

And so on. We'll come back to this in several places, including a discussion of plotting and how you set goals for yourself. For now, just consider that writers don't just have raw motivational emotion—you need to elaborate on it a bit.

PART IV: CREATIVITY

If we pretend to respect the artist at all, we must allow him his freedom of choice ... of innumerable presumptions that the choice will not fructify. Art derives a considerable part of its beneficial exercise from flying in the face of presumptions.

HENRY JAMES, "The Art of Fiction"

It's kind of fun to do the impossible.

WALT DISNEY, *Interview*

Everyone is a genius at least once a year; a real genius has his original ideas closer together.

GEORG LICHTENBERG, *Aphorisms*

15 Motivating Your Creativity

Unfortunately, an author's creative power does not always follow his will; the work turns out as it can, and often confronts its author as it were independently, indeed, like a stranger.

SIGMUND FREUD, Moses and Monotheism

The fun is the creative stuff, when you're sitting out there and you say, What the hell happens here? And all of a sudden Pow! And you're just lifted out of your chair by it. That is sensational!

WILLIAM KINSOLVING

People see the fruits of creativity as a pure, white light, shining brilliantly through the fog. Creativity is a magical thing, a precious thing, something beyond the tawdry efforts of a mere mortal. "You feel like God on the seventh day," wrote legendary mystery and religious writer Dorothy L. Sayers (in *Gaudy Night*).

This feeling—and seeing the output instead of the process—clobbers motivation for many people who could otherwise be highly creative. "I know I can't do that." But what if you can?

Imagine a prism, if you will. Usually we see the white light broken by the prism into all of the colors of the rainbow. But the reverse is also true: white light combines every color of the spectrum, the entire range. Ironically, the "purest" color of light is actually the most commingled.

So it is with writing, or indeed any creative task. Many, many different parts of a person come together to create. Inspiration alone could not be enough, or your average kindergartner would equal Shakespeare. People forget this is true, because like anyone else who knows their work, a good writer makes it look easy. The next time you read smooth, apparently ordinary dialogue, compare it to a real discussion, where people stutter, fumble, pause, wander, insert "um" and "ah," and generally throw a lot of friction into their prose. If you ever read a verbatim transcript, the clumsiness of ordinary speech will surprise you.

Look at the task of reading. We largely take this ability for granted—note how much of what we do depends on it, from various work tasks to storm warnings on television to our daily news. And yet it is so phenomenally complicated that behavioral biologists point it out as the product of exogenous evolution, meaning we had to evolve to do it—though we did so accidentally.

Reading requires you to coordinate your eyes together, make short "jumps" called *saccades* to read a few words at a time (a task so difficult that 10 percent of first-graders—a six-year-old animal—cannot do it), read the shapes, interpret those images as words, link them to their definitions, do a grammatical analysis, link them to related memories, and, oh yes, make sense of the sentences—not to mention remembering plot, character, and setting—and all of this so fast that you can read an amusing billboard and laugh at it as you pass it on the highway at a mile a minute. Sounds more like juggling flaming chainsaws, doesn't it? And yet most people do it casually, without thinking. In many of us the coordination of these myriad abilities happens so smoothly that one pays no attention to the fact that they must *be* coordinated.

Creative efforts, such as writing, reflects the same complexity, with an even wider spectrum of elements required. Writing requires everything reading does, plus a whole set of things related to being creative effectively.

The art of motivating your writing has to do, at least in part, with coordinating all of these different elements, so that when combined they produce that pure white light.

Creativity is not just one thing! It includes

- underlying motivational energy and enjoyment;
- traits of how you think and create;
- the way you see yourself, your work, and the world;
- skills of various kinds around work, managing yourself, and managing your creativity;
- key pieces of knowledge about yourself and your work;
- knowing and managing the outside environment to allow these elements to function.

If one piece of the spectrum goes badly awry, the color of the combined light will be tainted—or at least tinted. This happens even to highly experienced and productive writers; if their lives change in some unforeseen way, they find their productivity declining or halting for a time. One key advantage experience brings is the ability to make up for missing pieces and continue anyway—perhaps going at a slower pace but still functioning, knowing one can function and can get past obstacles. Every time a writer gets past a temporary block, he or she becomes more aware that blocks *are* temporary.

This book goes into some detail on the colors of this spectrum of creativity, in part to abbreviate the time required to gather sufficient experience, but you should keep in mind that people differ in their approaches, so not everything will apply to you.

16 The Seven Deadly Myths of Creativity

Writing's not terrible, it's wonderful. I keep my own hours,
do what I please. When I want to travel, I can. I'm doing what
I most wanted to do all my life. I'm not into the agonies of
creation.

RAYMOND CARVER, *Writers on Writing*

Generally in this book I deal with the motivation to write, without commenting on the quality of writing, or how you go about improving it, other than practice. However, when discussing how motivational science can support and drive art, I have been startled by people who actively resist this idea. I have concluded that one of the chief obstacles to motivated writing is what people think writing is. But creative effort is as susceptible to motivation as any other effort. I'd like to debunk a few of the myths, using some of the science available, so we can get back to the art.

When trying to distinguish writing from everything else, sooner or later someone will say that it is a *creative* endeavor. I do too. But these people use this as a weapon, fighting off those who suggest that creative endeavors are work like any other endeavor. You can find my response below, but let me quote a few of the weapon-wielders first.

The mystics say creativity is mysterious. Mere humans cannot define Creativity (and they usually use capital letters, for some reason), for it is being touched by God.

Then there are the snobs: you require a good education to truly create at the peak of your ability, they say. Your IQ needs to be high. Really sensitive work comes from certain social classes.

I find that the former will not only wait for lightning to strike to begin writing but also assume that every word is pure gold when they hear the thunder—a terrible burden to lay on God, to my mind. The latter are the kind of people who cannot accept that Shakespeare was common instead of noble, educated in an ordinary school and not by tutors; likewise, they assume they write well simply because they have been educated and score well on standardized tests, which in truth fail to correlate at all with performance in the real world, let alone measure anything as slippery as writing.

And finally, there are the humble: "I'm not really creative. I'm no Einstein."

It gives me great pleasure to say that when you look at the evidence, all three groups are incorrect. Some writers work like crazy to hone their prose, others possess neither a high IQ nor advanced degrees, and still others don't think of themselves as creative and yet turn out marvelous work. These are all *myths*— something many people believe that is nonetheless wrong.

What's bad about these myths? They can inhibit someone's writing—either that of the person who believes them ("I'm not creative, therefore I can't write"), or a writer near the person who believes themt ("You need a degree to really write, therefore you can't, because you don't have one"). In motivational terms, these myths are *personal blocks*, internal obstacles to success, and they may be the biggest blockers of motivation to write.

Let me lay down a guiding principle now for our discussion in this chapter: *all* human beings are creative. It belongs to our genetic heritage. Some possess more creativity than others, but I have never met anyone absolutely devoid of the stuff. All of these myths, on one level or another, try to deny this fundamental fact. With creativity as a given, though, you can put motivation to work using it.

I think the confusion begins when one sets too high a standard for creativity. A person who takes a set of apparently mismatching clothes and accessories and puts together a fetching ensemble is being creative, in a power-motivated way (thinking about impact). When you follow your wanderlust and try to identify a new, more efficient route to work, you are being creative in an achievement-motivated way (thinking about efficiency). Helping your kids make posters or jury-rigging that hardware is creative. Once when I was trying to fix some plumbing (not an expertise of mine), I realized that I lacked a wrench of the proper size and could not unscrew the pipe by hand. Suddenly I thought of applying a rubber jar opener to improve my grip, and it worked. The satisfaction of that task remains with me, and I find no difference between that feeling and the satisfaction of composing an essay, a short story, a simulation, or a sketch.

Creativity is combining unexpected things into something new, but you don't have to set unreasonable standards for what that is. The claw hammer was a marvelous invention in its time (it still is). The Pyrex dish came about accidentally (but creatively), when a scientist's wife complained about unevenness in cooking from her metal pots and pans. The scientist happened to work with special laboratory glassware, common enough in chemistry, that was heat resistant and transferred heat more evenly than metal. He gave her a battery casing made from this glass, and she baked a cake in it. Thus was a new kind of cookware born. While we're on food, trying a new combination of spices and ingredients to create your dinner is creative (even if it doesn't work).

You don't have to be Picasso or Shakespeare. You have all you need to be creative. But sometimes you may have an erroneous view of what that means. I would like to puncture a set of suppositions that even highly talented and productive writers may hold. I call them the seven deadly myths, because they can be fatal to your creativity. (There may be others I haven't identified, but it sounds pretty catchy this way, doesn't it?) Here they are:

1 Heredity: "Creativity is born, not made."
2 The Muse: "Creativity comes of its own accord—I must wait on the muse."
3 Solitude: "I have to be alone in a quiet place to be creative."
4 Discipline: "I must be disciplined to be creative."
5 Similarity/The "Right" Way: "I must write the way X does, or I am not really a writer."
6 Completeness: "Creativity must spring full-blown, like Athena from the brow of Zeus."
7 Worth/Belonging: "I don't belong here; I'm not one of the creative."

HEREDITY

If you believe that creativity is born, not made, why are you reading this? As noted above, creativity is inherent in the human brain. One theory of creativity, by psychologist David Perkins, is the "generate and select" theory. Basically, you *generate links* between different things and extend the links farther and farther out. Then you *select* the combinations that work. Take the typical good mystery plot. It may start with:

The butler did it.

Then proceed to:

The police *think* the butler did it.

Then later become:

The police *thought* the butler did it, but decided the evidence proved them wrong. But—aha!—in fact the butler *did* do it, and planted phony evidence.

See the links? You keep moving farther and farther from the original idea, but you can see the steps, moving from "did it" to "didn't do it" to "did it but looks as if he didn't." That's the generator in action.

The "select" mechanism comes into play when you go too far, or when there are too many choices. Let's carry on with our example:

> The police think the butler did it, but the detective thinks he didn't. In fact he did do it, but instead of creating an airtight alibi in which he didn't (because airtight alibis always appear suspicious to the detective), he deliberately set up a way to make them *think* he did it, but made them question themselves, so they would be afraid he didn't do it and avoid trying to convict him on inadequate evidence.

Sounds kind of strained, doesn't it? Time for the selector. Back up a notch, this one's too silly. The selector tells you when to stop, or when to cut to the chase.

That's all there is to it: idea generator, idea selector. That doesn't sound too complex, does it? But to generate *effectively*, it helps to have a lot of connections to make. This is a legitimate reason for why people say to "write what you know." It gives you more resources with which to play. The more you know about a subject, the more complex and interesting are the relationships you can establish between pieces.

Motivation channels creativity: it controls what you are interested in being creative about. Power-motivated people think about managing information in a way that creates maximum impact. A classic writing technique is to play on people's expectations and then surprise them. This comes from knowing how people will react, which is a highly power-motivated skill. Achievement motivation, on the other hand, may lead someone to be highly creative about better ways to do things—better methods or interesting ideas. Some science fiction writers have to design whole worlds before they write; this is probably achievement-motivated creativity at work.

While people do vary in their creativity, and where it can be used, you can develop it. Numerous books can help you do just that. Furthermore, you can hone it on your own just by using it.

Remember: If creativity is hereditary, you've already got it.

THE MUSE

Creativity is something built into the human brain; it is not imposed from outside. Circumstances can certainly inhibit your creativity, but it is still there. You don't walk when the mood strikes you; you walk because you need to get from point A to point B. Likewise, creativity can work for you on demand.

Like any form of exercise, the more you practice your creativity, the easier it gets. People who write nonfiction professionally, such as journalists or technical writers, find the idea of "writer's block" strange—they have no time for such luxuries. Some fiction writers feel the same way. Tom Wolfe, a journalist and fiction writer, sums it up: "With a gun at my temple, the work is just as good as what I write when I'm waiting for the muse that's never there, who's strumming the harp in the sky." And yet some become hooked into the myth that fiction is different. It isn't really so: the more you do it, the better you get. One simple cure for writer's block is to form associations that work; if you get into a block, leave your desk at once. Try to ensure that when you sit down at your writing desk (or computer, or what have you), you are accustomed to writing. If you deliberately link productivity with every time you sit down, after a while you will associate the mere fact of sitting down with productivity, and the setting will arouse your motivation to write.

If you associate creative effort with something that does not really contribute to your productivity—say drinking or a full moon—then you will be less productive. Don't wait on the muse—she won't wait on you.

Remember: The muse is you!

SOLITUDE

Being alone may reduce distractions, but that doesn't make it necessary. Isaac Asimov wrote regardless of what went on around him, because he had to. He started writing while working in his father's candy shop, where he was constantly interrupted. Mihalyi Chiksamahalyi wrote about "flow experience"—the most creative period of thinking—taking place after about twenty minutes of steadily working alone, but for some people (known as "extroverts") the most creative time is working with others and trading ideas around a table. You can either block distractions out, or get into an environment that washes them out (like a bus or a plane), or simply produce less efficiently.

Jane Austen wrote a sentence or even a phrase at a time into a book set on a sideboard, because that's all she had time for. You'd be surprised how much you can produce that way, if you are willing to work at it. However, those with significant amounts of Power or Affiliation Motive are more likely to be distracted by people around, which is why it *does* take more work and concentration. If you can get solitude, it might help; on the other hand, a writer's group or workshop may also help you work out new ideas. Many people find the idea of a blank page intimidating, knowing that what goes on that page must come only from them. For these people, a supportive group can help. Groups are not necessary or even desirable in some cases (despite what some people will tell you), but it is a viable option. We'll talk about workshops later. Some people get energized by knowing there are people around, as long as they don't actually speak to them instead of writing.

Remember: Solitude is in your head, not in the environment.

DISCIPLINE

Discipline implies that you have to consciously work at something or it won't happen. If you allow yourself to enjoy the process of creating, you don't need discipline. Motivation works better than discipline for most people; motives *supply* energy, whereas discipline *drains* energy. If writing is always a chore, then perhaps you shouldn't be doing it. Not that you don't have to force yourself to perform on some occasions, but don't confuse regular writing with tight discipline. They aren't the same thing.

Here's Carole Nelson Douglas, who writes prolifically in multiple genres: "Discipline doesn't do it. Yes, in a minor way, discipline keeps a writer at the keyboard when there are Nazi midget transvestites on *Geraldo,* or never-before-seen varieties of bird in the backyard. Or popovers in the oven. But the greater factor is stability: in the writer's life situation and in the writer's head. There certainly won't ever be much stability in the writer's publishing climate." In other words, *manage* yourself rather than *force* yourself.

Insisting that the only way you should write is through forcing yourself to do so is masochistic at best. As Barry Longyear once said: "Don't beat on yourself." A good portion of this book is about motivation rather than discipline. Where discipline comes in handy is to get you started when you *don't* feel like it.

Remember: Discipline is for the bad days, not every day.

SIMILARITY/THE "RIGHT" WAY

"There are nine-and-sixty ways of composing tribal lays / And every single one of them is right!" So said Rudyard Kipling ("In the Neolithic Age"). No two writers use exactly the same style. Nor do they have the same habits. Saying, as one writing book does, that you "must learn Latin to write" is dangerously narrow-minded thinking. Joseph Conrad wrote great works in his second language, English (Polish was his first). Poe wrote sentences averaging forty-five words long; Hemingway averaged ten. *Bright Lights, Big City* was written in the second person, virtually the only published novel to have done so successfully. Flaubert invented the idea of a single viewpoint for a novel. The ancient Norse used alliterative poetry to tell epic tales, the ancient Greeks a chorus. Rex Stout plotted completely in his head before setting pen to paper. Heinlein invented some characters, got them in trouble, and tried to get them out, typically using the plot he called "The Man Who Learned Better." Philip K. Dick wrote each successive chapter to explain the previous. Tolkien never plotted at all, writing *The Lord of the Rings* as he went and rewriting it later. Some writers outline, others do not, some do both for different works. One cliché is "write what you know," but that would eliminate nearly the entire *corpus* of science fiction, which is based on "what if" and invention. *Don't limit yourself.*

One student of creativity named its "Three B's": bed, bath, and bus. In other words, most of his good ideas came in one of those three places. It has been said that Einstein always took great care while shaving, because that is where his best ideas occurred to him, and the jolt of an idea would cause him to jerk and cut himself. None of the Three B's help much in terms of training oneself to create more (despite humorist Douglas Adams spending inordinate lengths of time in the bath), though on the other hand, when fantastically prolific short-story and novel writer Fredric Brown occasionally ran dry, he took a long bus trip to someplace boring so that the boredom forced him into creativity. I wouldn't want to rely on that, though, and neither did he.

That does not mean that other writers haven't learned skills through experience, thought, and training. It does mean that the same skills do not apply to all people—at least where creativity is concerned. I suspect that people feel this way for a number of reasons related to their motives. If achievement-motivated people look for the most efficient method, why not use one that works for someone else? If you are affiliation-motivated, it might be an issue of trusting someone you like. If you are power-motivated, it might be a case of being impressed by someone famous. I advise you to find what works for you, instead of going with your gut.

Remember: The only writer you have to write like is you.

COMPLETENESS

The myth that creativity must spring full-blown like Athena from the brow of Zeus was held by no less a person than Charles Darwin. In his story of how he came up with evolution, he claimed that he had a burst of insight while reading Malthus that enabled him to identify the process of natural selection. Since Darwin kept detailed, dated notebooks of his daily thoughts and reading, the evidence to prove this actually exists. Scholar Howard Gruber read the notebooks carefully, came to the day when Darwin read Malthus, and found ... nothing. No brilliant insight, no recorded leap of creativity. A continued study of Darwin's notebooks revealed exactly the opposite: ironically, evolution *evolved* in his notebooks. In retrospect it may have seemed sudden, but in fact the idea came piecemeal. You don't have to work in "a white-hot burst of creativity," as Alfred Bester put it. Not that it isn't nice, but for longer works, it can't be done anyway.

Mozart typically wrote in first draft, but that doesn't mean he never thought about it first—just that he didn't *write down* his first thoughts. As noted above, Beethoven is equally praised, but he tinkered with his work over and over again.

Some assume that great work must come spontaneously from the soul, that there is no (conscious) control over it, or that editing would only damage it. Writers who have a particularly lyric style tend to have fans who believe that their stories came from such an illumination, rather than hard work. John Crowley (*Little, Big*), a person who writes in such a way, once expressed himself at length—strongly—regarding this illusion. And it is an illusion: he labors over his phrases, adjusting every line and sweating over it. When hearing him talk about this, I got the distinct impression that he resented the assumption that he didn't have to work for his marvels.

Konstantin Stanislavsky, the man who invented "method acting," came up with it because he was a mediocre actor watching a great actor. He could not imagine that the subtleties he saw could come from "acting," so he decided that it came from identifying intimately with the character. Unfortunately, evidence exists that he was wrong. The man he supposedly studied (but never spoke to directly) actually spent hour after hour honing the craft that made his art possible, rehearsing expressions, movements, and voices.

This may not seem particularly encouraging, but look at it this way: you can make your creative work better, and you don't have to pray for that one perfect moment to come rolling out. No one has to know how much effort you put into it. No matter how many drafts you write, they only publish the last one.

Achievement-motivated people, particularly those who are more focused on efficiency, will not be surprised by this; incremental improvement comes naturally to them. To the power-motivated, however, where big impact is key, this may feel disappointing. Not at all—it means that you don't have to worry about the earlier drafts so much, because the final draft will have greater impact.

Remember: You only publish your last draft, not your first.

People seem to feel that there is some magic criterion that forever marks you as "a creative person." Furthermore, you don't really belong to the company of other writers unless you bear this mark of Cain.

Some people establish targets, that they think will in turn establish them. "This means I am officially a creative person, an author." People who think this way often get surprised when they reach that point and nothing seems any different. Instead of ignoring the idea entirely, they decide another criterion must exist, farther down the line. "When I get an agent." But you still are not published, right? "When I am published." But what if it was only paperback? "When I have my first hardcover." "My *second* hardcover." "My first award." "When my book is in Brentano's on Fifth Avenue in Manhattan." "When my book is on the *front table* at Brentano's." "When I win the Nobel Prize for Literature."

When does it stop?

Never. This attitude can be part of the "imposter syndrome"—"I don't really deserve this, and the minute they find out, they'll take it all away. I'm not really a creative person. I have to work very hard to do this." So that makes it worse? You're not naturally creative, so you work twice as hard to come up with something just as good as the "naturally" creative person, so it can't be that good. And you say you aren't creative!

Creativity is a process, not a target. Achievement-motivated people are particularly prey to this concern, in that what was good enough today isn't good enough for tomorrow—if they achieve a target, that means it is time to raise it. It is vital to acknowledge what you have done and set it against its proper context: most people never even *start* to write.

Remember: You don't need a creative license!

FORGET THE MYTHS

Isaac Asimov once said that if *he* could be a successful writer, anyone could. You use creativity for all of the arts, but also all the crafts. Writing is a craft as well as an art, and crafts can be learned. You may not be Shakespeare, but we already have a Shakespeare. Furthermore, not everyone likes Shakespeare. Some remarkable people read a wide range of books that are good in ways different from the Bard. My late mentor, the famous, brilliant, and creative psychologist David McClelland, read mysteries for fun. So does President Clinton. John F. Kennedy—a creative writer in his own right—liked (and made famous) James Bond novels.

There is *no single criterion* for establishing yourself as a legitimate writer—except the one you set for yourself. Allow me to present some excuses people could make for "not being a real creative person." To drive the point home, I also list a famous creative person who fits that criterion.

EXAMPLES FROM HISTORY

Excuses for Not Being Really a Creator	Actual Creative Person
"I only wrote one novel."	Harper Lee: *To Kill a Mockingbird*
"I've never written a full novel, only short fiction and essays."	Harlan Ellison: winner of several Hugo Awards, Nebula Awards, the pen award, the Edgar, the Raven . . .
"I've only written some plays and poems."	William Shakespeare
"I've only written nonfiction."	Charles Darwin: *The Origin of Species*, etc.
"I only wrote one book, and it was nonfiction."	John F. Kennedy: *Profiles in Courage*
"I only sold one piece, and that was to a relative who felt sorry for me."	Vincent Van Gogh

You can write for yourself if you want. You can write for others. But the fact that you are writing at all makes you a writer. Nothing more, nothing less.

Setting additional goals can help you become a more successful writer, as in having more people read your work, but that means you are a working writer, not a person who is yet to become a writer.

John F. Kennedy said it well: "There's always room for one more good one."

PART V: GOAL SETTING

There are only two tragedies in life: one is not getting what one wants, and the other is getting it.

OSCAR WILDE, *Complete Works*

Obstacles are those frightful things you see when you take your eyes off your goal.

ATTR. HENRY FORD

17 Overview of Goal Setting

*I write when I'm inspired, and I see to it that I'm inspired at
nine o'clock every morning.*

PETER DEVRIES, *The Observer* (London), 1980

Much of this material has been incorporated into other chapters, but let's talk about the principles that underlie goal setting and why it matters.

When I say "goal setting," I mean the process by which you identify targets for producing something—prose, a finished edit, a limerick, etc.—before you do it. In other words, the plan for productivity. Too restraining, you say? Too bureaucratic? Why bother with laying out what you plan to do before you do it?

First of all, because goal setting *works*. According to stacks of research, your chance of finishing your book, story, epic poem, etc., improves by doing some kind of goal-setting process.

"Okay, I want to write a 75,000-word book by tomorrow that will be a best-seller."

Perhaps not *any* kind of process, however. In fact, different kinds of goals apply to different situations, and they depend both on how much information you have and how far ahead you are planning. For some of what follows I am indebted to the work of fellow motivational psychologist and McClelland student Richard Boyatzis (*Primal Leadership*). The types of goals he picks out are frequently discussed, but I'm using his naming conventions. He identifies three:

- rational goals (also known as "SMART" goals)
- direction and domain
- muddlin' through

The first is best for short-range or highly organized goals, such as word count. The second is better for long-range, more nebulous goals, where you know the basic thrust but not necessarily how you will get there: goals around genre or size of work, for example. The third is good for very little *unless* you really have no reason to prefer one choice over another, so you wing it. It is inefficient but sometimes useful for gathering information.

Let's spend a little time referring to the work of Boyatzis on goal setting, going in order from least to most specific:

MUDDLIN' THROUGH

This is really the absence of goal setting: pure trial and error, doing things until one works. In the business world, one example of this process is the introduction of automatic teller machines or cashpoints (ATMs). When they were developed, no one had any idea how and where they should be placed. How do you set a goal for establishing ATMs when you do not know where they will be?

What happened is that people tried everything. ATMs were placed inside banks, on the outside walls of banks, in isolated kiosks, in special places within malls, in grocery stores — everywhere. With time, it became possible to gather sufficient data to determine where future ATMs could be built—moving to a new kind of goal setting.

In writing, this is not an efficient way to set goals. However, to some extent all writers may be forced into this, in two ways. First, there are people who will claim that this *is* the process of art: accidental discovery of a process or style you can make your own. This philosophy assumes that Picasso stumbled onto cubism through random experimentation and was bright enough to see its potential or at least intrigued enough to keep using it. The counter-argument is that Picasso had a profound understanding of the history and practice of art and worked deliberately to violate certain conventions based on ideas from the pioneering work of others, pushing it until it became uniquely his. I lean toward the latter interpretation for Picasso (you might have guessed), which really puts him in the realm of "direction and domain" goals, but I wouldn't completely eliminate the factor of chance in art, either. Even if you succeed with this approach, "muddling through" is still not particularly efficient.

The second way this becomes forced upon a writer is in terms of getting your work out. If you come up with your own idea, your own direction, the only way to know if people want to read it is to try to sell it. You have to keep sending it around until it sells or you decide to try something different. William Gibson was not able to sell cyberpunk until the market was ready for it — at which point he invented a new subgenre the minute his novel was published. Anne Perry wrote ten novels that never sold before selling her British Victorian-era mysteries. But those first ten were set in different times and places. She just kept writing until something sold—and in the United States rather than her native Britain, oddly enough. She said at one point that she would never leave the Victorian setting again, because it sold. It took a long, weary time to find her forte, but she did. Interestingly, as of this writing she has just published a fantasy novel, so perhaps she feels she can finally afford to experiment.

DIRECTION AND DOMAIN

These goals are rather more focused but not what you would call detailed. When you can clear away some of the underbrush, you determine the *domain*. Anne Perry determined her domain (Victorian-era Britain) and could then focus in on that. Many (if not most) writers tend to have some domain focus from the beginning, some area that compels them. A genre, such as science fiction, mystery, romance, or horror, is a domain. A "hardboiled mystery" or "hard science fiction" or "Regency romance" is a smaller domain. A length (short-short, short story, novelette, novella, novel, series) is a domain as well. People with special knowledge or interest may choose a domain that builds on their strengths: Aaron Elkins, a physical anthropologist (specializing in bones) wrote mysteries starring—surprise!—a physical anthropologist. Barbara Mertz, a.k.a. Elizabeth Peters, an Egyptologist, writes mystery novels related to Egyptology. Many science fiction writers are engineers or scientists: Heinlein, Asimov, Clarke, etc. Domains are delimiters, defining the area in which you want to work, or the playing field for your game. Football, baseball, cricket, basketball? Choose your game.

A direction is just what it sounds like. What do you want to do within your domain? Most writers start with "Sell what I write!" But you can also try to extend what you do, or tell a particular story, or offer a lesson. Kurt Vonnegut learned to write in order to tell the story of his traumatic experiencing of the firebombing of Dresden during World War II; his direction was to get to that point. He did not know, when he started, how many years he would require or how he would get there other than in the domain of science fiction novels and short stories.

Do not forget that you can pick a *new* domain, too. If you have an interest in a period, for example, no one says you have to be an academic expert already to do well in it. Shelby Foote considers himself a novelist, but his research into the Civil War (for his novels and ultimately for his three-volume history) was so thorough that Ken Burns used him as a historical reference and interviewee for his television series *The Civil War*. Similarly, science fiction writer Harry Turtledove is a historian specializing in the Byzantine Era, but he has since applied his historical training to so many other times and places that he now has a reputation as a master of the "alternate-history" story, where things diverge from the history we know. He won several awards for the Civil War–era story *The Guns of the South* and also set a series in an alternate World War II. After anthropologist Aaron Elkins, described above, had success with his Gideon Oliver anthropologist series, he began a series about an art historian.

This kind of goal is very good for long-term focus, since it narrows your direction but does not define it completely. Where it fails is in daily work.

RATIONAL GOALS

These goals are rather more concrete and detailed; they are designed to accomplish specific, relatively short-term tasks—up to years, potentially, but typically of a shorter duration. When you have your direction and domain, the logical next step is to start thinking about how to get there. A shorter goal is to write a book. Then you can set up structure around measuring your progress. When done fully, rational goals closely resemble the problem-solving model, and for good reason: they use all of the same elements.

These goals have very specific characteristics, and you are likely to run across them in many works designed to help you set and accomplish goals:

1   **Specific.** They need to be precise, not vague.
2   **Measurable.** You need to be able to know how far along you are.
3   **Moderate risk.** The goals need to be challenging but still attainable.
4   **Time-locked.** A goal needs a deadline.

Ideally, you want some of the first two kinds of goals—preferably together. For example:

Direction and domain goal:

> "I want to be a successful mystery writer who writes 'tea cozy' mystery series with good characters and who is read by at least a small but loyal audience that follows each book in the series; and I want that audience to grow for each book."

Rational goal:

> I will write at least 600 words in a single writing session, four days a week, or at least 2400 words in the entire week.

These latter goals are my restatements of the goals set by my wife when she got rolling on her Laura Fleming mystery series. Her direction and domain goal is pretty much the same (though she has added others around expanding her scope), but her rational goals have evolved as her abilities have grown—which is as it should be. I'll use her again later, because she is a natural at goal setting, and I have particularly detailed access to her thinking.

To complete the set, I'll give you an example of a "muddlin' through" goal: "I want to be a writer some day." Pithy, but useless. Lots of people want to be writers. Few do it, and even fewer publish.

Let's take a look at each criterion in detail. These apply to *any* goal, of course, but I want to give you some solid writer's examples.

Specific

If it isn't specific, you don't know when you have reached it.

Bad example:

"I want to write." Write what? Mysteries? Nonfiction? If you write a letter, have you reached your goal?

Good examples:

"I want to complete a first draft of a mystery novel." A good early goal.

"I will write four pages a day every day." A typical goal, used by many.

"I will finish my short story over this weekend."

Measurable

If it isn't measurable, you don't know how far along you are toward your goal. This is essential to helping your progress as well as your outcome—it is a pleasure to be able to say "I am three-quarters of the way finished."

Bad example:

"I want to write a mystery story." Of what length? How much counts? You could write multi-book series, novels, novellas, short stories, essays, short-shorts, limericks, or haiku. When do you get that "warm feeling" that Heinlein described?

Good examples:

"I will write 600 words four days a week."

"I will generate five scene cards today."

"I will have enough to show my writing group this month."

Challenging but Realistic

This is absolutely key. If you do this well, you are really incorporating the other three criteria. However, this is the most difficult element because the degree of challenge and realism varies from person to person.

Bad examples:

"I will sell a novel this year." Is this realistic if you have never sold before? On the other hand, it would not challenge Isaac Asimov enough. Stephen King wrote under the name Richard Bachman to assure himself that he could sell a book on its own merits and not just on his name—a way of checking his ability but also raising the bar again.

"I will write some prose people can read and enjoy." This might be so easy that you never complete it—or even start! After all, you could do that any time. This may partially explain those annoying people who say "I've often thought that if I could just sit down for a while I could write a book." What book? And obviously they don't consider it a challenge to generate 75,000 words of coherent, readable, organized prose—which is why these people are annoying to professional writers, who know just how difficult it is. Not to mention why those people virtually never actually do what they say.

Good examples (remembering that everyone is different):

"I will write one scene a day." Kelly Tate set this goal (which could include a number of cards of scene description), and her long-range (direction and domain) goal was to eliminate her stack of scene cards. She set this first goal to be time sensitive. When you have no more than four hours a day to write (thanks to your kids), you had better set an achievable goal. One scene was about right, and she experimented to ensure that it was.

"I will write 200 words a day on average and definitely 1400 words per week."

"I will write one sentence of my doctoral dissertation every day." This graduate student had a terrible fear of writing, and this was the way she ensured that she would *keep going*. One sentence felt safe, even every day. Frequently she exceeded this goal, but her fear made more than that seem unrealistic.

"I will write eight hours a day, five days a week, and six hours a day the other two, unless forcibly removed from my typewriter." Isaac Asimov probably didn't set this goal consciously; it was just what he did. It worked for him.

"I will break out from the limitations and low rates of pulp science-fiction magazines into anything and everything: slicks, books, motion pictures, general fiction, specialized fiction not intended for science fiction magazines, and nonfiction." Robert

Heinlein's goal when he returned to full-time writing after WWII. He succeeded by the end of the 1940s.

"I will sell a novel not under my own name." Stephen King, as above.

Time-Locked
If your goal isn't time-locked, you won't have a deadline.

Bad example:

"I will write some fiction someday" is so realistic that it isn't energizing. It won't push you until you are on your deathbed eighty years from now, at which point you will probably have other things on your mind. And what happens if you get hit by a bus?

Good examples:

"I will write two limericks this weekend."

"I will write 600 words today."

"When I sit down for my four hours today, I will write one scene."

"I will finish 2400 words this week."

As you can see, these goal-setting criteria often overlap. This is inevitable for the good goals; it is the bad ones for which we need the separate criteria. At any rate, if you can answer "yes" to the question "Does my goal meet all four criteria?" then your odds of actually meeting it go up sharply—as much as 70 percent.

However, before you just copy down some of the goals listed above, let's be sure they are the right kind for you.

18 Goal Issues: Finding Your Balance Point

*If everything seems under control, you're just not going fast
enough.*

MARIO ANDRETTI

Now that you know the basic criteria for a good goal, there are other issues that surround the process of successful goal setting, that enable the precise attainment of that magical balance point or "hot spot" implied by the Yerkes-Dodson Law.

The underlying purpose for a calculated goal-setting process comes from taking the law and making it useful for you. The art of goal setting, and indeed of this entire book, is to *identify and use the degree of aroused motivation that leads to maximum sustainable performance.* That varies widely from person to person, making some investigation and thought necessary.

In my experience people often understand the goal-setting criteria above very well in the theoretical sense but hit a brick wall when it comes to actually using them. So here are Kelner's Rules of the Balance Point, a few thoughts to ponder as you set your goals.

1. Different people need different goals.
2. "Challenging" and "realistic" depend on your perceptions.
3. The balance point of appropriate motivation changes according to external issues.
4. The balance point changes according to internal issues as well.
5. Give yourself flexibility in your goal setting.

DIFFERENT PEOPLE NEED DIFFERENT GOALS

The inverse of this ("everyone should use a single goal") is an extension of the myth that you should write like someone else. In my research I interviewed people who wrote one sentence a day and people who wrote four thousand words a day (Asimov could theoretically write 40,000 words a day; L. Ron Hubbard wrote even more); people who wrote for an hour, four hours, or all day and into the night. Do not be afraid to select a goal that works for *you*, regardless of what anyone else might think. The fable of the tortoise and the hare applies: the person who wrote one sentence a day *finished* her lengthy doctoral dissertation, and that is all that matters. If a goal doesn't work, move it. Anthony Trollope said, "Three hours a day will produce as much as a man ought to write." But Anne Bernays thought it was "shameful" that on her best days she wrote only about three or four hours. Others write eight hours a day. Do not focus on *how much* you do but on what *feels right*, so you can continue to do it. Setting high goals that inhibit your writing will not do you any good at all.

Naturally, motivation applies here as well, since motives are about achieving different kinds of goals. The motives you bring allow you to set different goals. If you are highly affiliative, it may not be reasonable for you to spend a weekend alone writing. But you could conceivably do a writer's workshop with your writing friends. If you are highly achievement-motivated, you can set more goals around the process of writing, which may be rewarding in and of itself.

"CHALLENGING" AND "REALISTIC" DEPEND ON YOUR PERCEPTIONS

At one time, my wife found herself running behind on a deadline—there had been some deaths in the family and other issues. She studied the schedules and decided that she had to write two thousand words a day—double what she had set for herself previously, though she had hit that number on some occasions. Toni had been a professional technical writer for years and in the course of having published two books and a short story was normally writing 1,000 to 1,200 words a day. What do you think her productivity was after setting this goal? Zero. The goal appeared too high.

But that was just it: the goal *appeared* too high. Toni turned to me to help her, and I made a suggestion: set *two* goals of one thousand words each—one for the morning, one for the afternoon. I knew Toni was perfectly capable of writing two thousand words a day, but I suspected that the goal seemed too huge and was daunting her. People cannot reach for an impossible goal. There is a myth (often found among coaches and managers) that deliberately setting the goal too high forces people higher. In the long term or even the short term, this fails. People know when the goal is impossible. If you do the best job you can and still fail (and then get punished for it) because of an unrealistic goal, why bother to do your best work? It certainly isn't energizing to throw yourself at a job when you know you can never make your target.

On the other hand, some goals are possible but do not appear possible. If I went up to you and said, "You have to write a 72,000-word book. You have one year. Can you do it?" What would you say? Probably a resounding no! On the other hand, if you break it down into bite-size morsels, "chunking" it:

72,000 words in a year is . . .

6,000 words a month, which is . . .

200 words a day, which is . . . the length of the above one-and-a-half paragraphs from "But that was just it" to "no!"

That doesn't sound so bad, does it? Let me make this a concrete suggestion: take the big goal and break it down into its components, or you will not be able to accurately assess the degree of challenge. By the way, Toni modified her goals. She set herself a primary goal of 1,000 words per day—her normal goal—but twice a day. Others could do this with an *option* for a second 1,000-word goal. She felt she could manage that, and it put the decision back into her hands. You see, she could confidently hit the first goal, which meant she had one success already as she went into her second goal. She started producing again, and in fact usually hit that 2,000-word mark, but she gave herself both smaller chunks and an out in case she was not able to hit the mark. She regained her pace and was only slightly (and acceptably) late.

In terms of the motivational subcategories, this affects your anticipation of success or failure—something well worth managing!

THE BALANCE POINT CHANGES BASED ON EXTERNAL ISSUES

The amount of time you have available, for example, may not be entirely within your control. Saying you will write 1,200 words a day is not appropriate if you are working two (other) jobs already and you write slowly. If something happens that throws you off, you may need to reassess your goals, because what was reasonable may now become unrealistic. I mentioned deaths in the family above; suddenly dropping everything and flying somewhere is guaranteed to derail your plans. Consider it a "block in the world"; you either need help, or you need to adjust your goals, but either way you need to fix the unattainable.

The best example I can think of is having a baby, one of those changes that is impossible to predict exactly. Your entire life transforms not only in some predictable ways but also in ways that depend on the nature of the baby and your relation to him or her. All you can do is revert to "muddlin' through" goal setting and hope to narrow it down to direction and domain as soon as you can.

If you have a baby who goes to bed early, sleeps through the night, and wakes up happy, then you can manage your time well. But what if your baby is colicky? Suddenly you could be up at any time at all, perhaps driving your child around to soothe him or her, short on sleep and long on aggravation. To make matters worse, this is not a predictable issue; not even from month to month, because infants change so rapidly.

What can you do? There is, as you may suspect, no easy answer here. All you can do is *reassess the realism*. Mystery writer Charlaine Harris abandoned her writing for the first five years that she had kids; others get an au pair; still others just keep writing at a slower pace. One writer I know worked immediately after the baby was born, relying on her husband to take extra time with the baby while she completed an almost finished project. It strained them both, but it worked, and she felt comfortable taking time off after that project finished, within the first month or so.

Also remember that things change, and therefore you can change again with them. This is profoundly frustrating to very organized people, but sometimes life is like that. Colic usually only lasts the first three to four months; kids go to school; other people can help you.

You cannot ignore the potential external blocks. You can try to manage them, if you stay alert to them as they happen. Some even plan for a disaster per month, because, sure as shootin', it will happen. If not, well, add another goal!

THE BALANCE POINT CHANGES BASED ON INTERNAL ISSUES

Not only does the outside world change, but you change as well. Remember how much of this book is about individual perception and ability. When you start, four hundred words a day for a novel may seem overwhelming. After you have published a couple of volumes, it still may not be easy, but it will not be overwhelming any more. Your development or re-evaluation shrinks the internal block.

I recall a person who wrote a long and complex doctoral dissertation and said, "After that, I knew there would never be anything as bad again." (You know, that might have been me!) At any rate, going through the mill can give you self-confidence. Likewise, public announcement of a goal has been found to increase the chance of its accomplishment, but it can also increase the pressure so high that you fall over the top of the bell curve and start sliding down on performance, unless you know you can do it. Confidence allows you to use that public announcement, instead of letting anxiety freeze you up.

Greater confidence also usually means you can pick up speed. Furthermore, one *might* hope to get better over time. One day science-fiction writer Geary Gravel found that he did *not* have to go over his drafts obsessively, that his first draft actually looked pretty good! This meant that he could do almost all of his polishing in a second draft, so he cut the time for a novel substantially. Toni increased her goal-per-day to keep pace with her own interest.

I have a friend who occasionally found himself driving late at night—well, early in the morning, actually—in a state of exhaustion. His solution (and no, I don't recommend it) was to increase his speed "until it got interesting again." In a way (a crazy way, to be sure), he used the Yerkes-Dodson Law to overcome his exhaustion: to push himself back up the energy curve until sheer panic would keep him awake. Similarly, if writing at thirty miles per hour no longer challenges you, start picking up speed.

The Yerkes-Dodson bell curve continues to shift upward. What challenged you yesterday does not challenge you today. So move the curve, or you may find yourself losing steam.

GIVE YOURSELF FLEXIBILITY IN YOUR GOAL-SETTING

I suppose nearly all of the above comments boil down to this single statement. By flexibility I don't mean vagueness or fudging—take your goals seriously, and act on them. What I mean is that goals do not occur in isolation. They must fit you, your abilities, the circumstances around you, and so forth. This may be as simple as giving yourself a fallback. Toni set a goal of six hundred words a day for four days a week—so she could adjust which days she wrote as needed—but also set a fall-back goal of 2,400 words for the entire week, so if things went *really* badly she could do four days' worth of writing on Sunday. That is what I mean by flexibility: not compromising your performance, but allowing it to happen multiple ways *when necessary.*

SUMMARY OF A GOOD GOAL

A good goal should be

- specific, measurable, challenging but achievable, and time–phased;
- right for your level of challenge;
- based on your current perceptions of what is challenging enough;
- affected by external issues;
- changeable based on your internal issues;
- equipped with built-in flexibility (e.g., fall-back goals).

EXAMPLES OF THINGS YOU CAN INflUENCE FOR GOALS

- Quantity of writing: number of words, pages, lines, etc.
- Quality of writing: first-draft or free-written material with misspellings vs. spell-checked, grammatical, final draft material
- Quantity of edited pages: number of pages revised/added
- Time of accomplishment: how much over what period (speed of writing)

- Time available for accomplishment
- Fallback goals over longer periods
- External rewards (candy, reading a book you've postponed, sex)
- Internal rewards (emotionally satisfying rewards, e.g., writing the fun sections)

PART VI: THE PROCESS OF WRITING
HOW IT WORKS, WHAT YOU DO

Writing is a craft. You have to take your apprenticeship in it like anything else.

KATHERINE ANNE PORTER, *The Saturday Review*, 1962

First I get some characters into trouble. By the time I can hear their voices, they're usually out of trouble.

ROBERT A. HEINLEIN, quoted in *Starlight*

19 Styles of the Creative Process

*I've got a great idea for a novel. If you just write it, I'll split
fifty-fifty with you.*

A REMARKABLY ANNOYING PERSON,
SPEAKING TO A PROFESSIONAL WRITER

For some people, finding that writing does not require simply "applying your
fundament to the furniture" comes as a shattering blow. Because we are a verbal species and dialogue composes the majority of most fiction, people come to
the erroneous view that all you have to do to write a book is to somehow sit
down and "talk to the typewriter," and after a sufficient time you will have a
volume. Unless you are Isaac Asimov, you probably can't do that. And he's dead.

MOZARTIAN AND BEETHOVENIAN

There are two types of people in this world: those who divide people into two
types, and those who do not. (I fall into both groups.) Motives divide people into
at least three, but in this section I want to discuss two basic styles of the creative
process: the Beethovenian and the Mozartian. Note that we are not talking
about "style" in the literary sense—that is, the pattern of words, sentences, paragraphs, and themes that make a writer recognizable. I am referring instead
to the writing process by which prose or poetry are generated, not what comes
out the far end of the pipe. "Beethovenian" and "Mozartian" are nicknames
attached to the ends of the spectrum of creative practice, which happen to be
well represented by the composers Wolfgang Amadeus Mozart and Ludwig van
Beethoven.

Mozart's music sheets were nearly all first drafts—completed music going
straight from his head onto the paper with little or no correction. The *Mozartian*
creator does most of the work in his or her head, writes largely in first draft, and
does not require editing. (At least, that's what the writer thinks. Editors and

readers may believe otherwise!) Likewise, legend has it that Shakespeare never blotted a line when writing his scripts. His contemporary and friend Ben Jonson commented, "Would that he had blotted a thousand," but perhaps he was just jealous. Rex Stout, the author of the Nero Wolfe mysteries, never put word to paper until he had organized the entire book in his head. He wrote entirely in first draft. Isaac Asimov, who only bothered to use his word processor for novels, also fit into this category. He wrote, "I think at ninety words per minute, and I write at ninety words per minute." His frequent columns and articles were always first drafts, but he organized them well for easy reading, even when dealing with arcane aspects of science.

I heard Asimov speak on several occasions, and it struck me that, apart from a strong (and somewhat startling) Brooklyn accent, his speech *exactly* matched his prose. It was measured, literate, and precise—and about ninety words a minute. Furthermore, he could extemporize at will; he had gifts that enabled him to quickly produce organized, smooth prose and then speak it at once. As I listened, I understood that to him, writing was merely speaking on paper. Since he spoke well, he wrote well.

Beethoven, by contrast, fought with his music, trying to make it different from what had gone before—including, and especially, the music of Mozart. These are the people who agonize over words, who tear up drafts and start over, whose pages are more red ink than black. These writers and creators are the people who must struggle to find the *exact* right word.

James Joyce spent seventeen years writing *Finnegan's Wake,* revising constantly. Award-winning writer (and dyslexic) Samuel R. Delany, in his memoirs *The Motion of Light in Water,* shows a page from one of his books that is virtually *all* edited. Editor and writer Judith Merril told a story about when she had locked herself in a hotel room to complete three writing assignments on a short deadline. After writing steadily all day, churning out volumes of prose, her friend Delany came by beaming. Merril, who was in a bad mood indeed, knowing how much she had to do, asked him what made him so happy. "I have written a perfectly *wonderful* sentence," he said, "and it took me only *twenty minutes!*" Sitting in her hotel room with stacks of paper she had written *that day*, Merril was struck by the dramatic differences between the two of them, and how fortunate she was. She lacked time, not writing ability or fluency.

"I have rewritten—often several times—every word I have ever published. My pencils outlast their erasers," said Vladimir Nabokov. "I can't write five words but that I change seven," moaned Dorothy Parker. Others, not so driven to change, may simply be unable to keep the entire work in the brain. Some of us, unlike Rex Stout and his mental mysteries, need to write it down and look at it once in a while. People carry around with them a varied set of intellectual gifts, and memory is one of many.

I have often helped my wife as she thought through her mystery plots, and if I made a suggestion she could instantly pull apart the threads of the story and show the links from my suggestion to other parts of the book that were affected. If you cannot do that, you are unlikely to be Mozartian, but I hasten to note that my wife is not wholly Mozartian either. I suspect that you are unlikely to be a mystery writer either, at least if you feel the need to change your plots after you write them. On the other hand, some rewriting becomes unnecessary once you have practiced eliminating mistakes. My wife's first novel went through several complete drafts; her fifth had one complete draft and a thorough run-through of editing.

In brief, Mozartians tend to create all-of-a-piece and more or less fully developed prose (or art or music or accounting or whatever you happen to be creating), while Beethovenians tinker, edit, revise, and alter their way to completion.

There is no inherent superiority to either type; they are simply different ways of being creative. It would be foolish to say that Mozart's music surpasses Beethoven just because he liked it the way it fell out the first time. Likewise, I am not about to suggest that Beethoven possessed more talent because he took more time to revise. In the end, both were stupendous, and that is what is important: the quality, not the quantity. Some Mozartians would benefit from a course in rewriting, and some Beethovenians need to learn when to quit. Time and effort provide the experienced writer with the ability to alter approaches as necessary—just one of the massive set of skills that practice provides.

Of course, these two types stand at extreme ends of a spectrum. Most people fall somewhere between a pure Beethoven and a pure Mozart, rewriting to some degree but perhaps having an occasional short work pour out of the typewriter (Alfred Bester called these "pianolas," meaning that they played themselves out without conscious intervention).

The advent of the word processor has altered this typology somewhat, in that you can change your words so quickly that you might not even notice you are editing (in fact, I wonder if the word processor in effect expands the boundary of the writer's mind; instead of holding things in your memory, you hold them in your computer's buffer). Nevertheless, the general rule applies: some people edit a lot, and some don't. Some writers ignore spelling, punctuation, or even grammar until the second draft; others never let a typo go by, even in their notes. Some don't make typos at all. (Aren't those people irritating?)

You may wonder what this has to do with motivation. Having motivation alone is not enough—"Now he tells me!" you think—for it must be fed through your various traits, abilities, and skills. As a result, the Mozartian writer's problems are different from the Beethovenian's. Often the biggest problem for motivating Mozartians is to get going and not to lose momentum if they stop.

It was said that Michelangelo, who sculpted with a speed so fantastic that chips flew about him like rain as he labored, quit working on the statuary group that included *Moses* because for once in his life he made a mistake on one of the other figures and as a result chose to abandon the group, never to return. Whether or not this is true, it does provide a good example of one kind of

Mozartian artist. For someone who can't put something on paper until it is complete, getting to that point may cause a kind of mental constipation. In motivational terms, the idea of starting over may feel ridiculously large.

Alfred Bester described having to build up his steam by pacing back and forth as he gathered the threads of his story and then bolting for the typewriter. When writing interviews for *Holiday* magazine, he had an area of the office that everyone avoided because he paced back and forth there, presumably building up to that critical point on the Yerkes-Dodson bell curve. But you can also imagine a Mozartian writer like Samuel Taylor Coleridge, who only managed to write the first part of "Xanadu" because of the "person from Porlock" who knocked on the door at that wrong moment and derailed the drug-induced vision that had guided him.

The problem for most Beethovenians, by contrast, is to *keep* going, instead of editing so often that you just give up. A few Beethovenians do not quit, but they will not stop revising, either. Had friends not forcibly removed the manuscript from his hands, J. R. R. Tolkien would have rewritten *The Lord of the Rings* over and over again, as he did with *The Silmarillion* for three decades. His Beethovenian perfectionism made it nearly impossible for him to finish a manuscript. In fact, *The Silmarillion* was only published because he died! Tolkien rewrote so often that his son's compilations of his earlier drafts and previously unpublished works now far exceed that of his other published works—indeed, they nearly triple that number, the last time I looked. This man would not quit. Or there is *Blue Bayou* author Dick Lochte's experience: "Each time I'd return to the manuscript, I'd begin by reworking that first chapter. Before long I had a brilliant first chapter, but I'd grown tired of the book" (*Writer's Digest*). Beethovenian style can wear you out, especially with too much Achievement Motive, which can lead to perfectionism.

As I noted above, this is a wide spectrum of creative styles. In this book you will find suggestions for making your writing process more rewarding in the motivational sense, but everyone's style of writing is a bit different, and Mozartians and Beethovenians often require different approaches. I have tried to supply suggestions for both sorts. For yourself, I recommend a general guideline: if a tactic *seems* inappropriate to the way you write, it probably is. Do not assume that all suggestions will work for you, or that if one fails, you should give up. Remember Mozart and Beethoven, and try something that works for you.

Remember: Mozart and Beethoven were both excellent, but they created very differently. Use the suggestions that work for you and pass on the ones that don't.

---

20 Steps in the Writing Process

Let's take a little time to examine just what the writing process entails. Here we get into a dicey area, but I'll try to stay objective. Different people write differently, of course, and even those who use this exact process won't necessarily call each step by the same name. These are just names to describe certain steps in the typical writing process. Feel free to substitute your own.

FICTION	NONFICTION
1 Generate ideas	1 Identify topic
2 Plot	2 Research
3 Characterization	3 Lay out material
4 First-draft writing (description, dialogue)	4 First-draft writing (prose, captions)
5 Editing	5 Editing
6 Rewriting	6 Rewriting

This is a partial and general list. For example, you could write whole books about word choice, paragraphing, chapter breaks, even punctuation, and some have (for example, see *The Well-Tempered Sentence,* a marvelous guide to those strange marks that pepper written English). Some people have written whole books about screenplay writing. Some writing endeavors combine aspects of nonfiction and fiction; for example, historical mysteries or Regency romances require a good deal of research in addition to all of the other tasks, enough to exclude the more casual writer.

Why is this important? Because different motives drive different tasks. I have seen far too many people fail to complete a doctoral dissertation because, while they can do research and analyze data, they are incapable of writing or even just completing the writing they have started. Alas for them, you must have a completed document, not just nifty results. As we proceed through the motivational sections, we will refer to these different tasks, but first let's walk through the lists and discuss the nature of each item.

GENERATING IDEAS

Unfortunately, this is the easy part. People who fear that editors will "steal" their ideas do not realize that ideas are cheap—good use of them is what is rare and precious. ("I think it may be said that the more worthless the manuscript, the greater the fear of plagiarism," said publisher Sir Stanley Unwin.) Regardless, motivation does come into play here—perhaps not for an initial idea ("Gosh, what if Sherlock Holmes came to the twentieth century to hunt a serial killer?") but for the plot complications, subplots, and additional characters that occur in any novel.

IDENTIFYING A TOPIC

This can relate to your motivation, too. Again, many Ph.D. candidates never make it because they try to pick an "easy" topic rather than an interesting one, forgetting that they have to live with that topic for years. Professional nonfiction writers may have fewer choices, but they can try to work in an area where most of the topics (or at least some element of them) interest them. Journalists must cover a lot of dull stories, but they also get the excitement of constant change, fast-moving events, and interesting people.

PLOTTING

Contrary to popular belief, this isn't just sitting back and watching a story happen. It includes issues such as pacing, story, character development, and tension building. Motivation can affect any of these. Someone who likes dwelling on the intimate life of individuals might slow an action plot down to a crawl in order to get extensive, detailed dialogue. Hemingway experimented with the idea of deleting something from the story in such a way that its *absence* would strengthen the rest of the story. What would you choose to delete? Are you more interested in a plot that moves lickety-split, tumbling along, or a plot that moves with smooth and stately grace, building up layer on layer?

RESEARCHING

For some people this is the best part; for others it is the part you leave until last. A third group uses research to trigger ideas that may evolve into a story. A fourth group manages to avoid it by writing present-day fiction or a certain kind of pure fantasy. Some works require years of research to complete thirty days' writing. Samuel Johnson said, "The greatest part of a writer's time is spent reading, in order to write; a man will turn over half a library to make one book." The kind of research one likes to do, and the ability to sustain it when you need it, derive from motives. For some people the very process of research is motivating.

FIRST-DRAFT WRITING

People fear the blank page—or the blank screen, if you prefer—that mocks their efforts. Others love the pristine whiteness the way kids love a field covered with snow: as a place to leave a mark. Both behaviors come out of your motives. It might even be the *same* motive for different people. The first draft is obviously critical: if you don't write a first draft, you can't have a last.

EDITING

Do you love tinkering with prose? Adjusting this word here and tightening this sentence there? Or do you dread it, not wanting to damage your marvelous writing? Some people take pleasure (motives, again!) in reading over their own work, knowing that they will make it that much better. Others struggle and sweat over it until they reach a point where they will abandon their work rather than have to change it. Depending on the degree of change required, almost all writers might have a balking point. Motives can push you past it, for example, by imagining the outcome (the motivating goal) to energize yourself or by seeking out help.

REWRITING

Virtually all professional, published writers rewrite; Neil L. Albert says that he redoes his outline twenty five times. Whether you love it and spend hour after hour on it, or you don't like it and do it anyway, you clearly depend on your motives to carry you through. Since you are getting less of the obvious joy of creation or the visible accomplishment of piles of pages, engaging your emotions in rewriting is key!

21 Parts of the Work

There are three rules for writing the novel. Unfortunately, no one knows what they are.

W. SOMERSET MAUGHAM, *Writers on Writing*

BEGINNING, MIDDLE, AND END

The desire to write grows with writing.

ERASMUS, *Writers on Writing*

The three toughest parts of a long or short work have different challenges for your motivation. Even after the book is finished, you have not finished your job—you still have to *sell* your piece. (I won't abandon you there, either. There are ways to bridge that gap between finishing this work and starting the next, while trying to stay motivated to do the things writers must to market their work.)

Please note that "beginning" and "end" refer to the process, *not* to the work itself. You can write a book in any order you wish. Some like to start at the beginning and write until they reach the end, for example, Rex Stout or Robert A. Heinlein. Others skip around, writing scenes as they see fit and filling in the gaps later. Jeremiah Healy writes his Cuddy mysteries in reverse order, the same way he managed his cases as a lawyer: start at the end with the desired result, then determine the immediately previous step needed to get to that end, then the step before that, and so forth. He works completely backward, one chapter at a time. To confuse matters further, you can write a complete book in one order and then rewrite it in a different order. Tolkien wrote *The Lord of the Rings* forward but then rewrote it backward.

We will start with the initial gleam in your eye and follow through to the completion of the work, keeping in mind that not all of these steps look the same for everyone and that you may choose to write in an order not described here.

THE BEGINNING

Every author does not write for every reader.
SAMUEL JOHNSON, *The Life of Johnson*

First, you have to have an idea. That's your department. I can only suggest areas you might find interesting. Past studies have suggested that leisure-time reading matter correlates with motive patterns. This makes sense, if you consider a book to be a way to find enjoyment or release. When you are unencumbered by conscious needs or external requirements, you will tend to read what you *like*—and that is strongly influenced by your motives.

This assumes, of course, that you will want to write what you like to read, like Disraeli: "When I want to read a good book, I write one." This can be far from the truth, though. Many writers are omnivorous in their reading habits; others purposefully venture outside of their specialties when they write. Tolkien, for example, was a comparative philologist with special expertise in Northern European and British languages and literature; he drew on this expertise in writing *The Lord of the Rings* but spent most of his time writing scholarly papers and translating works. Although one may argue that his giant saga only gave him a place to play with fictional languages, he brought far more to bear than linguistics. His place descriptions, for example, are so exact that a professional cartographer had little difficulty creating an atlas from them.

Values also play a part. Most professional writers feel the desire to make an impact on others; the impact is not usually random. Values provide the focus for what point they wish to make.

Other authors, such as Robert Graves, write novels to support other writing habits: "Novels are the prize dogs I raise to sell to support my cats"—meaning his poetry. Mario Puzo wrote *The Godfather* for exactly the same reason. I know many mystery and science fiction authors who *avoid* reading in their genres so they will not contaminate their writing. Alexander Jablakow, for example, finds himself too critical of science fiction to enjoy it anymore. He reads a great deal of history, which ultimately inspires and influences his fictional worlds.

In any case, the purpose in this book is to *get* you writing—once you get started and hook into your own motives, *what* you write can be almost incidental. However, it does not hurt to stack the deck in your favor. If you have trouble writing what you have chosen, perhaps it is not your first interest and you need to find ways to make it more engaging.

I do not refer to inspiration here, by the way. The idea of waiting around for inspiration to strike is romantic but not very realistic. Shakespeare wrote two plays a year, consistently; Philip K. Dick wrote and published twenty-six short stories one year and twenty-seven the next. Inspiration as an outside force had nothing to do with it; in the latter case, being able to feed himself had a *lot* to do with it. I am suggesting only that you will find more emotional arousal around an issue that corresponds to your motives and thus builds in some positive reinforcement right at the beginning.

I have to assume that you know what you like to read, but you may find another genre of interest as well. As we discussed above, research has indicated the kinds of literature people with a given motive tend to read; you may discover a previously untapped area of interest in which to write:

The person high in the Achievement Motive tends to read how-to books, nonfiction, and mysteries—books that include or imply goals or include useful facts or means to reach goals. There may also be a concern for innovation and clever ways to solve problems—hence the fascination with a unique method of murder in mysteries. Solving puzzles may also be interesting, as a challenge.

The person high in the Power Motive reads political biographies, books about scandals, political thrillers, psychology, and religious works—books about the use (and abuse) of power, or an interaction with powerful figures (including God), or ways in which to influence people or understand how they may be influenced. I hasten to remind you that the Power Motive need not be Machiavellian; the desire to influence is unconscious. The power person may just be interested in seeing how people react, and may well enjoy reading fictional accounts of actions they would never do personally (thus flushing them out of their systems).

The person high in the Affiliation Motive reads romances and books with well-developed characters—books about the interaction of people in relationships. It is probably not an accident that romances are divided up into extremely precise types where the protagonists are clearly defined as people: age 25 to 27, little experience with men, modern, dresses well, professional. A person interested in the real guts of relationships thinks about these details, because every detail changes the nature of the relationship.

If you are having trouble writing, it may be because the subject matter bores you, or because you approach it the wrong way. "Write what you know" is a cliché for writers; I would also add "write what you like," because you will be more sensitive on those wavelengths. Some writers talk about writing a "commercial book" to make enough money to write what they like. Some may be able to do this (when they have a choice), but I find it foolish. You will be more effective writing what you enjoy, and more genuine as well.

When I interviewed Philip Craig, he discussed his process for writing and how he got started. After writing some eight or nine novels that did not sell, he and his wife sat down and actually analyzed several books then on the bestseller list. They did not enjoy them much, but they did identify a pattern, which included things such as a middle-aged man of the world involved with a younger attractive woman, a murder, an exotic or unusual setting where people would like to go, and so on. So he wrote a novel incorporating all of these elements—and he sold the first book of his ongoing series set in Martha's Vineyard. Interestingly, while he stuck to his "formula," he still writes novels that interest him. Having a high Power Motive that is very socialized in nature, he has written stories about the *misuse* of power. In one of his recent novels, *A Deadly Vineyard Holiday*, he writes about the young daughter of a president vacationing on Martha's Vineyard, who slips away and embroils the protagonist in a plot filled with secret service men, intrigue, and so on. The book came about because President Clinton and his family came to the Vineyard, and Craig started to mull over the issues of being a child in the corridors of power. He thinks about power but has a deep ethical distrust of it. In a sense, his sensitivity to the Power Motive and the nature of power allows him to warn of its dangers more effectively. The formula came from outside, but the plots are his. He gets enormous satisfaction from the process of writing (except rewriting), because his process and product are closely linked to his motives.

Could you actually write a "commercial novel" totally unlike you? I won't be foolish enough to call it impossible, but imagine the challenge of writing in a genre in which you find *no* emotional satisfaction at all.

I have read stories written by people trying deliberately to present a motive pattern different from their own, but they always fail to disguise it.

On the other hand, *writing* in a genre is not the same as *reading* in the genre. Many mysteries do indeed include some kind of mechanism (usually) for committing a crime in a way that makes it difficult to discover, allowing for the achievement person to try and figure it out. However, making the mechanism a centerpiece of your story leads to a dull story. (Although I did meet a woman at a mystery convention who *only* read for the puzzle and disliked characters.) In other words, all work and no play makes Jack (or Jill) a dull writer. Consider that the classic and best known mysteries have interesting characters   often so interesting that the mystery itself becomes secondary, or at least mixed in with the relationships. Dorothy Sayers, creator of the Lord Peter Wimsey stories (and a fine prose stylist), deliberately wrote *Busman's Honeymoon* as "a romance with detective interruptions." I might also add that Agatha Christie has sold more copies of her books than Shakespeare—and she's catching up on the Bible. While she was famed for her intricate plots, she never failed to have identifiable, if not complex, characters. Hardly anyone alive has not heard of Hercule Poirot or Miss Marple.

Early science fiction writers often made the mistake that, as they were celebrating science and progress, they needed to lecture on the origin and theory behind every technological miracle in their stories, rather than discussing how people interacted with them—a classic example of assuming your audience has the same interests and motives you do (in fact, this can be a clue to a person's motives.). I don't wish to insult any writer (who after all wrote for an audience and a particular time) by quoting serious work, but I feel safe in quoting Randall Garrett and Lin Carter, who parodied this style hilariously in their story "Masters of the Metropolis":

He paused to board a *bus* which stopped at regularly-spaced intervals to take on new passengers. The *bus*, or Omnibus, was a streamlined, self-propelled public vehicle, powered by the exploding gases of distilled petroleum, ignited in a sealed chamber by means of an electrical spark. The energy thus obtained was applied as torque to a long metal bar known as the "drive shaft" which turned a set of gears in a complex apparatus known as the "differential housing." These gears, in turn, caused the rear wheels to revolve about their axes, thus propelling the vehicle forward smoothly at velocities as great as eighty miles every hour!

You can imagine what the *actual* stories were like. These stories were often written by engineers who found fascination in how things worked—an Achievement Motive–based attitude—rather than the power perspective of having an impact or the affiliative perspective of enjoyable, sympathetic characters. This need not block good writing (especially nonfiction) unless you also lack craft. Knowing everything about your field is insufficient if you cannot write a meaningful and interesting sentence; and in the early days of science fiction, many did not understand their craft. Fortunately for the field, other writers knew better, or at least made their lectures entertaining. Since the audience had motives that made them sympathetic to the writers, everyone felt satisfied. As readership shifted, the typical writer shifted too. Stories that would sell in an instant in 1955 would never sell today. The audience has changed, as has the quality of the writing. Nevertheless, you can choose to write whatever you like; as long as the motivation comes from inside, who cares about the genre of the material? It is silly not to write what you *enjoy* writing. Just remember that not everyone has the same motive pattern as you.

STARTING YOUR FLOW

As indicated above, subjects tend to line up with motives. But there are other approaches that intertwine with your motives and may define how you write your stories. The story process is driven by different things, and I do not claim to have them all, but here is a reasonable list.

- **Plot:** You work out an intricate (or straightforward) plot, and that is what interests you or keeps you moving—you want to see it play out, in the same way that assembling a puzzle can hold your attention for hours. This could apply to the power-focused thrillers of Robert Ludlum or the achievement-focused mysteries of Agatha Christie.

- **Ideas:** You have a fascinating idea: What if so-and-so happened? This is most common in science fiction, for obvious reasons, but it is also found in mysteries (what if you had a nearly perfect, undetectable murder method: Dorothy Sayers's *Suspicious Characters*, sometimes called the "gimmick" mystery approach), thrillers (what if the Soviets invent a silent sub, but its commander is willing to bring it to the West: Tom Clancy's *The Hunt for Red October*), and the like.
- **Characters:** You have an interesting character you want to follow around or put in interesting settings. In one interview, Donald Westlake described how he came to write his humorous caper novels featuring the unlucky John Dortmunder; he had come up with a crime that was basically so silly (stealing an entire bank that was temporarily in a trailer) that his regular crime-novel protagonist "turned it down." He was wondering what to do when this sad-faced individual turned up and said with a sigh that he would take it. This person became John Dortmunder, the unluckiest brilliant criminal you can imagine. The book became *Bank Shot*, which started a successful series that has been going on for years now.
- **Scenes/settings:** Philip Craig told me that he wrote one novel in order to get to a scene. He had grown up in Colorado and wanted to set a scene on a certain cliff there. He wound up moving his character from Martha's Vineyard to Colorado for one novel just to get that scene written. Some writers, including Carol Higgins Clark and Mary Higgins Clark, set a scene in a place they would like to visit and then actually go there. Dorothy Gilman's Mrs. Polifax series is written the same way. In a sense, this is also tax-driven, since it meant the trip was tax-deductible. You find your inspiration where you can.
- **Research:** Some writers write their books so they have an excuse to do research. While some find it the most difficult and boring part, others get joy from it. Sharan Newman said that this was the best part of writing for her; she takes great pains to ensure total historical accuracy, supported no doubt by her advanced degrees in medieval history.

SITTING DOWN AND WARMING UP

Hemingway's first rule for writers was to apply the seat of the pants to the seat of the chair. Some people sit down and promptly start writing; others need to find ways to warm up to the task. Hemingway himself sharpened twenty pencils before he wrote—standing up, by the way, because of a previous injury. I distinguish these activities from superstitions and the like because they are inextricably linked to the process of writing for their users.

Since these are idiosyncratic, I will group these into larger categories and cite a whole batch.

- **Music:** One writer I met at a conference wrote an entire book to a single soundtrack; he had to put this on to inspire him, and he played it over and over until he finished. Unfortunately, when I met him he had been unable to start a second book. I suggested that that music was now irrevocably associated with that first book, and that he needed a new score. Many writers write to music—including me, at this moment—and it has been suggested that engaging the right hemisphere, where music is processed, may "liberate" one's writing, which comes primarily from the left. Along these lines, Harlan Ellison recommends movie soundtracks, particularly those of Ennio Morricone (*The Good, the Bad, and the Ugly*). The advantage of such music is that it lacks lyrics and therefore does not engage the verbal centers of your brain and distract you from writing words by making you listen to them instead.
- **Inspirational reading:** Some writers get ready to write by reading someone else. Willa Cather read a passage from the Bible; Stendhal said in a letter to Balzac, "Whilst writing the *Chartreuse,* in order to acquire the correct tone I read every morning two or three pages of the Civil Code." Playwright and screenwriter Neil Simon reportedly saw a stage show called *Something's Afoot* (a murder-mystery musical comedy, if you can believe it) that inspired him to go home and write the screenplay for *Murder by Death.* I have seen both and certainly see a family resemblance in theme.
- **Setting up targets:** If one of the unconscious goals of a writer is to have an impact (the Power Motive, remember), it helps to remind yourself of whom you might have an impact upon. Henrik Ibsen hung a portrait of August Strindberg over his desk, saying, "He is my mortal enemy and shall hang there and watch while I write." The writer's equivalent of a dartboard with a portrait, I suppose.
- **Trips:** Fredric Brown took boring bus trips. George M. Cohan actually rented an entire Pullman railroad car drawing room and traveled until he finished a project, writing up to 140 pages a night. Some writers take trips to gather material, but they also want to write off the trip on their taxes. Many writer's conferences have

been paid for this way. Roger Zelazny describes writing a chess-playing unicorn story ("Unicorn Variations"), selling it in three places, and thereby paying for the Alaskan cruise on which he wrote it.

- **Relaxing in the tub:** Ben Franklin had the first bathtub in America and liked writing in it; Edmond Rostand, author of *Cyrano de Bergerac,* wrote in the tub to avoid interruptions from his numerous friends—arguably an example of removing distractions as well. On the other hand, Douglas Adams took lengthy baths to *avoid* writing.
- **Stimulants:** I considered titling this "drugs," but let's be more tactful than that (I drink caffeinated sodas, after all). Coffee, tea, tobacco, and other stimulants are long-time favorites of many writers, as well as others no longer legally available. Sigmund Freud used cocaine earlier in his career and cigars his entire life (as did American poet Amy Lowell, who bought 10,000 of her favorite brand when shortages looked likely in 1915)—even when diagnosed with cancer, Freud could not give up his beloved cigars, which he claimed he needed to think. Alexander Pope and Balzac drank strong coffee—the latter, fifty cups a day; Dr. Johnson could put away twenty-five cups of tea at a sitting. Please note again that if you assiciate a moderate stimulant with writing, then it might help; if you are driven to excess, you have an inconvenient and possibly dangerous habit. Balzac's death is partially attributable to caffeine poisoning, after all. You might increase your productivity over a limited time but shorten your lifespan—and I could hardly recommend that.
- **Positioning:** I already mentioned Hemingway's vertical stance, but that was in some ways physically required. Truman Capote, on the other hand, felt he had to lie down to write. Mark Twain and Robert Louis Stevenson also liked horizontal composition. Lewis Carroll and Virginia Woolf wrote while standing up by choice, and we may presume that Jane Austen wrote standing up because she wrote only a sentence or two at a time in passing.
- **Rehearsing:** Just get your fingers warmed up and in the habit of typing words. It doesn't have to make sense—yet.

GETTING TO THE BEGINNING

This book will not be useful to you unless you are really ready to begin producing prose. It may help to discuss methods of garnering and organizing ideas to the point where you do want to take action.

The traditional writing method taught in high schools today generally goes like this:

1 Jot down ideas
2 Winnow ideas
3 Make a tentative outline
4 Research
5 Revise outline according to research (plot)
6 Begin writing from outline.

I have yet to meet anyone who actually *follows* this method strictly except in very limited circumstances—such as high school writing classes. (Though I am certain some wildly successful writer out there does exactly this.) If you ask one hundred writers how their writing process goes, you are likely to get one hundred responses, none of which resemble the above. Some outlines never get written until after the book is finished—in order to submit an outline to a publisher. I am not about to recommend that you start to use this method if you do not now; I am using it as a summary of nearly all of the tasks a writer *may* undertake before writing, and a means for logically laying them out for our convenience here. In that way, we can sort out the options available to you to get your writing started.

JOTTING DOWN IDEAS

The achievement-oriented individual is interested in the new and different— hence the large numbers of achievement-oriented science fiction readers looking for well-designed futures and mystery readers who seek a new and innovative crime. Writers in these genres need to remember that ideas are not enough but that a good one can get them going, especially if they have a sufficient backlog of ideas stored up to support it. The classic device for storing fleeting ideas is the "commonplace book," in which you jot ideas, insert newspaper clippings and photographs, store anything that triggers your ideas, or may someday. Items may sit for years, but don't worry about that. The idea is to give you a mine for your notions, so that when you need something *right now,* you can consult your book and find something waiting.

Alfred Bester, a partisan of this method, relied on it so heavily that he satirized himself in the mystery-thriller *Who He?* as a person who was completely dependent on his commonplace book and went into a frenzy when it went astray. A commonplace book is a good place to acknowledge your innovative thoughts; as you fill pages with jotted notes, you can measure the number of ideas you have available. Darwin's books were so detailed that we can trace exactly what he read and thought on a given day.

For the power-oriented person, such a book is a place to put things that evoke a response—that have a profound emotional impact: dramatic scenes, striking pictures (in the days of pulp magazines, editors often commissioned stories to fit a completed cover painting), ways to influence people, descriptions of people who influenced *you*. Then you can refer to it to find a description of an effect you desire in your own work.

The affiliative person could put in descriptions of relationships in all of their myriad forms, and the outcomes of those relationships.

For all three types, jotting down notes and keeping them is a way to store your motives up for when you need them, in the form of motivating ideas. If they don't have power to move you, then they probably will not help you.

When making a jot list for immediate use, you can use this same dividing line—does it arouse your excitement? Of course, some kinds of writing just aren't that thrilling—but on the other hand, a subject that is boring to the writer will bore the reader as well. If you find a topic that requires sections that lack interest for you, perhaps you should jot down some ideas for making those sections more interesting.

FREEWRITING

This is an alternative form of jotting, where you sit down and begin writing about anything that comes to mind. This technique is particularly helpful when you do not know what you want to do, but know you need to start writing. Anything will do: the preamble to the Constitution, "Now is the time for all good men," whatever; after a few lines you are likely to get so bored with the task that you start generating more interesting ideas. This is likely to work best for those with achievement or power motivations, but it could work for anybody. This can be, in effect, a free-association session, where you let your motives run wild.

The usual caution on freewriting is that you do not stop to criticize it. It must be *free*, or you will choke off the flow. If you suddenly begin focusing on a specific plot, go with it; do not bother to fix the beginning until the time is right.

OUTLINING

The Mozartian writer may choose to outline completely before writing a lengthy work, or not outline at all. The Beethovenian, on the other hand, may choose to write and rewrite an outline before beginning and then still diverge from it. Whatever works is fine. Just do not let anything limit you. Any writing technique that stifles your motivation, no matter how apparently useful, will work against you in the long run. It may appear, for example, that outlining will make your writing far faster, especially if you are the apparently disorganized type that writes your novel or textbook completely out of order. Note that I said *apparently* disorganized; after all, no movie script is filmed in order, for very good reasons that have nothing to do with the plot. If, however, you hate outlining so much that it sours you on the production of prose, then you will have made it impossible to use that outline.

If you like or need outlines (and not necessarily at the beginning, either: some people like to write isolated scenes, order them roughly, and then outline the remaining plot around them), then you should try to motivate yourself to do them as you would your other work. Make sure, again, that the reinforcement is appropriate to your motives, so you will look forward to it. Keep the scope distinctly different from that of prose writing; it is a different process, after all. Do not count hundreds of words; count dozens. Or better yet, count heads and subheads. For the achievement person, make columns listing each level of heading: Roman numerals, capital letters, Arabic numerals, lower-case letters, etc., as below:

DATE	I	A	1	a	1)	a)
March 17, '91	4	10	26	23	3	3
March 18, '91	5	12	32	32	6	3

This kind of recording can be easily placed in a spreadsheet, should your mind work that way, and graphed or charted.

PLOTTING

Within the limits of what I do, I can satisfy myself. [My stories] do not rely on plot. Mine rely almost entirely on character.

ELMORE LEONARD, *Writer's Digest*

A story is: the king died, the queen died. A plot is: the king died, the queen died of grief.

E. M. FORSTER, *Aspects of the Novel*

I never work out a plot—I always say that plots belong in cemeteries.

KINKY FRIEDMAN

Outlining can link closely to the process of plotting. A plot organizes your characters and keeps them moving in the right direction, leading (and misleading) your readers. Some basic plot types are so well known that they have become clichés:

> **Romantic:** Boy meets girl, boy loses girl, boy gets girl.
>
> **Mystery:** Crime occurs, police are baffled, red herrings distract, detective penetrates to the truth.
>
> **Epic:** Naive protagonist meets mysterious stranger who leads him to his destiny, overcoming obstacles in himself and the world, finally becoming a hero.

And so on, and so on. These plots recur, with numerous twists, over and over again. Why? Why does *Romeo and Juliet* follow the romantic cliché (with the tragic twist that "boy-gets-girl" occurs in death), Agatha Christie the mystery cliché, *Star Wars* the epic cliché? Just how many plots are there, really?

Many people will tell you that there is a limited number. Scholars of this subject and writers have pegged it variously at one, fifteen, forty-five, sixty-four, and probably other numbers as well. The single-plot camp sees something like this "quest" plot:

- Hero starts quest
- Takes action to goal
- Encounters obstacles in self and world
- Struggles forward despite despair, maintains hope
- Gets help to overcome obstacles
- Reaches consummation of goals

I've missed some subtleties, but I've covered the bases. Now I don't necessarily hold to *any* theory that limits range (witness Douglas Adams's *Hitchhikers' Guide to the Galaxy,* about "the end of the world and the happy-go-lucky days that follow"), but I think most would agree that this quest plot (also known as the "monomyth") has power to move. It includes Odysseus, King David the Israelite, Luke Skywalker, Bilbo Baggins, and many others.

Why? Motivation, by gum! Remember the problem-solving model? The model reflects a pattern of thought about getting to a goal. Well, since the monomyth is about getting to a goal, shouldn't they have something in common?

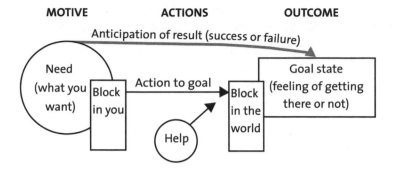

Figure 7. The problem-solving model

How the Problem-Solving Model Compares to the Monomyth

MONOMYTH	MOTIVE
Goal	Stated need (goal) (N)
Action	Instrumental activity (Act)
Obstacles in self	Blocks personal (Bp)
Obstacles in world	Blocks world (Bw)
Despair and hope	Goal Anticipation (Ga+ & Ga-)
Help (mentor)	Help (H)
Consummation of goals	Goal state (G+ & G-)

The monomyth is motivational—and I mean that literally as well as literarily. It echoes a piece of our brain, it makes sense. Not that it is necessarily the best plot, but it is a *recognizable* plot. For example:

Motive Subcategory	Romance	Science Fiction	Mystery
N	Boy meets girl	Person discovers truth/destiny	Person discovers crime, must solve
Bw	Boy loses girl	Person exiled, lost	Person alienated from normal life
Act	Boy seeks girl	Works behind scenes	Investigates
FA	Fears lack of merit	Fears death or loss	Fears being wrong
Bp	Loses confidence	Loses confidence	Loses confidence
SA	Resolves to go on	Girds loins	Finds purpose
Value	Moral/selfish	Moral/selfish	Moral/selfish
H	Support from friend	Support from secret mentor	Unexpected ally
G+ (or)	Boy gets girls	Achieves destiny	Solves mystery
G-	Loses girl to death (e.g. *Love Story*)	Big Brother wins (e.g. *1984*)	Real villain gets off (various)

Of course, you can (and should) apply this to yourself as a writer:

- **N**   I want to write a book/story/essay.
- **SA**   I think I can do it; I can imagine my book on the shelf or my essay in the magazine.
- **FA**   I'm afraid no one will like it/buy it.
- **Bw**   I can't find an agent/publisher.
- **Bp**   I'm no good as a writer, I can't plot, characterize, etc.
- **Act**   I'm writing, sending queries, etc.
- **H**   I have emotional support (spouse/friend), writing support (workshop, editor), selling support (agent).
- **G+**   I've finished! I sold! I have an agent! I'm on a ten-best list! I've got a hardcover! I've won the Nobel Prize!
- **G-**   It's a bomb (ideally followed by "I'm doing better on the next one!").

Don't ignore any of the subcategories—miss one, and you may sink your efforts (though some are not good to dwell on, especially personal block, world block, and failure anticipation). Note that in addition to the obvious influence of motive thinking, positive affiliation parallels the trusting attitude you may need to get it done—that is, that you will be taken care of, that things will work out, that God will provide. This also scores in motive assessment as positive goal anticipation (Ga+) and help (H).

THE MIDDLE

Often enough, writers get a perfectly wonderful idea with no place to go. I have stacks of them piled neatly in my computer. I assume that you have gone beyond that stage and instead seek to continue a beginning (or an end, for that matter).

At this stage the motivational writing strategies described above become most useful: in the midst of a story, with an idea at least partially developed. When the challenge is just to keep going, use these tools.

However, it may be difficult to sit down at the typewriter (or keyboard, or quill pen stand) in order to get this going. This is more of a challenge for some than for others. Many achievement people will not stop at all once engaged. They are internally motivated anyway (in the sense that they do not look for external stimuli to write), so they are unlikely to be greatly distracted, except perhaps by nearby individuals.

The power person, on the other hand, may have trouble getting down to cases. Useful tactics may include looking at that big red sign with your word count, talking to someone sympathetic about the book, or just sitting down and staring until you get tired of looking silly. You might also refer to the "Sitting Down and Warming Up" section above.

If you are telling a story of some kind, speaking it aloud to someone or even to yourself may be your best tactic. Besides the value of hearing the words roll (assuming you speak well), you will see that your words have an impact on someone else. When they want to know what comes next, you will want to tell them. Make sure they are responsive, or you may kill your book.

Remember that everyone has different tastes—as mentioned above, some of this comes from your motive pattern. If you are reading the wrong book to a person, they will not respond.

The affiliation person may do the same, but with slightly different intent. They want a positive impact on the person, or in some cases, a feeling of affection for themselves or even their written characters. A detailed literary analysis is not what they want. They want positive reinforcement and personal support, to reassure them that they are good people, or that they are sensitive and likable, or simply that they belong to something larger than themselves.

NATURAL BREAKS

For many writers, there are clues to when they need a break, or when they need to try another take on what they have done so far. These clues range from greater difficulty with writing to rage to physical symptoms, so it is difficult to describe them with a single term. I'll call them incidents.

An incident occurs when you should be plugging along and suddenly something happens. Here are some real writers' examples:

A SLOWDOWN OR STOPPAGE:

[I had] a sense of being stuck in doing things—in the assumptions I was making. I felt it. I would sit there and I found it extremely hard to move forward. It takes four hours to write one paragraph.

SARAH SMITH

I just can't do anything. I want to write, but I don't. I just play Pac-Man or solitaire or something. It means I need to think for a while longer and when I'm ready it will go again.

TONI L. P. KELNER

THE CHARACTERS GO AWRY:

If something's going wrong the characters go dead.

SARAH SMITH

DRIVING YOURSELF TOO HARD:

On my first book, I was kind of obsessive. My goals were too aggressive. I exhausted myself ... I hit a wall—I couldn't tell if what I was writing was good or not.

KELLY TATE

For some individuals, no such stoppage occurs. They simply continue writing. Presumably even Isaac Asimov paused to eat, however. Eating and typing at the same time is hard, unless your lunch can go through a straw.

REWRITING

Despite the vast amount of outlining and thinking I do, when it comes to writing there's always new inspiration. My method of work is to get a very good idea of what I want to cover and assign a time percentage to it. I will rewrite each page, and then each few pages, moving ahead very slowly with the handwritten page. When I finish a whole section, I go back and type what I've rewritten. That is an extensive rewriting process—largely with language. Usually it will be taking out much and then getting new ideas to put in. Then I'll read it again, pencil it, and give it to a typist to type. It's not necessary to do much in the way of rewriting [after that]—it's largely a matter of cutting, changing words, catching an inconsistency.

JOSEPH HELLER, *Writer's Digest* (October 1977)

The revision process is fascinating to me. Some of my poems have gone through sixty or more drafts by the time I'm satisfied. I think it's very important for poets to have others read their work, get all the criticism they can as well as be extremely self-critical.

MAY SARTON, in a profile by Lois Rosenthal, *Writers Digest* (1989)

Some enjoy rewriting. Some do not—they feel that the pure joy of generating prose is somehow compromised by tedious backtracking and tinkering. For those people, it is important to keep motivation high—unless you are Isaac Asimov, Mozart, or Shakespeare, you will probably need *some* rewriting. We are not discussing quality here, but the process of writing. Even the best prose needs rearrangement, tinkering, or transfer to another book.

Obviously, many of the tools described above to motivate writing do not assist rewriting. Counting "new words," for example, might work against you if you tend to overwrite and edit down at the next session. Here are some different approaches:

Internal Measures of Progress
These are particularly helpful to the Achievement Motive.

- Count the number of pages you have rewritten. Each time you rewrite them, you can count anew.
- Keep track of the number of words reduced (works best if you are a person who overwrites and then cuts).
- Count the number of lines altered in any way, right down to the comma.
- Edit from beginning to end in order, and keep track of your page numbers. Set goals for pages covered, either by deletion or by addition (i.e., you can either edit five pages, or edit one page and write four additional pages. I did that on this book for my first full edit pass.)
- Track the percentage completed. You can do this in two ways: per-

centage of old text covered (that is, I have rewritten my first thirty pages of 300, or 10 percent, even though I expanded them to sixty pages), or percentage of the total that is now done (sixty done out of what is now 330, or roughly 18 percent).

External Measures of Progress
These are often helpful to the Power and Affiliation Motives:

- Get an outside person to praise you for how much better it is.
- Tell a writing group about your progress.
- Do your editing in bright red ink, set yourself specific time goals for specific chapters, and post your progress and/or show your pages.

Rewriting may appear to be a trivial point, but in fact it may be the single biggest differentiator between those who sell and those who do not—either because of bad rewriting or because of not rewriting at all.

As mentioned elsewhere, Dick Lochte never finished one of his novels because he kept rewriting the first chapter. So by the time he had a perfect beginning, he had lost interest in the rest of the book. By contrast, Philip R. Craig never sold his first eight or nine completed novels because he would send one out, get a rejection, and then start another book rather than try to rewrite. Craig gives credit to his word processor for making rewriting more interesting for him. Tinkering with words on a word processor, where all of the formatting and refitting is done for you, greatly reduces the pain of rewriting. In a few years the concept of "draft" may well be obsolete except in arbitrary or external terms— that is, the first draft is the one you send out for rejection or happen to print out, rather than the first one you write out on paper. Many writers find it easier to tinker with a document onscreen than to have to redline and retype. Sarah Smith uses her PC to write and rewrite as follows: "I generally start by reading over a little of what I did the previous day, then keep writing. I often go back and change little bits in previous stuff I've written. It generally takes one 'write' and 150 rewrites, changing things around, which you can do with a computer."

As you can see, rewriting can be very important indeed: Lochte failed to complete a book because he did too much too soon; Craig failed to sell a book (or eight) because he did not do enough. Beethovenian writers are clearly more vulnerable to this kind of issue; if you know yourself to be one, prepare to do a lot of rewriting. If you think you are a Mozartian writer, remember that Philip Craig got a lot of rejections for non-rewritten books. Be sure you really *are* Mozartian. Perhaps you just (ahem) possess a great deal of self-confidence. Mozartian writers (or any other kind of creator) are relatively rare, especially at book length. Even Isaac Asimov needed his word processor for his novels. As someone once said: "It isn't writing—it's rewriting." Or, as Peter DeVries put it: "I love writing—it's the paperwork I can't stand." Rewriting is the purest form of paperwork. Be ready for it.

APPROACHING THE DENOUEMENT

Finishing a book is just like you took a child out in the yard and shot it.

TRUMAN CAPOTE, *Writers on Writing*

There is a curious phenomenon to be observed in some writers: they find it difficult or nearly impossible to finish anything. If they genuinely have no end in mind, well, that happens often enough. But what of those people who have an end in mind, or at least a completion (I do not assume you write from beginning to end), but cannot bring themselves to put it on paper?

There are many reasons for such behavior; some may lie in the realm of clinical or therapeutic rather than motivational psychology. For our purposes here, I can propose some reasons that can be understood in motive terms and then dealt with.

The most obvious reason is that once writing has become rewarding, you do not want to stop: the end of a work (be it a short story, an essay, a text book, or a novel) symbolizes the end of writing and the end of the enjoyment thereof. This is irrational, but no one said people had to make sense. The solution is neat enough: start something else before you stop. It need not be much; just knowing you have more writing to do might be enough. Writing is a discontinuous process: starting, stopping, and starting again. But if you keep *some* process going, the discontinuities will not affect your writing motivation. Do avoid getting so involved in the next work that you neglect the first, though—I can just see a writer surrounded by almost finished volumes churning happily away at the next. And lest you think this is a fantasy, listen to Erica Jong (*Writers on Writing*): "I went for years not finishing anything. Because, of course, when you finish something you can be judged . . . I had poems which were rewritten so many times I suspect it was just a way of avoiding sending them out."

THE END

Writing every book is like a purge; at the end of it one is empty . . . like a dry shell on the beach, waiting for the tide to come in again.

DAPHNE DU MAURIER, *Writers on Writing*

For me it is torture when I finish a novel. The good time is
when I'm writing. When I am finished it's no more fun.
UMBERTO ECO, *Writer's Digest*

Umberto Eco writes large, very successful books. For you, the words "The End" may be wonderful words indeed, because you have finished your book! Now what? Well, it is awfully easy to lose your motivation to do anything more when you have reached an obvious stopping place such as an ending; so I recommend that you find ways not to stop. Shift gears: for example, start looking for an agent or a publisher before you finish.

It may be quite difficult to consider marketing before you are even finished—unless you have a high need for power, in which case you may find the idea of marketing more alluring than writing. But when the book is finished, it does allow you to keep moving.

If you already have an agent or publisher, start the next book or story. After completing a manuscript, you may not feel like writing ever again; but in most cases this feeling will pass. Do not feel that you have to work *hard* at it. Remember that the idea here is to engage your enjoyment. Fool around—write something completely different. Hunter S. Thompson started *Fear and Loathing in Las Vegas* as a brief article for *Sports Illustrated*, who rejected it savagely, as he would say. So there he was: a professional journalist working on a very heavy straight story (the murder of Chicano journalist Ruben Sálazar) that could conceivably get him killed, who unwound at night by letting his fingers run wild over this bizarre, comic story. Thus was Gonzo Journalism born—or at least acknowledged. Other creative people like to use a different medium entirely: painting, or acting, or something else. Woody Allen, who writes, acts, *and* directs, plays jazz sax in Manhattan for fun. As long as you feel consistently creative, do not worry about it. You will come back when you want to.

And let us not forget that some people need the mental rest that playing around can give. After a sufficient time, you may begin writing of your own accord. If not, go back to the beginning and work on jump-starting yourself.

Some studies indicate that people find restoration in switching hemispheres—of the brain, not the earth. That is, if you are doing something primarily left-hemispheric, such as writing or editing, you should alternate with something right-hemispheric, such as drawing or sports. One study even suggests that you can jump-start one hemisphere into primacy by blocking a nostril and breathing on one side for a while. (Werntz, Bickford, and Shannahoff-Khalsa, "Selective Hemispheric Stimulation by Unilateral Forced Nostril Breathing," *Human Neurobiology* (1987) 6:165–71). Again, a single action like that is too simplistic for practical use by anyone, but the basic principle is applicable everywhere: alternate kinds of tasks. When you exhaust your brain, go exercise your body.

THE NEXT ONE

Some writers talk about the "second book problem," meaning that you may have said all you had to say in the first book and can write no more. If this is actually so, then quit! You are in excellent company. Miguel de Cervantes wrote only one novel of note: *Don Quixote*, which happens to be the single most significant and influential work of fiction in Spanish to date—more so than any single work in English, including Shakespeare's. On a less prominent note, *To Kill a Mockingbird* was the only novel written by Harper Lee, and apparently she felt perfectly happy with that very successful book, play, and movie.

But that is not true of many writers, who get hooked. Once you learn to write and become able to keep writing, it is hard to stop, no matter how little you may feel you have to say. After all, Shakespeare had only a couple of mildly original plots in all of his plays. It didn't bother him—don't let it bother you.

When moving on to the next work, if you set your standards too high, you won't achieve them. For maximum accomplishment, you should set a moderate but challenging goal. Don't expect to write your second novel immediately. In fact, expect it to be harder than the first. It may not be, but be ready for it. Take your time, and set your daily goal lower if you have to—but write something, even if it is gibberish. Write enough, and you will begin to force yourself to make sense of it.

Whether you choose to outline first or not is a matter of taste. Some swear by it, but on the other hand, Tolkien wrote his three-volume *The Lord of the Rings* over ten years with no idea where it was going. Of course, good plotting would probably have made it shorter—but who knows what we would have lost?

I have said it before: there is no one best way to write, and there are no easy answers. You must work to make writing something you *want* to do, and whatever method you use is fine.

Mozart went from his head to the paper with virtually no changes. Beethoven went through many, many drafts and edits on his music. These two styles can be applied to virtually any kind of creative endeavor, including writing. Don't let the *other* type of person sway you in the way you choose to go about your work. That includes yourself! The second book will certainly be different from your first, if only because you have had practice. You might find yourself unexpectedly better.

22 Motivate Your Selling!

You must put your work before an editor who will buy it.
ROBERT A. HEINLEIN'S THIRD LAW OF WRITING

*"I don't want to take up literature in a money-making spirit,
or be very anxious about making large profits, but selling it
at a loss is another thing altogether, and an amusement I
cannot well afford."*

LEWIS CARROLL, *The Annotated Alice*

Until now, I have primarily focused on the actual process of writing. I have tried to give a comprehensive view of the different issues you bring to the task of writing. In one sense, my job is done. However, yours will not be. If you do in fact have the motive profile shared by most professional writers, you will not be satisfied by having finished a work—you will want to publish it.

Today's publishing industry makes it virtually certain that you will have to spend a significant amount of time working on selling what you have written. After all the work you have done to actually write, it can be very depressing to know that you have only just begun the process of publication.

In the course of studying writers, I inevitably became familiar with the process of selling and marketing as well. I see no reason to stop with the writing if I can contribute to the publication—as I noted earlier, I read too—and given the daunting obstacles facing the writer who wishes to be published, motivation is clearly essential.

Realistically, thousands of people are out there competing for an editor's attention. Editors, being only human themselves, have their own personal likes and dislikes, which may cause them to fail to appreciate your unique brilliance. Calvin Trillin tells of soliciting stories for a book called *Authors' Atrocity Stories about Publishers*. He received enough material for a twenty-volume series but couldn't find anyone who would publish it. He was kidding (more or less), but there is a real truth there. People become sensitive about their ability, or lack thereof, to publish.

If you sell your book, it is the unhappy truth about publishing that, with few exceptions, you must then go on and spend time selling the book to readers. Many writers spend almost as much time marketing as writing. Some spend more.

I cannot tell you the best way to go about selling as such, though I have some experience and knowledge, if only from assisting my wife in her efforts. But we can discuss the ways in which you can apply your motives to the job.

Robert Silverberg describes this encounter in *Reflections and Refractions*:

> [A] woman . . . told me that she had in fact written an entire novel, a detective story, but had never found the courage to send it to an editor. Nevertheless she wanted to be a published writer. I pointed out, not entirely gently, the little lapse of logic in her behavior. Pick a publishing company, I said, and send your book there, or else stop pretending that you're interested in a writing career . . . I figured that was the last I would ever hear of her; but no, no, just the other day I noticed a half-page ad in the *New York Times Book Review* for what I think was her fifth novel, quoting from ecstatic reviews of her earlier books and listing all the awards she has won. She is big stuff, these days, in the mystery field. So she was a real writer after all—with a slight under-confidence problem that I suspect she has long since outgrown.

Heinlein's Third Law, again!

GETTING AN AGENT

At one time writers could sell directly to an editor, who would sometimes hold their hands as they rewrote their works. Today, no major publishing firm dedicates that much time to individual writers unless they produce megabucks, and most of those writers have the clout to demand no editing. The first hurdle now (for writers of book-length works, especially) is getting an agent, who often takes up the role of counseling the writer. I'll start here because the process is similar to getting a publisher, and because if you get an agent you can put your motives back to work writing. I didn't call this book *Motivate Your Marketing!*, after all.

The first thing you should know is that you need not reinvent the wheel when it comes to finding a market. Numerous resources exist to support the writer seeking a buyer. That might boost your motivation right there. Many big, thick books list nothing but agents and markets: *Writer's Market* and *The Writer's Handbook* are updated annually. Both include articles on how to lay out a manuscript, how to write query letters, even how much postage to use. They are both available in bookstores and libraries everywhere.

If you want more, you can buy or borrow writer's magazines that have interesting articles on the art, craft, and business of writing. Some people may find them inspirational and often more directly applicable to their work. Others may get mad enough at an opinion they disagree with to propel themselves. *Writers Digest* and *The Writer* are two of the highest-circulation magazines available, but you can also find magazines associated with specialty writing, such as screenplays or poetry.

The process of acquiring an agent is as tiring as sending to publishers, and more discouraging, since getting an agent certainly doesn't guarantee publication. However, a good agent will take you on because he or she believes in you and your work and its potential. Remember that an agent's livelihood depends on your sale.

This gives me an opportunity to revive a conversation we had earlier about motivational feedback loops. Some agents offer to assess and/or edit your work for a fee. Many imply that their editing will help you get sold, and that they will be more willing to take it on afterward. Let's look at this logically: does an agent in this position get more money from (a) trying to sell your book, or (b) charging an editing fee for your book and *then* trying to sell it? Looking at the larger picture, which will provide the steady income for such an agent: the occasional and risky sale of the rare good work, or the surefire editing fees from many, many, many hopeful writers?

You get the idea. While extrinsic motivation alone is not an ideal resource for extended effort, it can certainly focus your energies. Agents who charge "reading fees" have no motive to see your work as good and indeed may not care. Therefore, get an agent whose income derives from selling your work, and avoid the "readers." A goodly number of top editors and agents share my opinion, incidentally, but I'm making the motivational argument here rather than the ethical one.

Maintain your motivation while getting an agent exactly as you do while selling your book, except know that you are one step farther away from actual publication. Set up goals and send out several samples. Be careful not to have a full manuscript out to more than one person at a time. The convention is that you can send out as many letters of inquiry as you want—after all, they don't commit you or the agent to anything—but if an agent is serious enough to ask for your entire manuscript, it is only polite to repay their investment of time with your exclusivity until they turn you down or take you on. This is the time during which you need to find something else to do. It takes finite time to read a work, and agents always have more than one to read. So find some way to keep yourself focused while you wait.

You have several opportunities here. First, you can write something else. If you time this right, you can have several works out at once and keep writing, too. You could also prepare a list of the next few agents you wish to approach, so that you can immediately send another wave of queries. If it depresses you to anticipate failure that way (why else would you need an agent list?), think of it as insurance. If your book doesn't get picked up, you don't skip a beat getting it out again. If your book does get picked up, you can burn the list ceremonially in celebration. If you prefer, you might also keep that list, so you can see the progress you have made. If it depresses you to see a long list of rejections (I'm being realistic here—most writers go through multiple rejections at various points), then be careful about reading over the list, except when you need to avoid sending a second query (on the same work) to the same person.

GETTING PAST REJECTION

I discovered that rejections are not altogether a bad thing. They teach a writer to rely on his own judgment and to say in his heart of hearts, "To hell with you."
SAUL BELLOW, the New York Times, 1985

I still get stories turned down by editors occasionally, you know, and so does every other well-known science-fiction writer I can think of —if God were a science-fiction writer, He'd get rejected once in a while too, editors being what they are . . .
ROBERT SILVERBERG, Reflections and Refractions

"Cold-calling," which requires you to push yourself in front of someone who does not know you or your product and has no reason to buy what you are selling, sounds like a brutally difficult task, but there are tens of thousands of salespeople who love it or at least don't see it as an obstacle. Top salespeople have certain traits in common; chief among them is the ability to withstand failure and even ignore it.

One method is to consider every "no" to be that much closer to a "yes." Knowing that, for example, Frank Herbert sent *Dune* to over twenty publishers before he got it accepted means that you could get rejected nineteen times without expecting an acceptance—more if you think Herbert wrote better than you do. You are *bound* to get rejected; therefore, you want to get the rejections out of the way first. Especially since once you get anything accepted, everything gets easier. You have more connections, more people to talk to, more resources in the industry. After a while, people call you to submit a short story to an anthology, or a new magazine drops you a line asking for submissions, and so forth.

A second method of surviving rejection relates to attributional style. As noted above, psychological researcher Robert Seligman has studied salespeople for years, and he finds that when they get rejected, they tend to see the reasons for rejection as:

- **External to themselves.** "He didn't want what I was selling—I had nothing to do with it".
- **Situational.** "She could not tell me yes while she was right in front of her boss—she had to tell me alone."
- **Time-linked.** "I got him when he was about to go on vacation—no way he would buy when he was walking out the door."

Putting this all together, a good salesperson describes a failure as happening because "in this time, in this place, this person did not want it." By implication, this means that in the right time and the right place, the right person *will* want it. In a sense it removes the blame, so that no non-sale (and salespeople have many) feels like a personal failure. Accumulated failure becomes self-perpetuating: people start to believe they will fail, and amazingly enough, they do.

Another part of this relates to the concept of managing your goals. As we have discussed, an overlarge goal tends to crush motivation. If each rejection feels like an indictment of your ability to write, then the goal of selling will begin to appear more and more overwhelming, moving you down the "arousal curve" and farther away from your optimum performance. This is a fancy way of saying that if you get rejected several times running and attribute this to incompetence on your part, it will be hard to keep going.

I remember one study where I and my colleagues compared highly successful versus only moderately successful salespeople, and we found that the most successful people tended not to remember failures, or if they did they did not dwell upon them. They learned from them and moved on. The lesser folk would mull over their failures and reenact them mentally. Doing that once or twice may help you learn, but doing it repeatedly racks up a larger tally of failure. Let me tell you about one extreme case of overcoming failure. A salesperson had just made a huge sale, so mammoth that he stood to get around a quarter of a million dollars in commissions, as I recall. The sale, which he thought he had in the bag, fell apart at the last minute—the day they were to sign on the bottom line, in fact. I asked him what he did. He said, "I went into the bathroom and I threw up. After that, I got up and started calling people to get a new appointment." And that was it!

Try to remember that an editor might have numerous reasons to reject your book, or that an agent can decide not to represent it for reasons you do not know. Do not assume that their rejection of your writing means that *you* are bad. Below I have accumulated some actual reasons for story rejections, collected from various places. Some are easily fixable—sending to the wrong market, for example. Others relate to personal taste, such as whether an agent wants to fight for it. Just remember the difference! You can fix fixable things; personal taste varies from person to person. Translate these facts into optimism. For example, change "I can't get a publisher to save my life" to "I haven't found the right agent/publisher *yet*." Don't try to rewrite your work unless you have received the exact same criticism over and over again, or you decide as an artist that it is necessary. You must try to sell it before you rewrite it!

Actual Reasons for Publishers to Reject Your Work
- They don't publish my genre (e.g., Harlequin Romances don't take westerns).
- They have several writers like me already; they're afraid they can't sell another (e.g., a mystery writer with a white female regional amateur detective).
- They have no money to pay for an advance or the printing of a book because: (a) they spent their new author budget; (b) they just sank it all into acquiring a big-name writer; (c) they are bankrupt; (d) they are too small.
- They only print X number of books a year, and they're booked for the next two years.
- They automatically reject unsolicited manuscripts.
- They have a backlog of new authors.
- They have a backlog of manuscripts in the "slush pile" (unsolicited manuscripts) that they are still reading.
- The editor has changed, and the new one has different tastes.
- They have eliminated that genre.
- They have reduced that genre list to their biggest names.
- They are eliminating that publishing line and are just finishing out the ones they have already bought.
- The market is saturated; sales are declining on this kind of material.
- They only publish lesbian fiction. (This happened to my wife! Worst thing was, they really liked the book but felt they couldn't publish it.)
- The editor is unsympathetic with the kinds of problems I write about, e.g., coming-of-age stories, being Jewish in America, intellectual-philosophical-suicidal college students.
- The editor disagrees strongly with my politics or opinions as expressed in the work.
- The publisher's lawyers fear libel suits from my work.
- The topic just isn't salable to a large enough audience to justify a major investment.
- The editor had a bad day.
- The editor read three superb submissions in a row, and yours suffered by comparison and through exhaustion.
- The editor just didn't like it.

Actual Reasons for Agents to Reject Your Work
- The agent liked it but didn't love it and in a tight market doesn't feel up to the challenge of pushing it.
- The agent didn't understand it.
- The agent does not sell that genre.
- The agent is overworked and afraid to take on another author.
- One of the chief agents and other key staff just left to start another firm.
- The agency is understaffed.
- The agency is overstaffed and afraid to take on a writer who is not established (and therefore needs more work to sell).
- The agent died. (Yes, it's been known to happen!)
- The agent didn't like it.

I realize that some of these excuses sound lame at best, but you will recall that I said these were *actual* excuses, not *sensible* excuses. Pick up the newsletter of any writer's organization and you will find laments about, for example, the trend of publishers spending an entire budget on one blockbuster writer when they could probably have dozens of solid sellers with the same money. Nevertheless, these excuses are no more lame than those the actual people gave. Just be sure not to tell people you consider their excuses inadequate—often enough, they are just trying to be polite. If they really hated your work, do you really want to know that?

And let's be fair here: do you want an agent selling your life's work in a lackadaisical manner? Do you really believe a publisher should put their entire company (and all of its employees) at legal risk for you?

In publishing terms, here are some things you might say to yourself, both in terms of attributions and next steps:

- They don't publish my kind of book right now. (I'll check *Writer's Market* for ones that do.)
- The editor hates coming-of-age stories like the one I happened to write this time. (I'll send it to another editor.)
- Their list is full this year, but there are others.
- One agent doesn't like it, but I might be able to send it to another—even in the same agency!
- This editor does not like it, but maybe he will leave this publisher.

And so forth. Remember George Scithers: "Editors do not reject people. They reject pieces of paper with writing on them." The most important thing is to *keep going*. After getting a rejection letter, one writer I know insisted on identifying a new target and writing a letter to them on the day she was rejected, so she could immediately have a new opportunity for success.

This lesson applies to many things in life, naturally; having something else ready to go means you never have too much time to brood.

Remember what John Jakes said in *Writer's Digest*: "Be persistent. Editors change; tastes change; editorial markets change. Too many beginning writers give up too easily."

CHANGING STRATEGIES OVER TIME

Most of the strategies described here are aimed at those just getting started. If you get fired up, you won't need me looking over your shoulder. However, it may be helpful to supply some suggestions for modifying your motivational technique for continued success.

A person with a strong Achievement Motive loses patience with the same goals. They should continue to rise. The challenge is not to push them too high to be accomplished. Achievement Motive run wild may disable the almost intuitive sense of what is a *moderate* risk by focusing only on doing more, more, more! So if you raise your minimum word-count goal for the second book, be ready to lower it again if the new level is not working. Try to keep it higher than last time (if that is your chosen tactic), but even a single word is a gain.

The power-motivated writer (apparently the majority of published writers, as you will recall) is still trying to impress someone and therefore may raise the stakes well beyond last time, making it impossible to deliver. The power-motivated would do well not to raise the goal unless it will (a) impress someone to do so, and (b) still be a reachable target.

The affiliative writer still wants to do something nice for someone; it might be a good idea to find out that the previous work has done so. Sending it out to friends and relatives may supply a sufficient store of this satisfaction to continue; if there is a strong response, there may be a smaller need for continual positive reinforcement during the writing of the second work. Reviews are unlikely to be helpful, as few of them are directed toward assuring a writer that he or she is likable.

SELF-CONFIDENCE

This is an important point that I have not addressed directly here until now. If you believe that you can never write a book (or essay or short story), all of the motivation in the world cannot overcome your own thoughts. The best way to convince yourself that you can write (regardless of whether it is good) is to start writing and keep writing. As you grow more sure of your mastery of the writing process (in the sense of its continuation), you may need less frequent feedback. Your own internal motives will keep you going fine.

If you think that nothing you write is worth reading, well, you are reading the wrong book. I have to assume that you are past that point. Nevertheless, I have advice to offer from other writers: you write for yourself first. The artist has one model and one audience member with him or her at all times: himself or herself. Many books were thought to be unsalable by one editor or another—*Jonathan Livingston Seagull* (more than forty publishers, by one count), *Dune* (twenty-seven rejections), *A Confederacy of Dunces*, *Auntie Mame*, and so on. Just take it to another editor. Anne Perry, who writes meticulously researched mysteries set in Victorian London, did not sell a book in ten years of writing. When she did, she sold it in the United States rather than in her native Britain. Years (and many books) passed before any of her work was published in Britain.

If nothing else, you must think that someday you can write something worth reading. Kurt Vonnegut built a career as a writer in order to write one book. Remember that Ray Bradbury commented that he thought every new writer should write a million words' worth of material—to be thrown away. A mere sixty thousand is enough for a short novel, so he suggests you toss away over sixteen novels' worth of material. Why? To learn the craft, nothing more. He does not think your first million words are likely to be worth reading. He speaks from personal experience—he thinks his first million were bad writing, even though some of them got published. Writing is a development process, and no one expects you to be Shakespeare the first time out. (If you are, well, I look forward to reading your work.) No writing work is truly wasted. Save it, think about it, start a new work, and come back to it if you feel the need. John Fowles felt he had to rewrite one of his (published!) novels completely, and he is hardly alone in this: Marion Zimmer Bradley rewrote several of hers. Even the best may worry about their work.

Stephen King chose to write under the name Richard Bachman in order to test himself—could he sell under another name? So don't worry if the first book is a whiz-bang. Just do your best, and with practice it will get better. As John Creasey said: "Nine out of ten writers, I am sure, could write more. I think they should and, if they did, they would find their work improving even beyond their own, their agent's and their editor's highest hopes" (*Writers on Writing*).

On that note, let us return to thinking about you.

PART VII: DEVELOPMENT
MANAGING AND CHANGING YOURSELF (AND YOUR WRITING)

The artist is nothing without the gift, but the gift is nothing without work.

EMILE ZOLA

23 Demotivators

I hesitated to write this section. Why? Because while awareness of obstacles and inhibitors is useful, getting frightened of the wide range of them is not. Realistically, there are many things that can demotivate you—and just as many that can remotivate you. One of the critical factors is your optimistic perspective on your writing practices; that is, do you believe you can solve the problems and move on?

Nevertheless, this section *is* useful, if only to help you manage your circumstances in order to avoid their occurrence. Below I list a few obvious (and perhaps not so obvious) demotivating factors. Remember that they *are* within your control. Don't use these as excuses not to write, just as warnings as you plan how to write around them.

THE ENVIRONMENT IN WHICH YOU WRITE

This can be a myth ("I have to have a quiet office with no interruptions") if it is overemphasized, but it is fair to note that your writing place occupies a great deal of your time. You should feel comfortable in it. As Kelly Tate told me, hers had to be "a place I can enjoy spending some time in." She realized that she did not like her writing room, so she bought some pictures, some plants, and some curtains and set it up in a way she found pleasant. If it gets in your way, deal with it. Ellen Kushner was an editor in New York and wrote constantly on the subway, which for some reason was inspirational to her, perhaps because it was pretty much the only time she had, and the pressure propelled her there. When she went to writing full time (or nearly full time), the lack of pressure and the large amounts of time daunted her. She started finding ways to take up her time, and she wrote more.

Creativity expert Mihalyi Chiksamahalyi has studied the phenomenon of "flow experience," when people are functioning at their peak, and for this to occur in a creative effort such as writing, people typically require at least twenty minutes of uninterrupted time. I think it is safe to assume that there are exceptions to this, and one probably does not need to be in a flow state to edit or even write decently, but it is still worth remembering.

There are more basic and obvious issues, however. Noise, temperature, smells—all of the basic senses—can distract you. The key here is not to give up, but to try and manage your environment. For example, if you are in a noisy area and find it difficult to concentrate, put on some music (add some "signal" to cover up the "noise"), or put on some headphones. At worst, put in some earplugs. One writer with whom I am closely associated has hearing aids, which she sometimes turns into the world's most expensive earplugs by turning *down* the volume so that she can't hear anything or at least can screen out most minor nuisances.

If temperature is your bugaboo, deal with that. Too cold? Put on a sweater. Too hot? Write in your skivvies. Way too hot? Go someplace air-conditioned and write there—a library, for example.

Environment is an issue, but it is a manageable one, if you use a little of your creativity on it.

OTHER PEOPLE

I've referred to this on several occasions. People can be the worst problem you have, especially those who don't believe in your dream. In some cases their opposition isn't even malicious but merely insensitive. A person may feel they have done you a favor by saving you from failure, disappointment, and low pay. It is hard to tell someone who genuinely cares about you that they have done you wrong. But they have.

Remember: It isn't their place to say.

Loved ones, I'm sorry to say, have the worst impact, because you are most open and sensitive to their criticism and influence.

It may be as little a thing as "Writing? What do you do that for?" That's what writers generally do, you know. Or the classic "I know if I had time, I could write one of those bestsellers." Yeah, right. Like Stephen King just has more time than you do. To the dedicated craftsperson, this is incredibly insulting. Try substituting their job for "write one of those bestsellers," and see what they say. An artist friend of mine made the mistake of saying "I could write a book, if I only had the time" to my wife, who promptly shot back "And if I only had the time, I could paint a picture." (To his credit, he said "Touché.")

Not everyone will agree with me here. James Blish, the noted science fiction writer, literary critic, music critic, and expert on James Joyce, pointed out that a thin-skinned writer is not worth having around, that there are plenty of other talented people out there. He was a critic in order to improve the quality of writing, and to some extent if you as the writer are not willing to try to improve, then you shouldn't try to write at all. However, Blish once said that a certain young writer was never going to get good, and that writer went on to become Harlan Ellison, multiple award winner. Blish, I note, apologized handsomely in print and became a friend of Ellison, who credited Blish with teaching him about the English language.

My point here is that developing a thick skin may be helpful, but ignoring the critics and practicing may be just as helpful.

Let's test out a few phrases, and some snappy answers you can give to them, at least until you develop your own.

"What do you want to do that [i.e., write] for?"

Have you noticed that for some reason everyone feels comfortable asking someone with an artistic job this incredibly rude question? Here are some possible answers:

- "I love reading, so I always wanted to write."
- "I can't help it."
- "It's a disease."
- "I'm a writer."
- "What do you eat for?"
- "What do you do what you do for?"

"Don't make much money at that, do you?"

- "That's not why I do it."
- "So?"
- "How much do you make at what you do?"
- "Stephen King does all right."

"What makes you think you can write/publish, anyway?"

- "Effort, study, and practice."
- "Experience."

- "What makes you qualified to judge?"
- "Just look at what else gets published!"

Feel free to come up with your own snappy answers. Even if you are too polite to say them, it is satisfying to think of them!

24 Superstitions

I'm no more superstitious than most writers—which means that
if I lost my lucky coffee mug, I'd be looking for another job.
JOE HALDEMAN, *Dealing in Futures*

Above I described a myth or two that had to do with the magical nature of creativity and when it takes place. Cross those with your view of yourself and your
role, and you may get superstitions. Since most people consider creativity a
mysterious and magical happening, who knows what could affect it? Anything
may influence the unpredictable. Some people write at night, others in the
morning. Some insist on a quiet room, others can write in bedlam. Most superstitions occur around inspiration and have been mentioned above. Generally I
distinguish superstition from beliefs and myths because it often requires some
sort of ritual behavior that is designed to invoke its magic. I have carefully considered the evidence, and my comment on this may surprise you: Go ahead!

If a superstition helps you write, who am I to tell you otherwise? The placebo
effect has its own power and legitimacy. And who knows? Maybe wearing a
crystal *does* help, at least for you. Rudyard Kipling required extremely black ink
(never blue-black, which he described as "an abomination to my Dæmon"); Truman Capote and Alexandre Dumas *père* required specific colors of paper—yellow for Capote, and rose, blue, and yellow for nonfiction, novels, and poetry,
respectively, for Dumas, who was so adamant about this scheme that he had his
ghostwriter and assistants use the same colors. Mystery writer Tony Fennelly,
who has studied under astrology masters, arranges much of her writing and
marketing by the stars. She once sent off a package to her agent at exactly 6:50
in the morning in order to get the proper benign influence (she stayed up late
to do it—she is not a morning person). In this case it turned out well.

I do *not* endorse astrology or any other belief here (I believe in keeping my
personal beliefs, outside of the faith in your ability to write, out of this book);
but if you do, you can use them to help you. Invoke St. Clare against sore eyes, St.
Vitus against oversleeping, or St. Mathurin for protection from fools, clowns,
and idiots (always useful when the reviews come in). Burn incense, or call upon

higher powers. Barry B. Longyear, the award-winning science fiction author, uses a "God Box" when he gets a problem; he writes it down on a piece of paper, puts it in the box, and lets God take care of it—that is, for all intents and purposes he forgets it. It works for him, and it might for you.

I have one important caution, however: make sure your belief *helps* your writing instead of inhibiting it. For example: if you think you can only write in longhand in a bus to Detroit, you are making it mighty hard on yourself and greatly limiting your efforts unnecessarily. Even a literary light like T. S. Eliot was not immune to superstition: he was convinced that no one ever wrote anything worth anything after winning a Nobel Prize. Since he had just won one, this did not exactly encourage him. I would prefer that you agree with Toni Morrison: "I don't wait to be struck by lightning and don't need certain slants of light in order to write." Superstitions only help you if they support your writing, not if they make it easy for you to hide from your responsibilities. If you don't want to write or are afraid of it, then stop. Don't invoke a superstition to take the blame.

25 Recharging Your Motives

*I write whenever it suits me. During a creative period I write
every day; a novel should not be interrupted. When I cease to
be carried along, when I no longer feel as though I were
taking down dictation, I stop.*

FRANÇOIS MAURIAC, *Writers on Writing*

Motives generate energy, but no source of energy is limitless. If, as we think,
they relate to specific neurotransmitters in the brain, you can certainly drain
them dry, as it were. You might drive yourself into exhaustion first, but you still
face the problem of restarting once you get yourself rest.

Some folks can wipe out their energy on one particular task rather than
drain their motive overall. Just because writing does not require hard physical
labor does not mean that you cannot tire yourself doing it. An extended mental effort is draining in its own right. Roughly half the oxygen your body collects
goes to the brain. There is a reason for this.

For those who exercise regularly or perform hard physical labor, there is no
equivalent for aching muscles in your brain, but tired is tired. If you feel physically tired, you cannot perform physical tasks, no matter how alert you may be.
If you are mentally tired, you cannot perform mental tasks, even if your body is
in tip-top shape.

Ask anyone who has finished a long doctoral dissertation, for example. Few
feel thrilled by the prospect of an immediate return to the keyboard. Mine was
over two hundred pages (of small print), with sixty-two tables (some three
pages long!). The thought of putting any more numbers in columns and rows
could have pushed me over the brink.

An extended effort focused not only on one task but one *motive* can drain
you really dry—especially if that motive is not your strongest. I saw this once
with an individual who was trying to be friendly to others on a professional
basis with only the barest shred of Affiliation Motive to help. To make matters
worse, she had to stay with the same small group for two weeks, both days and
evenings. By the end of the day all she wanted to do was hide. She knew how to

do the *behaviors* of affiliation, but she could not get up the *energy* even to social-ize with one of her most familiar colleagues. This issue becomes particularly salient when you are working out of your weaker motive. Eventually you run out of "natural" energy and start forcing it, draining yourself.

Well, how do you recharge?

If you are first-stage tired, you're just tired of the task. In that case, you might be able to sustain a different task with the same motive. If you're tired of writ-ing alone, go out and socialize, or attend a conference of fellow writers and fans. Many find that listening to others discuss work gets them inspired and excited about moving again, or so frustrated by listening to those other bozos that they want to go back to the keyboard and show them how it's done! A caution: if you are working out of a lesser motive, try not to drain your motivation in the *wrong* task.

If you are second-stage tired, you're out of motivational energy. Rest. Take a significant break. By that I do not mean just switching gears and doing some-thing else, if that other task requires the same motive. Do something com-pletely different. Writing that is primarily power-motivated could allow you to use the Achievement or Affiliation Motives to recover. Solve puzzles. Play soli-taire. Go have a picnic. Play with your children. Again, watch what you choose. It should interest and engage you, but not too much. Some studies show that 40 percent of the activity on personal computers consists of playing solitaire. I know a writer who had to remove the game from his hard drive after three days because after he bought a computer he literally failed to do anything else with it. This is a successful published author of a number of books, and had two or three in print when he bought his computer. His (successful) action falls under the category of managing your external setting, by the way—remove the temp-tation, and you will remove the concern.

Once you have truly exhausted yourself, don't try to start too soon. In some jobs, a solid two-week vacation is necessary to completely clear the mind of past worries. Why should writing be any different? If the option exists, you might need that two weeks. Several writers (including my wife) take a break after a major accomplishment, such as turning in a manuscript, especially since dead-lines tend to promote high-speed, high-volume writing, which wears you out that much more.

Even then, you might not want to start with the same thing. You might want to shift to the first option: try something different for a while. Many writers, especially in the mystery field, write multiple series. This prevents staleness; after living in one character's pocket for months or more, they go to some other character. That way they maximize productivity *and* get a rest from their main character. I don't mean that you have to spend exactly half your time some-where else. Take Rex Stout, the author of the Nero Wolfe mystery series: he wrote primarily Wolfe stories, both short and novel length, but periodically he would write a novel about someone else. He filled the majority of the fifty-odd books he wrote with stories about Wolfe, but he also wrote two about detective Alphabet Fox, one about Inspector Cramer (a character who shows up in the Wolfe series), and a few that stand alone. Agatha Christie had several series (Hercule Poirot, Miss Marple, and Tommy and Tuppence) but also some mysteries that stood completely apart from any series.

Or you can do something related to writing and very useful (once you have finished your book). Concentrate on marketing: go visit bookstores, prepare a cover letter for your press kit, talk to your publisher's publicist.

Other writers do something dramatically different: mountain climbing, painting (Churchill painted as well as wrote histories), whatever. Just be aware that if you start back writing and you feel tired just sitting at the keyboard, it might be too soon. If you have had your two weeks or so, you may need to re-energize yourself about writing. In that case you might want to *arouse* your power motive in appropriate ways: inspirational music or movies, for example. Ideally, you should be itching to get back to work. If writing feels like a punishment instead of a reward, there might be a good reason.

As always, this assumes that you should enjoy the process or at least find it to be acceptable work. People who must write for their daily bread either enjoy it or at least don't consider it painful.

26 Motivate Your Learning

All want to be learned, but no one is willing to pay the price.
JUVENAL, *The Sixteen Satires*

Grow or die—it applies to writing as well. You can improve—in plotting, in speed, in confidence—or you can rot away on the vine. Even highly experienced writers sometimes begin to cannibalize themselves, becoming self-parodies rather than speaking genuinely. Preventing that process requires learning. Most people, sadly, think of learning as unpleasant work. They have lost the gift of children to simply absorb. But when you are learning about something enjoyable, you may find you forget it is learning.

When I was in college, we called fun courses "gut courses," meaning that we could do it from the gut rather than from the head. I recall examining the required reading list for one such course and realizing that it had nearly a thousand pages of different texts, some quite difficult—but the class was so much fun that people could not see it as being real work. That is what we aim for, and for good reason.

Writing, or indeed any creative endeavor, does not come from nowhere. Not even from the muse. It comes through work, practice, and learning from your mistakes. Can you be born with talent? Of course! But if you were born deaf, don't expect to be an opera singer. You simply lack the tools to do the job. The best potential writer in the world who does not read might as well have a bucket over his head.

Some might think I am being overly optimistic, that it isn't possible to improve beyond a certain degree. Here's Kurt Vonnegut's view of that: "This is what I find encouraging about the writing trades. They allow mediocre people who are patient and industrious to revise their stupidity, to edit themselves into something like intelligence."

Elsewhere in this book I refer to Kipling's "nine-and-sixty ways" to write. All of them depend on learning how to use the tools of a writer, but they *can be learned.*

It has become a common insult that the modern artist "doesn't know how to draw." People make jokes about Picasso's distortion of "obviously" correct proportions. People forget that any two-dimensional image of a three-dimensional object must have translated the object's information in novel ways. What modern audiences see as "right" is no more true to reality (whatever that is) than Picasso's work. Furthermore, Picasso was a very fine representational artist, when he chose to be; I remember seeing an exhibition of his drawings, one of which came from the period when cubism was at its height. It was a beautifully detailed, highly realistic pen-and-ink portrait of a friend, done for a birthday. To break the rules, you must first know what they are.

I mention this because the process of being continuously creative is often coupled with continuous learning. Again, we have a need for motivation. Why learn at all? Why not repeat one's own expertise? Well, it can be boring, for one thing, and that isn't good for motivating oneself to write. The Achievement Motive is only aroused by a fresh challenge.

In any case, if you are not a published author, your best chance is to learn the craft well enough to sell. Yes, there are authors who were good but underappreciated; an entire book, *Rotten Rejections,* chronicles some of the worst rejections of the best authors and stories. But I prefer to think like Pasteur: "Chance favors the prepared mind." Or, if you prefer, Thomas Jefferson: "I find that the harder I work, the more luck I seem to have."

Given that, how do you keep learning? I will remind you again that Bradbury thought you should write a million words to be thrown away. He sold a respectable chunk of those first million words, but he did not consider it good work, especially once he learned more. Please note that "salable" is not the same as "good." Likewise, Robert Silverberg became a selling machine in his earlier days. He once told the "dean of science fiction," Robert Heinlein, that he had sold two million words in the past year. That's at least twenty-six novels! Heinlein's comment deflated him somewhat: "There aren't that many words in the English language. You must have repeated a few." With time, Silverberg realized that he had enough quality to publish, especially in a market that was desperate for readable, competent material, but he lacked the ability to do more than that—to really engage people. He was fortunate enough to get advice from several gifted people. But how do you keep working? How do you know if you are good enough? How do you get through that first million words, if that is what you need?

Link the learning with a natural process. Many writers see their lives as if they are writing, transferring their experiences into fictional terms in the same manner that Picasso could transfer a three-dimensional image into a two-dimensional canvas. It has become habitual. As Dorothy Sayers noted of her fictional writer Harriet Vane in *Gaudy Night,* "In that unpleasant habit of the novelist, of turning over the memory in her mind to turn it into a scene in a book . . ."

Some like to use different learning techniques, however, such as workshops or even brute force. For example, several highly prolific writers consider their success to be due primarily to hard work rather than talent, including Stephen King, Robert Silverberg, Kurt Vonnegut, and Isaac Asimov. In *Robert Silverberg's Worlds of Wonder: Exploring the Craft of Science Fiction,* Silverberg describes the various books he read (H. D. F. Kitto's *Greek Tragedy; In Search of Wonder,* by Damon Knight; *The Issue at Hand,* by "William Atheling, Jr." (actually James Blish); Thomas Uzzell's *Narrative Technique*), the mentors he had (James Blish,Damon Knight, H. L. Gold) and the various turning points in his career, such as the time when he realized that though he was selling everything he wrote—which at one point was "two short stories a day and a novel in two weeks"—he still was not writing as well as he should. Ultimately, he describes an endless process of learning from multiple sources, and he recommends, "The process of becoming a writer involves discovering how to use the accumulated wisdom of our guild, all those tricks of the storytelling trade that have evolved around the campfire over the past five or ten or fifty thousand years. Others can show you what those tricks are. But only you can make a writer out of yourself, by reading, by studying what you have read, and above all, by writing."

Alfred Bester discovered how to write *mostly* by writing, and by making mistakes. He credits comic books with giving him a place to be bad—a place to sell and survive but at the same time learn. At one point he describes a conversation he had about his discovery that if you had two plots play against each other it was "tremendously exciting!" The other man, an experienced writer, stared at him and said, "You mean you have never heard of plot and counterplot?" He does not describe it as an *efficient* way to learn, but he did learn. Bester also cites a mentor, someone who can greatly accelerate one's development; Robert Bloch cites Lovecraft as an influence, for example. Bester's case reveals a couple of patterns: you learn if you keep doing it, and a mentor can help.

Asimov loved stories so much that he started to write his own in a copybook. Since he loved an audience, he often read stories aloud to his friends, so one time he read his own story. To his amazement, the friend treated it like any other story—he wanted to know what happened next.

Sharyn McCrumb relates that in her very Southern family all the women tell stories in the kitchen and were very refined in this art. Her own writing has its roots in this tradition of storytelling, and the desire to be able to tell your own stories by learning from them too.

Kurt Vonnegut, as mentioned elsewhere, became a writer solely to write *Slaughterhouse Five,* but it did not happen magically. He worked at his craft and experimented with approaches. His sophistication changes markedly between his early work and the point when he thought he was finally ready.

Philip R. Craig not only learned a new approach, he determined what the approach would be first. As an academic, he took the logical approach: he bought a stack of bestsellers and studied them. He developed a list of things that were necessary and then used them systematically. Some people may see that as constraining. Go ahead—but he sold that book, and a lot of books since.

Hemingway was a journalist who worked quite deliberately at his craft of writing. As a professional writer, he did not expect the muse to strike. In his letters he spends a good deal of time talking about his techniques and experiments. He thought about ideas and then tried them out.

People have studied the process of how to learn, and not everyone learns the same way. David A. Kolb has identified four learning styles into which most people tend to fall. However, you need not limit yourself to one; in fact, the best learning comes from using multiple styles in rapid succession.

What does this look like when learning to write?

- **Concrete experience (feel):** just start writing, and see what happens. Many writers start this way—just trying to tell a story.
- **Reflective observation (watch):** listen to writers at conferences, read writing books and memoirs, observe writers at work. Many science fiction fans-turned-writers did this through fanzines, reading criticism, and studying. Robert Silverberg was one.
- **Abstract conceptualization (think):** create a pattern, principles, lists of steps; create a set of concepts. Phil Craig did that when he compiled his list of what a bestseller looked like.
- **Active experimentation (try):** apply learned principles to one's own writing. Hemingway would experiment with ideas by applying them to a story.

Or put them all in a row! Try writing an exercise for fun, take it to a writer's workshop where people can tell you what to do; work out for yourself what you think the key principles are; apply them to your story.

Another example: go to a conference where writers talk about their craft, and listen; organize their descriptions into a list of items; do a writing exercise trying something out; start fresh with trying something out.

Or do it backwards! It doesn't matter; just do it, and you will learn more effectively.

In any case, you can apply these principles to anything—not just writing. If you use them to research a topic you need to write about, you will retain more of the information. Sharan Newman set her fourth Catharine LeVendeur mystery novel on a twelfth-century pilgrimage, and she wound up taking the pilgrimage path herself. It is a commonplace that when you immerse yourself in a subject, you learn it faster. To this day I recall the Spanish word for an overhead cable car (*transférico*), which I learned nearly twenty-five years ago because I was in Madrid and looking for one. It takes me a good week to get back to basic conversational Spanish, but I remember that word even now.

BASIC PRINCIPLES OF PERSONAL CHANGE

1   **Change only happens if you want it.** You cannot force yourself to change if you don't really want to, and neither can anyone else—for the long term, anyway.

2   **Change can come from inside and from outside.** You can change yourself or you can change your environment in such a way that your ability to write is enhanced.

    To create internal change, develop, shift focus, learn something, set a value, make a decision. Use the Competency Acquisition Process as described in Chapter 31.

    To create external change, set a structure, arrange for someone outside you to affect you, organize your environment so it organizes you.

    For example, learning how to set a schedule for yourself is an internal skill; setting the schedule is creating an external change method.

    Or, having to write only in dark nights because of a superstitious dread of moonlight could certainly limit your output. Internal change: break your fear of moonlight. External change: write in an inside room with no windows to block the moonlight. So it's the bathroom—so what?

    In the somewhat silly second example, you can choose either to change yourself or to change the environment to support you as you are. But you can also do both: use the "write inside" option to smooth your path as you eliminate your phobia. As long as it helps, do it!

    Smokers quit their habit more easily when they have an *array* of tools: nicotine patches, rubber bands, hypnosis, and so on. Likewise, the more supports you have, the better.

3   **Change can come in many ways.** If one does not work, try another (or more than one). Remember that there is no single way to write. Likewise, while there are principles for personal change that are reliable, the best methods will vary from person to person. In studies of the effect of therapy, the single most important predictor of success is the therapist-client relationship itself (with some exceptions, particularly around phobia treatment). Similarly, if you find that one technique or one particular writer's group fails to help you, change it. Don't assume you can't do better.

4   **Change can be painful and slow.** Expect this and prepare for it. People generally do not wish to change. The intellectual acknowledgment of a need to change is not the same as being

able to change, and it certainly does not make the change process any less painful. If you are unleashing your existing motivation, you may find it highly pleasurable as the floodgates open, but if you are imposing structures on yourself, you may chafe a bit. Remember the intention, and your own commitment.

27 Workshops

The best book is a collaboration between author and reader.
BARBARA TUCHMAN, Practicing History

The primary distinction of the artist is that he must actively cultivate that state which most men, necessarily, must avoid: the state of being alone.
JAMES BALDWIN, "The Creative Process"

Many writers participate in writer's workshops. These groups vary widely, from support groups that meet to read each others' stories and eat dinner, to carefully structured organizations with a charter and a set of bylaws, to online gatherings. A related idea is the "amateur publishing association," or APA (pronounced "apa"), which goes the extra step of accomodating publishing as well as writing—the former much less difficult than it once was, thanks to inexpensive desktop publishing and Web-based forums.

Practically speaking, these various groups tend to overlap in function, providing both support and feedback. As John Hall Wheelock noted, "Most writers are in a state of gloom a good deal of the time; they need perpetual reassurance." Workshops also exist in which professional writers or creative writing teachers provide this feedback for fee-paying participants.

Many writers swear by workshops; one acquaintance once critiqued a story by saying "this is good enough that you should find a workshop for it." The recipient of this note was astonished at the assumption that a workshop would be the obviously necessary next step. Those who rely on workshops may use them at every step of their writing processes: ideas, outlines, rough drafts, later drafts. Others may get some limited criticism (say at an early stage) and leave it at that. Others have no interest in them at all.

Workshops can be a powerful tool. The Inklings, which included C. S. Lewis and J. R. R. Tolkien, was a kind of workshop. The Mañana Literary Society was a group that included what would be some of the best names in science fiction, including Robert Heinlein, Cleve Cartmill, "Anthony Boucher," and others; its avowed purpose was "to permit young writers to talk out their stories to each other in order to get them off their minds and thereby save themselves the trouble of writing them down." The Algonquin Club (known to the members as the Vicious Circle) gained fame for its quips, but a good deal of real work was accomplished there as well; people tend to forget that the legendary Algonquin Round Table members were all nobodies when they started their meetings. Harold Ross got the capital to start *The New Yorker* from his winnings at a poker game hosted by the club. A mystery writers' group has met at Kate's Mystery Books in Cambridge, Massachusetts, for years. I have seen numerous groups on America Online, via listservs, and through other online organizations, working on writing exercises to a fortnightly challenge (in "Theme Park," everyone who wants to can try writing about a particular theme), short stories, and even novels, one chapter at a time.

What can a workshop do? The answers vary. The only thing more complicated than understanding one person is to understand two and the relationships between them. Nevertheless, the workshop can have profound effects, because it supports all three motives, under the right circumstances, and helps you manage them as well.

BENEFITS OF THE WORKSHOP

Here are some of the things a workshop can provide:

- A temporary arousal of the motives you need: bringing out the Achievement Motive, for example, when you are ready to start cutting prose, or the Power Motive when you need to consider the impact of a scene more closely.
- An engagement for the motives you have: the impact on others hooks the Power Motive; meeting a challenge (even just producing your share of prose) snags the Achievement Motive; meeting with and helping people you like and trust pulls in the Affiliation Motive.
- A cultivation of the behaviors and thoughts of a professional writer that is focused on actual practice: there is a way to develop a trait, ability, or capability—even difficult ones—that may sound painfully simple when it is stated (you should remember it from the section on developing your motives): first, learn to *recognize* it when you see it demonstrated well. Second, *understand* what is going on inside and outside the head of the person demonstrating the characteristic. Third, *assess yourself* against what you have

seen. Fourth, *experiment* with doing it yourself. As you master it, *practice the skill* and get objective *feedback* on how you are doing. This practice was used to develop the Achievement Motive, but it applies to any characteristic. A workshop allows all of these steps to take place at one time and another.

- Substitution of others' viewpoints for your own in an area of weakness
- Emotional support (for any or all three of the motives).
- An opportunity to "Fool the watcher" by helping you to hold back the self-criticism that can stop you, in three ways:
    1 "It's just for them, not for real." Writing for your trusted group instead of the anxiety-provoking "professional market" can lower the perceived level of the challenge—you could not possibly satisfy the reviewer for the New York Times, but you know your fellow workshoppers.
    2 Shoring up self-confidence by getting "real" feedback instead of the "watcher." Drown out the self-criticism with the feedback of others. For some people, outside feedback can carry far more weight, especially if it comes from a professional. Even negative feedback may feel better, if you focus on something that you can improve rather than on something insurmountable, which is what self-criticism tends to zero in on ("I don't have the soul of a writer"). Remember good attribution is time- and place-focused. A group can focus on the prose rather than on vague, self-perceived inadequacies.
    3 Unconditional support when necessary to silence the watcher.
- Hard feedback on performance: supporting the Achievement Motive's desire to ask "How am I doing?"
- A chance to show off and impress people: supporting the Power Motive's desire to have an impact on or influence over others.
- A "safe" environment to experiment in new fields.

DANGERS OF THE WORKSHOP

The workshop has three main dangers:

- reinforcing the wrong things;
- tearing itself apart with its own strengths;
- seducing people away from their writing.

First, workshops that give positive support for a fledgling writer help that writer develop their craft. But workshops that tend to see everything as outstanding do their participants a disservice. While it may support your motive to write (over the short term), it does nothing for your *ability* to write. This may be prevented by having a balance of feedback. As noted above, studies have suggested that ideal performance feedback should be at the ratio of four positive comments to one negative. Indeed, there is reason for this beyond the issue of quality (which is not part of the scope of this book—or of motivational psychology per se, for that matter). Unabated praise starts to lose its force. People cease to believe it to be genuine, at which time it fails to motivate: "Well, he liked it, but he likes everything. Maybe he just has bad taste."

When I was an apprentice in a summer stock company, I assisted the prop mistress. She asked my opinion as we selected furnishings for the sets. I would dismiss something I found inappropriate as "tacky." Unfortunately, I limited my critical vocabulary to that one word. She turned to me once and said, "You know, I don't know if you have great taste—or no taste at all." After that, I became specific as to what I liked and disliked, and we could actually discuss the quality. "I think the light-colored Scandinavian-style furniture would be inappropriate for this family of characters, not only because they are Edwardian English people but also because they are ostentatious and therefore more likely to want large, ostentatious furniture." She decided that I did have some taste, after all. The same principle applies to feedback.

I doubt that I have to delineate the demotivating aspects of entirely (or overwhelmingly) negative feedback—if one has a fragile ego, it can be nearly destroyed by ongoing abuse. If one has a strong ego, it can still be shaken, or at least over time one's faith in the other person's critical judgment is bound to falter.

The second danger of the workshop is that its strongest force—the varied dispositions, talents, and motives of the group—can tear it apart. A group without careful management can and *will* disintegrate—or explode—from the conflicts it must inevitably engender. Remember that motives are *nonconscious*. That means that people may not know the forces driving them. A quick and strongly achievement-motivated person, impatient with a slow exposition, may finish sentences for a power-motivated person who wants to let the words roll out impressively. This latter person in turn gets incensed by the "obviously deliberate" insult. The former cannot understand what annoyed the second: "But it's faster." The latter cannot understand why the former would do such a thing: "Did you consider my feelings here? I'm trying for something more than speed of downloading."

Dissimilar levels of talent can inhibit as well. Different people have different gifts. Two people may have equally exceptional final products but they will have reached them through their own uniquely meandering paths. If one misinterprets a single gift as representative of them all (for example, someone who writes speedily seen as someone who writes *well* and speedily), one may set an unrealistic goal for oneself. Resentment then follows.

The same applies to relative time before pecuniary success. One person may sell their first work. Another may sell their tenth, or hundredth. Neither is necessarily superior to the other, but a great deal of resentment can build up between the "amateur" and the "professional." In the science fiction community this has produced the odd phenomenon of the "dirty old pro." Fans—who may write stories, essays, or poems that are published in their own "fanzines"—have turned on a fellow fan who dares to publish professionally. The implication is that you have left the ghetto—and how embarrassing for those left behind! A *good* group can share in success (see below), but even so you have to allow for human feelings. One can only go so long congratulating one's luckier (or more talented) fellows with a genuine smile. After a while the felicitations will be uttered through clenched teeth. Anger propels some people to produce, but others only become anxious and depressed. One obvious defense here: Leave the workshop, temporarily or permanently. Remember that this is not failing as a writer. No matter how much workshoppers like their practice, *it is not the same as actually writing.* If you think a workshop will help, find another group whose chemistry supports your own. As I have said, the single strongest variable predicting the success of therapy is the relationship between the therapist and the patient—if it does not work, you should find another therapist, not give up on the problem. Likewise, other workshops are available to help with your writing problems—or you can skip them. For many writers, workshops would only get in their way. Dickens didn't need a workshop; Stephen King doesn't either.

The third kind of danger is the seduction of the workshop. When taken to extremes, it can becomes a serious obstacle; for example, when you can write only for a workshop, the orientation of your audience has altered. Belonging to a workshop then becomes a superstition: "My work won't be any good unless they look at it." The workshop can also remove your sense of personal responsibility for your work: "I'm afraid to try alone," or "I can't do it without them. I'm not good enough." In this case, people may have lost the self-image of being a writer, instead seeing themselves as only part of a writer, the remaining part being supplied by the workshop. This does not mean that the workshop may not provide elements a person may find difficult to supply on his or her own; instead, it means a person may choose to give up all elements of writing without that one key piece, and that can sink your long-term motivation. Fanatic workshoppers to the contrary, many great works of writing never went near a workshop, and never needed to.

A final kind of seduction may come about when people get hooked by their motives into activities that do not produce writing, such as editing. If you are editing someone else's work, you are not writing. Period. You may hone skills that assist your writing, but no more than that. This seduction is particularly treacherous if the workshop has not put guidelines in place to prevent it. One writer of my acquaintance has apparently made a hobby of critiquing new writers' first novels. She reads thoroughly and well, making numerous helpful observations, suggestions, and notations. Fortunately, she is still writing also—though more slowly than her fans would prefer. She appears to be much faster at editing than at writing. In my view, she has three reasons for this: first, she does intensive and thorough historical research, which can absorb a great deal of time before one ever touches a keyboard. Second, she rewrites frequently, testing out alternatives or linking units so much that she has a word processing program that can hold up twenty-four windows at once. Third, she spends a lot of time being a one-woman workshop; I can recall three novels she read out of the goodness of her heart for which she wrote a total of thirty pages of single-spaced criticism. This is a gift from heaven for the unpublished writer (one of whom was published shortly after taking large chunks of her advice), but it can be a deadly danger for the published one giving the advice. You will note that I do not reveal the name of this author.

This can seduce people of any motive pattern, hence its danger. The achievement-motivated person may be tempted by the ability to *make something better*. A person with this motive may often think about the costs and benefits of his or her effort, and in these terms the act of helping others scores high. If you can take personal pride in someone else's accomplishment (and some do), then for the cost of perhaps an hour or two, you can feel you have pushed a story from unpublishable to publishable. Great benefit—minimal cost.

The affiliation-motivated person may feel the appeal of doing something for others and then basking in the warmth of others' gratitude—depending on how positive the feedback is, of course. The affiliative person may be tempted to be more positive than is warranted, to get just that response. The social nature of a gathering may be irresistible to the affiliative person, and this could keep him or her coming—but not writing, if the rules of the group do not manage the output.

The power-motivated person can know he or she has affected someone's life and work—and possibly gotten that person visible to the world by helping the writer write publishable material. Furthermore, a workshop is a wonderful opportunity to display one's own talents and person to a more-or-less captive audience; the personalized power person may like the idea of being on stage and in charge far more than being the victim of the process itself. Again, a motive to avoid writing.

Thus perhaps a fourth danger: workshops can slow you down! Good workshops put limitations on the amount that is read, both to be equitable and to ensure that people critique a reasonable quantity. Very fast writers then must wait for their critiques, if they really want to use the feedback. This only applies to very fast and capable writers for the most part; that's why I don't see this as terribly serious.

SMALL GROUP RESEARCH

Many people have studied how small groups work and what interpersonal processes occur in them. Robert F. Bales made one of the best descriptions, using the system he calls SYMLOG, for systematic multiple level observation of groups. He found, as had others, that groups tend to *polarize*—that is, form small, focused groups sometimes in opposition—but he went further and found a way to observe how a group changes over time. In brief, he found that there are usually two groups: one group that is positive, group-focused, and willing to go along with authority for the sake of the task; and another loose coalition of those who are more individualistic and rejecting of authority.

You can think of these as the "let's go along with the gang, huh?" group and the "why should I do what you want?" group. As you might expect, extreme polarization prevents a group from complete and effective functioning.

Polarization does not last, however. An extreme focus will frequently shift and flow, thanks to people who move into the *Moderator* or *Scapegoat* roles: the former works to bring the groups together, and everyone loves to hate the latter. Either way, the two groups will tend to merge, and perhaps realign around the moderator or scapegoat, with some joining the moderator or moving away from the scapegoat.

Studies have suggested an ideal array for an effective group and group leader. The group should be positive, group-oriented, and willing to accept authority and focus on the task. No one should be overly emphasized. The leader should be the same as everyone else, but with a stronger dominance to help influence the group.

When participating in a workshop it is important to remember that a group is not fixed, nor can it be made so. An effective group is a dynamic equilibrium with enough flexibility to include everyone yet enough rules to correct itself as necessary. Otherwise, the potential polarization will literally tear the group apart.

Not every group will get along. Nor will the members of a good group always get along. You need not like the people—you need only work well with them. If you cannot even work with these folks, you do neither yourself nor the group any good. Effective workshops, like the Cambridge Science Fiction Writers Workshop, evolve and change. They have turnover (several have come and gone from CSFW, and sometimes even come back), as people find they were not suited for this kind of group work or sometimes have a personality clash that is too strong to allow for functional criticism. There is nothing wrong with this; if anything, it is not sensible to assume that any group of people will invariably get along—yet that is probably the commonest error of a new group. "We all write—we can form a workshop!" But if one person despises another's writing, or does not respect the other as a person, it will not work.

You need not like everything others write. You must acknowledge, though, that this is your taste, not some standard chiseled in stone. While I (and many others) believe in minimum requirements for writing craft, there is always a point where two people can never agree, no matter how similar their tastes in other respects. When you hand over your pride and joy to be hacked and bloodied, you may feel as Abraham did in sacrificing Isaac. But like Abraham, it can be important over the long run to bear up to it.

Still, nobody said you had to *like* it.

THINGS TO WATCH

When looking at a group, watch for several things. SYMLOG tells us that people express certain values and behaviors (which may not match) around the three dimensions of dominance-submission, positivity-negativity, and forward-backward, and that these interact with each other over time.

Motives tell us that different people like different things and may have different emotional or unconscious agendas in what they do. These agendas are also essential for understanding what drives people.

Writing styles come into it as well: some people like to outline and find it rewarding. Others write at apparent random, as the muse strikes.

And always remember: *people want to be good writers*. Criticism hurts when it is untempered by respect for the individual as someone trying hard to learn a difficult craft and turn it into art. There is no one way to write! If you cannot accept that, *never* join a workshop unless its members all resemble you exactly—an unlikely possibility, especially since writers often change as they mature.

Below is a list of ten process guidelines taken from those participating in successful workshops, and from the field of group psychology. I hesitate to call them the Ten Commandments of Effective Groups, especially after the Abraham reference earlier, but it sure is tempting:

1 Trust in others' abilities.
2 Mutual respect for each other's efforts.
3 Mutual respect for each other as people.
4 Enough self-confidence.
5 Willingness to protect and maintain the group as an entity.
6 Awareness of the ultimate shared goal.

7 Knowledge of what you like and don't like.
8 Clear and fair expectations of each other.
9 Someone to manage the rules and/or do the work.
10 Desire to grow and improve

The alert reader will already have noticed a pattern here. The first five are all about *group cohesion*—in other words, what keeps the group together: trust, mutual respect, and willingness to believe that one is truly part of the group. The next four (6–9) are about *clarity of purpose and practice:* understanding what the group is doing, and how. The final item stands alone, but it is far from the least important: the *focus on improvement*. We will come back to this pattern below, but let's look at the specifics first.

1 **Trust in others' abilities.** You need not consider everyone outstanding, but you should trust that everyone is good at *something*. Ideally, you should be able to state what that is—"Joe knows how to plot well" or "Jane can target inconsistencies in characters every time." This may take a while to establish. At first, you may want to keep an open mind, and watch what strengths people show.

2 **Mutual respect for each other's efforts.** The first item tells you to trust that people have ability. This one tells you to respect what they do with it. A workshop is an opportunity to develop one's writing. Therefore, you should not expect deathless prose in a first draft. Respect the effort, not the outcome. A Beethovenian writer is no less competent than a Mozartian writer—in the long run. Some people write much slower than others.

3 **Mutual respect for each other as people.** You must go beyond basic respect for the work to respect for the person, or you will not be able to work together over the long term. You do not have to like each other—but you do have to respect each other. This is good advice for life in general and well worth repeating here. If you see a fellow workshopper as the scum of the earth, I doubt you will be very helpful to that person—and if he or she senses your feelings, don't expect helpfulness in return. This kind of conflict can also polarize a group in the ugliest manner.

4 **Enough self-confidence.** The members of the group must have enough self-confidence (or support) to deal with the time when one person sells and one person does not. This is critical, considering the wide range of speeds at which different people produce their work, let alone the idiosyncrasies of the publishing world. Workshops demand either personal self-confidence (if you

are the slower one) or good emotional support of others (if you are not), and preferably both. A good group can share in the success of any member; everyone had their part to play, even if it was just to force the other person to come up with a new way of saying things. I see many people thanking their workshops in acknowledgments these days.

5 **Willingness to protect and maintain the group as an entity.** From my time spent with members of the Cambridge Science Fiction Writer's workshop (and others), as well as interviews with several of them, I observed a tendency to protect the group for its own sake. If someone applied to the group and one workshop member hated the submitted sample, no one would push to get that person in, even if they liked that person. Furthermore, they did not all get along with each other; people joked about each others' styles of criticism (though not of their writing) and personality quirks. Many would avoid going to parties together. But they were willing to put up with each other to protect the mysterious gestalt of the functioning group. This is important. If individual problems outweigh the focus of the group, then the group will collapse into individual squabbles. You have to be willing to put up with some eccentricities for the sake of the group. Since I looked at CSFW, I have seen the same behavior among other groups, and self-managed work teams in businesses as well.

6 **Awareness of the ultimate shared goal.** Keep in mind your goal: to generate publishable, quality written material. Not to create only your kind of written material; not to change the world. Set a goal that you can all agree on, and remember it. Make sure that the goal lines up with your writing, rather than just being nice to each other, for example. See my comments on practices that support writing rather than stand apart from it. If you get together as friends also, be sure to manage the time so you can move smoothly from the social to the practical.

7 **Knowledge of what you like and don't like.** This applies both to you and to the other members of the group. Being objective makes you effective. If you hate "coming-of-age" stories, then you might want to moderate your criticism, or at least make it clear that you dislike the subgenre so much that Shakespeare himself could not write one you liked. Likewise, if you know that another member of the group dislikes the type of story you have written, you can shield yourself from the fallout.

8 **Clear and fair expectations of each other.** Resentments build rapidly if there is a perceived inconsistency or inequity. In dealing

with people, your intentions mean very little; the perception of the *other* person is what counts. Objective expectations will help keep personalities out of the mix. Some examples include:

- Everyone edits, everyone writes. It is tempting, as noted above, to get hooked into just editing or just writing. Some online writing workshops actually kick you off if you do exclusively one and not the other. It is not fair to criticize and not get criticized, or vice versa. It produces an imbalance of power.
- Be no meaner to others than they are to you. Some people can take brutal feedback without blinking. Some only pretend to do so. Some can't even do that. Try to respect the other person's feelings.

9 **Someone to manage the rules and/or do the work.** Every effective group has a person who monitors the process, or who keeps track of who is applying and handles their submissions, or who maintains the rules. For groups where no one wants the work, rotation may be the best option. Sometimes no one wants to be the banker in Monopoly. I hasten to note that if that person is a writer, special care must be taken to ensure that their writing and criticism time does not become overly hampered by their facilitation duties. Cut this person some extra slack. I have seen groups give extra benefits to the coordinator (including extra royalties on shared books) to keep that person happy and part of the group. It's usually worth it.

10 **Desire to grow and improve.** A group is at best a dynamic equilibrium, not a stable object. The more willing you are to accept changes (in people, process, etc.), the better your chances to sustain the effectiveness of the group over time. In this manner you can grow together and also self-correct. Part of this derives from the achievement-motivated desire to improve, but part of it also derives from the willingness to be open and to trust that the group *can* move.

Note the pattern again: group cohesion, clarity of purpose and practice, and focus on improvement. There are three categories here: the trust and respect that goes along with the affiliative motivation (group cohesion); clear understanding of intent and approach (clarity of purpose and practice); and achievement motivation (focus on improvement). In other words, the combination of two motives and one external factor. Let's look at one real example of a group and see whether this holds up.

CASE STUDY: THE CAMBRIDGE SCIENCE-FICTION WORKSHOP

As part of my research for this book I interviewed and measured the motives of three of the eight members of the Cambridge Science-Fiction Workshop: Sarah Smith, Alexander Jablakow, and David Alexander Smith. Each had distinct impressions of the group and what it did for them. Since the whole is often not just greater but qualitatively different from the parts, this case study focuses on how the group works, not how the individual members as such react to it.

The group was founded about 1982; it has gone through several iterations, but one relatively constant set of members has stayed for around ten years. They use techniques derived from other successful groups (e.g., the Clarion workshop) and have developed themselves through years of testing. They share their experiences with participants in mini-workshops at science fiction conferences, giving people this set of tools:

- Names and addresses of workshop participants.
- A "critiquing manifesto" that lays out the principles of the group (e.g., "Why are we here?" and "How do we critique?").
- Organizational notes, including the logistics (e.g., monthly meetings) and how the agenda is set.
- Specific critiquing rules for a session.
- Variations from the norm (e.g., doing a novel rather than a short story).
- A list of useful vocabulary accumulated over the years from their group and others (e.g., POV (point of view), "nowism" (putting something current into the future, such as a wristwatch on Captain Kirk), and so forth).
- Writing aphorisms: useful things that have been said and done that may not have direct application but could be inspirational.

I would like to quote some of the CSFW's notes, with annotations based on some of the concepts we described above. As always, different groups operate differently.

1. WHY ARE WE HERE?

> We're here to help one another produce our best fiction. All other goals are subordinate to that. If you want to work out personal issues in your fiction, that's fine, but if the results are bad fiction, you can't defend yourself by saying your life happened that way.

This exemplifies the "affiliation plus achievement" criterion described above, with a dash of socialized power. "Help one another" is affiliation; "best fiction" is achievement. Note the example used for excluded goals: working out personal issues can be construed either as self-centered (and thus not group-focused) or anxiously affiliative. This is a clear shared goal and guideline that can help determine the rules of engagement.

2. HOW DO WE CRITIQUE?

> [A] two-edged commitment: (A) Tell the truth, (B) Criticize the prose, not the writer.
>
> As a *critic*, comment on anything that moves you. Line edit if you want. Argue with the character motivation. Question the rubber science. Suggest alternate plot lines.
>
> At the same time, *you must respect the author's right to tell his own story*. Figure out what the author's objectives are, and then figure out how to help the author achieve them. You may not like heroic fantasy, but if you're critiquing an author who does, you have to provide suggestions for making it more fantastic or more heroic. You're not here to demand that an author change his agenda. You can suggest other agendas, but if the author declines them, you must help the author go his way, not yours.

This lays down the specific role of the participant: anything is fair game, but the author is the final determinant of the story. It is not a collaboration. This allows for Kipling's principle that every single way of "composing tribal lays" is right, but it also implicitly focuses on achievement (make it better) over affiliation (be nice to people by holding back criticism). It also includes the issues of mutual respect and "know what you don't like," and it considers how they apply to the group. Several points from the CSFW notes follow from this:

> A *You Must Do the Work.* You're not here reading for pleasure. You're here because other people have agreed to work on your material. And they won't do that unless you work on theirs.

A clear statement of equity: do mine, and I'll do yours. This reinforces the goal of helping one another to create the best work.

> B *Be General First.* If something bothers you over and over, state the general issue first.

A good guideline for coaching overall: state the general principle that will enable someone to avoid the specific examples for themselves in the future.

    c *Then Be Specific.* "Why do you feel it's slow?..."

An essential partner to the above point that is related to goal setting. The critic should not simply say "It's too slow"; this comment is too vague to suggest specific improvement. Instead, try this: "I found the long descriptions of scene bored me and interfered with the action." Then you must cite a specific example, both to illustrate and to allow editing to take place: "In the scene with the executive, you spent an entire page describing the contents of the desk and the office, but only four pages on the entire scene, which was critical to establishing the relationship between the protagonist and the executive."

> The author, of course, doesn't have to take your suggestion, but the act of examining an alternate story line is enormously helpful. All too often, writers see their stories as having no options— they *must* occur a particular way.

A vital point. Respect the other person, and as a participant realize that their perspective may assist you. Also stated to me by CSFW participants: hearing other options may help you understand what you like about your choice, and how to strengthen those traits, whether or not others like it.

3. HOW DO WE LISTEN?

> As an author, you must absorb what is said to you. That doesn't mean you accept it or reject it, it means you listen to it. You take it seriously as being motivated for your benefit.
>
> Being critiqued in a roundtable workshop is no fun. You sit there, naked and exposed, as someone goes over your flaws with a microscope. Ouch! And a bunch of other people who've also read your material agree with the critic. Double ouch! ...but intellectually you're realizing that a good chunk of what's being said is dead right. So you don't even have the normal defense of rationalizing that your critic is full of beans.
>
> How do we get through this and come back for more? *Because the prose gets better.* Just like exercise ...
>
> Wouldn't you rather hear the problems from a few folks in private than have editor after editor recognize them, reject your story, and never tell you? Or worse, have your story published

with the flaws there for all eternity, for hundreds of people to notice and cluck over?

Note the Power motive here: "Because the prose gets better" sounds like Achievement motive until you hear: "hundreds of people to notice and cluck over."

That's why in our workshops:

A No outsiders. You can't be vulnerable with other people if there's somebody who can take free shots.

Interestingly, the CSFW follows this so scrupulously that even when doing mini-workshops, most of the CSFW members will submit a piece, even though they are the teachers rather than the students. Of course, they do believe in this technique, which supports an egalitarian philosophy, so from their point of view more people might equal more benefit.

B Everyone must submit periodically.

Equity again; you can't just do the parts of the workshop you like, or hold yourself aloof altogether.

C You have to build trust. You have to come to believe that people really are trying to help you, otherwise you'll close up to the comments.

Positive affiliation: you can trust that people will help you.

D Things are written down. You can react to them later, after the pummeled feeling subsides.

Memory is a poor servant of accuracy. Studies indicate that 80 percent of the witnesses will be flat wrong about an event they just witnessed. A person who has just seen a crime—a dramatic, memorable event—will be mistaken as to the height, dress colors, hair color, build, and actions of the criminal even immediately afterward. When subject to emotional stress (and getting criticized is certainly that!), a person loses the ability to recall exact words.

E Over time, we become very respectful of one another. We hold nothing back in terms of identifying and pounding problems ... but we're all extremely solicitous of each other's intentions.

A restatement of the honesty-plus-respect or achievement-plus-affiliation goal.

4. WHAT ABOUT GIVING AWAY IDEAS?

> We've had people get very upset when given ideas or asked for ideas . . .
> You don't have to accept it.
> As long as things are reasonably reciprocal, everybody wins.
> If you stick with it, sooner or later everybody gets published.
> When that happens, each person in the workshop can share in that wonderful feeling, because everyone contributed to making it happen.

This refers to socialized power—feeling satisfaction from having had a positive impact on another person; or in an even more sophisticated fashion, feeling strengthened from the strengthening of another. Reciprocity is key here; the workshop members assume that as people get published, they improve in their ability to assist *you* to get published.

Note that the CSFW meets virtually every characteristic I described above. This is not accidental. They took rules from other successful organizations, experimented to find out the best combination for themselves, and grew. They now protect each other and the fragile creature that is their workshop to maintain its effectiveness over time. Even those who are not dedicated workshoppers acknowledge the usefulness of the group, and they know that.

A PICTURE OF A SUCCESSFUL WORKSHOPPER

I've spent a good deal of time on the process of a good working group, and this is important, because the best group of people in the world may ruin themselves without the right process. "Never go into business with friends and family" is a truism, but for good reason. For most people, the nature of the relationship with those individuals is deeper and more important than the immediate business needs, which is good for personal relationships but can be bad for the business.

Turning this around, some characteristics support an effective working group, and research into self-managed work teams has identified a number of them. Self-managed work teams are just what they sound like: a group of individuals who can successfully do good work, and who reinforce each other's behavior as necessary to improve performance, without a fixed or formal leader. In the ideal state, there is no manager at all. This describes a workshop very well: nobody with formal authority tells the other writers what to do; no one holds individual responsibility for the performance of the group. While this research is highly debated, there have been some interesting findings that seem to apply to a host of different jobs and roles.

First, the motives. The Achievement Motive is key for getting things done and moving forward; the Affiliation Motive is key for keeping people together and maintaining the group. Both can act for the good of a group.

A person with only the Achievement Motive engaged will tend to act for personal accomplishment—it is easier and more satisfying to control the steps. Such a person will chafe under the needs of a group to maintain itself: "Why should I care about feelings and process? We've got a job to do!" Out of disgust or impatience, they will start working on their own, or jettison the group, or try to force things in a single direction.

Alternatively a person with only the Affiliative Motive engaged will act for the personal harmony of the group, taking care of the people involved. Since a normal task of a writing group is to criticize, this person may spend more time being nice to people than giving them the feedback they really need. The good of "the group" starts to become paramount, regardless of whether the group gets anything done.

But a person who combines both motives has an ideal profile:

- wants to do well (Achievement Motive);
- likes being part of a group of people (Affiliation motive);
- wants the group to succeed (achievement and affiliation, or team achievement).

This is the key to getting a group to work effectively. As noted above, the Power Motive drives most published writers, but it can threaten a group. If group members focus on the persuasion of others rather than on the improvement of the work, they won't have a group for long. Instead of everyone trying to get the best possible outcome, people will spend time getting others to agree that their work is fine just the way it is—or that someone else's work has to be redone in only *this* way.

Seems like a paradox, doesn't it? Power Motive drives the individual to write, but Achievement and Affiliation Motives enable an effective team. Not many people have all three measuring high, do they?

Here is where we return to the concept of *values*. You do not have to have the motive to carry out the behavior. You can be laden with Power Motive and *act* as an achievement-plus-affiliation person. Indeed, the well-socialized power-motivated person might want to do so, because it will have the most positive impact on the group.

I know that sounds circular, but bear with me. Here is the logic:

1 I want to influence others (Power Motive).
2 Therefore, I want to write (value).
3 For whatever reason, I have decided to join a group.

4 To succeed as a writer (influencing others), I need to make this group work for me.
5 I can't force people in the group to help me, I need to influence them (Power Motive).
6 The best way to get their help is to help them and make sure the group is successful (achievement and affiliation value).
7 If the group succeeds, I succeed, and I get to influence people (Power Motive).

If you already have some combination of achievement and affiliation, the specific issues become different, but the basic answer is the same: be a good team member by choosing to act like one.

28 When You Are Not Writing

In the course of this book, it may appear that I blithely assume that you write constantly or want to do so. I do, if that is what *you* want. In practice, however, few of us get the opportunity to write full-time. In fact, many people find that a difficult job indeed. Writing is a solitary activity; those with a very strong Affiliation or Power Motive (and as we have seen, most professional writers have the latter) may find it intolerably lonely if they are forced to write day after day.

Most writers do not spend all of their time writing, even if they write full-time. Science fiction writer Alexander Jablokow describes his full-time writing process:

> I work at the same time . . . morning . . . sometimes I just sit there, but I am there. I use the old trick of rewriting some of last night's work to get started. Sometimes I'm hot, sometimes not. I usually pick up something to read—the danger of keeping books in your writing office—then write a little bit, then wander around, then come back . . . if you graphed out my time, there would be a little peak early in the morning, then a long gap, then a longer peak, then a gap, then a longer gap. Eventually I'll catch hold and write steadily. If I write six pages a session, four of them are in the last hour to hour and a half, and the remaining two are in the previous three hours.

Contrary to popular belief, you do not have to churn out pages every hour to be productive—unless you are doing it to survive, of course. Six pages a day, five days a week equals approximately 120 pages a month. A 70,000-word book-length manuscript will have 280 250-word pages (longer books will have more, naturally; James Clavell's *Shogun* weighed in at 1,200 paperback pages, roughly 420,000 words or over 1,600 manuscript pages). You can theoretically write a first draft at that pace in two and a third months, which some writers consider very fast indeed.

Realistically, many interruptions and natural pauses happen to your writing. Not to overstate the obvious, but you do have to eat and sleep sometime. You may have to deal with a day job, as most writers do. You may have to deal with the needs of children or your spouse. Sometimes, you may just want a rest from writing. Some writers get depressed at the end of a novel; others love to get the monkey off their backs. Frankly, you may not be cut out for full-time writing. Even if you are, you may not want to write every minute of the day. So the question here becomes not the maintenance of a pattern of behavior (writing), but the care and feeding of yourself (and your motives) when *not* writing.

You may want to consider your other motives. Motives are sources of emotional energy. They don't go away just because you have no opportunity to use them; instead, they build up a tidal wave of energy. If they do not find some outlet, you may find yourself irritable, frustrated, or restless. Robert Heinlein tried to retire from writing at one point, before he realized what a source of satisfaction it was for him. Here is what he said in *Expanded Universe:* "I retired ... This went on for about a month when I found that I was beginning to be vaguely ill: poor appetite, loss of weight, insomnia, jittery, absent-minded—much like the early symptoms of pulmonary tuberculosis, and I thought, 'Damn it, am I going to have still a *third* attack?'" Then an editor asked him to make some minor rewrites to a story. "I sat down at my typewriter to make the suggested changes ... and suddenly realized that I felt *good* for the first time in weeks ... Once you get the monkey on your back there is no cure short of the grave ... If I simply loaf for more than two or three days, that monkey starts niggling at me. Then nothing short of a few thousand words will soothe my nerves."

This is an extreme case of writer's addiction in a man of not terribly good health, but it illustrates the cost of suppressing motives. They are natural forces within you, and you may not ignore them for long if they have great strength. Indeed, they parallel other kinds of addictions. After one has developed a tolerance to a drug, higher and higher doses are required to create pleasure, but one will keep taking it to stave off the pain of going without. Sounds grim, doesn't it? Realistically, most writers are not crazed junkies willing to do anything to get their fix (well, except maybe the late Dr. Asimov). Of course, even if they are, at least they don't wind up selling the stereo to get some more writing done.

Getting back to the subject at hand, the real point of this discussion is that your productivity will increase if you maintain a balance of satisfaction suited to your own pattern of motives. You can't ignore your motives, so you might as well adapt to them.

Some people avoid reading within their genre so they can stay focused on writing instead of reading. Alexander Jablokow and David A. Smith do that, because they have trained themselves to be so critical that reading science fiction is "not relaxing," in Jablokow's words. Philip Craig only came into mystery fiction by accident (there was a murder in the book he was trying to sell), and he reads mostly the classics, not current works, with few exceptions. A number of writers I know make a point of not reading fiction at all while in the process of writing their own work, because as one put it: "I would rather finish [reading] a work of fiction then finish my own book." Some manage to read in a different genre—science fiction instead of mystery, for example.

Some of this may be natural procrastination, but some of it may be motivationally powered. A motive is what you think about when you do not have to think about anything; remember that externally motivated actions are not the same as internally motivated. Jablokow, who, like virtually all the people I studied, is largely power-motivated, may not find the process of criticism itself very satisfying, when he really wants to see a dramatic situation laden with emotional energy. Reading critically lacks a free-flowing nature. Alternatively, it takes a lot less energy to get satisfaction from reading than from writing. Interestingly, in Jablokow's case he continues to read Power-Motive material (such as histories of Eastern Europe or psychological thrillers like Ruth Rendell and P. D. James), but his profile is very much dominated by that motive. Similarly, David A. Smith reads mysteries when not writing science fiction, generally of the hard-boiled variety.

You may feel the need to rotate your focus from time to time. This can refresh you and give the emotional energies time to recharge. The motives can provide powerful energy, but you must use all of the motives you have sometime. And keep in mind that the way in which you use them may have its own price. Your Achievement Motive could propel you to lift that weight just five more times, to use a nonwriting example, but that might be five more times than your stressed muscles can take. By the same token, if you find yourself running a fever or getting eyestrain, perhaps you should lay off the keyboard for a while. Besides, many writers speak of the value of taking time off to learn something that feeds into the writing. "I cannibalize my life," said Harlan Ellison—but he has a life filled with experiences worth cannibalizing that he did not gather in his office. Isaac Asimov resisted writing an autobiography for years because he thought his life was rather dull. Most of his working life—eight to ten hours a day, virtually every day—was spent typing in a small, windowless room. Somehow, he managed to produce four large volumes anyway, but never mind. As long as you produce reliably and to a reasonable extent, it is okay to take a break. Anxiety can hamper your output, too.

29 Support Systems

"Solitude, competitiveness and grief are the unavoidable lot of a writer only when there is no organization or network to which he can turn."

TONI MORRISON

Writers appear as lonely figures, toiling away in a garret at midnight with no one around for miles. No committees have gained fame for their masterworks of literature, it is true, but by the same token no man (or woman) is an island. Just because the task itself is typically (though not always) solitary does not mean that you must isolate yourself from all society.

Even if you exclude collaborators, many writers depend on the emotional and even literary support of friends and lovers. While Thoreau wrote his salute to the natural life in Walden Woods, he had Sunday dinner with his mother every weekend. And a quick perusal of acknowledgments and dedications will reveal a remarkable number of people "without whom this could not have been written."

People are embedded in a web of other people. That web can work to your benefit or against you. Your challenge as a writer is to make the best use of the web, or to shield yourself from the worst of it.

A large scientific literature exists showing that support systems are vital to emotional health, the defeat of adversity, and success in life. At its simplest, a good network can provide information. At its most complex, it can provide jobs, emotional support, financial support, and opportunities to sell your work.

WHAT IS YOUR NETWORK?

Below is a simple list of categories of people cobbled together from frequent sources of support. You can add to it as you wish. The important thing is to mark whether you see these people as having a positive, neutral, or negative impact on you in terms of support. That is, someone who helps you is "positive," someone who makes you feel depressed or angry is "negative." Someone who does not fit into either category (or perhaps fits into both) would be "neutral." Here's what such a table might look like:

Social Support	Positive	Neutral/Both	Negative
Wife	x		
Grandpa	x		
Joe Friend			x
Agent	x		
Sister			x
Jane Friend	x		
Totals	4	0	2

Normally such a table would be applied to life overall, which is a useful task in itself. I suggest taking it a step further and measuring these people's impact on your writing. Someone who has a positive impact on your social life might have a negative impact on your writing, especially if they say "Oh, knock off that writing and let's have some fun!" Someone who wants you to see writing as boring, difficult work has a negative impact no matter how much fun they are otherwise.

Let's put together a table. Below I have gathered a list of obvious and less obvious suspects that can support your work as a writer. Some may be specific to writers. Don't limit yourself to the categories or people I happen to suggest. It can be helpful to have multiple lists, one for each of the categories below:

Family: Parents, grandparents, siblings, children, spouse/significant other, in-laws, aunts/uncles

Friends: Past and present

Work support: Boss, employees, peers, human resources

Community support: Minister, church members or groups, fraternal organizations

Writer's support: Agent, editor, publisher, publicist, writer's workshop, other fellow writers, writer's organizations (e.g., Authors Guild, Mystery Writers of America, etc.)

Anyone else you can think of: Teachers, mentors, etc.

I'll put more explicit directions below, but first, put down as many or as few of these people into a table as you need to. Check where people come out, and add them up. Don't be afraid to add names—we want this to be a complete list. To use the support systems list:

1 Go down the list one person at a time, and assign specific people where appropriate. For example: The grandparent might be your mother's father, who encouraged you to write and has a complete collection of your articles in the high school newspaper.

2 For each person, determine whether he or she provides overall *positive support* or *negative support* or *neutral* or *no support*. Check the appropriate column.

3 Add up totals at the bottom. Look at the overall balance. Do you have more positive support than negative?

4 Look at the people you checked as positive. Is there a pattern here? Who are they?

5 Look at the people you checked as negative. Is there a pattern here? Who are they?

6 Add these people to your writing plan: get support from those who give it and find ways to circumvent the negative impact of those who don't. For example: when you are feeling down, call a fellow writer (who is a positive impact, naturally) and commiserate. If you know your mother is coming into town and she will occupy your time, don't set a goal of writing when she is there— it will only set you up for failure. (See section V: "Goal Setting.")

Simply comparing the numbers of positives and negatives alone may give you a clue as to how easy it is for you to write; it is hard to maintain motivation in the absence of support, and even harder in the presence of opposition.

Note that your motives affect this as well. The affiliation-motivated person is more susceptible to being "guilted" out of work to be with people. The power-motivated person might choose to skip writing in order to be visible somewhere, or to appear at a conference or with a group. Only the achievement-motivated are relatively immune to all of this, but even they crave feedback on performance that might come only from someone outside themselves.

That is the negative side. On the other side, a good friend can give the uncritical support an affiliative person needs to keep writing alone ("I'm proud of you for your writing. We can get together when you're done."), or the feedback needed to propel the power-motivated person ("This is very impressive, you had me completely absorbed in your work. I want to read your next book—hurry up!") or the achievement-motivated person ("You're making excellent progress —much better than your previous draft. You want details? Okay . . .").

The process of creating this list may give you some insight, but remember that it is too simple to capture the real world. The same person may be a very positive impact or a negative impact, and you may be able to help that change.

For example, many people suffer negative remarks from their families regarding their writing. "What do you want to do that for? You're just wasting your time anyway." Then, when they win an award for their writing, their families fall all over themselves to say how proud they are. Well, you can make them a support instead of an obstacle. Don't make enemies of them by maligning them in your acceptance speech; sigh and be glad that they are turning around.

For many people, they just don't understand. Perhaps their family members are simply not well educated, or they lack a value around reading and writing. You can still recruit them into your support system if you want to, and if you can find ways to do so.

To interpret your support system list:

1   **Grand totals.** This section will help you see whether you generally feel supported or not. Questions to ask yourself here include:
    • Do I have supporters? How many?
    • Do I have obstacles? How many?
    • Do I have more supporters than obstacles? (Positive greater than negative?)
    • Are most of my supporters mixed?

Think about how many people you have here. Granted, you only need one supporter (and some do without that for periods of time), but it is nice to know whether you have enough of a network that you don't have to rely on only one person.

Also, know your obstacles. The worst obstacles are those people whom you like and care for but who do not help you write. You can hardly write off your family (so to speak), but they might not be helping you either. Those people you have to manage or educate. One writer told me that she had her children trained not to come to her office door unless there was a significant amount of blood still flowing.

2   **Balance of positive and negative.** Questions to ask yourself include: What is the balance of support I have?
    If you have three supporters and fifty obstacles, this might be a clue as to why you are finding it hard to write. Of course, if the three are your spouse, child, and parent, while your obstacles are people at work, this might not be a problem.
3   **Balance per list: are some predominantly positive or negative?** Questions to ask yourself include: What is the balance for each list? Are some areas more or less supportive than others?
    This will show you *where* your support is located. As noted

above, who is supporting you can make a big difference. If your only obstacles are at work, then don't talk about writing at work. This could become challenging if you are supported everywhere but at home, since most people write at home, but perhaps you can write during your lunch hour, or bring your family around.

4 **Key sources of support overall.** Questions to ask yourself include: Who are my best supporters? Where should I go to get consistent support?

This is a good time to create a short list of "Key Sources of Support" and "Key Obstacles to Writing." Who makes the biggest difference for you? Keep these lists handy for those down periods—*both* lists. Why? Two reasons. First, when you are down you want to know who you can call to get back up. Second, many people get down because someone put them there. If you know that such a person is on your "obstacle" list, keep in mind what my mother told me: *Remember the source.* Don't take the obstacles too seriously. Forewarned is forearmed.

A FAR FROM COMPLETE LIST OF WRITER'S ORGANIZATIONS

- American Crime Writers League (www.acwl.org)
- Authors Guild (www.authorsguild.com)
- Horror Writers Association (www.horror.org)
- Mystery Writers of America (www.mysterywriters.org)
- Romance Writers of America (www.rwanational.com)
- Science Fiction and Fantasy Writers of America (www.sfwa.org)
- Screenwriters Guild of America (www.screenwritersguild.com)
- Sisters in Crime (www.sistersincrime.org)
- Writers Guild of America (www.wga.org)
- National Writers Union (www.nwu.org)

30 Changing Your Motives

Don't try to teach a pig to sing; it wastes your time and
annoys the pig.

ROBERT A. HEINLEIN, *Time Enough for Love*

You may be asking yourself whether you have the motives you want, and whether you are stuck with them forever. Given that you may see your own motivational pattern as more of an obstacle than a benefit, this becomes a question of large personal import.

Fortunately, the answer is no, you are not stuck—up to a point. You *can* change your motives, using a lengthy and difficult process. Motives resemble muscles, in the sense that if you flex one, it grows stronger. But like muscles, only a repeated, steady effort over time makes a significant difference.

Fortunately or unfortunately, however, no one has ever managed to make a motive go *down*. I once worked on a study examined people with severe osteoarthritis—the crippling kind. We thought it might lead to a reduced Achievement Motive, since people would be unable to act on their desire to meet goals due to physical incapability. Nope. They measured exactly the same as the rest of the world. Unlike muscles, motives do not atrophy, nor do developed motives return to their former states. That's good and bad news. If you want to develop a motive, it's good news: whatever you develop seems to stick. If you find a motive blocking your efforts, it's bad news: you're stuck with it, so you will have to find some other way to manage it.

Remember: Motives can grow, but not shrink!

Early research work by David McClelland and his colleagues around the world in such places as India, Poland, and urban Washington, D.C. was devoted to developing people's need for achievement. The process was surprisingly simple (though not easy): teach people to see the motive in others, to understand the motive from the inside (that is, to understand how people with the motive think and act), and then to practice thinking in the motive, making sure they got positive feedback for successful use of the motive. With time, the natural reward systems of your body take over, and you will have a higher motive. I'll lay this process out in a list later.

One way to integrate a motive into your normal thinking is to practice writing appropriate stories. Writing "maximum achievement" stories gets you into a personal understanding of how an achievement-motivated person thinks. Likewise, writing "maximum power" stories helps you to practice thinking like an influence-motivated person.

If you know what people of a given motive pattern read and watch, you can do the same to match their motives. Saturate yourself in the appropriate material, and try to find it enjoyable on its own terms rather than your accustomed terms. Remember that everyone has all three basic motives; it's just a matter of degree. If you spend time building up your motive strength, it will stay strong (unlike a muscle).

Before trying to change, however, you should think long and hard about whether you need to do so. We know the commonest primary motive of published writers, but does that mean you cannot write if that motive is a close second in you? Of course not. You may just have to rearrange your priorities, or use your values to manage the application of your different strong motives.

Changing a motive is simple in concept but very difficult in practice. It can be done, though. I met a woman who set her mind to it and increased her Power Motive by nearly fifty percentile points (that is, she made herself more power-motivated than fifty percent more of the population, which moved her from below average to above average) in less than a year. But it demands much. You should not try unless both the requirement and your conscious values are strong and clear. The values, particularly, will carry you over the threshold of change to start making a motive satisfying in its own right.

Before you try to change, you should:

1 Set your values.
2 Do your research.
3 Find your reinforcers.
4 Find your sources of feedback.
5 Find your potential obstacles.

SET YOUR VALUES

First things first: you will work hard, so you must prepare yourself to do so. You must decide that this matters to you enough to make a concentrated effort. Then you can make your plans. You need not inscribe your new values on a stone tablet or even a piece of paper; you simply need to be clear in your own mind as to what you will be doing.

DO YOUR RESEARCH

The second step: start finding out the thinking patterns of the people you wish to emulate. This book is a starting point, but only just. You may find or deduce more, particularly by looking at other people who write what you want to write. Read what they read, or what they would like to read if they were not writing. Watch movies that appeal to your chosen motive-to-develop. I think watching movies in a theater can be helpful because the setting helps ensure strong involvement and emotional engagement. In other words, they don't make movies to bore you but to draw you in.

FIND YOUR REINFORCERS

Now that you have some idea of what you are doing, the third step is to find ways to reinforce yourself for doing it. All motives are found in everyone to some extent, so you can probably get at least a small amount of pleasure out of the process; allow this to happen. Beyond that, you may well need to create or use other rewards to help you practice your new method of thinking, at least until you master the basics. Link up what you want to do with the most effective reinforcers you can identify. Remember that ultimately you want the motive to operate on its own rather than being dependent on an outside source (e.g., candy), so the best means is to find ways you can fan the flames of your existing motive, however embryonic. I can't dictate any specific approaches; they must fit you. However, I do know this: one of the most effective ways to prevent yourself from manifesting your potential is for you to limit yourself. If you are unwilling to take satisfaction from a new kind of behavior, you won't. It can be as simple as that.

FIND YOUR SOURCES OF FEEDBACK

As your fourth preparation step, identify your best personal sources of feedback. This step couples with reinforcement, as good feedback *is* reinforcement, but finding a *source* of good feedback is a separate problem. Why is this important? People (this means *you*) are often not very good at judging themselves, particularly on motives, which you will recall are nonconscious in nature. Someone whose opinion you trust can support your efforts, both emotionally and practically.

FIND YOUR POTENTIAL OBSTACLES

Finally, know your enemies, the stumbling blocks and barriers to your effort, both internal (not wanting to work at it) and external (negative reinforcement from others). These are the folks who will prevent you from succeeding.

CHANGING YOUR MOTIVES: THE ACTUAL PROCESS IN DETAIL

At the beginning of this chapter I quickly described the steps to develop your motives. Immediately above I described the "homework" you must do first, so you go the right direction. Now it is time to lay out the development steps systematically. These steps are based on the work of David McClelland, as described in Boyatzis's book *The Competent Manager,* and are known as the "competency acquisition process."

1 **Recognition.** In other words, know it when you see it. Observe those who have the trait you wish (in this case, a motive) and see what they are doing that is different from you. "I don't know how he does it, but I can see what he does!"
2 **Understanding.** Know it from the inside. Learn the inner thoughts of the person with that motive (or trait, or whatnot). Be able to reproduce it, at least on paper. "I may not be able to do it, but I know how she does it!"
3 **Measurement of self.** Know how you stand against it. This will be difficult for motives unless you get a more precise measure through a picture story exercise or the like, but you can probably get a fair idea of how much of your life is based on a given motive from the self-assessment exercises included here. "I know how much I have of it!"
4 **Experimentation.** Try it out, and learn how it feels from the inside. One critical characteristic of science (as opposed to other major human endeavors, such as art, religion, war, or agriculture) is that failure is understood to be part of the process—that even negative results are good data. Try to take on the same attitude here. Your objective is not to succeed every time, because that is not reasonable or likely. Your objective is to *experiment,* and you should expect some failures along the way. Just learn from the failures (this is why science has been phenomenally successful). A 50 percent success rate can be pretty good at this stage. "I am trying it on for size."
5 **Skill Practice.** Once you can more or less consistently produce the behaviors and thoughts you want to develop, then you must

strengthen the ability through practice, so that it becomes reflexive rather than deliberate. "I am doing it regularly."

6 **Integration.** Make your new motive part of ordinary life. Once it becomes reflexive, you can move on to using it anywhere and everywhere you want. This step may seem obvious, but I also know about a phenomenon called *state-dependent memory.* In other words, some memories are closely associated with the situation in which you acquired them. This is one reason why some people claim to do tests better stoned than straight—if they studied while stoned, they *might* be able to recall better once stoned again. In a more typical situation, you might get into the habit of thinking in terms of your new motive only when you are working on your new motive. Instead, it should be everywhere.

7 **Feedback.** This tells you how you are doing, and takes you back to step three so you can reassess yourself and your progress. *This step is critical to continued improvement.* Feedback enables the process to happen accurately (you don't want to develop the wrong trait, or just find a new way to manifest the motives you have), it allows you to track your progress, and it charges you up to keep going. "I know how well I am doing in my growth."

To develop a motive means that you change the pattern of your thoughts. So above all, practice the thoughts. Everyone has them to some degree, and so do you. Build on what you have, and be patient. It takes a significant amount of time, even months, before a change in a motive becomes noteworthy. Don't look for instant success, but in time you can build a motive up—assuming you need to.

31 Last Words

*If only God would give me a clear sign! Like making a large
deposit in my name in a Swiss bank.*

WOODY ALLEN, Great Hollywood Wit

He who hesitates is last.

MAE WEST, Great Hollywood Wit

LONG-TERM RESULTS

Motives do not predict immediate choices; they predict long-term *patterns* of behavior over time. If this approach works for you, then it should apply over years, not just days. To do so requires hard work, but it will be worth it. This is not a get-writing-quick plan. Fortunately, the characteristics we are discussing can have enduring effects, once you have them linked to your writing practices the way you want them.

In a study of men and women in business, their motives were measured when they joined a company and then eight to twelve years later. The single strongest predictors of success later in life (at least for two-thirds of them) was the primary motive of the individuals as measured eight to twelve years before. Thus, motives can strongly influence your success in certain broad areas.

The individuals who were taught achievement motivation in the 1960s were also encouraged to meet in groups to discuss their accomplishments and compare notes. This was a means of obtaining feedback, a reality check, and some positive reinforcement—not unlike writing workshops. Some groups were still meeting twenty-five years later, and they were still applying what they had learned. They were, on average, highly successful entrepreneurs. Therefore, not only can motives influence your success long-term, but motives can be learned instead of "natural" and still have a profound impact.

Finally, you get better over time at things you keep doing, and that applies to writing as much as to anything else. If you get your motives properly engaged, start writing, and keep writing, you will find it gets progressively easier.

This is common sense for most things, but why writing? What about the creative flash, the voice of the muse that strikes by random chance? As Louis Pasteur put it: "Chance favors the prepared mind." Or, as Gary Player put it: "It's amazing. The more I practice, the luckier I get." You are better prepared to hear the muse if you practice listening.

As proof of this I would like to once again offer an extreme case: Isaac Asimov. He wrote nearly five hundred books in his long writing career, starting in his teens and continuing to the last chapter of his autobiography, which he wrote by hand on his deathbed. Every book was practice for Asimov for writing more. Five hundred practice rounds is a reasonable statistical universe. In examining the time it took Asimov to write each hundred books, Stellan Ohlsson ("The Learning Curve," in *Psychological Science*, 1992) found that it fit the standard learning curve perfectly: that is, the speed increased asymptotically. Asimov's first hundred books took nearly twenty years to complete. His second hundred took fewer than ten. His third took fewer than six. His last 190 books took less than seven and a half years all together.

This was interesting, because the learning curve had previously been studied only over short periods of time, usually under laboratory conditions. Asimov presented an unusual contrast, because he was doing a highly complex real-life task over many decades, and he nevertheless fit the curve perfectly.

This means you will get better, as long as you keep going. You don't have to write hundreds of books, but you must practice and keep practicing. If you do, you will get better.

IF ALL ELSE FAILS

The mass of men lead lives of quiet desperation. What is
called resignation is confirmed desperation.

HENRY DAVID THOREAU, *Walden*

Just writes to make his barrenness appear,
And strains from hard-bound brains, eight lines a year.

ALEXANDER POPE, *Essay on Criticism*

What if all this good work fails? You do the exercises, you write and write, and still you cannot sell, or even get someone else to read your work? Let's look it straight in the eye.

Mark Twain suggests that if you cannot get paid for writing within three years, you may fairly take that sawing wood is what you are intended for. I don't agree with that, having met too many good, successful writers who took longer, but the possibility exists.

Rather, I would like to leave you with a thought offered by Barry Levinson, the award-winning producer, director, and writer, when he was given his special award for lifetime accomplishment.

He started out writing comedy material, which for a long time he could not sell. Levinson's father, a retailer, did not really understand what his son did, but he would ask how business was going. Levinson would reply that it was tough, that he kept producing material but couldn't sell any of it.

"Well," his father would say, "at least you've got inventory."

You have inventory, too. You bring a unique insight, your own gifts, a lifetime of experiences—and that is before you begin actually writing.

I have mentioned David McClelland, the great motivational psychologist (and my mentor), who gave a rigor to the understanding of motives we now have. One of the fundamental drivers of his life and work, rooted in his Quaker belief, was the conviction that all people are of equal worth. In my years of study with him and without him, I have never found cause to doubt that every human being has some special worth. Whether you write successfully or not, I would be remiss if I did not reinforce that. Writing isn't everything.

But in any case everyone has a story to tell, everyone has motives, and everyone has inventory in their warehouse. Start there, and apply yourself, and you will write. Maybe not a lot, maybe not a bestseller, but you *can* write, and you will. Now go do it!

Remember: You can write!

I have described writing as a cross between a religious calling and a heroin addiction. There are a lot of bad things that go along with it, and a lot of ego gratification, grubbing for fame and money—visceral things. But that's part of it. Anyone who says otherwise is a saint or a liar, I guess.

ERIC S. NYLUND, AUTHOR OF *Dry Water*

True ease in writing comes from art, not chance,
As those move easiest who have learn'd to dance.

ALEXANDER POPE

APPENDIXES

APPENDIX A Discovering Your Motives Using the Picture Story Exercise

The basic measure of motives is one with some appeal for writers. It is called the picture story exercise (PSE), and it asks you to write stories to ambiguous pictures. In this way, you may write whatever you choose to write and let the motives emerge naturally. It is a difficult measure to fake, since people do not generally know what is being coded or why; even those who are knowledgeable are frequently unable to skew their stories.

The following pages contain a set of pictures commonly used for motivational research. For each one, spend no more than five minutes writing a story. For best results, do not study the pictures for more than a few seconds; just get a sense of the image and begin writing.

There are no right or wrong answers, of course, only motivational data. This is a self-analytic opportunity, not a test. Don't worry about your grammar, spelling, or handwriting; the only person who needs to see this is you.

To use the PSE:

1 Glance at picture #1 for a few seconds.
2 Begin writing a story. Do not take more than about five minutes. Try to write a story with a beginning, a middle, and an end, and try to answer the following questions in the course of the story: What is happening? Who are the people? What has led up to this situation? What is being thought? What is wanted? By whom? What will happen? What will be done?
3 Turn to picture #2, and continue.

When you are finished, refer back to Chapter 2, "Identifying Your Own Motives," and use the motive imagery found there to examine the stories. Read your stories over carefully for content—or get someone else to do so. Tally how many times you get each kind of imagery across all stories, and you can get a rough sense of your own primary motive or motives.

Picture 1

Picture 2

Picture 3

Picture 4

Picture 5

Picture 6

REALITY TESTING YOUR MOTIVES ON THE PSE

While the PSE is a reliable instrument, scorers are not; furthermore, the sensitivity of the PSE is high enough to pick up "noise" from events happening in one's life—accurate representations of your unconscious concerns at a given time that are largely unrepresentative of your life as a whole.

This section deals with some details about interfering factors ("artifacts" in technical language). The identifying your motives worksheet in chapter 1 can be used to "validate" or test your motive profile—the motives should be relatively consistent with each other overall. Doodles also offer an interesting, if unusual, cross-check.

Artifacts
1   **Drinking.** The need for power is associated with alcohol. Studies have shown that drinking more than two ounces of alcoholic beverages (two cans of beer, glasses of wine, shots of whiskey) will start to raise your power motivation—and not for the better. Personalized power, the need to prove or display yourself over others, gets stronger over time and more booze. After seven drinks (in a reasonably short period, of course), *all* motives tend to decline. The reasons for this latter finding are obvious enough, but the association of power and alcohol has no positively demonstrated reason.
2   **Recent trauma.** The need for affiliation tends to rise after an affiliative stress, such as a death in the family, a person moving out of the house, a relocation to a new place—all times when you would expect people to be focused on relationships and concerned with how they are going.
3   **Exhaustion.** This will depress your motives. When you have no energy to spare for anything, why should motives be an exception?
4   **Interruption.**
5   **Arousing circumstances.** Motives can be aroused over the short term. Repeated arousal can lead to more enduring increases.

CHECKING MOTIVES USING DOODLES

Studies of achievement-motivated people have indicated that they tend to doodle in certain ways. They tend to make S-curves (but *not* continuous waves) and diagonal lines, varying their line. They also tend to fill pages rather than leaving them blank. This has been applied even to ancient Greek pottery designs, and it appears to hold true. Unfortunately the same approach has not been used to identify power or affiliation.

APPENDIX B Case Studies

CASE STUDY #1: SCIENCE FICTION AND MYSTERY WRITER

Background
Had no formal writing training; sold one book "the hard way"—wrote it all himself without help—and then joined a writer's workshop, to which he has belonged for years. Several books and short stories published. Editing a collection assembled by the group.

General Behavior
A very meticulous person, for the most part; a self-employed individual who also acts as the administrator of the writers' workshop when some kind of special work is required. Hates wasting time; organizes his time to maximize his resources. Plans his writing.

Approach to Writing
No structure at first, just wrote as he felt: "Much more difficult than now." Wouldn't go back over his work; didn't want to break the momentum.

Only occasionally does he feel like writing powerful scenes—runs with it when he feels that way.

A true believer in workshops: would not write any other way and volunteers his time to do one-time workshops to get other people involved.

Key Learnings
- Evolution came through assurance and the influence of the workshop.
- Came up with a "zero draft" to relieve the stress of producing a first draft: a draft that was purely for creative purposes.

General Progression of Motivation
> **Middle** Used lots of structure: wrote an outline, then followed it faithfully.

Recent "I know when to move away from the structure." However, still uses an outline so carefully that when he decides to change elements of the plot as he writes, he goes back and revises the outline as well.

Now Less time for writing but still wants to help run the workshop.

Third book was "three to four times as efficient" as first book.

CASE STUDY #2: MYSTERY WRITER AND TECHNICAL WRITER

Background

Writing since age eleven or so, originally intended to become a scientist but switched her major to English in college. Became a technical writer and began writing fiction in her spare time. Partially deaf, she learned to read lips but tended to stay in the background in crowds until she acquired hearing aids in adulthood.

General Behavior

Sometimes perceived as quiet and shy, she is actually neither; she is an acute observer who is also an irrepressible smart-aleck in a comfortable situation. Tends towards negativity at low moments and constantly questions herself—not in a neurotic way but in a self-analytic manner that sometimes inhibits her writing briefly.

Approach to Writing

Wrote science fiction short stories and was rejected repeatedly; moved to a different part of the country and wrote a mystery set near her old home. The contrast she saw between her current home and her previous showed her she had something distinctive to say, which she had taken for granted in her home environment. She began writing mysteries set in the present-day, in a first-person, distinctly regional voice. From the beginning, she "just plain enjoyed writing," creating worlds for herself where she could be an adventurer. Will work on a schedule by choice, but knows points where she must stop and recharge; sometimes she finds herself stalled, and invariably this is because she needs to think through her plot and characters further before proceeding.

Key Learnings
- Understanding the endpoint of a novel-length work, so she can measure progress toward that goal.
- Learning to set and track goals for herself.

- Learning to adjust goals for herself.
- Finding ways to keep going in the face of rejection, for example by sending out new works before the old can be sent back.

General Progression of Motivation

Early The first book took the better part of a year and was totally rewritten at least once with a changed plot and language; the second book, using a more organized approach, took nine months.

Middle Started challenging herself on each progressive book to keep her series (and herself) fresh. Increased speed steadily but then ran into trouble when first child was born: unpredictability of baby's schedule made it difficult to work even when time was available. Increased confidence; when asked to write a short story, she said "sure!" though she had never published one before. She has sold a number of them since.

Current Much more adept at managing herself around an unpredictable schedule, partially through the use of outside resources (a regular babysitter, her husband) and partially through a higher tolerance for chaos developed through raising two children.

CASE STUDY #3: SCIENCE FICTION WRITER

Background

Full-time writer, but writes only four hours a day or so. Enjoys pop history; thinks of it as visiting alien worlds. Saw *Shogun* as a "first contact" science fiction novel. Enjoys novels where mysteries are posed and then revealed. Likes histories of Eastern Europe and Russia (he is of Russian descent), ancient history, the history of religion, French histories. Rarely reads science fiction because he gets too critical, thanks in part to his workshop experience, and so he does not find it relaxing. He doesn't think he could write mysteries because he is "too straightforward." Always surprised by the end of a mystery. Likes being in the hands of the author. Particularly likes P. D. James, Ruth Rendell, Dorothy Sayers, Tony Hillerman, and James Ellroy.

General Behavior

Gregarious and friendly, very thoughtful in his discussion, laughs frequently.

Approach to Writing

Starts with a scene, either a visual hook (i.e., a very vivid image) or an emotional charge. One story he enjoyed writing was entirely dialogue, with no visuals at all, but the relationship of the characters was important.

After the hook, he goes back to the beginning and writes to get to that point.

He belongs to a workshop but uses it selectively rather than as a true believer. He gave me the impression that he felt he commanded his work, merely using the workshop as a source of useful advice, and therefore he could easily write without it. Indeed, he wrote one recent book almost completely without the workshop, showing only an early fragment and then not returning. Even before that, he tended to keep his distance from the workshop. While others turn in early drafts or even outlines, he virtually never turns in either.

His stated reasons for using the workshop are:

- Outside perspective: he uses this to help him find his *own* way through the story rather than following other's suggestions slavishly.
- People satisfaction: he likes scaring people with a whole new novel.
- Gives as well as he takes, and enjoys the giving.

General Progression of Motivation

Steadily improving; has won awards for his work.

CASE STUDY #4: THRILLER WRITER

Background

This woman started writing as an escape from a terrible, abusive marriage. She felt trapped because she did not have enough money to get out and survive, and she had children to support. She felt helpless to fight back overtly. But motives can't be kept down for long: she found a way to feel strong. In her spare time she started writing novels.

General Behavior

Thoroughly enjoyed being around people and had a very outgoing personality. Not afraid to strike a provocative and risqué pose for a publicity shot; had a fine sense of marketing and management of relationships—she was perhaps the only writer I have ever known (out of scores of them) who managed to connect with book distributors and was very successful in getting them interested in her. Took her work very seriously, but definitely had a sense of humor.

Approach to Writing

She wrote novels that came straight from her feelings: violent stories where men were killed in awful, satisfying ways, or romantic stories set far away from reality as she knew it, such as romance/science fiction novels.

Despite what you might think, she set herself daily goals, and tracked her performance day after day, including producing wall charts of her performance. While still married she hid herself away and wrote in bursts.

General Progression

When I interviewed her she had just reached a critical point in her career: she had received not one but two major contracts, one in the six-figure range, which allowed her to free herself from her abusive husband. However, she was totally blocked. We discussed that perhaps she had too strongly identified her writing with escape: with the pressure gone (an extrinsic motive of sorts), she could no longer write. I suggested that she begin with a very low goal, such as one sentence a day, just to get herself jump-started, which was an idea she had already had. At last check she had managed to publish another book but had not delivered on her contract. She has since joined the staff of a magazine that caters to her genre and organizes conferences.

APPENDIX C Sample Development Plans

We need not worry much about writers. Man will always find
a means to gratify a passion. He will write, as he commits
adultery, in spite of taxation.

GRAHAM GREENE

In this appendix I am going to show you some examples of how to decide what you might need to change. Specific recommendations appear at various points throughout this book, so I won't attempt to consolidate them here. Instead, I want to focus on the big picture of change: what enables it to happen?

In addition, I have taken a few motive profiles and other characteristics and identified a key challenge of each, and then proposed some options for change. These are examples of development *ideas,* not requirements. Only you can determine the direction of your development; these may or may not work for you, but they may trigger some workable notions that will work for you. Then you can lay it all out in more detail and depth, using the goal setting principles described above.

The following are sample motive profiles.

HIGH ACHIEVEMENT, LOW POWER, LOW AFFILIATION

> **Challenge** Might need to develop Power Motive, and has a strong Achievement Motive that could either support efforts or block them.

> **Comment** Achievement-motivated people might well see publishing as a long shot, which indeed it is. The amount of effort that goes into a slender chance of being published looks like a losing deal. The need here is to harness the Achievement Motive to support the long-term goal of increasing the Power Motive.

Option 1 Structure: set up a system of targets and writing goals to keep motivation going independently of publication.

Option 2 Thought: develop Power Motive.

Option 3 Focus your writing on your best (or most manageable) chance of success.

HIGH POWER, LOW ACTIVITY INHIBITION (SELF CONTROL), LOW ACHIEVEMENT, LOW AFFILIATION

Challenge To successfully manifest and channel the Power Motive though writing takes a great deal of activity inhibition. Being low on that can make it difficult to apply the Power Motive to the task of writing.

Comment People with the right motive but a low activity inhibition may find themselves petering out quite rapidly on longer works or giving up after only a single rejection. Power-motivated people want to have an impact, but without activity inhibition they may find it difficult to postpone gratification of that desire when they can go do something easier.

Option 1 Focus on short works: essays, articles, short stories. Hoard your discipline.

Option 2 Structure: set up a habit, rhythm, or plan to manage your time for you. Invite help to move you along.

Option 3 Thought: develop your activity inhibition. Not easy!

HIGH AFFILIATION, LOW POWER, LOW ACHIEVEMENT

Challenge Writing out of a different motive, or developing the Power Motive; resisting the Affiliation Motive which may interfere with the act of writing.

Comment Affiliation Motive can easily block writing, since writing is essentially a solitary process and does not necessarily earn you friends as such, whereas creating an impact will be satisfying to a power-motivated person whether they are liked or not. Restraining the Affiliation Motive and focusing on writing needs can be quite difficult, as affiliation is the most common human motive and everyone has someone to affiliate with, be it family, friend, or lover.

Option 1 Focus on short works: essays, articles, short stories. Arrange your time so you don't have to be away from people too long.

Option 2 Structure: set up a habit, rhythm, or plan to manage your time for you, with shorter, protected time periods in which to write, preferably supported and defended by a friend or partner as well.

Option 3 Thought: develop your Power Motive. Not easy!

HIGH ACHIEVEMENT, HIGH AFFILIATION, LOW POWER

Challenge To use the two motives that are not associated with published writers and that can both block writing efforts, or to develop the Power Motive substantially to overcome these obstacles.

Comment Having two motives that are significantly stronger than the one you want makes development much more difficult. It may be easier here to reorient the motives you do have, for example by bringing in a team to help you, as this profile is characteristic of effective team members.

Option 1 Structure: join a supportive and well-structured writer's workshop to help you manage your writing.

Option 2 Thought: develop you Power Motive. Not easy!

Option 3 Structure: set up a system of targets and writing goals to keep motivation going independently of publication as such, linking both of the other motives, e.g., using friends and goal setting.

FURTHER READING

REFERENCE BOOKS

Bartlett's Quotations, 17th ed. Boston: Little, Brown & Co., 2003.

Dictionary of Quotations. New York: Avenel Books, 1978.

The Writer's Market. New York: Writer's Digest Books, 1921– .

MAGAZINES

The Writer

Writer's Digest

BOOKS AND OTHER SOURCES

Asimov, Isaac (1995). *I. Asimov: A Memoir*. New York: Bantam Books.

Baldwin, James (1962). "The Creative Process." In James Baldwin and Toni Morrison (1998), *Collected Essays: Notes of a Native Son / Nobody Knows My Name / The Fire Next Time / No Name in the Street / The Devil Finds Work / Other Essays*. New York: Library of America.

Beckett, Samuel, and S. E. Gontarski, eds. (1995). *Nohow On: Company, Ill Seen Ill Said, Worstward Ho*. New York: Grove/Atlantic, Inc.

Bester, Alfred (1977). *Starlight*. New York: Berkeley Publishing Group.

——— (1953). *Who He?* New York: Dial Books.

Boswell, James (1992). *The Life of Samuel Johnson* (Everyman's Library, No. 101). New York: Everyman's Library.

Boyatzis, Richard E. (1982). *The Competent Manager: A Model for Effective Performance*. New York: Wiley.

Browning, Robert (1997). "Bishop Blougram's Apology." In Robert Browning and Adam Roberts, *Robert Browning*. Oxford: Oxford University Press.

Brown, Fredric, and Robert Bloch, eds. (1977). *The Best of Fredric Brown*. New York: Del Rey Books.

Carroll, Lewis, and Martin Gardner, eds. (2000). *The Annotated Alice: The Definitive Edition*. New York: W. W. Norton & Co.

Davenport, Basil, ed. (1969). *The Science Fiction Novel: Imagination and Social Criticism*. Chicago: Advent Books.

Eshbach, Lloyd Arthur, ed. (1964). *Of Worlds Beyond: A Symposium*. Chicago: Advent Books.

Faulkner, William (1958). Interview in Malcolm Cowley (1977), *Writers at Work: The Paris Review Interviews, First Series*. New York: Penguin Books.

Freud, Sigmund (1967). *Moses and Monotheism*. New York: Vintage Books.

Gaiman, Neil (1988). *Don't Panic: The Official Hitchhiker's Guide to the Galaxy Companion*. New York: Pocket Books.

Garrett, Randall (1986). *Takeoff!* Norfolk/Virginia Beach: Donning Co.

Gaskell, Elizabeth, and Elisabeth Jay, eds. (1998). *The Life of Charlotte Brontë*. New York: Penguin Classics.

Gass, William (1958). "The Artist and Society." In *Fiction and the Figures of Life*. Boston: Godine.

Ghiselin, Brewster, ed. (reissued 1996). *The Creative Process*. Berkeley: University of California Press.

Haldeman, Joe (1986). *Dealing in Futures*. New York: Ace Books.

Heinlein, Robert A. (1980). *Expanded Universe*. New York: Ace Books.

Hendrickson, Robert (1994). *The Literary Life and Other Curiosities*. New York: Harcourt Brace & Company.

Heffron, Jack, ed. (1995). *The Best Writing on Writing, Volume Two*. Cincinnati: Story Press.

Henderson, Bill, and Andre Bernard, eds. (1998). *Pushcart's Complete Rotten Reviews and Rejections: A History of Insult, a Solace to Writers*. Wainscott, N.Y.: Pushcart Press.

Hodges, Jack (1992). *The Genius of Writers: A Treasury of Facts, Anecdotes, and Comparisons*. New York: St. Martin's Press.

James, Henry. "The Art of Fiction." InLeon Edel and Mark Wilson, eds. (1984). *Henry James: Literary Criticism, Volume One: Essays on Literature, American Writers & English Writers*. New York: The Library of America.

Jong, Erica (1974). "The Craft of Poetry." In William Packard, ed. *Craft of Poetry*. New York: Doubleday.

Juvenal (Juvenalis, Decimus Iunius) (1999). *The Sixteen Satires*. 3rd ed. New York: Penguin Books.

King, Stephen (2000). *On Writing: A Memoir of the Craft*. New York: Pocket Books.

Kipling, Rudyard. "In the Neolithic Age." In *The Seven Seas* (2002). Ripon, North Yorkshire: House of Stratus, Inc.

D. H. Lawrence. Letter, 31 Oct. 1913. *The Letters of D. H. Lawrence, Volume 2.* In George J. Zytaruk and James T Boulton, eds. (1981), Cambridge, Cambridge University Press.

McClelland, David C. (1985). *Human Motivation.* Glenview, Ill.: Scott, Foresman.

Menanader. Maurice Balme, trans. (2002). *Menander, the Plays and Fragments.* Oxford: Oxford University Press.

Mencken, H. L., and Terry Teachout, eds. (1995). *A Second Mencken Chrestomathy: Selected, Revised, and Annotated by H. L. Mencken.* New York: Knopf Publishing Group.

Montgomery, Lucy Maud (1923/1983). *Emily of New Moon.* New York: Bantam Doubleday Dell.

Ohlsson, Stellan (1992). "The Learning Curve for Writing Books: Evidence from Professor Asimov." *Psychological Science*, 3(b): 380–82.

Parker, Dorothy (1976). "The Little Hours." In *The Portable Dorothy Parker.* New York: Penguin Books.

Pope, Alexander (1994). *Essay on Man and Other Poems.* New York: Dover Publications.

———(1971). *Essay on Criticism, Part II.* In *Works.* New York: Classic Textbooks.

Powell, Lawrence Clark (1973). *Books in My Baggage: Adventures in Reading and Collecting* London: Greenwood Press.

Raudsepp, Eugene, ed. (1981). *The World's Best Thoughts on Success & Failure.* New York: Penguin Books.

Redman, Alvin, ed. (1959). *The Wit and Humor of Oscar Wilde.* New York: Dover Press.

Richter, David H. (1998). *The Critical Tradition: Classic Texts and Contemporary Trends.* Boston: Bedford Books.

Reynolds, Sir Joshua (1997). *Discourses on Art.* New Haven, Conn.: Yale University Press.

Sand, George (1976). *The Letters of George Sand.* New York:Gordon Press.

Sayers, Dorothy L. (1995). *Gaudy Night.* New York: HarperTorch.
> A novel about being one of the first women through Oxford, examined as an older but wiser mystery novelist years later. It says a lot about the academic and writerly mind and the creative process.

Schopenhauer, Arthur. *Counsels and Maxims from the Essays of Arthur Schopenhauer.* Project Gutenberg. www.gutenberg.org.

Scithers, George H, Darrell Schweitzer, and John M. Ford (1981). *On Writing*

Science Fiction (The Editors Strike Back!). Philadelphia: Owlswick Press.
Written by the then-editors of *Isaac Asimov's Science Fiction Magazine*, the premier magazine of its genre.

Shalit, Gene, ed. (2002). *Great Hollywood Wit: A Glorious Cavalcade of Hollywood Wisecracks, Zingers, Japes, Quips, Stings, Jests, Snappers, & Sass from the Stars*. New York: St. Martin's Press.

Silverberg, Robert (1997). *Reflections and Refractions*. Grass Valley, Cal.: Underwood Books.

——— (1987). *Robert Silverberg's Worlds of Wonder: Exploring the Craft of Science Fiction*. New York: Warner Books.

Stendhal (1840). Letter to Honoré de Balzac, October 30, 1840.

Stoppard, Tom (1969). *Rosencrantz and Guildenstern Are Dead*. New York: Grove Press.

Thompson, Hunter S. (1982). *The Great Shark Hunt*. New York: Warner Books.

Thoreau, Henry David (2002). *Walden and Other Writings of Henry David Thoreau*. New York: Modern Library.

Trillin, Calvin (1983). *Uncivil Liberties*. Garden City, N.Y.: Anchor Books.

Tuchman, Barbara (1982). *Practicing History*. New York: Random House.

Wilde, Oscar (1989). *Complete Works of Oscar Wilde: Stories, Plays, Poems and Essays*. Vyvan Holland, ed. New York: Harper and Row.

Williams, Rose, trans. & ed. (2001). *Latin Quips at Your Fingertips*. New York: Barnes and Noble Books.

Wilson, Edmund. "The Historical Interpretation of Literature." In David H. Richter (1998). *The Critical Tradition: Classic Texts and Contemporary Trends*. Boston: Bedford Books.

Winn, Dilys,ed. (1984). *Murder Ink*. Rev. ed. New York: Workman Publishing Co.

Winokur, John (1990). *Writers on Writing*. Philadelphia: Running Press.

Yerkes, Robert M. and John D. Dodson (1908). "The Relation of Strength of Stimulus to Rapidity of Habit-Formation." *Journal of Comparative Neurology and Psychology* 18, 459–82.

Zelazny, Roger (1987). *Unicorn Variations*. New York: Avon Books.

FL

The toughest bunch of Rebels that ever lost a war, they fought for the South, and then for Texas, as the legendary Floating Outfit of "Ole Devil" Hardin's O.D. Connected ranch.

MARK COUNTER was the best-dressed man in the West: always dressed fit-to-kill. BELLE BOYD was as deadly as she was beautiful, with a "Manhattan" model Colt tucked under her long skirts. THE YSABEL KID was Comanche fast and Texas tough. And the most famous of them all was DUSTY FOG, the ex-cavalryman known as the Rio Hondo Gun Wizard.

J. T. Edson has captured all the excitement and adventure of the raw frontier in this magnificent Western series. Turn the page for a complete list of Berkley Floating Outfit titles.

TRIGGER FAST

BERKLEY BOOKS, NEW YORK

Originally published in Great Britain by Brown Watson Ltd.

This Berkley book contains the complete
text of the original edition.
It has been completely reset in a typeface
designed for easy reading, and was printed
from new film.

TRIGGER FAST

A Berkley Book / published by arrangement with
Transworld Publishers Ltd.

PRINTING HISTORY
Brown Watson edition published 1964
Corgi edition published 1969
Berkley edition / November 1983
Second printing / October 1985

ISBN: 0-425-8191-5

A BERKLEY BOOK® TM 757, 375
Berkley Books are published by The Berkley Publishing Group,
200 Madison Avenue, New York, New York 10016.
The name "BERKLEY" and the stylized "B"
with design are trademarks belonging to
Berkley Publishing Corporation
PRINTED IN THE UNITED STATES OF AMERICA

CHAPTER ONE

The Rosemary-Jo Lament

STANDING waist deep in the cool clear water of the swimming hole Freda Lasalle rubbed soap over her slender, naked young body. Overhead the sun, not yet at noonday height, gave forth enough warmth to make this outdoor bathing both pleasant and possible.

Only rarely these days did Freda, daughter of the ranch's owner and sole woman of the house since the death of her mother, have a chance to bathe and swim in such complete freedom. The two cowhands her father hired were poor spirited men who would be only too willing to hide and watch her bathe, drooling over the sight of her naked beauty. However, her father took the two men to town with him earlier that morning and she had the ranch to herself.

Freda did not intend to miss such a chance. She had cleaned out the kitchen stove as her first chore after breakfast and wanted to wash the soot and grime from her body. Until her father returned from Barlock with supplies she could do nothing about making a meal so she took the time to bathe, stripping off her clothes in the house and running naked to the water, then plunging in to splash happily around.

The girl made an attractive picture as she stood working the soap lather into her short brown hair, although the only witness appeared to be the redbone hound which lay on the bank and watched her. She stood almost five foot six, a slim, willowy girl in her late teens, blossoming forth into full womanhood. Her face had charm, without being out and out beautiful. It was a warm, friendly face, one a man would not easily forget. Given another couple of years her figure would fully ripen and as yet the Texas Panhandle weather had not

1

made her skin coarse or harshened the texture of her hair.

She looked at the small frame house with some pride, then ducked her head under the water to rinse the soap from her hair. The house might be small, but she kept it spotlessly clean and neat. Between the stream and the house stood a small pole corral, empty now, but large enough to hold the small remuda and harness horses they owned. To one side of the house stood a barn, stable and a couple more small wooden buildings, to the rear was a chicken pen and beyond that a backhouse.

On the side of the river away from her home a bank rose fairly steep in most places, but sloping down more gently to a ford below the swimming hole. Beyond the bank, a mile away, lay the two mile wide strip along which, by convention, the cattle herds stuck as they trailed north by the Lasalle place to the Kansas railheads. The passing herds caused little trouble and, as yet, the first of the new season had not come up from southern Texas.

Ever since her father came home from a Yankee prisoner-of-war camp, a sick man whose doctor warned he must get out into the dry plains country or die, this small ranch had been Freda's home. In the early days their neighbours helped them build the house, showed Lasalle much he needed to know, joined in with such communal tasks as gathering the free-grazing herds of cattle and cutting out each other's stock. The great trail drives wending their way north proved to be a boon to the small ranchers in this section. To the trail bosses they sold their surplus stocks, thus saving the expense of shipping the cattle north to market. True they might have made more money in Kansas, but the long drive north would eat that same money up, even if a small outfit handling maybe a couple of hundred head could have got through alone. Often too the trail bosses would turn over unwanted calves born on the way north and in that way helped bring new blood to the range.

In many ways it had been a lonely life for Freda, especially since her mother died. She grew up in healthy surroundings, free as a bird. Before her mother died she rode the range like a man, she could handle a horse, use a shotgun well enough and also could cook, mend or make clothes, do the chores a woman in a lonely ranch was expected to do.

Now she wondered how long the happy life might continue. To the north and west ran the great Double K ranch, the Lindon Land Grant, one of the huge open-range outfits for which

Texas had long been famous. When Lindon owned and ran it the Double K took its share in the local round-ups, helping out the smaller and less fortunate folk. Then old man Lindon died and his sole kin, back east, sold out the holding to an Englishman called Sir James Keller. At least so rumour had it for nobody had seen the mysterious new owner.

They felt his presence though. Two days before Brent Mallick, the local Land Agent and attorney for the Double K, paid a visit to Lasalle's and offered to buy them out. Freda remembered how Mallick smiled when her father refused the offer. There had been neither amusement nor friendship in the smile, nor on the faces of the two tough looking men who accompanied Mallick. She shuddered as she thought of Mallick's smile, with its implied threat—

> "A Yankee rode into West Texas,
> A mean kind of cuss and real sly,
> He fell in love with sweet Rosemary-Jo,
> Then turned and told her goodbye."

The redbone hound came to his feet even before Freda heard the pleasant tenor voice singing an old cowhand song. She threw a startled glance to where the bank of the stream hid the singer from view. From the sound of his voice he must be coming straight towards the house.

> "So Rosemary-Jo told her tough pappy,
> Who said, 'Why *hombre* that's bad,
> In tears you done left my Rosemary-Jo,
> No Yankee can make my gal sad.' "

The second verse of the Rosemary-Jo Lament came as Freda hurriedly waded out of the water. She grabbed up the towel from the shore and then ran for the house, the redbone following and helping scatter the chickens which scratched and pecked before the house.

> "He whipped out his two trusty hawg-legs,
> At which he warn't never slow,
> When that Yankee done saw them a-spitting,
> He said, 'It is time for to go!' "

*   *   *

Even as Freda reached the house and dashed inside, slamming the door behind her, she heard another verse of the song. The windows of the room stood open and as she could hear the singer clearly, she knew he must be close. She could hear the sound of more than one horse's hooves.

> "He jumped on his fast running pinto,
> Lit out like hell for the west,
> When Rosemary-Jo got her a fortune,
> He come back and said, 'I love you best.' "

Still drying herself Freda went to where she could peer out of a window and see the top of the river bank. Three riders came into sight, halting their horses at the head of the slope. Three cowhands from their dress, each astride a big, fine looking horse. The singer led a packpony which looked to be carrying their warbags and bed-rolls.

> " 'No no' cried she in a minute,
> 'I love me a Texan so sweet,
> And I'm going down to San Antone town,
> My sweet, loving Texan to meet.' "

The singer lounged in his saddle at the left of the party. Sitting his huge white stallion with easy grace, there appeared to be something wild, almost alien about him. His black, low-crowned, wide-brimmed Stetson hat thrust back from curly hair so black it almost shone blue in the light and the face it framed looked to be Indian dark, very handsome, babyishly innocent and young. From hat, down through tight rolled bandana, shirt, gunbelt, levis trousers, to boots he wore but one colour, black. The blackness was relieved only by the white, ivory she guessed, hilt of the bowie knife at his left side and the walnut grips of the old Colt Dragoon revolver hanging at his right.

The young rider's white horse moved restlessly, allowing her to see the low horned, double girthed Texas rig. That went without saying, a man who dressed in such a manner would use that kind of saddle. She also saw the butt of a rifle under the rider's left leg.

* * *

"So the Yankee went to the back country,
He met an old pal, Bandy Parr,
Who captained the Davis' State Police,
And a meeting they held in the bar."

They did not appear to be in any hurry, she thought, finishing drying herself and grabbing up clothing. The rider at the right side took her attention next for she could never recollect seeing a finer figure of a man. He towered over the other two, three inches at least over the six-foot level. For all his great size, the width of his shoulders, the tapering to a slim waist, he sat his seventeen hand bloodbay stallion with easy grace. He looked to be a light rider, the sort of man who took less out of his mount than a smaller, though less skillful person.

His costly white Stetson carried a silver concha decorated band, was on the same pattern as the other two's. It set on a head of golden blond hair, shading a face which had a classic, handsome cast of feature like those of a Greek god of old. His tan shirt had clearly been made to his measure, the bandana around his throat looked to be pure silk. In his dress he seemed to be something of a dandy, yet he also looked remarkably competent and those matched, ivory butted Army Colts in his holsters did not look like decorations, but hung just right for fast withdrawal.

"Rosemary-Jo got word to her pappy,
He fogged on his strawberry roan,
And said, 'From that ornery critter,
I'll save Rosemary who's my own.' "

By now Freda was struggling into her dress. Her head popped out of the neck like a squirrel peeping from its den-hole in a sycamore tree. She looked at the center man of the trio. She gave him barely more than a glance for, compared with his friends, he faded into nothing.

He didn't look tall like the other two, being at least six inches under the wiry six-foot length of the black-dressed, baby-faced boy. If his clothes were of as good quality as those worn by the others he did not have the flair to show them off so well. A costly black Stetson sat on his dusty blond hair. The face under the hat seemed to be handsome, though not as eye-catching as that of either of his friends. His shoulders had a width and appeared to be sturdy enough, but he faded into nothing compared with the giant build of the big blond. Even the brace of white handled 1860 Army Colts which rode butt forwards in his holsters did nothing to make him more noticeable. Freda smiled as she glanced at the gunbelt. The small, insignificant cowhand must badly want everyone to think of him as a real hard *hombre* and tried to improve the impression by going armed in the same manner as his friend.

> "Now the Yankee went down to San Antone,
> Met the Texas boy out on the square,
> But his draw was too slow, and as far as I know,
> That Yankee's still lying out there."

With the final verse of the song ended the three men rode slowly down the slope. At that moment, for the first time, Freda realized her position, alone in the house and far from any help. Three strangers, gun-hung and handy looking, came riding down towards her. They could be hired hard-cases from Double K for by now all the old cowhands of the spread were gone, being replaced by men whose ability with guns exceeded their skill with cattle.

Freda turned from the window and headed to collect the shotgun which hung with a Le Mat carbine, over the fireplace. She took down the ten gauge, two barrelled gun, checked the percussion caps sat on their nipples and then stood uncertain as to what her next move should be.

"Hello the house!" called a voice from outside. "Can we ride through the water?"

Which did not seem like the action of a hard-case bunch coming to scare her father into selling the ranch. The girl realized she might be doing her callers less than justice with her suspicions. She crossed the room, leaned the shotgun by the door, opened it and stepped on to the small porch.

"Come ahead," she called.

The Lasalle family might be poor, but they still offered hospitality to any passing stranger.

Slowly the big paint stallion, ridden by the smallest man, moved into the water, followed by the white, bloodbay and pack horse. Freda studied the horse, seeing it to be as fine looking and sizeable as either of his friends' mounts. It didn't look like the kind of horse one would expect so small and in-significant a man to be afork. Probably it belonged to that handsome blond giant and he allowed the small cowhand to ride it. Yet at that the small man must be better than fair with horses for the paint stallion did not look like the kind of animal to accept a man on it unless the man be its master.

Just as the men came ashore Freda felt something was wrong. Then she realized what. She had not fastened her dress up the back! The men were ashore now and she needed to think fast, to gain time to make the necessary adjustments. A flash of inspiration came to her.

"Take the horses around back," she told the three men. "Let them graze while you come in for a meal."

Not until the three men rode around the house and out of sight did Freda move. Then she stepped back into the house and began to fumble with the dress fastenings. At the same moment she realized that apart from a few eggs the ranch could offer its guests nothing by way of food.

The front of the house consisted of one big room, serving as both dining and sitting room. The kitchen and three small bedrooms all opened off the front room, a handy arrangement from the girl's point of view. She entered the kitchen, saw the coffeepot stood ready and looked to her skillet ready to fry eggs. Through the window she saw her guests removing the saddles from their horses.

Freda opened the kitchen door and stepped out, getting her first close-up look of the three men. The blond giant looked even more handsome close up and Freda wished she had donned her best dress instead of this old working gingham. She hardly gave the small man a glance, although his face did seem older and more mature. The dark boy seemed even younger now he was in close. His face looked innocent—until one looked at the eyes. They were red hazel in colour, wild, reckless, savage eyes. They were not the eyes for such an inno-cent face. If the youngster was, as she had thought at first glance, only sixteen they had been sixteen dangerous and hard-living years to give him such eyes.

"Howdy ma'am," greeted the small man, removing his hat as he saw her and showing he had some strength in his small frame for he held the heavy double girthed saddle in his left hand. "Thank you kindly for the offer."

"Sure is kind, ma'am," agreed the giant, his voice also a

Texas drawl, but deep and cultured. "Our cooking's not what it used to be."

"And never has been," grinned the dark boy, looking even younger and more innocent as he swept off the Stetson hat.

Watching the men walk towards her Freda wished she had taken time out to put on a pair of shoes and tidy her hair which still fluffed out and showed signs of washing. Yet there had been time for none of it and she must make do as she was.

Each man laid his saddle carefully on its side clear of the door, by the wall of the house. No cowhand worth his salt ever rested his saddle on its skirts, or placed it where clumsy feet might step on it. A cowhand took care of his saddle for without it he could not work.

"Go on through and sit a spell," she told them, indicating the door into the front room. "I'll fetch in the coffee."

By the time Freda arrived with the coffee she found her guests sitting at the table, their hats hanging by the storm straps on the back of the chairs. Her eyes studied them, knowing them to be strangers to this part of the range.

"You're from down south, aren't you?" she asked, pouring the coffee into cups.

Under the rules of rangeland etiquette the host could ask that much without giving offence. It left the guests free to tell as much or as little as they wished.

"I didn't think it showed," drawled the dark boy.

"You aren't looking for work hereabouts?" she went on, hoping they were not. Such men would stiffen any fighting force and they would be powerful backing if they aimed to ride for Double K.

"Work, ma'am?" asked the blond giant. "The word near on scares us off our food."

"I tell you, ma'am," the small man went on. "In all the years I've known this pair I haven't once got them to do a hand-stroke of work."

Freda could hardly restrain a smile as she noted the way the small man spoke. He really must be wanting to impress her, make her believe he gave the other two orders, or was in a position to have to put them to work. Then she thought of the big paint stallion, a real valuable animal. The small man must be the son of a rich ranch owner and the other two hired to be his bodyguard. Yet neither of the tall men looked like the sort to take pay for being a wet-nurse.

The small man's eyes flickered around the room. It looked neat, clean, tidy without being so fussy a man wouldn't dare breathe in case he messed something up. None of the furniture looked new, but it had been well kept and expensive when new. The drapes at the window were clean and colourful, and enlivened the atmosphere. Over the fireplace hung a Le Mat carbine, one of the old type known as the "grapeshot gun". The upper of the twin, superposed barrels took the nine .42 balls in the chamber. The lower barrel had no rifling and threw out either a .50 calibre grapeshot, or a charge of buckshot when needed.

Despite its brilliant conception the Le Mat was a weapon long out of date, yet the house showed no more modern weapons—except for the shotgun leaning by the door.

Following the small man's gaze, Freda gulped as she saw the gun. Nobody would keep a shotgun in such a position as a normal thing. Her eyes went back to the small man once more.

"Menfolks not at home?" he asked.

"Not just now," she replied, then went on hurriedly. "They'll be back any time now."

"Huh huh!"

He left it at that. The girl shut her mouth, holding down a remark about the men her father hired, one much more complimentary than they deserved. Some instinct told Freda she need not fear her guests even though she was alone.

The small man's eyes were on her face; they were grey eyes and met a gaze without flinching. Nor was there any of the slobbering stare of her father's hands in the way he looked at her. His eyes did not try to strip her clothes away and feast on her young body. He looked like a man with close women kin. He also looked in a manner which told Freda her last words had not fooled him one little bit.

Suddenly she became aware of the strength in the small man's face. She knew her first impression could have been wrong; there might be much more than was at first apparent about this small South Texas man. Her eyes dropped to his gunbelt, seeing the fine workmanship in it—and how well worn and cared-for it looked. He had none of the habits of a show-off, nor did he in any way, by voice or gesture, call attention to the fact that he wore two guns like a real bad *hombre*.

"I'm afraid we're clean out of everything but eggs," she

said, wanting to prevent her confusion showing.

"Lon," drawled the big blond, "you've got a head like a hollow tree. What about those pronghorn steaks in the pack?"

"Ain't your fault we done got 'em, any old ways," replied the dark boy who then turned to Freda. "There I was, ma'am, trying to sneak up on that lil ole rascal. Then this pair comes—"

"How about you-all sneaking through the door, sneaking to the pack, sneaking out the steaks, then sneaking back and giving them to the lady," put in the small man. "You being so sneaky and all."

Freda noticed the way the small man addressed his friend. He spoke like a man long used to giving orders and having them obeyed. The black dressed boy came to his feet and performed the remarkable feat of draining his coffee cup while bowing gracefully to her.

"Reckon I'll have to apologize for this pair, ma'am," he said. "I can't take them no place twice. Folks won't even have them back to apologize for the first time."

He replaced the cup on the saucer and headed out through the kitchen. Freda followed and in a few minutes he returned carrying a burlap sack and several thick antelope steaks wrapped Indian-style in leaves.

"You-all take the thickest for yourself, ma'am," he told her. "We're riding greasy-sack, so take whatever you need out of the bag."

The girl understood his meaning. To ride greasy-sack meant that they had no chuckwagon along and so carried their food in a burlap bag. She opened the bag to find it contained potatoes, carrots, onions and a few cans of tomatoes, corn and peaches.

Since the arrival of the three men Bugle, the redbone hound, had stuck pretty close to his mistress, showing no sign of friendship, following her into the kitchen. Now his tail wagged as he caught the scent of fresh meat.

"You come friendly all of a sudden," drawled the dark boy. "Is it me or this here meat you're in love with?"

"I can't take your food!" Freda gasped.

"Don't let that worry you, ma'am," he replied, tossing a two pound steak to the waiting jaws of the redbone. "Too much food makes Mark 'n' Dusty get all mean and ornery. Only with Dusty, him being the boss, you can't most times tell no difference. Say, was it all right for me to feed your dawg, ma'am?''

Freda nodded. She thought she had the three men sorted out now. The dark boy's name appeared to be Lon and from what he just said about Dusty being the boss it ought to make the small man's name Mark, for he was not likely to be the other two's employer.

At that moment the small man came to the kitchen door.

"Whatever Lon's telling you, ma'am," he said, "it's likely to be all lies."

"Just telling the lady what a sweet, kind 'n' loving nature you-all got, Dusty," Lon replied. "Course, like you said, it's all lies."

The words puzzled Freda more than ever. The small man's name appeared to be Dusty and that made him the boss. Then she thought she had the solution, Dusty was their boss' son and they treated him in such a manner as a result of it.

"You wouldn't be looking for the Double K, would you?" she asked.

"Double K?" Dusty replied. "That's the old Lindon Land Grant, isn't it?"

"It was. Lindon died and an Englishman bought it."

"We've never been this way before, have we, Lon?" drawled the small man. "I run my herds over the eastern trails, it's better for us that way."

Once more Freda noticed how he spoke; as if he was the trail boss when his ranch sent a herd to market. Yet he did not seem to speak in a boasting manner, or to be trying to impress her.

Through her cooking and the meal which followed Freda tried to understand the man called Dusty. The other two regarded him as their boss. Yet, from the banter which flowed between them, they were also good friends with much in common.

"You mean you came along the stream?"

The words came in a gasp from Freda as the import of something Mark just said sank into her puzzled head. A blush came to her cheeks for if they had been riding the bank of the stream they must have seen her bathing.

"Why else do you reckon we'd put up with Lon's caterwauling?" asked Dusty, a smile on his lips. It was a friendly smile, not the leer of a venal sneak who would sit watching a nude girl in the privacy of her bathing.

Then Freda understood and the blush died away. The three men must have spotted her from a fair way back down the river. To avoid causing her any embarrassment they swung from the bank edge and rode parallel to it but well clear, with Lon singing to warn her of their presence. They also took their time, allowing her a chance to get to the house and dress before riding in.

Tactfully, and in a diplomatic manner, Dusty swung the conversation away from the subject. Then Lon started her laughing with an exaggerated story of how he hunted and shot the pronghorn, which had tasted so delicious, despite having his two friends along.

The meal had ended but Freda wanted her guests to stay on and talk. She felt starved for company and good conversation and for the first time realized how lonely her life was.

Suddenly Bugle raised his head, looking across the room from where he had laid since finishing his steak. At the same moment Lon's youth and levity fell from him like a discarded cloak. He looked older, more alert—and deadly dangerous.

"Your pappy run seven—eight men, Miss Freda?" he asked.

"No, why?"

"There's that many coming up right now."

Then the others heard the sound of approaching hooves, coming at a good pace towards the river bank, down it and through the water. This had a special significance. The stream marked the boundary of the ranch house and nobody but the owners and their hired help had the right to cross without first calling for permission to do so.

Freda rose to her feet and darted to the door, opening it and stepping out. Eight men came across the stream, riding towards the house and halting their horses in a rough half-circle. They looked a hard bunch, with guns hanging low at their sides. She only knew one of the eight but could guess at the purpose of their visit.

The man she knew was called Preacher Tring—he'd been at Mallick's left hand when the Land Agent offered to buy them out. Now it looked as if Tring had returned to make sure the Lasalle family did sell out.

CHAPTER TWO

The Name's Dusty Fog

FREDA stepped across the porch and halted at the edge of it looking towards the eight men, not liking what she read in their eyes. They, with one exception, were men in the thirties or early forties, and with one exception wore cowhand dress— but they weren't cowhands.

Preacher Tring sat in the center of the group. A big blocky man with heavy rounded shoulders and a nose hooked like a buzzard's beak. He wore a round topped hat of the style circuit-riding preachers favored. His white shirt looked dirty, the black tie crooked. His sober black suit also looked stained and rumpled as if he'd worked hard in it that day. Around his waist hung a gunbelt, a brace of Navy Colts riding the fast draw holsters. Slouching in the saddle of a fine black horse Preacher Tring looked like a particularly evil buzzard perched ready to slash the eyes out of a corpse.

"What do you want?" Freda asked.

"We've come to move you folks on," answered Tring, his voice a harsh croak which was well suited to his looks. "Boss made you a good offer for this place. Now he allows you've had time to think about it. Price still goes, even after the place gets wrecked."

"How do you mean, wrecked?"

"Going to wreck the place, gal," Tring answered, waving a hand towards the buildings, then down to the corral. "Then happen your father doesn't sell out it won't just be the place we wreck."

Freda grabbed Bugle's collar as the dog stood by her side, his back hair rising and a low growl rumbling from his throat. She knew the men would shoot down her dog without a second

13

thought and did not want that to happen.

"You wouldn't dare!" she gasped.

Without even troubling to reply Tring turned his horse and rode towards the corral. He unshipped the rope from his saddlehorn, tossed the noose over the right side gate post and secured the other end to the horn. Turning his horse he rode forward slowly until the rope drew taut. The big black threw its weight forward to try and drag whatever lay behind it.

Laughing and making coarse comments the men sat their horses and watched Tring. They did not trouble to look at the house, knowing the quality of Lasalle's hired hands and expecting no opposition except maybe from the rancher himself. Only Lasalle could not be at home or he would be outside and facing them.

"Go on, Preacher!" yelled the youngest of the bunch, a brash, tall youngster in his late teens and who clearly considered himself the hardest rock ever quarried. "Get off and push!"

This brought a roar of laughter from the others and a snarled curse from Tring. He often boasted of his horse's strength and pulling power, so did not intend to allow the animal to make him a liar.

Tring spurred his horse cruelly. Steel shod hooves churned up dirt as it threw weight against the taut rope, trying to tear the corral's post from the earth. The man cursed savagely as the post held firm. He raked his struggling horse from neck to rump with sharp-rowelled petmakers, but to no avail.

From behind Freda came the crash of a shot. The rope split and the horse, suddenly relieved of the strain, stumbled forwards, throwing its rider over its head. Tring's companions turned to see who dared interfere with the Double K.

The small Texan stood in the doorway of the house, smoke rising lazily from the barrel of the Army Colt in his right hand. He looked at the hostile group of eight hard-case riders.

"I'm taking cards," he said. "The name's Dusty Fog."

With that the sleek Colt pinwheeled on his finger and went back to the holster at the left side of his body. He stepped forward, passing the girl, to halt between her and the men.

Only it was not a small, insignificant cowhand who passed her. Now he seemed to have put on inches, and to exude a deadly menace. Never again would Freda think of him as being small.

He faced the men, hands thumb-hooked into his belt, eyes watching them, daring any of them to make a move.

Snarling out incoherent curses Preacher Tring sat up. He had lost his hat and his head was completely bald, which added to his general air of evil. He forced himself to his feet and looked at the small Texan. From the expression on Tring's face, Freda thought he would grab out his gun and shoot down this impudent stranger who came between him and his desires. In the heat of the moment Freda clean forgot about the other two men and did not wonder why they failed to stand alongside their boss at such a moment.

"Easy Preacher!" a man spoke hurriedly, urgently. "He's speaking true. That there's Dusty Fog all right. I saw him when he brought the Rocking H herd to Dodge against Wyatt Earp's word."*

Not until then did Freda fully realize who her small guest really was. She could hardly believe her eyes or ears as she looked at the small Texan called Dusty Fog.

She'd heard the name often enough, but never pictured the famous Dusty Fog as anything but a handsome giant, a hero of the same kind she read about in books. In the War Between The States she, and almost every other southern girl, dreamed of Dusty Fog as their knight in armor. He had been the boy-wonder, the Confederate Cavalry captain who, at seventeen, made the Yankees wish they'd stayed at home and who carried a fighting cavalryman's reputation as high as that of Turner Ashby or John Singleton Mosby.

Since the War his name rose high as a cowhand, a trail boss who ranked with Charlie Goodnight, Oliver Loving, Stone Hart, the pick of the trail bosses. It had been Dusty Fog and his friends who tamed the bad Montana mining city called Quiet Town,† after three lesser men died in the trying. He was the segundo of the great OD Connected ranch in the Rio Hondo country. He had ambidextrous prowess with his matched bone handled guns. His speed of drawing those same guns and his accuracy in shooting were all legends. Now he

* Told in TRAIL BOSS
† Told in QUIET TOWN

stood before Freda Lasalle, a man of five foot six at most, a man she had dismissed as nobody and hardly spared a second glance.

Tring also thought of all he had heard of Dusty Fog and liked none of it. The small Texan stood alone, facing eight of them—or did he stand alone—where he was two other men were likely to be.

The tall, handsome blond stood at the corner of the house. He stood with empty hands but that meant little for rumour had it that Mark Counter could draw and throw lead almost as fast as Dusty Fog. In his own right that handsome blond giant had a name himself.

If anything Mark's reputation as a cowhand stood higher than Dusty's. He had a name for being somewhat of a range country Beau Brummel who helped set cowhand fashions now as he had once done amongst the bloods of the Southern army. A rich man in his own right, son of a prosperous Big Bend rancher, Mark still rode as a hand for the OD Connected, working as a member of the floating outfit and siding Dusty in any trouble to come along. His strength was a legend, his skill in a rough-house brawl spoken of with awe and admiration wherever it was seen. How fast he could handle his gun was not so well known. He rode in the shadow of the Rio Hondo gun wizard for all that he stood a good six feet three inches tall.

Small wonder the hired guns from Double K looked uneasy when they saw Mark Counter all set to back his *amigo* against them.

Slowly Tring lowered the hands which had hung like curved talons over the butts of his Navy Colts. He'd been set to chance taking Dusty Fog with odds of eight to one in his favor. Eight to two were far from being bad odds, even eight to those two—then the odds dropped to a level where Tring did not intend bucking against them.

A sinister double click announced another man stood at the side of the house opposite Mark Counter. Not one of the assembled gunhands thought it to be a trick of their ears, or imagination. That showed in the way they looked towards the dark boy, noting the twin barrel ten gauge in his hands.

Freda also looked and felt surprise. This was not the innocent looking boy who talked and joked with her inside the house. The clothes might be the same, but the face was a mean, cold, slit-eyed Comanche Dog Soldier's mask, alert, wolf-cautious and watching every move.

They called him Loncey Dalton Ysabel, the Ysabel Kid, *Cabrito* depending on how well folks knew him. Three names, but they all added up to one thing—a real dangerous *man*. His father had been a wild Irish-Kentuckian border smuggler, his mother the daughter of Chief Long Walker of the Comanche and his French-Creole squaw. That marriage brought a mixing of bloods which produced a deadly efficient fighting man with an innocent face and a power of danger inside him. He had the sighting eye of a backwoodsman of the legendary past and the same ability to handle a rifle. He could use his Dragoon Colt well enough when needed. From his French-Creole strain he gained an inborn love of cold steel as a weapon and an ability to use that James Black bowie knife which would not have shamed old Jim Bowie himself. Tied in with that came the skill of a Comanche Dog Soldier at riding anything with hair, ability to follow tracks where a buck Apache might falter and the keen eyes which came in so useful when riding scout. He could move through thick brush as silent as a shadow, speak seven languages and fluent Spanish. All in all it made the Kid a real good friend—or right bad enemy.

From the way he stood and watched the Double K men he was no friend.

"Don't see how all this comes to be your concern, Cap'n Fog," Tring said, in a much milder tone than he usually adopted. "These here nesters—"

"Stop handing us that bull-droppings, *hombre*!" growled Mark Counter, moving forward to flank Dusty and face the men. "These folk don't plough. They run a brand and keep cattle. That makes them ranch folks."

The youngster in Tring's bunch thought he was real fast with a gun. He had come through a couple of cowhand backing-down sessions and didn't reckon this trio would prove harder to handle than the others.

He swung down from his saddle to step by Tring and face the two Texans in his toughest and most belligerent manner, even though he wasn't showing good sense.

"Who asked you to bill in?" he asked in a tough voice.

"We're in, boy," Dusty answered, sparing him hardly a glance. "You, *hombre*, get afork your hoss and take your pards off with you."

Tring wasn't fixing to argue. He bent and took up his hat, placing it on the bald head. Tomorrow would be another day. The Texans would be riding on soon and he would return. Freda Lasalle was going to wish he had not when he came back. Or maybe Lasalle would pull out in a hurry when he heard what had happened—or what might have happened had not those three interfering Texans been on hand.

So Tring turned to collect his horse. His backers did not want trouble, he could read that on their faces. Only the fool kid wanted to make fuss, bring off a grandstand play.

Full of brash conceit and over-confident both in himself and the ability of the others to back him, the young hard-case took a pace forward.

"Listen, you!" he said to Dusty. "Our boss sent us to do a job, and we aim to do it, so you can smoke off afore you get hurt."

Dusty did not even look at the young man, but threw a glance at Tring as the bald man mounted his horse.

"Call him off, *hombre*," Dusty said gently, "or lose him."

Tring made no reply. He watched the young gun-hand, wondering if he might be lucky and give the rest of them a chance to cut in.

"Listen, you short-growed ru—!" began the youngster.

He stopped faster than he started, and without finishing his speech, for a very good reason. Dusty Fog glided forward a step. His right fist drove out and sank with the power of a mule-kick into the youngster's stomach. The young gunny's hand started moving towards the butt of his Army Colt as Dusty stepped forward. He failed to make it. The hand which he meant to fetch out the Colt clutched instead at his middle as he doubed over croaking in agony.

Instantly Dusty threw up his fist-knotted left hand, smashing it full under the youngster's jaw, lifting him erect and throwing him backwards into the horses. Then the gunny slid down into a sitting position. Through the spinning pain mists and bright lights which popped before his eyes he saw Dusty

standing before him and again tried to get out his gun. Dusty
jumped forward, foot lashing out in a kick which ripped skin
from the gun-hand, brought a howl of pain from the youngster and sent the Colt flying.

Bending forward Dusty took a double handful of the
youngster's shirt and hauled him erect, shook him savagely,
then let him go. The youngster's legs were buckling under him
as Dusty's right fist lashed up at his jaw. Mark Counter
winced in sympathy as the blow landed. The youngster went
over backwards, crashing down and made no attempt to rise.

Dusty looked at Tring, his eyes cold and hard.

"You always let a boy do your fighting?" he asked.

"Boy played it on his own," snarled Tring, hating backing
down but not having the guts to take Dusty up on it. "We
ain't after fuss with you."

"Fussing with a gal'd be more your game," drawled Mark.
"Wouldn't it?"

Never the most amiable of men, Tring still managed to hold
down his anger and resentment at Mark's words.

"The boss made these folks a fair offer for their place," he
said. "He wants more land to build up his holding. We just
figured to toss a scare into the girl and her pappy. Didn't mean
her no real harm."

Freda watched everything, still holding Bugle's collar. She
wanted to say something, take a part in the drama being
played out before her. Dusty did not give her a chance for he
clearly aimed to handle the entire affair his own way. She went
back to shove Bugle into the house then came towards Dusty.

"We aren't selling," she said.

"You hear that?" asked Dusty.

"I heard it!" Tring replied.

"We'll be going up the trail today. But we'll be coming back
this way and if these folks aren't here and unharmed, *hombre*,
you'd best be long gone or I'll nail your hide to the door.
Understand?"

"I understand, Cap'n Fog."

"Then get that kid on his horse and ride out of here."

A growled order from Tring brought two men from their
horses to help the groaning youngster to his feet then into his
saddle. Freda watched them, seeing the conspicuous way they

kept their hands clear of the guns at all times. This puzzled her for, from what she had heard, Double K hired tough hard-cases.

Under the right circumstances Tring's bunch might have been hard and tough. Yet every last one of the seven who were capable of thought knew they faced three men who were with but few peers in salty toughness and were more than capable of handling a fight with guns or bare hands.

So the Double K's hard-case bunch got their horses turned and headed off, leaving behind an undamaged house and a Colt Army revolver lying where the youngster let it fall.

Among the other men, thinking himself either hidden from view or unsuspected of being able to do any harm, the youngster leaned forward over the saddlehorn. The way he hung forward he looked like he was still too groggy to do anything, but his left hand drew the rifle from his saddleboot. They passed through the river and rode up the slope. This was his chance. Thirty yards or more separated him from the three Texans and the girl. It was a good range for rifle work and not one at which a man might make an easy hit with a fast drawn Colt. He could turn, make a fast shot at that small bond runt who whipped him. Then he and the rest of the boys could make a stand on the rim and cut the other two down.

The horse was almost at the top of the slope when he wheeled it around in a tight, fast turn and started to throw up the rifle. The move came as a surprise to the other Double K riders. It did not appear to be so much of a surprise to the people against which the move had been directed. The youngster saw that almost as soon as he turned the horse.

Always cautious, more so at such a moment, the Kid stayed right where he had been all the time and did not join Mark and Dusty before the house. After watching Dusty hand the hard-case youngster his needings, the Kid rested the barrels of the ten gauge on his shoulder although his right hand still gripped the butt, forefinger ready on the trigger and hammers still pulled back.

From his place the Kid saw the leaning over and might have passed it off as a dizzy spell caused by the whipping Dusty had handed out. Then the Kid noticed the stealthy withdrawal of a rifle and he waited for the next move.

"Dusty!" the Kid snapped, even as the youngster swung his horse around.

With men like the three Texans to see was to act. Neither Dusty nor Mark had seen the rifle drawn, but they were watching for the first treacherous move, ready to copper any bet the other men made.

At the Kid's word Dusty went sideways, knocking Freda from her feet, bringing her to the ground. She gave a startled yell, muffled for he stayed on top of her, shielding her with his body. The girl heard that flat slap of a bullet passing overhead, but the crack of the shot was drowned by the closer at hand roar of the shotgun.

Even as he yelled his warning the Kid brought the shotgun from his shoulder. Its foregrip slapped into his waiting left hand, the butt settled against his shoulder and he aimed, then touched off first the right, then left barrel. He expected the charge to spread at thirty yards and was not disappointed in it. He did feel disappointed when the men let out howls, including the youngster who jerked up in his saddle, screamed in pain, turned the horse and headed after his bunch as they shot over the bank top and went from sight, although their horses could be heard galloping off beyond the rim.

Freda managed to lift her face from the dirt and peer out by Dusty. She saw Mark kneeling at one side, holding his right hand Colt at arm's length, resting his wrist on his left palm and his left elbow on his raised left knee. Her eyes went to the other side of the stream. She could see no bodies, nor any sign of Tring and his men.

Holstering his gun Mark walked to her side, she saw him towering above her. He bent down, gripped Dusty by the waistbelt, and with no more apparent effort than if lifting a baby hoisted him clear of the girl. Then in the same casual manner Mark turned and tossed Dusty at the Kid who came forward muttering something under his breath and too low for Freda to catch—which in all probability was just as well. Ignoring the choice and lurid remarks made about himself, his morals, descendants and ancestors by his friends, Mark bent and held a hand toward Freda.

"If you throw me I'll scream," she warned.

"Ma'am," Mark replied, gallantly taking the hand and

helping her rise. "I never throw a real good looking young lady away."

By the time Freda stood up again she found the Kid and Dusty had untangled themselves and the Kid came forward bearing the ten gauge and showing a look of prime disgust at such an ineffective weapon.

"What the hell have you got in this fool gun?" he growled. "I reckon to be bettern't that with a scatter."

"I charged it with birdshot. There's been a chicken-hawk after the hens and so I—"

"BIRDSHOT!" the Kid's voice rose a few shades. "No wonder I didn't bust their hides. Landsakes, gal, whyn't you pour in nine buckshot?"

"Because I didn't think I'd need it!" she answered hotly, the reaction at her narrow escape almost bringing tears.

"Easy gal, easy," said Dusty gently. "Lon's only joshing you. It's just his mean old Comanche way. They've gone and they won't be back."

"Not today," she agreed bitterly, thinking of the morrow and the visit it would surely bring.

"Nor any other day," Dusty promised. "We'll call in at the Double K and lay it plain before the new boss. If he makes fuss for you we'll make it for him on our way down trail."

CHAPTER THREE

Wire Across The Trail

IT took Freda a couple of minutes to catch control of her nerves again. She made it in the end, helped by the thought of how lucky she had been. Tring and his men might have done much worse than wreck the buildings and rip down the corral on finding her alone at the house. She thought thankfully of the unfastened dress, it caused her to request the three Texans take their horses around back and then come in for a meal. That gave her a chance to fasten the dress. It also kept the horses out of sight. Had Tring and his men seen three fine looking animals such as Dusty, Mark and the Kid's mounts out front they might have waited in the background until the visitors departed.

"Whyn't you call in the local law?" Mark asked.

"In Barlock?" she replied. "There'd be more chance of help in a ghost town."

"Well," Dusty drawled, "We'll ride in and see their boss. It might do some good for you."

"Riders coming in, Dusty," remarked the Kid, walking towards the side of the house with his hand hanging by the butt of the old Dragoon and the despised shotgun trailing at the other side. "Three of them, coming from back there a piece."

Freda ran towards the Kid, sudden fear in her heart. She reached the corner of the house at the same time he did, staring across the range to where three men rode towards them, following the wagon trail into town. She clutched at the Kid's right arm, holding it tight.

"Don't shoot, Lon," she gasped. "It's my father!"

"Wasn't fixing to shoot, so let off crushing my dainty lil

23

arm,'' he replied. "You-all near on as jumpy as those other pair.''

"Something's wrong. I'm sure something's wrong,'' she went on.

"Won't get any righter until we know what it is,'' Dusty answered, coming to the girl's side.

None of the approaching trio rode real good horses. Two were youngish, cowhands; although not such cowhands as the OD Connected would hire. The third looked in his late forties, sat his horse with something of a cavalryman's stiff-backed grace. It showed even slumped up and dejected as he looked. His clothes were not new, but they were clean and neat—and he didn't wear a gun. The three Texans saw this latter point even before they noticed the rest. A man without a gun was something of a rarity anywhere west of the Mississippi and east of the Pacific Ocean.

Nearer the house the three men split up, the hands making for the door which led into the room they used as living quarters. The older man rode forward, halted his horse and swung down from his saddle. His face bore a strong family resemblance to Freda, now it was lined and looked exhausted, beaten, like the face of a man who has taken all he can and wants to call it quits.

He came forward, hardly looking at the three Texans, laid his hand on his daughter's arm and shook his head gently.

"We're licked, Freda,'' he said. "Mallick has taken over the two stores and won't let any of us small ranchers buy supplies unless we pay cash.''

"But Matt Roylan has always known our credit is good,'' she answered.

"Yes, but the Double K has taken over Matt and Pop Billings' notes at the bank and will foreclose if they sell. I saw Mallick, he said we could have all the supplies needed and he'd take it out of the price he offered for our place.''

"He can't pull a game like that!'' Dusty said quietly stepping forward.

"He's done it,'' George Lasalle answered.

"And the local law stands for it?'' Mark asked.

"Elben, he's town marshal, takes orders from the Double K and has men supplied to back him.''

Never had Freda felt so completely helpless and so near to

tears. They must have supplies, food at least, to tide them over until the first drive came up trail and they could sell cattle to the trail boss. Then they would have enough money to straighten their account, as they had in previous years.

"Sloane sold out," her father went on. "I saw his wagon before Billings' store, taking on supplies. Mrs. Sloane was crying something awful."

Then for the first time he seemed to become aware that there were strangers, guests most likely, present. Instantly he shook the lethargy from him and became a courteous host.

"I'm sorry, gentleman," he said. "I shouldn't be troubling you with our worries. Have you fed our guests, Freda?"

"We had a good meal, sir," Dusty replied. "Your daughter's a fine cook."

At that moment the two hired hands emerged from their room carrying what looked like all their gear. Without a word they swung afork their horses and rode away, not even giving a backwards glance. Dusty watched them, thinking how he would not take their kind as cook's louse even, but most likely they were the best hands Lasalle could afford to hire. Now it looked like they were riding out.

"Where're they going, papa?" Freda asked.

"They quit. A couple of Double K men saw them in town and told them to get out while they could. I told them I couldn't afford to pay them but they said they were going anyway."

"But we can't manage the place without their help," Freda gasped. "You can't gather and hold the shipping cattle alone and we have to get a herd to sell so we can buy supplies."

"Never knew that ole hoss of mine so leg-weary as now, Dusty," Mark remarked in a casual tone.

"Ole Blackie's a mite settled down and ain't willing to go no place at all," drawled the Kid. "And it looks like this gent needs him a couple or so hands for a spell."

Lasalle and his daughter exchanged glances. He did not know who these three young men might be, but he knew full well what they were. They looked like tophands in any man's outfit, seventy-five-dollar-a-month men at least and he could not afford to pay for such talented workers.

"Happen Mr. Lasalle here can let us stay on a spell we'll have to get word up to Bent's Ford and warn Cousin Red not to wait his herd for us," Dusty remarked more to himself than the others. He turned to Lasalle. "Take it kind if you'd let us stay on and rest our horses. We'll work for our food and bed."

A gasp left Freda's lips. She could hardly believe her ears and felt like singing aloud in joy. After seeing the way Dusty, Mark and the Kid handled the eight Double K hard-cases and made them back off, she did not doubt but that the ranch would be safe in their hands.

"We haven't much food," she said, "but the way you told it none of you do much work either."

From the grins on three faces Freda knew she had said the right thing. Her reply showed them she had the right spirit and knew cowhand feelings. Her father did not take the same lighthearted view.

"Just a moment, Freda," he put in. "These gentlemen are welcome to stay over and rest their horses, but we won't expect them to work for their food."

"Why not?" asked Dusty. "The way this pair eat they need work, or they'll run to hawg-fat and be good for nothing when I get them back to home."

"But—but—!"

"Shucks, give it a whirl, sir," interrupted Dusty. "Mark here's good for heavy lifting which don't call for brains. Lon might not know a buffalo bull from a muley steer, but he's better than fair at toting wood for the cook."

"And how about you?" asked Freda. "What do you do?"

"As little as he can get away with," Mark answered.

The girl laughed and turned to her father. "Papa, this is Captain Dusty Fog, Mark Counter and the Ysabel Kid."

It took Lasalle a full minute to reconcile Dusty's appearance with his Civil War record, or his peacetime prominence. Then Lasalle saw the latent power of the small man, recognized it as an old soldier could always recognize a born leader of men. His daughter was not a victim of cowhand humor. This small man was really Dusty Fog. He still did not know what he could say or do for the best.

Then his daughter took the matter out of his hands, made a decision of her own and showed him that she was a child no more.

"I'll show you where the hands bunked," she said. "You

running off wielding a broom to good effect on the hard-case crew.

All in all Dusty seemed far more interested in the closing of the trail than in being thanked for a very necessary piece of work.

"Lon," he said. "Reckon you could find Bent's Ford, happen you was looking for it?"

"Likely, but I'm not looking."

"You are. Just as soon as you've thrown a saddle on that white goat out back."

"Be late tonight when I get there," drawled the Kid.

"Happen that fool Blackie hoss makes it," grinned Mark.

"Ole Blackie'll run hide 'n' tallow off that brown wreck you ride," scoffed the Kid. "I'll make Bent's tonight all right, only I might find the hard boys have been here and took off with your guns."

"I'm here to protect them, Lon," Freda put in.

"Sure, with birdshot in both barrels. Say, reckon you can throw up a bite of food to eat on the way, something I can carry easy."

She sniffed. "I'll flavor it with birdshot. Just remember that I've nothing in the house, except for what's in your greasysack."

"Do what you can," Dusty suggested. "Then Mark and I'll take you into town and buy supplies."

"Mallick won't let us buy anything on credit," Lasalle pointed out.

"We never said anything about credit."

An indignant flush came to Lasalle's cheeks as he caught the meaning of Dusty's words. He thrust back his chair and came to his feet, facing the small Texan across the table.

"I can't accept charity—"

"And none's being offered. Man, you're the touchiest gent we come across in many a year. This's a loan until Stone Hart arrives and you can sell some stock."

"And any way you look at it Dusty and I'm going to eat our fair share of that same food."

Freda stepped to her father's side and laid a hand on his sleeve, her fingers biting into the bicep.

"We accept," she said and her voice once more warned her

can move your gear in and then I'll find you some work."

"I'm beginning not to like this here job already," the Kid told Dusty in an audible whisper. "This gal sounds too much like you and I'm all for a day's work—providing it's spread out over three days."

With that the three cowhands started to follow Freda, leaving her father with his mouth hanging open, not knowing how things came to happen. Then he recalled a piece of news overheard in town, something which might interest the three cowhands.

"Mallick's started wiring off their range. He's already fenced off the narrows all the way along their two mile length from the badlands down to where they open out on to his range again. He doesn't allow any trail herds to cross the Double K."

"He's done what?"

Lasalle took a pace backwards before the concentrated fury in Dusty's Fog's voice as the small Texan turned back towards him. Mark and the Kid had turned also and they no longer smiled or looked friendly.

"Put wire across the trail, clear across the narrows. Says any trail herd which wants to make the market has to swing one way or the other round his range."

The girl looked from her father to the three cowhands. She knew cowhands hated barbed wire and fences of any kind. She knew all the range arguments about wire; that cattle ripped themselves open on the spikes; that a man might ride into such a fence during the night hours and not see it until too late. She also knew the hate went deeper than that. From the Mississippi to the Pacific a man could move or let his cattle graze without being fenced in. He could ride where he wished and had no need to fear crossing another man's land as long as he obeyed the unwritten rules of the range. Through all that expanse of land there were few if any fences and the free-roaming cowhands wanted to see it stay that way.

"How about the herds already moving north?" Mark asked quietly. "This's the trail Stone Hart uses and he's already on his way."

"I think we'd all better go into the house and talk this out," Lasalle replied, but some of the tired sag had left his shoulders now and he seemed to be in full command of himself.

He led the way around the house side and in through the front door. The Kid collected the fallen Army Colt, although Lasalle paid no attention to it, or to the shotgun which the Kid leaned against the door on entering. He waved his guests into chairs and rooted through the side-piece drawers to find a pencil and paper. With these he joined the others at the table and started to make a sketch map of the outline of the Double K. It looked like a rough square, except that up at the north-eastern corner the narrows thrust out to where it joined the badlands. All in all Lasalle drew quite a fair map, showing his own place, the other small ranches and the general lay of the land.

"Did some map-making with the Field Engineers during the War," he remarked. "This's the shape of the Lindon Land Grant. We ranch here. This was the Doane place, but they've sold out. This's the Jones place and the last one here is owned by Bill Gibbs. The town's back here, out beyond the Double K's south line. If the new owner can buy us out it will make his spread cover a full oblong instead of having the narrows up here."

Taking the pencil Dusty marked the line taken by the north-bound trail herds. He tapped the narrows with the pencil tip. Freda noticed that he handled the pencil with his left hand, yet he drew his Colt with his right. He must be truly ambidextrous, she thought.

"And he's run wire down this way," Dusty said. "From the badlands up that way, right down to where the river starts to curve around and down to form his south line."

"So I've heard. I haven't been out that way."

"Which means any drive that comes up is going to have to swing to the west," Mark drawled. "Or go east and try to run the badlands."

Lasalle nodded. "Mallick claims the trail herds won't cross Double K."

"Which'd mean the drive would have to circle right around their range to the west, lose maybe a week, maybe more's drive, or cut east and face bad water, poor graze, worse country and the chance of losing half the herd," said Mark quietly. "I can't see any trail boss worth his salt doing that."

"Me neither," agreed the Kid. "What do we do about it, Dusty?"

"Wait until the Wedge comes up and see what Ston[e] to do."

"Huh!" grunted the Kid, for once not in agreeme[nt] Dusty's reply. "I say let's head up there to the narro[w] haul down that fence."

"The Double K have twenty men at least on the spr[ead] Lasalle put in. "They have such law as exists in this ne[ck] the woods. Elben has eight men backing him in Barloc[k] being paid by the Double K."

"Which sounds like a powerful piece of muscle for a[n] just aiming to run a peaceful cow outfit," drawled D[usty] "Have you seen this new owner?"

"Nobody has yet, apart from the hard-cases stopping crossing their range. They say the new owner hasn't ar[rived] yet, that he bought the place without even seeing it."

"So we don't know if he is behind this wiring the ran[ge] not."

"No, Captain, we don't. Only it's not likely Mallick be doing all this off his own shoulders is it? It'd take four mile of barbed wire to make a double fence along t[he] rows and that runs to money."

Changing hands Dusty started to doodle idly on the This ambidextrous prowess was something he had tau[ght him] self as a child, mainly to take attention from his lack o[f] He thought of Englishmen he had known, a few of t[hem] not enough to form any opinion of such men as a w[hole] none of those he had known ever struck him as bein[g] to make trouble for folks who couldn't fight back.

"We ought to head over and see if this English ho[me] home, Dusty," growled the Kid, sounding Comanch[e]

"It'll wait until we've a few more men," Dusty re[plied]

"Hell, after they come here today—"

Lasalle stared at the Kid. This had been the Tring's visit received a mention. Freda hurriedly arrival of the Double K men, their threat to the p[lace] their departure. The rancher's face lost some of then set in grim lines as he thought of what migh[t hap]pened had Dusty, Mark and the Kid not been on h[and] tempts to thank the three young Texans met wit[h] for they laughed it off and, the way they told it, I[.]

father not to argue. "Thank you all for helping."

"There's another thing though," Lasalle said, surrendering the field to his daughter. "Mallick has told the storekeepers they won't serve any small ranch folk unless they bring a note from him. He keeps a deputy in each store to make sure the owner obeys."

"Well now," drawled Mark idly, "reckon we could do something about that, don't you, Dusty?"

While agreeing with this big *amigo* on the point that they could do something about it, Dusty did not want to make war in Barlock until he had a fighting force at his back. While he and Mark could likely go into town and make Elben's deputies sing low, they might also have to do it to the tune of roaring guns and that could blow things apart at the seams. Dusty wished to avoid starting hostilities if he possibly could. It was not fear of odds which worried Dusty, odds could be whittled down and hired gunmen did not fight when the going got too stiff. With the Wedge at his elbow Dusty could make the hired hard-cases of Double K think the going had got too stiff, then likely put its new owner where he must make his peace.

Every instinct warned Dusty that more than lust for land lay behind this business. The Lindon Land Grant spread wide and large enough to satisfy a man, especially a man new to the cattle business. The entire area was well watered, that could not be the cause fo the trouble. So he must look deeper for the reason and when he found it would best know how to avert trouble.

Dusty wanted to meet the English owner if he could, Mallick certainly, to get the measure of his enemies, if enemies they should be. It might be that both were new to the west and did not know the cattleman's hatred of barbed wire, or the full implication of Lindon's Grant. If so, and they listened, he might be able to steer them in the right direction.

"What do you want me to do at Bent's, Dusty?" asked the Kid, breaking in on his pard's thought train.

"Leave word for Cousin Red to carry on up trail without us. I don't want him waiting at Bent's, or coming back to help us. That herd has to make the market. And don't spread the word about this wire trouble. I don't want this section swarming with hot-headed fools all looking for trouble."

"They'd likely be down here and rip down that fence," drawled the Kid. "Which same could sure show the Double K bunch how folks feel."

"And might start lead flying." Dusty answered.

He looked beyond the mere basic events. If Keller or Mallick aimed to keep the fence they had trained fighting men to help them. No matter what public opinion might think about the fences Keller had the law behind him in his right to erect one.

Before any more could be said Freda came in and announced she had food ready for the Kid's departure. So setting his black Stetson at the right "jack-deuce" angle over his off eye, the Kid headed out back to saddle his white stallion.

The girl followed him and watched the big white horse come to his whistle. She had the westerner's love of a good horse and that seventeen hand white stallion sure was a fine animal.

"Isn't he a beauty?" she said, stepping forward. "Can I stroke him?"

"Why sure," grinned the Kid, "happen you don't want to keep both hands. See, old Blackie here's mammy done got scared with a snapping turtle just afore he was born and he don't know whether he's hoss or alligator."

Freda studied the horse and decided that, despite the light way he spoke, the Kid called it right when he told of the dangerous nature of his horse. That seventeen-hand white devil looked as wild and mean as its master. So she refrained from either touching or approaching the horse. This was a real smart move for Blackie would accept the touch of few people, in fact only the Kid could handle his horse with impunity, it merely tolerated the other members of the floating outfit when circumstances forced them to handle it.

With his horse saddled ready to ride the Kid went astride in a lithe, Indian-like bound. He looked down at Freda and grinned, the grin made him look very young and innocent again. Removing his hat he gave her an elaborately graceful flourish with it, then replaced it.

"You get some buckshot in that gun, gal," he said, "and afore I get back here. *Birdshot,* huh!"

Before she could think up a suitable reply he turned the horse, rode around the side of the building, through the water and up the slope. He turned, waved a cheery hand, then went from sight.

Only then did she realize that he had not asked for directions to Bent's Ford. A momentary suspicion came to her for Dusty claimed they had never travelled this way before. Then the thought left her and she felt just a little ashamed of herself at having it. The Ysabel Kid needed no spoken directions to help him find his way across country. Out there, although the first drive of the year had not yet passed, he would find enough sign to aim him north and all the trails converged at Bent's Ford in the Indian Nations.

"Lon gone?" Dusty asked, coming to the front door as the girl returned to the house.

"No. He's sat on the roof, playing a guitar."

Somehow Freda felt in a mad gay mood, far happier than she had done for a long time. She gave a guilty start, realizing it must be the excitement of the day and the pleasure at having company which made her act in such a manner.

CHAPTER FOUR

A Pair of Drunken Irresponsible
Cowhands

"ABOUT these supplies?" Mark Counter asked as Dusty and Freda entered the room from seeing the Kid on his way to Bent's Ford.

"I've told, Mark," Lasalle replied. "Mallick won't let us buy any unless we sell out to him."

"Looks like we'll just have to go in and see Mr. Mallick," drawled Dusty.

"Poor Mallick," Freda remarked, the gay mood still on her.

Her father watched her and for the first time realized how lonely she must be out here miles from town. He wondered if they might be better to take Mallick's offer, leave the ranch and make a fresh home in a town where she could have friends of her own age.

Then he thought of the strength Mallick had in Barlock. With Elben, the town marshal, backed by eight gun-wise hard-case deputies, Dusty and Mark would be hopelessly out-numbered. They stood a better than fair chance of leaving town headed in a pinewood box for the boothill.

"It's risky—!" he began.

"Could be, happen we rode on in and started to shoot up the main drag," Dusty agreed. "Only we don't aim to. We'll just ride on in peaceable and ask him to act a mite more sociable and neighborly."

"And if he doesn't want to act more sociable and neigh-borly?" Freda asked.

"Don't reckon there's much we can do at all," drawled Mark, sounding mild but there was no mildness in his eyes.

" 'Cepting maybe try moral suasion," Dusty went on, just as mild sounding.

"Ole Dusty's real good at that, too," Mark said. "Yep. I can't think of a better moral suader than him. Excepting maybe his Uncle Devil and his cousin Betty."

"And what if Mallick doesn't fall for this moral suasion—whatever that might be?"

"Tell you, gal," Mark answered. "We'll likely hide behind you."

They left it at that, although Freda wondered what moral suasion might be. Her father was smiling now, looking more confident in himself all the time, more like the man she always remembered. Freda saw for the first time the strain he had been under for the past few years since her mother died. Now he looked better, ready to take on the world and its problems.

"Where at's your hosses, gal?" Mark asked, taking up his hat.

"Out back, grazing, I'll show you."

"I've seen a couple of hosses afore, gal, can likely tell them from a cow, happen the cow's not a muley. I'll hitch a hoss to your buggy for you."

Freda smiled. "I'll come along, there's a muley cow or two out back and I wouldn't want to drive into town behind it."

"Pick a couple of saddle horses out for us, Mark," Dusty put in. "No sense in going in there shouting who we are."

"Yo!"

With the old cavalry reply Mark turned and left the room with Freda on his heels. Lasalle watched her go, then turned to Dusty with a worried look in his eyes.

"I've never seen Freda act that way," he said. "It's—well—."

"Yeah, I know," grinned Dusty. "I've seen girls get that way around Mark afore. Don't worry, it won't get serious and you can trust Mark." He nodded to the old Le Mat carbine on the wall. "Does that relic work?"

Indignant at the slur on his prized Le Mat, Lasalle forgot his daughter's infatuation for Mark Counter and headed to the wall. He lifted down the Le Mat and walked to the table.

"Work!" he snorted. "I'll say it works. And I'll show Tring just how well if he comes back today."

Dusty grinned. "Way him and his bunch took off," he

drawled, "they were toting birdshot and they won't feel like riding anyplace today."

With that he took up the young gunhand's discarded Army Colt. He turned the weapon in his hands, checking its chamber was full loaded and that the weapon worked. It had some dirt in it, but the Colt 1860 Army revolver was a sturdy weapon and took more than a bit of dirt to put it out of working condition. He rubbed the dirt off the revolver, set the hammer at half cock and turned the chamber, making sure it would rotate properly.

"Here, let me handle that," Lasalle said. "You said the Kid used the shotgun on Double K?"

"Both barrels and a good ounce of birdshot, way they took to hollering when it sprayed out," Dusty answered. "So shove in some powder and pour a load of buckshot on top this time. It doesn't fan out but it's a mite more potent close up."

Outside Mark caught the best two of the ranch's small bunch of saddle stock and led them back to the house. He slung his saddle blanket on one horse, then the double girthed range rig while Freda watched. He felt her eyes on him and hoped she wasn't going to get involved in romance that could have no successful end.

Mark did not mind a mild flirtation but he made a rule never to become involved with a sweet, innocent and naïve girl like Freda. In his travellings around the west he had seen, and known intimately, a number of women who were either famous already, or would be one day. They were all mature women who knew what time of day it was and knew better than to expect anything permanent to come of romance with a man like him.

For all his worries Mark did the girl less than justice. Freda did not think of herself as being halfway towards marrying him. Some woman's instinct warned her it would be no use falling in love with a man like Mark. Yet she wanted to be near him, to see how he walked and talked, so that she might know the feeling again if it came with a more marriageable man's presence.

She pointed out the harness horse and helped Mark hitch it to the small buckboard wagon. Then they walked back to the house to find her father sitting at the sitting-room table with a formidable collection of weapons before him.

"We're ready to go, Dusty," she said.

"Reckon you can hold down the house while we're gone, George?" Dusty asked her father.

"Can I?" growled Lasalle. "I reckon with old Bugle here to give warning and all this artillery I just might be able to."

"Keep the shotgun handy then. It's got buckshot down the barrels—I saw to that."

Freda poked her tongue out at Dusty and headed for the door. He grinned, took up his hat and followed her out. Lasalle came to the kitchen door, the Le Mat carbine resting on his arm and the Army Colt thrust into his waistband. Freda could see the change in her father now. He looked almost as young and happy as he had on his leaves during the war, before being taken prisoner and sent to a Yankee hell-hole prisoner-of-war camp.

At first Freda kept up a light-hearted flow of banter with the two men as they rode by her on borrowed horses. They kept to the wheel-rut track the buckboard carved into the ground on many trips to Barlock, travelling across good range country with water, grass and a good few head of long-horn cattle grazing in sight of them. Freda saw the way Dusty and Mark watched the range, studying it with keen and careful eyes, watching for some sign of approaching danger, even while they laughed and joked with her.

Not until they were halfway to town did Freda mention the trouble.

"Why did you stay on to help us, Dusty?" she asked.

"It could be because I like you folks and don't take to Double K shoving you around," he replied.

"It wouldn't be because of that fence, too?"

"That's part of it," Dusty agreed. "The range has always been open and I'd hate to see it fenced. There's no need. A man's cattle can roam, feed anywhere the graze is good and not cut the grass down to its roots because they're hemmed in by a fence. Down home in the Rio Hondo our round-ups take a month and cover maybe three hundred square miles. We work with the other outfits, share the profits, take our cut. Any stock from out of our area is held until it's spread's rep. comes for it and we send men to collect ours."

"The fence blocks a cattle trail, Freda," Mark went on soberly. "Which makes it a whole lot worse. You didn't see

Texas right after the war. Not the way I saw it when I came though with Bushrod Sheldon on our way to join Maximillian. There were cattle every place a man looked and no market for them. Then we found a market up north and men started to move their herds up towards Kansas. It was the trail herd which saw this area opened up, the Indian moved on out. Men died on those early drives, more than do these days. They were learning the lessons we know now and a lot of times a man didn't get a chance to profit from a mistake. A code grew up, gal. The code of the trail boss, the way he and his crew lived on the trail. One thing no trail boss will do is risk losing his herd and that's what it'd mean to push 'round here."

The girl watched Mark, surprised at the sincere and sober way he spoke. She began to get an inkling of the way the cowhands felt about that fence across the narrows of the Double K.

"You know how Lindon got that Land Grant?" Mark went on.

"I'm not sure," she admitted.

"On the agreement that he kept the trail open, never closed it down. That was why he got the narrows, it's good winter graze and it lets the herd run through good food without being on his main grant land too long. Now the trail's closed there can only be the one answer—war."

"Would it come to that?"

"Likely," Dusty answered. "Stone Hart's coming north, be along most any day now. He's a good man—and a damned good trail boss. He won't waste time going all that way around when he's got clear right to cross. So Wedge'll fight, and if he can't force through the men following him north'll fight. Most of that fighting'll be done over your land, not on the Double K. At the end, no matter who gets their way, no matter who wins, you small folks lose out."

"How do you mean?"

"You make a living here, not much more. You need to sell your stock to make enough to carry you through," Dusty explained. "There'll be none of that. And once the shooting starts you'll be in the middle, stock'll go, maybe folks be killed. You'll be the ones who go under and that's what I'm trying to prevent. That's why I'm waiting for the Wedge to come."

"But would your friend allow that to happen?"

"Stone makes his living running contract herds for small ranch owners like your pappy. He'll have around three thousand head along with him, six or eight spreads shipping herds. Those folks are relying on Stone, just as you are on selling your stock. He never yet let his folks down and I don't figure he aims to make a start at it now."

"Won't there be trouble when he comes anyway?" she asked, watching Dusty's face and wondering how she ever thought of him as being small.

"Maybe," replied Dusty. "Maybe not. Only I've never yet seen the hired gun who would face real opposition and we'll have that behind us with the Wedge. If we can get through, talk this out with Keller, or whatever you called him, we might show him how wrong he is."

"Never knowed a gal like you for asking questions," Mark drawled in a tone which warned her the subject must be dropped.

"And I'd bet you've known some girls," she answered.

"Couple here, couple there."

"When did you first get interested in girls, Mark?"

He grinned at her. "The day I found out they wasn't boys."

Once more the conversation took on a lighter note and continued that way until they came towards the town of Barlock, buckboard and horses making for the main street.

Barlock was neither large nor impressive. Like most towns in Texas it existed to supply the needs of the cattle industry, growing, like the State itself, out of hide and horn, beef fattened on the rolling range land. The surrounding ranches supplied year-long custom for the cowhands had no closer place in which to spend their monthly payroll. During the trail drive season added wealth could be garnered from passing herds, their crews taking a chance of a quick celebration before leaving Texas.

All this did not mean that Barlock grew larger than any other weather-washed township out on the rolling plains. There were some fifteen business premises, two stores, two saloons, the inevitable Wells Fargo office with its telegraph wires and its barns and stables, a livery barn, a small house in back of town which showed its purpose with a small, discreet, red lantern. The rest were just like any other small town might offer, being neither more nor less grand.

Mark and Dusty now rode at one side of the wagon and the girl was surprised to see how they no longer kept protectively close to it. They passed into town, going by a blacksmith's forge, then the barber's shop.

"That's the Land Office," she said, indicating the next single floor, small wooden building.

"Saloon, ma'am," Dusty replied in a louder tone than necessary. "Why thank you kindly for pointing it out."

On the porch before the Land Office lounged two tough-looking men with prominent guns and deputy marshal badges. They appeared to be loafing, yet clearly stood guard to prevent anybody entering and bothering whatever might be in the office. Neither spoke, nor did they move, but studied the passing party with cold, hard, unfriendly eyes.

"Thanks for showing us the way in ma'am," Mark went on, also speaking in a far louder tone than necessary. "Let's find us a drink, *amigo*."

"Been eating trail dust for so long I need one," Dusty replied, then in a lower voice, for they had passed the Land Agent's office. "Where at's the jail gal. Tell, don't point."

Freda's finger had started to make an instinctive point but she held it down and answered, "At the other end of town, beyond the Jackieboy Saloon."

"We're going in this place here," Dusty said. "Wait out here for us. What's in that shop opposite?"

"Dresses."

"Couldn't be better. See you soon."

They swung their horses from her side and rode to the hitching rail outside the smaller of Barlock's saloons. Freda swung her own horse towards the other side of the street and jumped down. She crossed to the window of the dress shop and stood looking in the window, admiring a dress which would cost more than she could possibly afford.

Time dragged slowly. She wondered what might be keeping Dusty and Mark for there was no sign of either man. How soon would one of Elben's deputies get suspicious and come to ask her why she waited before the saloon? For five minutes she pretended to be examining the horse's hooves and the set of its harness, then leaned by the side of the wagon looking along the street.

The tall shape of Mark Counter loomed at the batwing doors. Freda heaved a sigh of relief. Then her smile of welcome died on her face as she watched the way her two friends came into sight.

For a moment Mark and Dusty stood on the sidewalk before the saloon. Then they started to walk towards the Land Agent's office without showing a sign that either of them had ever seen her before. Their hats were thrust back and they went on unsteady legs in a manner she knew all too well. They seemed to have spent their time in the saloon gathering a fair quantity of liquid refreshment. In fact they both looked to be well on their way to rolling drunk.

Hot and angry Freda stamped her way across the street on to the sidewalk behind them. She aimed to give them a piece of her mind when she caught up with them and to hell with the consequences. They had come into town to help her and the moment they hit the main street they took off for the saloon to become a pair of drunken irresponsible cowhands. She would never have expected it of either of them, yet the evidence stood plain before her eyes.

"Yippee ti-yi-ki-yo!" Dusty whooped, sounding real drunk. "Ain't no Yankee can throw me."

"Le's find another saloon 'n' likker up good," suggested Mark Counter, making a grab at the hitching rail on the end of the Land Agent's office and holding it to get his balance, allowing Dusty to go ahead. "Another lil drink sure won't do us any harm."

From his tone and attitude he already carried enough bottled brave-maker in him to settle him down. Freda came forward, her cheeks burned hot with both shame and rage. She saw the two deputies looking towards her friends and felt the anger grow even more. Dusty and Mark were headed for trouble, she hoped they got it.

"They sure didn't waste any time," said one deputy.

"Never knowed a cowhand who did," replied the other. "Nor could handle his likker once he took it."

"That big feller looks like he might have money. Let's tell them we'll jail 'em unless they pay out a fine."

"Sure. They'll be easy enough."

Dusty Fog looked owlishly towards the two men who blocked the sidewalk ahead of him.

"Ain't no Yankee can throw me!" he stated again, belligerently.

"You pair's headed for jail," answered the taller deputy. "Come on quiet, or we'll take you with a broke head."

"Jail!" yelped Dusty, fumbling in his pants pocket. "You can't do that to us. I got money—look."

He held out a twenty dollar gold piece before the men. Two hands shot out greedily towards the coin, both deputies eager to get hold of it. By an accident it seeemed Dusty let the gold piece fall from his fingers. It rang on the sidewalk and both deputies bent forward, reaching down to grab it.

Dusty's hands shot out fast, closed on the bending deputies' shirt collars and heaved. They shot by on either side of him, caught off balance and taken unprepared by the strength in the small Texan's body.

Out of control, the two men went forward into Mark's waiting hands which clamped on the outside of each head. Mark brought his hands together, crashing two heads into each other with a most satisfying thud. Both deputies went limp as if they'd been suddenly boned. They would have fallen to the ground only Mark gripped their collars again and held them up, leaning them against the office wall and jamming them there as if standing talking to them.

Turning fast, hands ready to grab at the butts of his Colts, Dusty looked along the street. Nobody appeared to have seen them for the street remained empty except for the girl. A girl whose face seemed to be twisting into a variety of different expressions. Relief, amazement, anger, amusement, they all warred for prominence on Freda's face.

Then Dusty was grinning, not the slobbering leering grin of a drunk, but the grin she had seen before, when he talked with her before leaving for Barlock.

"Lordy me, gal," he said, taking her arm and leading her to the Land Agent's door. "I'll never forget your face when we came out of that saloon."

CHAPTER FIVE

Moral Suasion

BEFORE any of the thoughts buzzing around in Freda's head could be put to words, before she had hardly time to collect her thoughts even, she saw Dusty Fog open the door of the Land Agent's office. Freda suddenly realized the reason for the piece of play-acting. By pretending to be drunk and incapable Dusty and Mark put the watching deputies off guard and enabled the two Texans to handle the matter without fuss or disturbance.

Wondering what would come next Freda followed Dusty through the open office door, into the hallowed and protected halls of Karl Mallick, Land Agent.

The office was designed for privacy, so that the occupants could talk their business undisturbed. There was but one large room, Mallick living in Barlock's best, in fact only, hotel. All the windows had been painted black for the lower half of their length and could only have been looked through by a person standing on tiptoes and peering over the black portion. The two deputies on watch outside whenever the office was in use prevented such liberties being taken.

It was a room without fancy furnishings. Nothing more or less than a set of filing cabinets in a corner, a stout safe in another, a few chairs, a range saddle with rifle and rope in a third. In the center of the room stood a large desk and at the desk, head bent forward as he wrote rapidly on a sheet of paper, sat Karl Mallick, Land Agent and attorney for the Double K.

Mallick had much on his mind as he wrote a letter. He set down the pen and began toying with the branding iron which lay on his desk top. He heard the door open and scowled. Only one man in town should be able to enter without knocking and he would be hardly likely to come around in plain daylight, not to the front door, unless something had gone bad wrong in their plans.

Raising his head, so his black bearded face looked towards the door, Mallick found he had visitors.

"What the—!" he began, coming to his feet as he stared at the small man and the girl who entered.

"Just sit again, mister," Dusty answered.

Behind him Mark entered, still supporting the two deputies, and dumped them in a heap on the floor. Mallick sat, but his right hand shot down to pull at the drawer of his desk, getting it open and exposing an Adams revolver which lay inside ready for use in such emergencies.

Whatever use Mallick intended to put the gun to never came off. Dusty let Freda's arm free and he lunged forward fast. His right hand trapped Mallick's left wrist as it lay on the desk top. With his left hand, gripping it between his second and third fingers, Dusty caught up the pen Mallick had laid aside. Moving faster than Mallick had ever seen, Dusty inserted the pen between the bearded man's two middle fingers. Then Dusty closed his hand, gripping down hard. With his hand scant inches from the butt of the Adams revolver Mallick stopped as if he'd run against an invisible wall. Pain, numbing, savage, agonizing pain rammed through his trapped hand. He could not cry out. All he could do was claw the right hand from the desk drawer and reach towards Dusty's trapping fingers.

Dusty released the hold before Mallick's hand reached his. He stepped around the desk, took out the Adams and thrust it into his waist band. Then he moved back and took his first look at the Land Agent.

Although he was tall and bulky Mallick did not give the impression of being a really hard man. He wore a good eastern style suit, white shirt and a neck-tie of sober hue. His face, what showed of it from behind the black beard, looked like the face of a man who spent some of his time out under the sun, which might be expected in his job. The eyes were light blue, cold and at the moment filled with hate as he studied his visitors.

He did not have the look of a western man.

Slowly his hand dropped towards the branding iron.

Having closed the door Mark Counter stepped forward and took up the heavy iron, handling it like a child's toy. He looked down at Mallick as he stepped back holding the iron between his hands, left below the handle, right at the head.

"Lead us not into temptation," Mark drawled, "just like the good book says. Feller tried to hit me with one of these things, one time when he got riled."

"What do you pair want here?" Mallick snarled, his accent sounding eastern. New York most likely from the way he spoke. "This's private property. You could be jailed for attacking those deputies and coming in here."

"Why *hombre*," replied Mark calmly. "We found these two gents all a-swooning away in the heat and hauled them in."

"And it's a trio, not us pair," Dusty went on. "You likely know Miss Lasalle. Her pappy came in to see you this morning. Allows anybody wants to trade at the store has to come and get a note from you."

"Where'd you hear a fool tale like that?" growled Mallick.

"I just told you *hombre*," Dusty answered, his nostrils quivering as he sniffed the air suspiciously. He threw a glance first at Mark, then at Freda. "Whooee! I thought that bay rum you used was strong, Mark."

"That's not mine," replied Mark, also sniffing.

"Don't look at me either," Freda gasped, also sniffing the sickly sweet aroma which aroused Dusty's interest. She was both surprised and puzzled by it and laid the blame on some lady visitor to Mallick, only if she used that kind of perfume she was not likely to be a lady.

"Smells like a Dodge City blacksmith's," drawled Mark.

"You ought to know," Freda answered, then blushed. A young lady should be unaware of the fact that a blacksmith, used in the way Mark spoke, had nothing to do with shoeing horses, but rather as acting as a pimp for ladies of easy virtue.

"I've better things to do than listen to you lot jawing," snarled Mallick, wanting the subject changed, although not for the obvious reason.

"That's where you're wrong, mister," Dusty drawled quietly. "You never had anything so important as seeing that we get the note to the store. See, old Mark here's an easy-going boy when he's fed. Trouble being we're staying out at Freda's place and they're short on food. And when Mark gets hungry he gets mean and riled."

"Which same I'm getting hunger on me right now."

Saying this Mark raised the branding iron before him and tightened his grip. At first none of the others could see any sign, except in the way Mark's face became set and grim. Then slowly, before the surprised eyes of Mallick and Freda, the stout iron bar began to bend. Freda saw the strain on Mark's face, saw the way his shirt sleeves, roomy as they were, went taut against the swell of his biceps as they rose and writhed under the pressure he put on. The bar began to bend, take the shape of a C, then an O. Not until it bent around in a full circle did Mark stop his pressure and toss the branding iron down before Mallick.

"Yes, sir," he said. "I can feel the hunger coming on right now."

Mallick made no reply. He stared down at the branding iron and the pallor which came to his face showed he appreciated the situation in full. Through all the Panhandle country he doubted if more than one man could equal the display of strength he just witnessed.

Footsteps sounded outside the building, and over the blackened lower part of the window showed a familiar hat's top. Mallick recognized it and so did Freda but she kept quiet. She did not need to speak, the flicker of relief which passed across Mallick's face warned Dusty and Mark, told them all they needed to know. The footsteps came to a halt before the door and a knock sounded.

"Mr. Mallick!" called a voice. "You all right, the boys aren't out here."

Even as Mallick started to rise, opening his mouth to utter a yell to the man outside, his plan failed. Dusty's left hand flipped across his body, the white handled Army Colt left his holster, its seven and a half inch barrel thrusting up to poke a yawning muzzle under Mallick's chin, at the same instant the hammer clicked back under Dusty's thumb.

"Get rid of him!" Dusty warned in a savage whisper, "or you'll be talking without a top to your head."

Mallick hired paid killers, men who sold their gun-skill to the highest bidders. He knew such men would never hesitate to carry out such a threat as Dusty made. Nor, looking at the small Texan's grim face, did he doubt but that his slightest hesitation would see a bullet crashing in his head. Mallick slumped back into his chair, sweat pouring down his face as he opened his mouth. He tried to keep his voice normal, and yet still convey a warning that things were wrong to the man outside. He hoped that for once in his life Elben the town marshal might show some sign of sense.

"It's all right, marshal," he called. "I told them to go along to the saloon."

Much to Mallick's relief the words prevented Elben from entering the room. He hoped the marshal might be following his usual practice of spending the afternoon in the saloon and would miss the two men, then mention the fact to the boss who would form his own conclusions and have a party down this way fast.

In this Mallick was to be disappointed. Elben shrugged, knowing no important business to be taking place inside. He strolled on, passing around the end of the building and heading down to the small house with the red light, having some civic duty to attend to, the collection of his weekly contribution from the madame to what they referred as election campaign expenses. From the house he returned, after a time to the jail.

While Elben attended to his self-appointed duties Mallick, one of the men who employed him, sat in the Land Agent's office hoping against hope that help would come.

"Write!" Dusty snapped, pointing to the pen and paper. "Make it *pronto!*"

Mallick did not argue. He had worked himself up the path to defiance when he saw Elben's hat passing the window. Only Dusty had pricked the balloon before it could be used and Mallick had nothing left with which to be defiant. He threw a glance to where Mark Counter took the rope from his own saddle, went towards the moaning deputies and began making a good fastening job on them. Then he took up the pen and began to write.

Having watched everything with puzzled, then smiling interest, Freda turned to Dusty and asked:

"Is that what you call moral suasion?"

"Rio Hondo style," Dusty agreed, taking the paper Mallick

wrote out and the letter, comparing the signatures on them. "It'll do. Hawg-tie him, Mark."

"Like a hawg," Mark agreed, gagging the deputies with their own bandanas. "I picked up your double eagle, out there, Dusty, want it back?"

"My need's greater than your'n," Dusty answered. "But keep it to send a telegraph message to Uncle Devil for me after we leave here."

With hands long skilled in securely tying things, Mark flipped the rope around Mallick's shoulders. Dusty sat on the edge of the desk and watched the hog-tying process, he also started to question Mallick.

"Like to see your boss," he began.

"He's not here yet," Mallick replied.

"When'd he be coming out here?"

"I don't know."

"Who ordered the fence built?" Dusty asked.

"Keller did!"

"You said he wasn't here," Freda pointed out.

"He sent a telegraph message. Told me to buy you folks out and fence his property."

"How long have you been out west, *hombre*?" Mark asked, quickly securing the man's wrists together.

"Long enough."

"You know how us folks feel about wire?" Dusty went on.

"Yeah. But Keller ordered me to lay it."

"He doesn't know how much land he's got then?" Mark said, thinking how much wiring a vast spread like the Double K would cost.

Mallick surged against the ropes and the expression which flickered across his face at the words surprised Dusty. Although he did not know what might have caused it the words had hit Mallick hard. Dusty could read facial expressions and knew fear when he saw it. He saw it this time in the bearded face of the Land Agent. Mallick threw a look at the wastepaper basket, then jerked his eyes away once more. Yet he left it too late. Dusty followed the direction of the other man's gaze. The basket contained only a small pile of pieces of paper as if a man idly ripped up something and tossed it in. Only an idle action and odd scraps of paper would not bring the fear and desperation to Mallick's face.

Bending down Dusty scooped the paper from the basket. Mallick gave a snarl of rage and struggled impotently against the securing ropes, but Mark held him down and Freda jumped forward with her own handkerchief to gag him. Once more the girl proved herself capable of cool and fast thought for neither Dusty nor Mark gave her any sign of needing help.

"What is it?" she asked.

Dusty spread open the crumpled torn pile of paper and looked down at it.

"A map of some kind. It'll take time to fit all this together right and we don't have time to spare, gal. I'll take it with me."

Fear, hate and worse showed in Mallick's eyes as he struggled impotently against the taut ropes which held him fast. He felt himself lifted to his feet, hauled into a corner where he could not be seen from the windows, then sat with his back against the wall while Mark lashed his ankles together. Mark knew his business, knew the discovery of Mallick and his crowd might mean death for the girl, Dusty and himself. So Mark aimed to see discovery was less likely. He dragged the now conscious and groaning deputies to where Mallick sat, propped them against the wall and used the last of the Agent's rope to secure their feet together. They now sat tied in line and it would be unlikely, if not impossible, that they could manage to roll, wriggle or crawl out into view, or even to where by kicking or stamping against the walls they might attract attention.

Freda crossed the room and looked down at the three bound men.

"We won't be selling, Mr. Mallick," she said.

"Let's go, gal," Dusty drawled, watching Mark lock and bolt the rear door.

Cautiously Freda started to open the front door, meaning to peer out and make sure their departure would be undetected. This action did not meet with Dusty's approval.

"Go on straight out, gal," he ordered. "Act like you've been to see Mallick on business, not like you're robbing the bank."

Holding down the comment which bubbled at her lips Freda stepped through the door. She had no sooner got outside than a hand caught her arm and turned her. She gave a muffled squeak, felt herself scooped up into Mark's arms. His face came down, lips crushing her own in a kiss. The girl struggled, her little hands hitting Mark on the shoulders. Then he released her and she staggered back a pace. Her right hand came around in a slap which jerked his head aside.

"Just because I talk friendly—" she began hotly.

"When you pair of love-birds have done," Dusty put in. "I've locked the door and we can move off."

Freda's angry outburst faded, contrition came to her face. Then she flushed red and glared at the two men. Mark put a hand to his cheek and grinned.

"That's a mean right hand you've got, gal."

"I'm sorry," she replied. "But you might have warned me. I've heard about you."

"Yeah," grinned Mark. "I could feel it. Anyway it spoils things when the gal knows what she's going to get. I'll see to getting word to Ole Devil and you take care of Russian Olga here, Dusty."

"Who's Russian Olga?" Freda asked, watching Mark walk along the sidewalk making for the Wells Fargo office, while Dusty headed her across the street towards the waiting buckboard.

"She's a gal we saw one time,"* Dusty replied. "Claims to be the female fist fighting champion of the world, only she got licked that time."

"Girls fist f— You're jobbing me!"

"Nope. There's a few of them about. Get the buckboard and head for the store and when we get inside don't be surprised at how I act. I don't want anybody thinking we're friends."

"Scared I might ruin you socially?" she asked with a smile.

"Call it that," grinned Dusty in reply. "That slap you gave Mark'd've helped if anybody was watching, wouldn't make you look real friendly with us. Only we had to stop anybody seeing me lock the door and Mark reckoned kissing you'd be as good a way of hiding me as any."

"And I slapped his face, poor Mark."

"He'll live."

Freda remembered where Mark was headed and a thought struck her.

* Told of in QUIET TOWN

"Won't your Uncle Devil object to your neglecting your work?"

"He'll turn the air blue and blister my hide, but he'll be behind me all the way and if this thing blows too big he'll get help here, happen we send for it. Now get in the buggy—and remember, gal, you've just been made to sell your home. Act like it, don't look so all-fired pleased with yourself."

When Freda entered Roylan's store she looked dejected almost on the verge of tears. Matt Roylan, sleeved rolled up to expose his muscular arms, leaned his big bulky, powerful frame on the counter and looked across the room towards the door. The lean, gun-hung hard-case with the deputy's badge also looked. He leaned by the cracker barrel into which he dipped his hand at regular intervals. His eyes studied the girl, then went to Dusty who followed on her heels.

"Supply her," Dusty ordered as they reached the counter.

"Says which?" asked the gunman.

"You want to see the paper?"

Dusty made his reply with a cold smile flickering on his lips. The lanky gunman studied Dusty, reading the signs in the matched guns, in those well-made holsters and the workmanship of the gunbelt. He knew quality when he saw it—and he saw it in the small Texan. Without knowing who Dusty was, the gunman knew what he was. Dusty belonged to the real fast guns, one of the magic handed group who could draw and shoot in less than half a second.

For his part Dusty tried to give the impression of being a typical hired hard-case, a man who used a brace of real fast guns to off-set his lack of inches. From the looks on the gunman and Roylan's faces Dusty had made his point, they took him at face value.

"You one of the boys from the spread?" asked the gunman, meaning to be sociable. "Mallick hire you?"

"Go ask him," Dusty answered in an uncompromising tone.

Watching from the corner of her eye Freda felt amazed at the change in Dusty. He seemed to be able to turn himself from an insignificant cowhand to any part he wanted to play. Right now, happen she didn't know him, she would have taken him for a brash, cocky and tough hired gunhand who knew he had the other man over a barrel in more ways than one. She saw that neither Roylan nor the deputy doubted that Dusty brought her from Mallick's office after forcing her father to sell out.

"You and your father are leaving after all, Freda," Roylan said, a touch of sadness in his voice as he looked at the note Dusty tossed in a contemptuous manner before him. His voice held such genuine sadness that Freda felt guilty at having to deceive him, yet she knew she did not dare take a chance on letting hint of her true position slip out.

"She's leaving, *hombre*," answered Dusty, saving Freda from needing to lie. "So shake the bull-droppings from your socks and make with some service."

In his own right Matt Roylan could be a tough, hard man. However he knew the futility of tangling with Double K in what now amounted to their town. He might jump the two hired hard-cases, lick them, although the small one looked fast enough to throw lead into him before he could bat an eye. Even if he did manage to lick the two men and throw them out, the Double K held his bank-note and would foreclose on him.

So Roylan stared to collect the order Freda gave him. Yet somehow, as he worked, Roylan got the feeling that Freda was not quite so grief-stricken as she tried to appear. The girl could not act well enough to continue her pose, at least not well enough to fool an old friend like Roylan. The storekeeper noticed this and felt puzzled by it. He threw a glance at Dusty who sat by the counter and dipped a hand into the candy jar to take one out. Roylan couldn't think how, but somehow Freda had gathered the note from Mallick, the girl was all right and things not so black as they looked. That would be impossible—unless the small Texan was not what he seemed. Yet he had the mannerisms of a tough hard-case hired gun.

One thing Roylan knew for sure, with the note from Mallick and the presence of one of the Double K's toughs, he stood in the clear. If it came out later that Freda managed to trick the paper from Mallick in some way all the blame could be laid on the deputy who accepted the note as genuine.

"How long've you been with Double K?" asked the gun-hand, giving Dusty a long and curious stare.

"Not long," Dusty answered truthfully. "You always this nosey?"

The gunman grunted and relapsed into silence once more, except for the crunching of the cracker he took out of the barrel. He did not know all the men out at the Double K but knew Mallick hired efficient men when he could find them, and this small Texan looked and acted efficient. One thing the deputy knew for sure. The Texan wouldn't take to having his word doubted and could likely deal harshly with any man who doubted it.

Freda felt tension rising inside her with every minute. She watched Roylan collecting the goods from the shelves. He seemed to be taking his time and she wanted to beg him to hurry. At any moment Mallick would be found and the alarm given. Then Dusty and Mark would need to face a hostile town, or at least such a part of the town as felt under obligation to Double K.

At last the order had been gathered and she paid for it. Then Roylan began to box it and carry it to her buckboard. Dusty watched this. The load did not look much after seeing the OD Connected's cook collect a chuckwagon full at a time, but the Lasalle family did not need such quantities of food and what they now had would be the difference between survival and being driven out.

Freda left the store, wanting to be outside so that she might see what happened around town. The gathering of supplies had taken some time and she thought Mark might be making his way towards her, but at first she saw no sign. Then Mark and another man left the Jackieboy Saloon. She saw Elben the town marshal and others she recognized as his deputies surround the pair in a menacing half-circle. A pair of riders came slowly along the street into town, beyond the Jackieboy Saloon but Freda gave them no second glance. She stared at the men before the saloon for another moment. Then she turned and darted back into the store.

"Dusty!" she gasped. "Mark's in trouble."

CHAPTER SIX

The Ysabel Kid Meets A Lady

HOLDING his big white stallion to a mile devouring trot the Ysabel Kid rode north. He found and now followed the signs of last year's drives with no difficulty for the sign lay plain for a man to see.

Ahead lay the fence. The Kid saw it and a frown came to his brow. Like Dusty and Mark he hated fences of any kind, probably more so than his friends for they would grudgingly admit some fences had their uses. To the Kid any kind of fence was an anathema. The free-ranging blood of his forefathers, all breeds which never took to being fettered and walled in, revolted against the sight of anything which might bring an end to the open range.

Touching the white's flanks the Kid swung to one side, heading down the stream which marked the boundary of Double K and which carried the barbed wire on the bank he rode along. Likely Double K had men watching the fence and he did not want to be delayed in obeying Dusty's orders while he made war.

The wire ended at a point where the stream made a sharp curve and formed the end of the narrows. After scanning the area the Kid allowed Blackie to wade into and through the water. At the other side he set his course across the narrows, in the correct direction, with the ease of a sailor using a compass to navigate his ship. All the range ahead of him looked good, plenty of grass, enough water, and dotted with small woods in which the cattle might shelter during bad weather. A man who owned such a spread should have no need to jump his neighbors' land for more grazing.

Caution had always been a by-word for the Kid. A man

didn't live as he'd lived during his formative years* without developing the instincts and caution of a lobo wolf. Not even in times of peace and on the safe ranges of the OD Connected did the Ysabel Kid ride blindly and blithely along. Always there was caution, always his eyes and ears stayed alert for any slight warning sound or flickering sight which might herald the coming of danger.

So the two men who appeared on a rim half a mile off to his right did not take the Kid by surprise. He heard one of them yell, saw them set spurs to work and send their horses forward at a gallop. As yet he did not speed up the big white stallion. Blackie could allow the men to come in much closer before he need increase his pace any. The Kid knew his horse could easily leave behind the mounts of the Double K men, happen he felt like it. One word would see the white running away from the pursuers, leaving them behind as if they had lead weights lashed to their legs.

"Couldn't catch up even if they wanted to, old Blackie hoss," drawled the Kid. "Which same they want to, and are trying to."

After dispensing this rather left-handed cowboy logic the Kid relaxed in his saddle. When the two men passed behind a clump of bushes out of sight for a few moments he bent and drew his rifle from the saddleboot. With the old "yellowboy" in his hands he knew he could handle the two men and prevent their coming close enough to bother him.

There had been a time, just after the War, when the Kid's handling of the pursuit would have been far different. Then he would have found cover and used his old Mississippi rifle (he did not own a Winchester Model of 1866 "yellowboy" rifle in those days) to down one of the following pair for sure and probably both if the other did not take the hint. Those days ended on the Brownsville trail when he met the man who turned him from a border smuggler into a useful member of society. It had been Dusty Fog who prevented the Kid sliding into worse forms of law-breaking than the running of contraband and gave him a slightly higher idea of the value of human life. So the Kid contented himself in having the rifle ready. If the men became too intrusive he could easily take steps to dis-

* Told of in COMANCHE

courage them, but he aimed to let them make the first move.

For a mile the Kid rode at the same pace and the men, knowing the futility of trying to close with him and his fast moving horse, clung to his trail like a pair of buzzards watching a trail herd for weak steers dropping out. Only the Kid was no weak steer, he didn't aim to get caught or to drop out.

A woman's scream shattered the air, coming from a small *bosque,* a clump of trees to the Kid's right. He brought the big white stallion to a halt, looking in the direction of the sound. It might be a trick to lure him close, to hold him for the two following men, only that scream sounded a whole lot too good for pretence. Then his ears caught another sound, low, menacing, one which set Blackie fiddle-footing nervously. The hunting snarl of an angry cougar.

Without a thought of the following gunmen, the Kid headed his big white horse forward fast, making for the *bosque.* Once more the scream rang out, than he saw, among the trees, what caused the terror.

The young woman stood back up against a tree, her face pale, her mouth open for another scream. On top of a rock, facing her, crouched for a spring, with its tail lashing back and forwards, was a big, old, tom cougar. To one side, reins tangled in a blue-berry bush, fighting wildly to get free, eyes rolling in terror, a fine looking bay horse raised enough noise to effectively cover the sound of the approaching white stallion and its rider.

Only rarely would a cougar, even one as big as the old tom, chance attacking a human being without the incentive of real hunger and the human being bad hurt, or without being cornered. Probably the cougar had its eye on horse-flesh, it's favorite food, and would have ignored the young woman. However fear carries its own distinctive scent and the cougar caught it, knowing the human being feared it. So the big tom changed its mind, decided to take the woman as being an even easier kill than the horse.

Bringing his brass-framed Winchester to his shoulder the Kid sighted and fired all in one incredibly swift move. The cougar had caught some sound Blackie made and swung its head to investigate the new menace. Even before its cat-quick reactions could carry it in a long bound to safety at one side, the cougar took lead. The Winchester spat out, throwing back echoes from the surrounding trees, the cougar gave out with a startled squalling wail, sprang from the rock, back arched in pain and hurling at the young woman.

Moving so fast the lever looked almost like a blur the Ysabel Kid threw two more shots into the cougar, spinning it around in the air and dropping it in a lifeless heap almost at her feet. The young woman stared down, trying to back further into the tree trunk, not knowing she need no longer fear the animal.

"You all right, ma'am?" asked the Kid, coming down from Blackie, landing before the girl and holding his rifle ready.

For a long moment she did not reply. She stood with her face against the trees, not sobbing or making any sound, just frozen rigid with the reaction of her narrow escape. Then with an almost physical effort, she seemed to get control of herself and turned towards him.

"Yes, thank you," she said in an accent which sounded alien and strange to the Kid's ears. "I'm afraid I was rather foolish. Mr. Dune told me there were mountain lions in this area, but I'd always heard they don't attack human beings."

"Don't often," replied the Kid, knowing she wanted to talk, to shake the last of her fear away. "This'n most likely was hungry and figured you'd make an easier meal than the hoss."

Holding the "yellowboy" in his right hand and sweeping off the black Stetson with his left, the Kid looked at the girl his timely arrival saved. Without a doubt she was one of the most beautiful young women he had ever seen. Maybe a mite taller than a man'd want, but not so tall as to appear gawky and awkward. She had hair as black as his own, neat and tidily cared for. Her face would draw admiring glances in any company and she'd come second to none in the beauty stakes. Her eyes, now the fear left them, looked warm, yet not bold. She wore a black eastern riding habit of a kind he had never seen before. A top hat sat on her head and a veil trailed down from the brim to fasten on to her jacket belt. Her outfit did nothing to hide the fact that she was a very shapely young woman.

She dusted herself off, knocking the leaves from her dress. "He took me by surprise, my horse took fright and tossed me off. You came just in time. Thank you."

"It wasn't nothing," replied the Kid, feeling just a shade uncomfortable in her presence.

"I can't remember ever having seen you around the ranch," she went on. "Of course Papa and I only arrived two days ago and I haven't met all the sta—cowhands yet. Mr. Dune warned me about the cougar, but I wanted to see one close up."

"Likely this old tom," replied the Kid with a grin, stirring the dead cougar with his toe, "wanted to see a real live gal close up, too."

For an instant a slight frown came to the young woman's face, then it was replaced by a smile. When the Ysabel Kid grinned in that manner he looked about fourteen years old and as innocent as a pew-full of choirboys who had put tintacks on the organ player's chair. No woman, especially one as young as this, could resist such a smile. She smiled also, it made her look even more beautiful.

The Kid looked to the young woman. From the way she talked she must be the Double K's new boss's daughter. He decided to ask if this was correct, then try and explain the dangers of putting fences around property, especially across what had always been an open trail.

Only he did not get a chance. The big white stallion swung its head in the direction they'd come, letting out a warning snort. It stood with ears pricked and nostrils working, looking for all the world like a wild animal. Reading the warning, the Kid turned fast, but he did not try to raise his rifle for he stood under the guns of the two men who followed him across the range.

"Just stay right where you are, cownurse!" one ordered.

The Kid stood fast, only he didn't let his rifle fall. He kept it in his hand, muzzle pointing to the ground, but ready for use. Then the girl stepped forward, coming between the Kid and the two men. She brought a worried look to two faces for the men could not shoot without endangering her life.

"It's all right," she said. "The young man saved my life, prevented a mountain lion from attacking me."

Still the two men did not lower their weapons, nor relax. The taller made a gesture towards the Kid.

"He's not one of our riders, Miss Keller," he said.

"Aren't you?" she asked, turned towards the Kid. "I suppose you're trespassing really, but we can overlook it this time. Put away your guns, please."

For all her strange sounding accent she made it clear that when she gave an order she expected it to be obeyed. The Kid watched the men and the girl, thinking how her tone sounded like Dusty's cousin, Betty Hardin, the voice of a self-willed young woman who was full used to be obeyed. Her last words had been directed to the two men.

They scowled, clearly not liking the idea, but holstering their guns for all of that. Their duty was to patrol the range and discourage stray drifters from crossing. Neither had seen Tring's discomforted bunch returning from the abortive raid on Lasalle's place and did not know anything about the Kid's part in it. They did know that they should have stopped him getting this far in. They should also most definitely have never allowed him to get so close to Norma Keller, only daughter of the new owner of the Double K. However Norma had given orders and they were instructed to obey her.

Norma turned to the Kid and looked him over with some interest. Once more he felt like a bashful schoolboy—then he remembered, in the early days he felt just the same when Betty Hardin looked at him.

"What are you doing on my father's land?" she asked coolly.

"Just passing through, ma'am, headed north to Bent's Ford, that's over the Indian Nation line a piece."

"I know!" she answered. "Do you make a habit of riding across other people's property?"

For a moment anger flickered in the Kid's eyes. Then he remembered that the girl was English, likely they did things a mite different over there. Only now she was in Texas and would need to change some of her ideas. He held down his angry reply and said:

"This here's always been open range country, ma'am. In Texas folks don't stop a stranger from crossing their land as long as he does no damage and makes no grief for the owners."

"I see," replied the girl, and her entire tone had changed. "Of course one must remember this is a new—I'm sorry if I snapped. Never let it be said the Keller family failed to conform with the local custom. Would you care to come to the ranch and allow father to thank you in a more suitable manner?"

For an instant the two men looked relieved, but the Kid shook his head.

"Thank you, no, ma'am," he replied. "I've got to make Bent's Ford as soon as I can. Got me a riding chore out from there and I can't miss it. Say, whyn't you have these boys here skin out that ole cougar, or tote it back to your place and have it done. It'll make a dandy footrug and you'll likely have a story to tell folks about it."

"Why yes, that's a good idea," she answered and turned to the men. "Will you attend to it, please?"

The word "please" might be there, but the Kid got the idea the girl aimed to have her orders carried out for all of being polite. He knew he could now ride on without needing to bother about the two men. He held his rifle in both hands, ready to handle any refusal, or try at holding him, but the men turned to walk towards the cougar.

Quickly the Kid swung afork his big stallion. He booted the rifle, removed his hat once more and gave Norma an elegant salute.

"*Adios*, ma'am," he said, watching the two men.

"Good-bye," she answered, looking at the white with appreciation showing in her eyes for she knew a good horse when she saw one. "If you are ever in this part of the country again drop in and see us. My father would be pleased to meet you."

"I'll do just that, ma'am," the Kid replied, setting his hat on his head.

Turning his horse the Kid rode out of the *bosque* and headed north once more, making for Bent's Ford. He knew neither of the men would follow him now, they would be too busy with the cougar. However the Double K might have more riders on it, men who also aimed to keep strangers away. He allowed Blackie to make a better pace and did not relax, not even after he left the narrows and passed over the Texas line into the Indian Nations.

Norma Keller watched the two men as they profanely tried to load the cougar on to one of their horses, a horse which showed a marked reluctance at having anything at all to do with such a creature. Then she went to her own horse and calmed it down feeling annoyed that she had not cared for the animal earlier. Not until she managed to quieten the horse and freed it did her eyes go back to the men. By now they had managed to get the cougar's body across the back of the horse and lashed it into place.

A smile flickered across her face as she thought of the innocent looking boy whose arrival saved her life. He looked quite friendly and so young to handle a rifle so well. The three holes in the cougar's body (she smiled as she found herself no longer using the term mountain lion) could be covered by the palm of her hand and any one would have proved fatal. She hoped the holes could be covered and somebody could tan and cure the skin for her.

The smile stayed as she thought of the way that the youngster spoke. She made a mental note to remember this was not the East Riding of Yorkshire, but a new country with different ways. In England no worker would have dared address her on such terms of equality and she found the sensation stimulating. Norma Keller was no snob. The upper-class to which she belonged rarely were snobs, that was the privilege of the newly-rich, the intellectuals who felt unsure of their position in life. She felt no snobbish class-distinction against the Kid, nor any annoyance at the way in which he addressed her. He spoke politely, yet without in any way being subservient. She wondered who he was, where he came from, what his position in life might be. Then she smiled still more. It would be highly unlikely that she ever met the boy again. Or was he such a boy? He seemed to be ageless. She wished she might get to know him better. He seemed to be so much better natured and pleasant than the rather sullen men hired by Mr. Mallick while she and her father travelled from their home in England, the home they would never return to again.

"All set, Miss Keller," growled one of the men.

"Good," she replied, allowing him to help her mount to the side-saddle she used. "Let's get that creature home before it stiffens and can't be skinned."

They rode back through the *bosque* and out at the far side. Norma threw her eyes over the range, searching for some sign of her rescuer, but seeing none. So she rode with the two men, comparing them with him and not to their advantage. There was so much she wanted to know about this new land, so much they might have taught her, but they seemed sullen and uncommunicative.

For a mile or so they rode in silence, then she saw a rider top a rim and head towards them, a man who looked familiar.

"That's Mr. Dune, isn't it?" she asked.

"Yeah," grunted the taller man. "That Dune all right."

Norma frowned for she did not approve of employees referring in such a manner to their foreman. However she made no comment for Norma had already seen a different standard of behaviour seemed common in this new land she and her father picked for their home.

Coming up at a gallop Dune brought his horse to a sliding halt, eager to impress Norma with his riding skill. He was something of a range-country dandy and fashion-plate, dressed to the height of cowhand fashion. Although only a medium-sized man Buck Dune fancied himself as quite a lady-killer, a gallant with a string of conquests which covered the length and breadth of the west.

Since the girl's arrival at the ranch Dune had tried to bear down on her with the full force of his charm and personality. Her father had money, more money than Dune could ever recollect seeing at one time and Dune was more than willing to find acceptance into the Keller family circle. Only the charm which attracted girls in the better class saloons, dancehalls and cat-houses; plus a few women not from that class but who should have shown better sense; failed where Norma Keller was concerned. Towards him the girl displayed a cool attitude. She always answered his greetings, asked questions and listened with interest to his answers but always with calm detachment, oblivious to his swarthy good looks, his neatly trimmed moustache, or the faint scent of bay rum which always clung to him. She treated him as a valued employee and made it plain that was how things would remain.

This morning the girl's flat refusal to allow him to act as her guide when she went riding left him feeling as awkward and shambling as a barefooted yokel boy. It had been an unusual feeling and he still did not know if he liked it or not.

"Howdy, Miss Keller," he greeted, removing his hat in a graceful gesture guaranteed to prove his genteel upbringing. Then his eyes went to the cougar's body. "Where did you get that cat?"

"I had an adventure," she replied, smiling and forgetting

that he warned her of the presence of cougars on the range. She did not notice his surprise at seeing the one her rescuer had killed. "A young man shot it when it tried to attack me."

Dune threw a glance at the two gunmen. He had clean forgotten warning the girl about the danger of mountain lions. It had been no more than an excuse to get Norma to accept his offer of guidance and company. Now it seemed she had really met up with a cougar and he lost the chance of acting as a gallant heroic rescuer.

He forgot that matter in something more urgent. His eyes stayed on the two gunmen but he remembered just in time not to say too much before the girl. If the young man was no more than a drifting cowhand it would not be too bad, for he would be unlikely to return.

"You'd best get it right back to the spread and skin it out," he said, hoping the men would read his words right.

It seemed they did, for the one toting the cougar started his horse forward, Norma at his side. The other man held his mount back, reading the message in Dune's eyes.

"Who was he?" growled Dune after the girl had ridden away.

"Some kid on a damned great white hoss," replied the other man. "It sure could move. We saw it from half a mile back and hadn't gone two hundred yards afore we knew there wasn't a chance in hell of us catching up to him."

An explosive snorted curse left Dune's lips. He let the veneer of charm fall from him and showed what he really was, a killer without moral or scruple. Tring's bunch had returned to the spread, most of them toting shotgun lead and cursing about it, although all might have accounted themselves lucky the gun carried no worse than birdshot which did no more than pierce their hides.

They gave livid and profane descriptions of the trio of men who, according to them, jumped them, held them under guns and pinned down helpless. Dune found the descriptions tallied with three men he had heard much of, although had never met up with. He remembered the Ysabel Kid, the descriptions he'd heard of that tall, dangerous young man. The descriptions often contained references to the Kid's horse, a seventeen-hand white stallion which could run like the wind.

"A tall, young looking, dark faced kid, dressed all in black?" he asked savagely. "Got him a Dragoon Colt and a bowie knife."

"That's him."

"And that's the Ysabel Kid!" snarled Dune, spitting the words out like they burned his mouth. "Which way'd he go?"

"Said he was headed for Bent's Ford."

"Reckon he was?"

"That's what he said. Was headed north all right when we put him up."

The two men sat their horses for a moment. Dune dropped a hand to the butt of the Tranter revolver holstered at his side. If the Ysabel Kid was headed for Bent's Ford he was going for some good purpose. Dusty Fog wouldn't send off his left bower* at such a time without good cause. And the Kid had seen Norma Keller. He had seen far too much to be left alive.

"I'll take your hoss, ride a relay after him!" growled Dune.

"And leave me afoot?" answered the other.

"Shout to your pard. Tell him I've got to go into Barlock in a hurry, that's for Miss Keller to hear. They can send another hoss out from the spread."

"What'll I tell Mallick, happen he comes out and wants to see you?" asked the gunman, swinging from his saddle.

"Tell him I've gone to Bent's Ford. That black dressed breed's seen a damned sight too much. He's got to be killed!"

* Left bower. Originally a term used in playing Euchre and meaning the second highest trump.

CHAPTER SEVEN

Jackieboy Disraeli

IN all fairness to Mark Counter it must be said he did not intend to get into any trouble at all.

After visiting the Wells Fargo office and sending a telegraph message which would eventually be delivered to the OD Connected house in the Rio Hondo country, Mark headed towards where he could see Freda's buckboard halted before the general store. In so doing he had to pass the hospitable doors of the Jackieboy Saloon. He saw that Dusty had collected both their horses and taken them down to the store and so would not have wasted time entering the saloon if it had not been for what he saw happening inside.

Mark glanced through the batwing doors, then came to a halt. He was a cowhand, a good one, he was also a cowhand who had seen the treatment handed out to less fortunate members of his trade when they found themselves in a saloon and at odds with the owners.

None of the crowd looked at Mark as he entered. Their full attention centered on the group at the bar. It was this same group at the bar which brought Mark into the room in the first place.

There were three men in the center of the bar, only they hadn't come to it for pleasure, or if the cowhand of the group had he sure didn't look like he was getting any of it.

"The boss told you to clear out of this section. There ain't no work here!"

The speaker stood tall, as tall as Mark Counter and maybe thirty or forty pounds heavier. From the slurred manner of his speech and the battered aspect of his face he had done more than his fair share of fist-fighting in the raw, brutal bare-

knuckle manner. He had powerful arms and big hands, and
was putting both to good use as he held the cowhand pressed
back against the bar.

Held with the huge man's powerful hands gripping, gouging
into his shoulders, the cowhand could do little. He stood six
foot, had good shoulders and lean waist but he looked like a
midget in the hands of the burly brutal bruiser who held him.
His face twisted in agony. It was cheerful most times, maybe
not too handsome, but friendly and pleasant. His clothes
looked northern range fashion, they were not over-expensive,
but his hat and boots both cost good money and his gunbelt,
while not being a fast-man's rig, did not look like a decora-
tion.

Standing to one side of the others a small, tubby man
watched everything with drooling lips and a sadistic gaze. He
was a sallow skinned man, his nose slightly large and bent. He
wore a light dove-grey cutaway jacket of gambler's style, snow
white trousers down which ran a black stripe, primrose yellow
spats and a pair of shoes which shone enough to reflect the
view around him. His shirt bore considerable frills and lace to
it and his bow-tie had an almost feminine look about it. He
stood relaxed at the bar, his posture nearer that a dancehall
girl than of a gambling man. Taking a lace handkerchief from
his cuff he mopped his brow.

"He understands now, Knuckles," he lisped in a falsetto
voice which might have brought down derision on him, but
did not. "Let him free."

On the order Knuckles released his hold. The young cowhand showed he had sand to burn. His right fist lashed
around, smashing into the side of the huge man's bristle-
covered jaw. It was a good blow, swung with weight behind it,
but Knuckles did not even give a sign of knowing it landed. He
grunted and his big left hand came back, slashing into the
cowhand's cheek and sprawling him to the floor.

"He's not learned his lesson, Knuckles!" purred the tubby
man. "Stomp him!"

Like an elephant moving Knuckles stepped towards the
dazed cowhand, lifting a huge foot ready to obey. Through
the pain mists the cowhand saw Knuckles towering over him,
tried to force himself into some kind of action.

Two hands descended on Knuckles's shoulders. He felt himself heaved back and propelled violently away from the bar. A mutter of surprise ran through the saloon as the huge bouncer went reeling and staggering backwards. Not one of the watching crowd had expected to see a man brave, or foolish, enough to tangle with the huge bouncer of the Jackieboy Saloon.

Nor had Knuckles. Caught with one foot off the ground he could do nothing to prevent himself reeling backwards. He smashed down to a table which shattered under his weight and deposited him in a heap on the ground.

"You shouldn't have done that, cowboy!" said the tubby man. "Now you've made Knuckles angry."

Which could have been classed as the understatement of the year. Knuckles had gone past mere anger. He snarled with rage, foam forming on his lips as he rolled over on to hands and knees. One hand clamped on a table leg he came to his feet holding it like a club in his fist. He attacked with a rush as dangerous as the charge of a long-horn bull.

Not a person in the room spoke as they watched. The big blond Texan looked strong, but no man had ever stood up to Knuckles in one of his murderous rages.

With the table leg raised Knuckles came in fast. Mark watched him, seeing the strength, noticing the slowness. Knuckles had been a prize-fighter but like most of his kind fought with brute strength alone, by standing toe-to-toe and trading blows until one of them could take no more. His instinct for fighting had become settled into his routine and he could not believe that any other man fought in a different manner. So he expected, if indeed he troubled to think about it all, that Mark would stand there to be hit with the table leg. Believing this he launched a blow that should have flattened Mark's head level with his shoulders. Only it did not land.

At the last instant, when most folks watching thought he had left it too late, Mark sidestepped the rush. The table leg missed him and shattered to pieces on the floor. Carried forward by his own impetus Knuckles lost his balance once more. He staggered forward a step and Mark, with a grace and agility a lighter, smaller man might have envied, pivoted around and threw a punch. The blow, driven with strength, skill and precision, traveled fast and landed hard. It crashed into and mangled still more Knuckles's fight-damaged right ear.

Knuckles shot forward, head down and with no control over

his body. The man's close-cropped skull smashed into the bar front and shattered through it. He disappeared behind the bar, knocking the bartender from his feet and preventing him from grabbing up the ten gauge shotgun which lay under the counter for use at such times. With a yell the bartender went down, Knuckles's heavy body on top of him.

A concerted gasp rose from the watching crowd. Everyone expected Knuckles to come roaring through the hole in the bar and stomp the big Texan clear into the floorboards. In this they were to be disappointed for it would be another four hours before Knuckles could move under his own power again.

"I don't like you, you nasty man!" hissed the tubby man from behind Mark. "I don't like you at all!"

The words brought Mark around in a fast turn. He found his aid in handling the matter unnecessary. Even as the tubby man's hand started to lift from his pocket with something metallic glinting in it, the young cowhand took a hand. He rose to one knee, his right fist caught the man in the fat belly and folded him like a closed jack-knife. Then the cowhand came to his feet, the other fist lashed up to catch the tubby man's jaw, jerking him erect and over on to his back. A nickel plated Remington Double Derringer came from the fat man's pocket, left his hand to fly across the room as he fell. The gun looked dainty and fancy enough to have come from the garter of a high-class saloon girl, but that made it no less deadly.

"Freeze!" Mark barked, hearing the rumble of talk from the crowd and facing them with his matched Army Colts in his hands, lined in their general direction.

They all froze for not one member of the crowd failed to notice how fast the guns came out, nor how competently Mark handled them. Apart from the whining and moaning of the tubby man on the floor not a sound came for a long moment.

Mark's nostrils quivered. He could smell a rich perfume which seemed to be vaguely familiar, yet he could not remember for the moment where he last smelled it. This time he could locate the source for the fat shape sprawled on the floor reeked of it. The perfume should mean something, Mark knew. The fat man smelled of the perfume, it rose and hung around him like a cloud.

"Look here, mister," said one of the customers in a conciliatory tone. "We don't know what set Jackieboy there and Knuckles on to the cowhand. Reckon anything between you and him's your affair and he ain't doing nothing much about it. But I got a chance of filling a straight here."

"Go ahead then," replied Mark, holstering his guns. "Only don't blame me if you miss filling it."

The young cowhand had made his feet now. He looked around the room, then said, "We'd best get out of here. Likely somebody's gone for the law."

"Sure," Mark agreed. "What started all this fuss?"

"There you got me. I came in, bought me a drink. Then I asked if there was a chance of taking a riding chore in these parts and the next thing I knew they was both of them on me. The name's Morg Summers."

From his talk Morg hailed from the north country. He looked like a competent cowhand, one who could be relied on to stay loyal to any brand into whose wagon he threw his bedroll.

"I'm Mark Counter," Mark answered as they walked side by side across the room. "Happen you got no other plans I might be able to put a riding chore your way real soon."

They reached the doors and passed forth. From the moment their feet hit the sidewalk both knew they were in trouble. It showed in the shape of the eight men who lounged around in a half circle before the doors. They wore deputy marshal's badges and looked as mean a pack of cut-throats as a man could want to see. Only this looked like the town marshal had extra staff, for Lasalle claimed but eight men worked for Elben and two remained safely hog-tied in the Land Agent's office.

In the center of the group, with a pomaded blond hair, a moustache and goatee beard stood the town marshal himself, looking like a fugitive from a Bill-show. He had a high crowned white Stetson, a fringed buckskin jacket, cavalry style trousers with shining Jefferson boots. A gunbelt supporting a matched brace of ivory handled Remington Beals Army revolvers butt forwards in the holsters. All in all he looked far too well dressed to be honest and much too prosperous for a lawman in a small Texas town.

"What went on inside there?" he asked.

"Enough," Mark replied. "You want to tell that swish to

keep his tame bear chained afore somebody throws lead into it.''

"Don't get flip with me!" Elben snarled. "I'm taking you both to jail on charges of assault and disturbing the peace.''

"I got assaulted and my peace disturbed too," Morg answered. "You going to jail the folks who done it?''

"Shut your mouth!" Elben replied.

"Happen I ever get to be a taxpayer you sure won't get my vote," Morg threatened. "How about it, Mark?''

Mark knew the men wouldn't chance using guns against him unless they were pushed into it. He also knew he could not risk being taken to jail. Any time now the men down in Mallick's office might wriggle their way free, or might be found. Before that happened Freda must be taken safely out of town. Mallick didn't look the kind of man who would let her being a woman stop him from roughing her up or worse. Two against eight were poor odds, but Dusty was on hand and could likely get to them in time to help.

The game was taken out of Mark's hands. A man darted from the saloon, arms clamping around the big Texan from behind. At the same moment the rest jumped into the fray.

While still held from behind by a man who had some strength in his arms, Mark brought up his feet, rammed them into the chests of the deputies who came at him from the front. He thrust out the legs and reeled them backwards. The man holding him staggered, but still retained his grip. To one side Morg Summers proved that he could handle his end in a rough-house even against odds.

A face appeared before Mark, a snarling face surrounded with pomaded hair. Elben moved forward snarling, "You lousy cow-nurses're going to learn not to play rough in my town.''

He moved his fist brutally into Mark's stomach, bringing a gasp of pain for Mark could do nothing to escape the blow. Even as Elben drew back his fist to hit again, Mark's boot lashed up. Fortunately for Elben the kick did not land full force. Had it landed with all Mark's strength the town marshal would not have risen for a long time. Even with the limited power behind it Elben jack-knifed over and collapsed holding his middle and croaking in pain.

With a surge of his muscles Mark flung the man who held

him first to one side then the other. The man lost his hold and went to one side. Mark shot out a fist which sprawled an attacker backwards, backhanded another into the hitching rail. Then they were at him from all sides. He fought back like a devil-possessed fury. This was Mark's element, in a fight against odds, tangling with hard-cases.

By the time Morg Summers went down four of the deputies lay stretched on the ground, one with a nose spread over most of his face and and all carrying marks from two pairs of hard cowhand fists. Sheer weight of numbers got them down in the end. Mark saw Morg go down, staggered one of his attackers and leapt to try and prevent the young cowhand taking a stomping. A man behind Mark drew his revolver and swung it. Mark heard the hiss of the blow and started to try to avoid it. The barrel of the weapon caught him a glancing blow, but one hard enough to drop him to his hands and knees. He stayed there, head spinning, brain unable to send any instructions to his body or coordinate protective movements.

"Get away from him!" Elben snarled, making his feet and looking down at Mark with an expression of almost maniacal rage. He waved back the remaining deputies who were preparing to attack the fallen Mark. "He's mine and I want to see his blood."

Mark heard the voice. It seemed to come from a long way off. The fight had been rough and not all the blows handed out by himself or Morg. He could not shake the pain from him, clear his head enough to protect himself. He did not see Elben coming at him, nor was the marshal more observant. Only one thing mattered to Elben, that he might take revenge on the blood giant who humiliated him before the town. Snarling in fury he drew back his foot for a kick, looking down at Mark. When he got through the big Texan wouldn't look so handsome, nor so high and mighty. Mark knew none of this. He shook his head to try and clear it and wondered why no more blows landed on him as he tried to get up.

In Roylan's store, Dusty heard the girl's excited words. So did the hired gunman, heard them and read their true meaning. He came up with a hand fanning his side, reaching for his gun. "You're not—!" he began.

Dusty wasted no time. Nor did he rely on his guns to stop the man. He came forward and left the floor in a bound, right, foot lashing out into the gunman's face. The man's body slammed backwards into the counter and clung there. Dusty landed on his feet and threw a punch the moment he hit the floor. His right fist shot out, the gunman's head snapped to one side. He went clear over the cracker barrel, landed flat on his back and did not make another move.

Before Roylan could catch his breath, long before he could get over this unexpected turn of events. Dusty faced him, a Colt lined on his chest.

"You go help your pard, mister," Roylan said quickly. "I'll take care of this here unfortunate feller as was supposed to be protecting me. I've got the note from Mallick to cover me."

Without a word Dusty hurled himself from the building, holstering his Colt as he went. He saw the crowd along the street and headed towards it on the run. Roylan caught Freda by the arm as she started to go after dusty.

"Who is he?" he asked, sounding real puzzled. "What happened and what's coming off, Freda, gal. How the hell did he make that kick and down the gunny. Where'd you get the note from?"

"He's Dusty Fog and helping us!" the girl replied as she tore free from his grip and raced after dusty.

She answered two of Roylan's questions, but not the third. Freda did not know of the small Oriental man down in the Rio Hondo. A man thought to be Chinese by the unenlightened majority, but known to be Japanese by his friends. To Dusty Fog alone this man taught the secrets of karate and ju-jitsu fighting. They stood Dusty in good stead and helped him handle bigger men with considerable ease as had the karate flying high kick Dusty used to set up the deputy for a finish in a hurry.

Along the street Elben drew back his foot and made sure of his balance, the better to savor the forthcoming kicking. He heard the thunder of hooves, saw his men scatter and fell back to avoid being trampled by two horses which raced at him. He opened his mouth to bellow curses and his hands dropped towards his sides.

The taller of the riders unshipped from his saddle, landing between Mark and Elben. He stood tall and slim, almost delicate looking. His clothes were Texas cowhand except for the brown coat he wore, its right side stitched back to leave clear the ivory grips of his low tried Army Colt. His face looked pale, studious almost yet the pallor was tan resisting, not one caused by sitting indoors or through ill health. His right hand made a sight defying flicker and the Colt seemed to almost meet it in midair, muzzle lining full on Elben's middle and ending his move almost as soon as it began.

"Back off, *hombre!*" ordered the slim man.

His pard wheeled the big horse between his knees, halting it and facing the deputies. He held a Winchester rifle in his hands, lining it full on them and ending their attempts to draw weapons. In appearance he was as much a Texas cowhand as his pard. Stocky, capable and tough looking, with rusty red colored hair and a face made for grinning. Only he did not grin now, his eyes flashed anger and he looked like he was only waiting for any excuse to throw lead.

"Is Mark all right, Doc?" asked the rusty-haired cowhand.

"He'd best be," replied the slim man called Doc, watching Elben's hands stay clear of the guns as he backed away.

"This's law matter you've cut in on!" Elben snarled, trying a bluff.

It failed by a good country mile.

"Kicking a man when he's down!" Doc growled back. "That's about the way of a yellow cur-dog like you, Mister, happen you've hurt Mark bad you'd best go dig a great big hole, climb in and pull the top on you."

At that same moment Dusty arrived. He came on foot, but he came real fast. Halting before the gun-hung deputies he looked them over. He clearly recognized the two riders for he did not ask how they came into this affair, or even spare them more than a single glance.

"You lousy scum!" Dusty said quietly, his grey eyes lashing the men. "All of you and they whip you down, put half of you in the street."

"Just a minute, you!" Elben snarled, seeing Dusty's lack of inches and getting bolder. "I'm taking all of you in."

"You and how many regiments of Yankee cavalry, loud mouth? asked the rusty haired cowhand. "This here's Dusty Fog and that's Mark Counter you started fussing in with."

That put a different complexion on things. Elben knew the names well enough. From the way the big Texan fought he could most likely be Mark Counter and where Mark Counter

was Dusty Fog mostly could be found. He could read no sign
of humor in the rusty headed cowhand's face, only deadly
serious warning.

Whatever Elben may have thought on the subject his
deputies acted like they sure enough believed this small man
really was Dusty Fog. They crowded together, those who
could, in a scared bunch. One of them indicated the two new
arrivals.

"That's Rusty Willis and Doc Leroy of the Wedge!" he
whispered in an urgent, warning tone.

This gave the others no comfort. Not only were the two men
named prominent as members of the Wedge trail crew, they
also had long been known as good friends of Dusty Fog and
Mark Counter. The Wedge hired hardy cowhands, men who
could handle their end in any man's fight and the names of
Rusty Willis and Doc Leroy stood high on the roll of honor of
the crew.

Freda arrived, dropping to her knees by Mark, trying to
help him to rise. She steadied him with her arm and gasped,
"Are you all right, Mark?"

That clinched it. The girl gave any of the bunch who might
have doubted them proof that the two Texans were who Rusty
Willis claimed them to be.

Slowly Mark forced himself up towards his feet, the girl
helping him. He pointed towards where Morg lay groaning.
The young cowhand had taken a worse beating than Mark,
due mainly to his being less skilled in the fistic arts than the big
Texan.

"See to him, gal," he ordered.

Turning Mark walked towards Elben, fists clenched. Dusty
caught his arm, held him back as Elben drew away.

"Leave it lie, Mark," he said. "Rusty, fetch that buckboard
from down there by the store. Bring the hosses with it. And
watch the door, there's one inside who might be on his feet
again.

Rusty turned his horse without wondering at Dusty's right
to give him orders. On the way to the store he substituted the
rifle for his Dance Bros. copy of a Colt Dragoon revolver. He
guessed that more than a dispute with the local law enforcement officers caused the trouble here. This town did not need
all the number of deputies who had been in the fight.

"I'll take that loud-mouthed fighting pimp now, Dusty," Mark said, loosening his gun as he gave Elben the Texans' most polite name for a Kansas lawman.

"You'll get on your hoss when it comes and ride out," Dusty answered, then turned his attention to Elben's men. "And you bunch'll go down the jail and stay there. If I see one of you between now and leaving town I'll shoot him on sight. Not you though, marshal. You're staying here. Happen any of them have smart ideas you'll be the first one to go."

Kneeling by the groaning cowhand Freda looked down at his bruised and bloody face. She felt helpless, scared, wondering if the young man might be seriously injured. The cowhand called Doc Leroy dropped to his knees by her side and reached out a hand. She watched the slim, boneless looking hands moving gently, touching and gently feeling. Doc Leroy looked up towards Dusty, showing relief.

"Nothing that won't heal in a few days," he said. "Have to ride the wagon for a spell."

By this time Rusty was returning with the buckboard and horses. He had seen the man he took to be owner of the store calmly club down a groaning deputy who tried to rise from by the counter.

Bringing the buckboard to a halt by the party Rusty leapt down, helping Doc get the groaning Morg on to the seat by Freda's side. Morg clung on, then pointing to a pair of dun horses which stood hip-shot at the hitching rail, gasped they were his string.

"Rest easy, *amigo*," drawled Rusty. "I'll hitch them on behind."

Dusty and the others mounted their horses. The small Texan jerked his carbine from the saddleboot and looked down at Elben.

"We're leaving, marshal," he said. "You shout and tell those boys of your'n that the first shot which comes our way brings you a lead backbone. See, you'll be walking ahead of us until we reach the city limits."

"And then we'll go back and tear your lousy lil town apart board by board," Rusty warned.

Freda needed no telling what to do. She started the buckboard moving forward with Mark, gripping his saddlehorn, kept by her side. Elben shouted louder than he had ever managed before, warning his men not to interfere. He spent the walk to the edge of the town sweating and hoping that none of the others wanted his post as town marshal for they would never have a better chance of getting it. All they would need to do was to pull a trigger and he'd be deader than cold pork.

All in all Elben felt relieved when he reached the edge of town and obeyed Dusty's order to toss away his matched guns. He prided himself in those expensive Remingtons, but they could be recovered and cleaned later, whereas he possessed but one life which could not be recovered if lead caught him in the right place.

Not until Dusty's party had passed out of sight did Elben return to the town. He found the owner of the saloon, Jackie-boy Disraeli, nursing a swollen jaw and in a fit of rage.

"What happened out there?" Disraeli screamed, sounding more like a hysterical woman than a dangerous man. "Why didn't you smash those men to a pulp for what they did to Knuckles and me?"

"That was Dusty Fog and Mark Counter, boss," Elben replied, hating having to call the saloonkeeper by such a name, but knowing better than to fail while Knuckles still lived. "They had that Lasalle gal with them and two of the Wedge crew. The girl was in to buy supplies."

Elben's voice shook. On the way back to town an awful thought struck him. He suddenly realized just what a risk he had taken. If his kick had landed on Mark Counter he likely wouldn't be alive now to think about it.

"So Lasalle's girl bought supplies," Disraeli hissed. "Then she must have sold out."

At that moment Roylan arrived with his story about how the deputy had been felled by Dusty Fog who then terrorized him and got away. The storekeeper tossed Mallick's note before Disraeli.

"Freda Lasalle had this and your deputy didn't say who Dusty Fog was," he said. "So I served her."

In this Royland cleared his name before blame could be fixed. He did not fear Disraeli and Mallick, but knew they could ruin him, so didn't aim to give them a chance. They had no proof of what happened in his place and he doubted if the deputy could say anything that might give the lie to his story.

Disraeli headed a rush for Mallick's office where they broke open the door and released an irate Mallick and his men. It took some time before the Land Agent could talk. He slumped in his chair, stiff and sore, glowering at Elben.

"We bring extra men to help handle the town and four cowhands ride all over you," he snarled, after hearing the story. "Elben, you're a— Hell-fire and damnation! They took that map I tore up and threw into the wastepaper-basket."

"I thought you destroyed it," hissed Disraeli. Only he, Mallick and Elben now stood in the office. "Why didn't you?"

"Because I didn't get a chance. They came before I could. Now there's only one thing to do. Get to Lasalle's place and kill every last one of them—and fast!"

CHAPTER EIGHT

The Ysabel Kid Meets
A Gentleman's Gentleman

A SMALL drifting cloud of dust on the horizon down to the south warned the Ysabel Kid he had somebody on his trail. He drew rein on top of a hill and looked along his backtrail. He saw the following rider at a distance where most folks could have made out only a tiny, indistinguishable blob. The Kid not only saw the man, but could tell he had two horses along. This in itself meant nothing for many men took their own string of horses along with them. The direction from which he appeared told a story. He came from the Double K area and the Kid knew few riders would get across without being halted by the hired guns and turned back in their tracks.

"He's after us, old Blackie hoss," drawled the Kid. "Dang my fool Comanche way of telling the truth when I'm questioned politelike. I should remember I'm a paleface, most times, and that as such I can be the biggest danged liar in the world without worrying."

The big white snorted gently, wanting to be moving again. With a grin the Kid started Blackie on his way again.

"Wonder what he wants?" he mused, talking to the horse, but never relaxing his wolf cautious watching of the trail ahead of him. The man was still too far behind to cause any menace. "Must be one of that bunch from this morning and looking for evens. Waal, he can have his chance when he comes closer."

Only the man did not seem to be pushing his horse to close up, nor riding the two mounts in rotation, travelling relay fashion. The kid knew he could make his tracks so difficult that he could delay the man—if he happened to be following the Kid's trail. The Kid told that pair of hired guns back on

Double K where he headed and the following man would not
waste time in tracking, but by riding straight for Bent's Ford
could be on hand when the Kid arrived. With that thought in
mind the Kid decided to continue to Bent's Ford, making sure
he arrived before the other man and so be able to keep a wary
eye on all new arrivals.

The sun was long set when the Kid saw the buildings, stream
and lake known the length of the great inter-state cattle trails
as Bent's Ford. The main house showed lights and even where
he sat the Kid could hear music from the bar-room so he did
not need to worry about disturbing the other guests by his arrival.

Why Bent's Ford had such a name when there appeared to
be nothing of fordable nature has been told elsewhere.* The
place served as a stopping off and watering point for the trail
herds headed north across the Indian Nations. On this night
however no herd bedded down near at hand. There were
horses in the corrals, two big Conestoga wagons standing to
one side, teamless and silent, the normal kind of scene for
Bent's most any night of the week.

The Kid rode steadily down towards the buildings. He could
almost swear the man following him had not managed to get
ahead during the dark hours. For all that he did not leave his
leg-weary white stallion in the corral. The horse stood out
amongst others like a snow-drift and would easily be noticed.
Also Blackie did not take to having strange horses around him
and could be very forceful in his objections.

Using the prerogative of an old friend, the Kid took his
horse to Bent's private stables and found, as he hoped, an
empty stall. He meant to attend to his horse before thinking of
himself. With Blackie cooled down, watered and supplied with
both grain and hay, the Kid left his saddle hanging on the
burro in the corner. He drew the old "yellow boy" from the
saddleboot and headed for the barroom.

Although busily occupied in wiping over a glass with a piece
of cloth, the bartender found time to look up and nod a
greeting to the new arrival.

"Howdy, Kid," he greeted. "Looking for Wes Hardin?"

"He here?"

"By the wall there, playing poker with the boss."

* Told in THE HALF-BREED

The bartender and the Kid exchanged glances and broad grins. The poker games between Wes Hardin, Texas gunfighter, and Duke Bent, owner of Bent's Ford, were famous along the cattle trails. In serious play and skill the games stood high for both men were past masters at the ancient arts of betting and bluffing known as poker. Yet neither had ever come out of a game more than five or so dollars ahead for they played a five to ten cent limit. This did not affect the way in which they played for they gave each deal enough concentration for a thousand dollar pot.

Before he crossed the room, the Kid looked around. The usual kind of crowd for Bent's Ford looked to be present. A few cowhands who spent the winter up north and were now either headed home or waiting in hope of taking on with another trail drive. Travelling salesmen, flashily dressed, loud-talking, boastful as they waited for stage coaches. A trio of the blue uniformed cavalrymen and a buckskin clad scout shared a table. None of them looked to have just finished a long, hard ride.

"Anybody new in, Charlie?" he asked.

"You're the first since sundown," the bartender answered.

"Check this in for me then," drawled the Kid, passing his rifle to the other man who placed it with the double barrelled ten gauge under the bar counter.

With his weapon out of the way, the Kid crossed the room towards where Bent played poker. He stood for a moment studying Bent's burly build, gambler style clothes and remembering the big man made this place almost single-handed, brought it to its present high standard by hard work and guts. Bent had been a cavalry scout, one of the best. He'd also been a lawman, tough and honest. And Bent was all man in the Kid's eyes.

With his back to the wall in the manner of one of his kind, Wes Hardin, most feared gunfighter in Texas, studied his cards. He was tall, slender, with a dark expressionless face and cold, wolf-savage eyes. Hardin wore the dress of a top-hand with cattle, which he was, he also wore a gunbelt which carried a brace of matched Army Colts in the butt forward holsters of a real fast man with a gun. He was that too.

"I'll raise you!" Bent said, fanning his cards between powerful fingers.

"Will you now?" replied Hardin. "I'm going to see that raise and up it."

The Kid watched all this, knowing the two men were completely oblivious of his presence. He moved around to see Hardin's cards, a grin came to his face and he did something no other man in the room would dare to do.

"Should be ashamed of yourself, Wes," he said, "raising on less'n pair of eights like that."

Slamming down his cards with an exclamation of disgust Hardin thrust back his chair and glared at the Indian-dark boy before him. The customers at nearby tables prepared to head for cover when guns roared forth.

"Hello, Lon," said Hardin, relaxing slightly when he saw who cut in. "What damn fool game you playing, you crazy Comanche. I was all set to bluff Bent clear out of the pot."

"Huh!" granted Bent. "You didn't fool me one lil bit." He raked in the pile of chips and started to count them. "Make it you owe me a dollar fifty, Wes."

"Bet you over counted, like always."

The two men glared at each other. They began a lengthy argument, each man casting reflections on the other's morals and general honesty. Things passed between them, insults rocked back and forwards, which would have seen hands flashing hipwards and the thunder of guns if spoken by a stranger.

Somehow the argument got sidetracked as, alternating between recrimination and personal abuse, they started to argue heatedly about a disputed call in a wild card game some three years before. Just what this had to do with the present disagreement passed the Kid's understanding as neither of the men had held the disputed hand, in fact had not even been in the pot where it came up.

A burst of laughter from the Kid brought an end to the argument and they turned their anger on him, studying him with plain disgust.

"What's amusing you, you danged Comanche?" Hardin growled.

"You pair are," answered the grinning Kid. "I've seen you both lose and win plenty without a word, in high stake games. Yet you're sat here whittle-whanging over who won a measly dollar fifty."

"You wouldn't understand it at all, Kid," Bent answered. "It's all a matter of principles, which same you've got none of."

"Man!" whooped the Kid. "Happen principles make folks act like you pair I sure don't want any."

Hardin's face grew more serious, though only men who knew him as well as the Kid and Bent would have noticed it.

"Where at's Dusty and Mark, Lon?" he asked. "I tried to make Moondog City, when I heard about Cousin Danny."*

"We handled it, Wes."

"Cousin Dusty all right now? He felt strong about that lil brother of his."

"He's over it now."

From the way the Kid spoke both men knew the subject was closed. He did not intend talking about the happenings in the town of Moondog. The sense of loss he felt at the death of Dusty's younger, though not smaller brother, still hung on. He did not offer to tell what happened when Dusty, Mark, Red Blaze and himself came to Moondog. They came to see how Danny Fog handled his duties as a Texas Ranger and had found him beaten to death. Danny Fog died because the town did not dare back him against Sandra Howkins' wolf-pack of hired killers. The Kid did not care to think of the days when he, Dusty and Mark stayed in Moondog and brought an end to the woman's reign of terror.

"Been any sign of the OD Connected herd yet?" asked the Kid, not only changing the subject but also getting down to the urgent business which brought him north.

"Nope, we haven't seen any sign of it," Bent replied. "You fixing to meet up with it here?"

"Was. Only we got us a mite of fuss down below the Texas line. Might take us a spell to handle it and we don't want Red Blaze coming down trail to help us, or waiting here for us to join up."

Due to having been followed the Kid was more than usually alert and watchful. So he saw the man who entered the saloon and stood just inside the doors, looking around. One glance told the Kid this man had not been on his trail, for the trailer had been a westerner and the new arrival anything but that.

He stood maybe five foot eight, slim and erect. His sober
* Told in A TOWN CALLED YELLOWDOG

black suit was well pressed and tidy, his shirt white and his tie of eastern pattern and sober hue. Though his head had lost some of its hair and his face looked parchment-like, expressionless, he carried himself with quiet dignity as he crossed towards where Bent sat at the table. Halting by the table the newcomer coughed discreetly to attract attention to himself.

"Has Sir James' man arrived to guide us to his residence, landlord?" he asked in a strange sounding accent.

"Nope," Bent answered, having grown used to being addressed as landlord by this sober looking dude. "Did you pass anybody on the way north, Lon?"

"Nary a soul," replied the Kid. "You all expecting somebody, friend?"

Swivelling an eye in the Kid's direction, the man looked him over from head to toe. The Kid had ridden hard all day and his black clothes did not look their best, but he reckoned that to be his own concern. To the Kid it seemed this pasty-faced dude did not approve of him or his trail-dirty appearance. This annoyed the Kid, never a man to allow a dude to take liberties with him.

Bent knew this and cut in hurriedly, saying, "Mr. Weems here's expecting one of the Double K to come and guide him and his folks down to the spread."

At first Bent had not taken to Weems. Weems came down from the north with two big Conestoga wagons, each well loaded, but drawn by good horses of a type rarely seen in the west, great heavy legged and powerful creatures which Weems called shire horses. The two wagons had been driven by a pair of gaunt men dressed in a style Bent had never seen before. Two women rode in the wagons and, strangely to western eyes, they did not ride together. Bent suggested that the men shared a room and the two women another. The suggestion was greeted with horror by all concerned, the two drivers insisting it wouldn't be proper to share a room with Mr. Weems and the pretty, snub-nosed, poorly dressed girl stated firmly she could not possibly use the same room as Miss Trumble.

It took Bent a short time to understand the social standing so firmly ingrained in these English travellers. They did not live by the same standards as the men of the West. To the girl, Weems called her a 'tween maid, it was unthinkable that she should room with so exalted a person as Miss Trumble who appeared to be a housekeeper of some kind. So he arranged for the girl to use a small room while Miss Trumble and Weems took two of his expensive guest rooms and the two men insisted on spending the night in the wagons.

"You-all work for Keller, mister?" asked the Kid, his voice sounding Comanche-mean.

"I am *Sir James* Keller's man," replied Weems haughtily and laying great emphasis on the third and fourth words.

"Never took you for a gal!" answered the Kid, getting more riled at the thought of a dude trying to make a fool of him.

Once more Bent intervened in the interests of peace and quiet. "Mr. Weems is a valet, Lon," he said.

"A valley?" asked the Kid, sounding puzzled and wondering if Bent was joining in some kind of a joke.

"V-a-l-e-t, not v-a-l-l-e-y," Bent explained.

"A gentleman's gentlemen," Weems went on, as if that would clear up any doubts the Kid still held.

"Like Tommy Okasi is to Uncle Devil," Hardin put in, helping to clarify the duties of a valet in a manner the Kid understood.

"Never heard ole Tommy called anything as fancy as a valet," drawled the Kid although he knew now what Weems did for his living.

"There's not likely to be anybody up here today," Bent told Weems. "If your boss hasn't anybody here in the morning you could send a telegraph message to Barlock and let him know you've arrived here. Or you could see if there's anybody going down trail who'll act as a guide. But you won't be able to start until the morning either way."

"Thank you, I yield to your greater knowledge."

With that Weems turned and walked towards the bar. Bent looked down at the cards, then raised his eyes to the Kid's face. The struggle between possible financial gains at poker and his keenness at quartet singing warred for a moment and music won out.

"Say, Lon," he said. "Let's see if we can get up a quartet and have us some singing."

Always when the Kid visited Bent's Ford on his way north or south, Bent expected a session of quartet harmony. He possessed a powerful, rolling bass and enjoyed throwing it into the melody, backing the other singers. The Kid stood high on Bent's list of tenors and the Kid was always willing to oblige. Knowing Dusty did not expect him to return before morning, the Kid could relax and enjoy quartet singing in good company.

"Let's go and find us some more singers," drawled the Kid.

"Got us a baritone," Bent replied. "Whiskey drummer over there. Now all we want is another tenor. How about you, Wes?"

"Never took to singing since pappy used to make me get in that fancy lil suit and go into the choir back home."

"I'll get around and ask, Lon," Bent said, as Wes Hardin refused to be drawn into the quartet.

The Kid and Hardin headed for the bar while Bent made a round of the room looking for a second tenor without which no decent quartet could exist. The two Texans took beer, further along the bar Weems leaned with a schooner of beer in his hand looking off into space and speaking with nobody.

"Not another tenor in the place," said Bent in a disappointed tone, joining the other two at the bar.

His words carried to Weems who walked towards them.

"I suppose there is no chance of getting started for the master's residence tonight?" he said.

"Nope, none at all," Bent answered.

"Then may I join your quartet?"

The other men showed their surprise for none of them thought Weems to be a likely candidate for joining in a quartet.

"You?" asked the Kid.

"One sings occasionally," replied Weems calmly. "I recollect the time Sir James' butler and I formed a quartet with the head keeper and head groom. Of course they weren't in our class, but we felt the conventions could be waived at such a time. Without boasting, we made a pretty fair quartet."

The meaning of Weems' words went clear over the heads of his listeners. Not one of them understood the strict hierarchy of servants in upper-class households. Nor were they greatly concerned with such things as conventions, being more interested in getting buckled down to some singing.

One problem might present itself, the choice of songs.

Weems could hardly be expected to know old range favorites.

"Shall we make a start with *Barbara Allen*?" asked Weems.

"Take the lead, friend," replied the Kid.

It took them but the first verse of the old song to know Weems could handle his part and was no mean tenor in his own right. The room fell silent as the customers settled back to listen to real good singing.

After four songs, all well put over and with Weems showing he could lend a hand at carrying a melody even if he did not know the words of the tune, Bent called for liquid refreshment. This gave the Kid a chance to talk to Weems and to try to learn more about Sir James Keller.

"What sort of feller's your boss, friend?" he asked.

"Sir James?" replied Weems. "A gentleman and a sportsman. My family has served his for the past six generations."

"Why'd he come out here?"

"I never asked."

The Kid grinned, warming to Weems. If anybody had questioned him about some of Dusty, or Ole Devil's business he would have made the same reply, in much the same tone. Clearly Weems felt the same loyalty to his boss as a cowhand did to the outfit for which he rode. However the Kid hoped to try and learn if Keller knew what went on around and about his spread.

"Maybe he reckons to make a fortune out here," drawled Wes Hardin.

"We already have a fortune," sniffed Weems, just a trifle pompously. "The master felt we might have a better chance of development out here. After all there is so little scope left in England these days. The whole country's going to the dogs. Why shortly before we sailed a junior footman at Lord Granderville's, in *my* presence, addressed the butler without calling him mister."

To Weems this clearly amounted to the depths of decadence, a sign of the general rottenness of the times. To the listening men it sounded incomprehensible. If a Texan called a man mister after being introduced it meant he did not like the man and wanted no part of him.

Bent took up the questioning and Weems, with the mellowing influence of a couple of beers, talked of the life he had in England. He might have been discussing the habits of creatures from another planet as he described the strict social distinctions between servants. It now became clear to Bent why a between-stairs maid did not consider herself good enough to share a room with so important a person as a housekeeper. The term brought grins to Texas faces. In their world a house did not mean a home and housekeeper sounded like a fancy title for the madam of a brothel. Weems broke in to a delighted chuckle as the Kid mentioned this, trying to picture the puritanical Miss Trumble in such a capacity. He talked on but there was no snobbish feeling in his words. To him it stood as a way of life, one with a code as rigid as that which ruled the lives of cowhands in their loyalty to their brand.

During the talking, even though absorbed by Weems' descriptive powers, the Kid stayed alert. He saw the stocky man who entered the bar room and stood just inside looking around with watchful eyes. For an instant he looked at the Kid, then his eyes passed on, but the Kid had noticed just a hint of recognition in them. The Kid studied the newcomer, noted his dandy but travel-stained clothes, the low hanging Tranter revolver from the butt of which a right hand never strayed. The man looked like a tough hired killer, one of the better class than the pair he'd run across on Double K, or the group he helped chase from Lasalle's, but one of their breed.

Possibly the man might be a guide come to take Weems and his party to the ranch. His next actions proved this to be wrong. The man did not cross to the bar and ask for information about the Weems' party. He sat with his back to the wall and close to the door, and ordered a drink from a passing waiter. Which same meant if he came from the Double K it was not to meet Weems, but to follow the Kid.

"Let's have another song," suggested Bent, getting in another round of beers. "Give us the *Rosemay-Jo Lament*, Lon."

"Why sure," agreed the Kid. "Soon's I've been out back."

Shoving away from the bar, the Kid headed across the room and out of the door. He gave no sign of knowing the man might be after him, but sensed eyes on him as he left the building. Two horses which had not been there when he entered, stood at the hitching rail. That meant he guessed right, the man was the same who followed him north.

For some moments after the Kid's departure Dune sat at the table and waited. Then he emptied his glass in one swallow, rose and walked through the doors into the night.

The night lay under the light of a waning moon, but he could see well enough for his purpose. He glanced at the two horses, they had brought him from the Double K although he did not travel at speed. He might have caught up with the Kid on the range but did not fancy taking such a chance. He had ridden steadily, keeping reserve energy for a hurried departure. Clearly the Kid had friends in the bar-room and they were not going to take kindly finding him murdered.

With this thought in mind Dune led the two horses to the side of the main building and left them. Then he walked around behind the building, making for the long, three-hole men's backhouse which lay some distance away.

To discourage his guests from staying inside too long, to the discomfort of other guests, Bent had three-quarter length doors on each compartment of the backhouse. This left part of the top and bottom open and tended to make the occupants take only such time as was necessary.

Only one compartment of the backhouse appeared to be in use. Dune saw this and could tell that it held the Ysabel Kid, for a gunbelt hung over the top of the door, a white handled bowie knife strapped to it.

Dune looked around him carefully as he drew his Tranter revolver. Apart from a small bush some twenty feet away he could see nothing and even the bush was nothing to disturb him. He did not aim to match up with the Kid in a fair fight and he had a good chance of avoiding the need to.

Taking aim Dune threw his first bullet into the door. He knew that the .44 bullets would make light work of smashing through the planks at that range. Twice more he aimed and fired, taking only enough time to re-aim and place the bullets a few inches apart, so they would fan across the interior and catch the Kid as he sat on the hole.

No sound came from the compartment. Nothing at all. Dune realized this as he triggered off his third shot. Realized it and the implication behind the silence. Even had his first bullet struck and killed the Kid there should have been some noise, if only his death throes.

"Finished?" asked a voice from his left.

Dune swung around, trying to turn the Tranter. The Kid's black-dressed shape loomed up from behind the bush Dune had dismissed as being too small to hide even a child. His gunbelt might hang over the backhouse door and show the hilt of the bowie knife as bait for a trap—but the old Dragoon was in his hand.

With a snarled curse Dune tried to line his gun. The Tranter never saw the day when its butt lent itself to fast instinctive alignment and Dune had time for nothing else. He fired, the bullet missed the Kid although it came close enough to stir his shirt sleeve. With a roar like a cannon the old Dragoon bloomed out a reply, flame stabbing towards Dune.

The Kid shot the only way he dare. For an instant kill. His round, soft lead .44 ball caught Dune just over the left eyebrow at the front and burst in a shower of bone splinters and brains out at the back of the head. Such was the striking power of the old gun that Dune went over backwards, thrown from his feet. The Tranter fell from a lifeless hand even before his body hit the ground.

Shouts sounded from the main building. Windows of the upper floor rooms opened and people looked out. Then Bent and Wes Hardin, both holding weapons, burst into sight, racing towards the Kid. Other occupants of the bar-room came next including some of the staff carrying lanterns.

"What happened?" Bent asked the Kid who stood strapping on his gunbelt once more.

"Take a look. That *hombre* sure messed up your backhouse door."

Taking a lantern from a waiter, Wes Hardin came forward and let the light play on the door. His eyes took in the three holes. From their height and position he could guess at what would have happened had the Kid been sitting inside.

"Who was he, Lon?" asked Bent, for he handled law enforcement in that section of the Indian Nations.

"Never saw him afore, until he walked into your place tonight. Any of these folks know him?"

Bent allowed the onlookers to move forward, but none of them could say who the dead man might be. Dune's face, apart from the hole over his eye, was not marked even though the back of his head proved to be a hideous mess when exposed to view.

The two horses did not help either, one came from a south Texas ranch, by its brand; the other from a spread which specialized in the breeding and selling of saddle stock.

"Nothing in his pockets to identify him," Bent stated, making a check. "Sure you don't know him, Lon?"

"Nope."

Bent threw a look at the Kid, knowing the sound of his voice. When that note crept into the Kid's voice it was no use asking him questions. So Bent shrugged and turned to order his men to remove the body.

The Kid found Weems at his side. They watched men carrying away the body headed for the stables where it could be left until morning when it would be buried.

"You killed him," said the valet, his face looking ashen pale.

Tapping the door by the line of bullet holes, the Kid nodded. "I reckon I did. He wasn't in this much of a hurry to get in and even if he had been there's two more empty holes."

"And you didn't know him?"

"Nope. He could have mistaken me for somebody else. Say, I'm headed down trail in the morning. Happen you feel like it I'll show you to Double K."

Weems gave the matter some thought. This soft-talking, innocent looking young man had just killed a fellow human being. True the other man appeared to have given good cause for the action, but in England people did not treat killing so lightly. However Weems had his duty to his master. He must get the two wagon loads of furniture and property to the house as soon as possible. He decided to take a chance. Like his master, Weems had been escorted from Kansas by cavalrymen from Fort Dodge, their colonel being a friend of Sir James. However Weems's escort were ordered to return at Bent's Ford where a guide from the ranch would be waiting. The guide had not arrived and Weems wished for no more delay. Who knew what a position Sir James might find himself in, alone, without the services of a good valet in the raw, primitive west?"

"I'll be pleased to have you along," he said.

"We'll pull out at sun-up then," replied the Kid. "Now I'd best get back inside, likely Duke Brent'll want to see me some more about that *hombre* I had to kill."

CHAPTER NINE

Keep Back Or I'll Kill You

DUSTY FOG turned in his saddle and looked back along the trail to Barlock. What he saw satisfied him and he slid the Winchester carbine back into its saddle-boot.

"They're not following us," he remarked.

Rusty Willis scoffed at the thought. "Course not. They know I'm along."

"You don't smell that bad yet," grunted Mark. "How you feeling, Morg?"

The young cowhand from the north country managed a wry grin and tried to ease his aching body on the buckboard seat. he didnt want the men, all well known members of his trade, to think him a whiner.

"Like one time a hoss throwed me off then walked over me. T'aint nothing but half a dozen or so broken ribs, all us Montana boys are tough."

This brought howls of derision from the others. Freda watched them and smiled, wondering if cowhands ever grew up so old as to take life seriously. She also gave a sideways look at Morg Summers; he seemed capable and honest, not bad looking either if it came to a point.

"Say Freda, gal," Mark went on. "Morg here's looking for a riding chore and you're looking for a hand or so. Must be fate in it somewhere."

"I'd have to be able to call him something more than just Morg," she replied.

"Why?" grinned Mark, watching the flush which crept to the girl's cheeks. "All right. This's Morgan Summers, from Montana, 'though why he'd boast about that I sure don't know. Morg, get acquainted with Freda Lasalle; my pard

97

Dusty Fog; and this pair are from the Wedge, but don't hold it again 'em. They answer to Rusty Willis and Doc Leroy and if you can't sort out which's which you north country hands are even less smart than I allow you are.''

"Rusty Willis's the best looking one," Rusty prompted.

"Howdy Rusty," Morg replied, looking at Doc. "I'd recognize you from your pard's description."

All in all Morg allowed he had made the right impression on the others. He wanted to make a good impression on them all —especially the girl who sat so close besides him and handled the ribbons of the buckboard so competently.

"I think we can manage to hire you," Freda stated, wondering if her father would agree, then she looked towards Mark in a coldly accusing manner. "What started the trouble in town?"

Leaving Mark to explain, or to keep the girl occupied, for his explanation in the first place bore little resemblance to the truth, Dusty turned his attention to the two Wedge hands. He had not seen them in a couple of years, but they looked little different. Doc still looked as studious and frail as ever, and most likely could still handle his gun with the old speed and skill. Rusty clung to his old Dance Brothers revolver, a Confederate .44 calibre copy of the Dragoon Colt and he did not look any less reliable for that.

"Where at's the herd?" Dusty asked.

"Down trail a piece," replied Doc. "Rusty and me cut on ahead to Barlock to pick up some makings. You look like you've found some fuss up here, Dusty."

"Man'd say you were right at that," Dusty agreed.

Then he told the story of their visit to Lasalle's and what came out of it. He saw the change in his friends' faces as he spoke of that wire across the narrows and Mallick's threat that no trial herd would go through his land. They did not offer any comment until he finished then Rusty let out a low exclamation, obscene but to the point.

"Clay Allison's about two days behind us and to the southwest," he went on. "Johnny saw him on a swing around the herd. There'll surely be all hell on when old Clay hears about that wire."

Doc nodded his agreement and Dusty saw nothing to argue about in it. They all knew Clay Allison, a Texas rancher and one of the real fast guns in his own right. If he arrived and found his trail blocked he would have a real good answer, roaring guns.

A thought hit Doc Leroy and he reined in his horse, looking at Dusty.

"If those yahoos from the Double K hit Lasalle's they likely went for the other spreads at the same time."

An angry grunt left Dusty's lips. He should have thought of that in the first place. However he did not waste time in futile self-recrimination, or in discussing the chance of the Double K making visits.

He rode forward to the buckboard and interrupted Mark's description of how he and Morg were saving the virtue of a beautiful salloongirl when the marshal's bunch jumped them, with Morg protesting his innocence in the matter of rescuing beautiful saloongirls.

"Reckon you can get this pair of invalids back to your place without us along, Freda?" he asked.

"I reckon I can. If lies were health Mark's sure well enough. You're not going back to Barlock, are you?"

"Nope," Dusty answered. "So don't get all hot and bothered. Doc's just reminded me of something I should've thought of sooner."

"What's that?" she asked.

"The same thing that bunch tried at your place might've been done to your neighbors, only more so."

Freda gave a low gasp for she had not thought of the possibility either. She instantly became practical and helpful, pointing off across the range roughly in the direction of the Gibbs' place, then how they would be able to find the Jones' house.

"Want me along, Dusty?" Mark asked.

"Not this time, *amigo*," replied Dusty. "Three of us should be enough and I'd like somebody on hand at Freda's in case that bunch comes back."

Although he would have much rather rode with Dusty, Mark knew his small pard call the game right. Not only would an extra pair of hands give strength to the Lasalle house if an attack came, but Mark himself needed to get off his horse and rest. That fight in town had taken plenty out of him, enough to make him more of a liability than an asset in the sort of conditions Dusty, Doc and Rusty might be running into.

Knowing hired gunmen, Mark guessed Tring would be smarting under the indignity of failure and in being fanned off the Lasalle place by a load of bird shot. He might easily gather his bunch and make for the Lasalle house to avenge himself and Mark wanted to be on hand when he came.

So Mark stayed with the buckboard while Dusty swung off at a tangent, riding with his two good friends of the Wedge. Mark grinned at the girl's worried face and said, ''Waal, there was ole Morg, with this beautiful blonde haired gal on his lap and all—''

''You danged white-topped pirate!'' wailed Morg. ''Whyn't you tell the truth for once in your life?''

''All right,'' grinned Mark. ''She wasn't beautiful, She was about two hundred pounds weight, had seven double chins—''

''Let's ignore him, Morg,'' suggested Freda, interrupting Mark's flow of descriptive untruth. ''You tell me what happened.''

Which brought her no nearer to knowing the truth for Morg reversed the story Mark told, putting Mark in his place in every detail.

''That I can well believe,'' Freda remarked at the end. ''Now—and I want to remind all and sundry that I am the sole cook at home—how about telling me what really happened.''

''A wise man once told me never to argue with the cook,'' Mark drawled. ''It all started when I saw Morg getting abused by that Jackieboy saloon bunch.''

This time Freda heard the true story. She felt grateful to Mark for having saved Morg Summers and almost wished she had not slapped Mark's face back in town.

For a time after leaving the buckboard Dusty and the other two rode in silence. Beyond expressing their regrets at the death of Dusty's brother neither Doc nor Rusty made any other reference to the happenings in Moondog. They were all good friends with past dangers shared, so did not need to go into words to show their true feelings. Dusty turned the talk to the wire and the other two growled their anger. All agreed on one thing. The fence must go. Rusty and Doc were all for war, although Doc, more given to thinking of causes and effects than his *amigo* saw how a wire cutting war might affect the inhabitants of the area.

''I can't see Clay Allison sitting back peaceable and talking,

Dusty," drawled Rusty Willis, "even if Stone will."

"I'm going to talk to them both," Dusty answered. "I'll ride down trail in the morning and meet up with Clay. He'll stand firm maybe, if I explain things to him."

"What sort of things?" Rusty asked.

"Like what'll happen to these folks up here happen a war starts over their land."

"That'd tangle their lines for sure," agreed Doc Leroy. "It'd be them who go to the wall if the trail herds were held up and grazed their land out, to say nothing of the fighting that'd be going on."

Then Rusty saw it. He had seen an area blasted wide open by a range war between two big outfits. There were three smaller places around the scene of the war and at the end of it all lay empty and deserted, the owners either killed or run out by the opposing factions.

They rode across the range and struck a track made by wagon wheel ruts which, according to Freda's directions, ought to lead to the Gibbs' spread. After following the tracks for a couple of miles they topped a rim and looked down.

"You were right, Doc," Dusty said quietly and grimly. "Double K didn't just call on Lasalle."

Neither Doc nor Rusty made any reply to this, Rusty growled a low, barely audible string of curses, but Doc said nothing. His long, slim fingers drummed on his saddle horn as his eyes took in the scene below.

The corral fence had been smashed down. The house's front door hung on its lower hinges, the top having been smashed open. Not a single pane of glass remained unbroken at the windows. Nor did the destruction end with the corral and main house. The outbuilding doors had been burst in, their walls battered into gaping holes. Not a living thing showed about the place. Several dead chickens lay before the house and the body of a big bluetick hound sprawled stiff and still by the corral fence.

"Let's go!" Dusty growled and started his horse forward.

Slowly they rode down the slope towards the house. Not one of them spoke as they studied the wreck of a well-kept spread and a neat, clean house.

"Keep away!" screamed a woman's voice from the house. "Keep back of I'll kill you!"

Hysteria filled the woman's voice, but the three men did not stop. They rode slowly on and halted their horses by the corral. Dusty started to swing down from his saddle when Rusty's voice, tense and warning, stopped him.

"Dusty! The door! Turn slow and easy!"

Turning his head Dusty looked towards the broken door of the house. He found himself looking at the barrels of a ten gauge shotgun. Behind the shotgun, holding it waist high but aimed at them, stood a pretty, plump, red-haired woman. Slowly Dusty swung down from his saddle and took a step forward, hands well clear of his sides, eyes never leaving her face.

She would have been a happy woman, full of the joys of life, friendly and kind, most times. Now her face bore marks of the strain she was under and he eyes were red rimmed, swollen with tears. She came through the door, a smallish woman wearing an old gingham dress and with a face which told that she had been through living hell that day.

"Keep back!" she repeated. "Haven't you done enough? My husband isn't even conscious yet! He can't do anything!"

"Easy, ma'am," replied Dusty, watching her all the time and stepping closer. "We're not from the Double K."

He might never have spoken for all the effect his words had on her. it did not even appear that the woman heard his words. She brought up the shotgun a trifle and Doc bit down a warning shout just in time.

"Watch her, Dusty!" he warned in a voice which sounded nearer a whisper than a shout. "One wrong move and you'll be picking buckshot out of your back teeth. She's scared loco and'd do it without even knowing."

Slowly as a snail crossing a leaf, Dusty moved forward. He did not for an instant take his eyes from the woman's face, trying to hold her attention on him. So far she had not pressed the shotgun's trigger but one fast move could cause her forefinger to close and send the weapon's deadly charge into him. Despite his earlier scoffing Dusty knew even a charge of birdshot at that range would be more than lethal and would blow a hole like a cannon's bore in him. One quick move, one sudden sound even, might cause her to press the trigger.

It was as deadly and dangerous a situation as Dusty had ever been in. Perhaps the most dangerous. If this had been a man bad mean and set on killing, Dusty could have handled things differently. Only this was no man, but a terrified woman driven to the verge of madness, hysterical and not responsible for her actions.

Perhaps Doc Leroy knew the danger better than Rusty, than Dusty even. For a time, before circumstances sent him home to Texas and to become a cowhand working for Stone Hart's Wedge, Doc read medicine in an eastern college. He did not complete the course but spent every spare minute when in town working with the local medicine man, learning all he could. On the trail he handled the doctoring chores which fell to the cook in most cases. He would take care of injuries, splint and care for broken limbs, diagnose various illnesses and produce their cures, within the limitations of his medical supplies. He probably knew more about the extraction of bullets than most eastern doctors ever learned. On two occasions, when driven to it by the force of circumstances, he delivered babies. So Doc had knowledge of the effect of hysteria. He knew the full danger of Dusty going towards the woman and he felt more scared than he had ever been in his life.

Still moving slowly Dusty made his way towards the woman, edging to the right with the barrels of the gun following him like iron filings after a magnet. He knew his friends were now clear of the shotgun's charge and there only remained the problem of getting the weapon away from her without taking its charge full in his belly. For the first time he looked down at the gun, seeing that the right side hammer only had been cocked back, the left lying safe and down.

An inch at a time, moving with the same slowness which covered all his moves since dismounting, Dusty's right hand went up, gripped the brim of his Stetson and removed it. He was close to the woman, but not close enough to chance a straight grab, not while her finger rested on the trigger. However the gun aimed at him, his friends were in the clear. He had brought them into this mess and must get them out of it without injury if possible. That was the way Dusty Fog thought and acted.

"Just take it easy, ma'am," he said, keeping his voice gentle and fighting to hold the tension out of it. His eyes were on her face once more. "Afore you can shoot you'll have to cock back the hammers."

The woman's eyes dropped towards the breech of her shotgun. For an instant her finger relaxed on the trigger. Instantly Dusty slapped his hat around, knocking the shotgun's barrels to the right while he made a fast side step to the left. For all that it was close, very close. The gun bellowed, he felt the hot muzzle blast and the hot rush of air and burnt powder stirred his shirt, but the lethal load, not yet spread on leaving the barrel, missed him.

Jumping forward Dusty grabbed the shotgun by its barrels and dragged forward at it. The woman gave a scream of terror, she tried to fumble back the second hammer but Dusty plucked the shotgun from her hands. She stood for a moment, staring at Dusty, while Doc and Rusty came out of their saddles and the mount Dusty borrowed from Lasalle took off for home on the run.

"Catch my saddle, Rusty!" Dusty yelled, giving the old range request for aid; for while the horse a cowhand rode mostly belonged to the ranch's remuda it carried his more precious and vital item of personal property, his saddle.

The words seemed to shake the woman out of her paralysis. With a scream she flung herself at Dusty, coming all teeth and fingernails, a wild-cat ready to use primeval fighting equipment to defend her home and husband. Dusty did not dare take a chance. He caught her by the wrists, holding her as she struggled with almost super-human strength, feet lashing out and arms fighting against his grip. He saw Rusty take off after his departing horse and felt relieved. Nothing in the west caused so much anxiety as a riderless, saddled horse. Dusty knew Mark would be worried if his mount came back to Lasalle's empty. He did not want his big *amigo* coming looking for him and leaving the Lasalle house with only a small guard.

For a moment the woman struggled, until Doc caught her by the arms from behind and held her. Then she seemed to collapse into herself. The shotgun, thrown to one side by Dusty when he found need to prevent her scratching his eyes out, lay on the ground but she did not look at it. Instead she lifted dull, lifeless eyes to his face and spoke in a strangled voice.

"All right. Do what you like with me, but leave my husband alone."

Dusty and Doc released her, but Dusty took up the shotgun and removed its percussion cap to make sure the weapon could not be turned against him. Then he stood with his back to the two, allowing the tension to ooze from him. In his time as a lawman Dusty had found cause to use a shotgun on a man, it was not a pretty sight. A man did not just shake off, and laugh at it as being nothing, almost winding up the same way.

Knowing how Dusty must feel, Doc gently turned the woman to face him. "Now easy there, ma'am," he said. "We're not from the Double K."

"Freda Lasalle sent us over," Dusty went on, his voice sounding just a little shaky still, and not turning around.

At that moment Doc threw a look at the partly open door of the house. What he saw brought an angry growl for his throat and sent him running for the house. Dusty turned and followed, seeing what Doc saw and forgetting his personal feelings in the urgency of the matter. The woman turned, watching them, looking as if all her will had been drained out of her. Then she heard hooves and turned to see Rusty riding back, leading the Lasalle's horse. He swung down from the saddle, left his horse standing with its reins dangling and the runaway fastened to the saddlehorn. Coming towards the woman he threw a glance at the stiff body of the bluetick hound.

"Nobody but a stinking Yankee'd shoot a good dawg like that'n," he said in a tone that boded ill for the man who shot the dog if Rusty ever laid hands on him. "Where'd I find a spade, ma'am? I'll tend to burying him."

He got no reply, for the woman turned on her heels and fled to the house, Rusty did not follow, but headed for the damaged barn to see if he could find a shovel.

Dusty and Doc were already in the house. The building, made on the same lines as Lasalle's home, had once been just as neat, tidy and pleasant. Now the front room looked as if a whirlwind had passed through it. The table had been thrown over, chairs broken, the sofa's covers slashed open to expose springs and stuffing. The cupboards were shattered and broken, crockery lying in pieces on the floor. Just inside the door, face down, head resting on a pillow lay the woman's husband, a tall, powerful looking man of middle-age. His back carried marks left by the lash of a blacksnake whip.

"Don't touch him!" gasped the woman, entering the room just as Doc went to his knees by the man.

"Get me some hot water, ma'am," Doc answered gently.

"Happen they've left you anything to heat it in. And I'll want some clean white cloth. I've got to get that shirt off and tend to his back."

At last the woman seemed to realize that her visitors meant her no harm. She made an effort, then led Dusty to the kitchen. It appeared the Double K restricted their efforts to the out-buildings and the front room for the neat kitchen remained intact and she had already been heating water when they rode up.

"What happened, ma'am?" Dusty asked, leading the woman from the room as soon as she gave Doc the water and cloth. Doc was never too amiable when handling a medical or surgical chore and it paid to steer well clear of him at such times.

"Some of the Double K men came to see us early on. They told us to sell out and leave. Said they would be back after they saw the Joneses. Later on they came back. Ralph told them he didn't aim to quit and they jumped him. Sam tried to help, but one of them shot him down. They lashed Ralph to the corral and whipped him, while one of them held me, made me watch. Then they wrecked everything they could and rode away. They said they'd be back tomorrow. I thought you—I thought—Oh lord! I nearly k-killed you!"

"You were scared, ma'am," Dusty answered. "You couldn't know."

The sound of digging brought her attention from Dusty. She looked to where Rusty Willis, who at normal times wouldn't have thought of touching the blister end of a spade, dug a grave for the dog.

Then she turned and started to cry, the sobs ripping from her, tears pouring down her cheeks in a steady flow. The anguish she must have held bottled up inside while she tried to do something for her husband and about the wreck of her home, boiled out of her. She knew herself to be safe and in good hands. Now she could be a woman and cry out her misery.

Dusty let her get on with it, knowing she would be better once the crying ended. He waited by her side and at last she dried her eyes, turning to him once more and showing she had full control of herself.

"I should help your friend. I was a nurse for a time in the

War. After the men rode away I managed to get Ralph inside the house. I had laudanum in the medicine chest, they hadn't touched it. I gave Ralph some to ease the pain. I didn't know what to do for the best. Can your friend do anything for my husband?''

"Reckon he can, ma'am? There was a time when a trail hand for the Wedge took sick, like to die. Ole Doc there, he went to work and operated with a bowie knife and a bottle of whisky. He saved that hand's life. Yea, I reckon he can handle your husband's hurts all right.''

At that moment they heard the sound of hooves. Rusty dropped the spade and fetched out his Dance. Dusty turned, hands ready to bring out the matched Colts. He knew only one horse approached but prepared to tell the woman to head for the house. It didn't seem likely that Double K would send one man to visit the ranch, but one of the hired guns might have the idea that a woman left alone and in a state of terror would be easy meat.

"Don't shoot!'' Joyce Gibbs gasped, seeing and recognizing the rider. "It's Yance. He works for Pop Jones.''

Riding at a fast trot the grizzled cowhand came towards the others. He halted his horse and threw a glance at Dusty and Rusty, then relaxed. Neither were the kind Double K hired.

"See they been here, too,'' he said in an angry tone. "They treat you folks bad, Mrs. Gibbs?''

"Ralph's hurt,'' she replied. "These gents came by and lent a hand. Have they been to your place?''

"Came in on their way through here. Told Pop to sell out and go. He allows to do it. Him and Maw's getting too old for fussing with that bunch. I'd've started shooting, but Maw said no.''

"When do they have to leave by, friend?'' Dusty asked, stepping by Joyce.

"Double K allow to come in tomorrow and make sure we're ready to up stakes and pull out.''

Studying Dusty, the cowhand did not see a small, insignificant man, he saw a master of their trade, a tophand more than normally competent with the matched brace of guns he wore. Yance did not know from where Dusty and Rusty came, but he knew they looked like the kind of men who could handle the Double K bunch. He hoped they would stay on and help the Gibbs family who were real nice folks and deserved better than to be driven out from their homes. Yance was more than willing to listen to any words of wisdom the small Texan might hand out.

"You head back to your spread," Dusty told him. "I'll try and get a couple or so hands over to you in the morning. If they haven't made it by ten o'clock tell your boss to upstakes and head for Lasalle's. Don't stand and fight."

"You at Lasalle's?" Yance asked.

"Sure."

"I'll tell Pop. Only I sure hope that you-all can get the men to us. I'd like to tie into Double K with some good men at my back."

He wasted no more time in talk. Turning his horse he headed for his home spread, but he rode in a more jaunty manner. Joyce saw this and wondered who the small man might be.

"Who are you?" she asked, then her face flushed red for such a question was never asked in polite western society.

For once Dusty took no offense at the words. He introduced himself and Rusty telling her who Doc was. Then he kept her talking while Rusty finished the grave-digging and buried the dog.

"They broke a tea set my mother gave me for my wedding!"she said suddenly, recalling something. Tears glistened in her eyes as she said the words and she clenched her fists, trying to avoid breaking down once more for the reaction still hung over her.

"One thing I promise, ma'am," Dusty replied. "The man responsible for this lot here's going to pay for it."

CHAPTER TEN

The Coming of The Wedge

BEFORE Joyce Gibbs could sink into despondency again she saw Doc come out of the cabin and started towards him with Dusty at her side.

"I've fixed his back, ma'am," Doc drawled. "Cleaned the wounds and got them covered. It's bad enough. He'll likely carry the scars until he dies and it'll hurt like hell for a time. But there's no injury to his spine as far as I can tell."

"We can't move him, then?" Dusty asked.

"From where he lies to the bed is all," Doc replied. "Happen you mean can we take him out of here."

"That's what I meant. Rusty, lend a hand to tote him to his bed. Then get your hoss and head back to the herd. Ask Stone if he can send a few of the crew to lend a hand up this ways. Tell him what's happened and that I'll likely come down and see him in the morning, but to get the boys here if he can spare them."

"Yo!" replied Rusty, giving the cavalry affirmative answer.

"Lasalle's place is over that way. Happen you see it, call on in and tell Mark I won't see him until morning."

Joyce watched the men heading into her house. It took some getting used to, the way the two men jumped to obey the small Texan, a man she would have passed in the street without a second glance. Of course she had heard of Dusty Fog, but never would she have pictured him as this small, insignificant cowhand.

Following the two men into the house she watched the gentle way they carried her husband into the bedroom and laid him on the bed, face down. She also blushed at some of the *sotto voce* comments Doc heaped on his friends if they did not

109

handle Ralph in the manner he felt correct. Already the laudanum had started to wear off and Ralph groaned in pain.

"Just stay by him, ma'am," Doc said. "Until he's sane enough to know better, I mean wtih the pain and all, and strong enough to get out of it, we'll have to make sure he keeps his face from burying into the pillow. I'd stay on, but I'll see what Dusty wants first."

He left Joyce with her husband and headed out to find Dusty watching Rusty ride off.

"What now?" Doc asked.

"We'd best put the hosses in the barn first, then get set for a long wait and maybe a fight."

They took their mounts to the stable and found that the damage had been done only to the outer walls. So they removed their double girthed saddles and left the horses in empty stalls, then headed for the house, taking the saddles with them.

Dusty spent the rest of the afternoon helping Joyce do what she could about the damage to the house. They set the table up and found that two chairs remained unbroken, but the rest were smashed beyond repair. Dusty swore again that he would make the men behind the raid pay for what they did and he meant it in more ways than one.

"Your husband's awake, ma'am," Doc said, just before dark as he entered the room. "Come on in and see him."

Joyce followed the slim Texan into the bedroom and found her husband, his face lined with pain still, looking at her although he still lay on his face.

"I'd like to thank you gents for helping us," Ralph Gibbs said, looking at Dusty who followed his wife into the room.

"There's no call for that," Dusty replied. "I only wish that I got here in time to stop them doing what they did."

"You fed our guests, honey?" Ralph asked.

"I did the best I could," she answered. "Used some of the chickens the men killed, made up enough for us all. I'll fetch you some broth in."

"You fixing on sticking here?" Dusty asked. "If you are, I'll have some men on hand to help fight off that Double K bunch when they come."

"I'm staying!" stated Gibbs firmly. "Although how I'll manage for food I don't know. That bunch told me the only way we could buy supplies was to sell out to Mallick and he'd give us a note for the store."

"I've got an answer for that," Dusty said quietly. "How about your market herd, did you get it gathered?"

"Not yet. I wanted to hire a couple of hands for a roundup but there's none to be had out this way."

"We'll see what we can do," promised Dusty. "So—Douse the lights Doc. We've got callers."

They all heard the rapid drumming of hooves and this time not just one horse but several.

Doc quickly doused the light in the room and Dusty darted across to blow out the lamp on the dining-room table. The house plunged into darkness and Dusty stood by a window. He heard a soft footfall and saw Doc coming towards him.

"You ought to be with her," Dusty said.

"That's what I thought," replied Doc and his teeth gleamed white in a grin. "Only I done fetched in, cleaned and loaded that old ten gauge and Mrs. Gibbs done got it by the window, swears to fill the hide of the first Double K skunk she sees out there. She'll do it, too, or I've never seen a gal who could."

"I reckon she will," agreed Dusty for he knew Joyce had regained control of herself and was the more dangerous for it. Now she could handle the shotgun in cold determination and she knew how to make the most of it.

Nearer thundered the hooves. Clearly if these were the Double K they did not expect trouble from Gibbs or his wife. Joyce suddenly realized the riders did not come from the direction of the Double K and she turned from the window to call out this information to Dusty. A voice let out a cowhand yell from the darkness, before she could speak.

"Hey Dusty, Doc! Don't go fanning any lead. It's us."

Which left a lot unexplained to Gibbs and his wife, but apparently satisfied the two men in the dining-room. After a brief pause a match rasped and the table lamp lit once more. Joyce saw Dusty resting his carbine against the wall then open the door they had repaired.

"I can't think of a better reason for shooting!" he called to the men outside, then looked across the room towards Joyce. "It's all right, ma'am. They're friends."

Saying that Dusty stepped out of the house to greet his old friends of the Wedge trail crew.

Six men sat their horses in a half circle before the front of the Gibbs' house. Six men who, apart from the OD Connected crew or some of his illustrious kin, Dusty would rather have seen than any others at such a time. Rusty Willis was one, leaning on his saddlehorn at the right of the party. Next to him, tall, slim, still retaining some of his cavalryman's stiff-backed grace, sat Stone Hart. He would have been a handsome young man had it not been for the sabre scar on his right cheek, a memento of a cavalry clash in the War Between The States. He wore cowhand clothes neither better nor worse than those of the others, but about him hung the undefinable something which sets a leader of men apart from the others. Stone Hart was such a leader of men. He rode as trail boss for the Wedge and that took a leader, not a driver of men.

"Rusty allows you found some trouble, Dusty," Stone said, his voice an even cultured deep south drawl.

"You called it right, Stone," Dusty agreed, then threw a glance at the woman in the doorway. "Can they light a spell, ma'am?"

"Of course they may," she answered, annoyed at being so lax in her hospitality. "Please get down, gentlemen."

Now she was no longer scared and half-hysterical, Joyce could tell quality when she saw it. Every man in that group looked like a tophand, even the medium sized, stocky man with the drooping moustache and the woe-begone look on his face. The rest did not look like hired hard-cases, but they did look like remarkably efficient fighting men. He alone did not fit into the picture, or the sort to be tied in with such an outfit as the Wedge. Later she found this man, Peaceful Gunn by name, would move easily two inches out of his way if he ran into trouble. His element was a fight into which he could plunge, all the time insisting he was a peace-loving and easy-going as a dove. Joyce knew something of wild animals and knew the dove, for all its being regarded as the bird of peace, was in reality amongst the toughest and most trouble-hunting of birds, always ready for a fight.

Next to Peaceful sat a tall, wide shouldered, freckle faced and handsome young man with a fiery thatch of red hair. He wore cowhand clothes and belted a low handing Army Colt. He rode as scout for the Wedge. Folks said Johnny Raybold, as the red head was named, could eat as much as would founder a good-sized horse although he preferred something more nourishing than grass. he had other good qualities and could be relied on in any man's fight.

While the other three men were not members of Stone Hart's regular crew, all carried a look of tophands who knew what their guns could be used for. They were the usual type of men he hired, tough, salty, loyal to the brand they rode for. Stone introduced them as Tex, Shaun and Billy.

The men trooped into the house at Joyce's invitation. She watched Peaceful as he peered around him a shade nervously. His moustache, which was capable of more expression than most folks could get from their entire face, dropped miserably and gave him the appearance of a terrified walrus.

"Where they at?" he asked in a tone which suggested they might be hiding under the table ready to jump him. "It's getting so a body can't ride a trail these days without running into fuss."

The rest of the men ignored Peaceful's words. Johnny Raybold gave out a whoop and held out a hand to Dusty.

"Where at's thishere wire, Dusty?" he asked. "And where's Mark 'n' the Kid?"

"What you want them for?" groaned Peaceful, his moustache drooping like the wilted lily on a cheap undertaker's lapel. "They'll only help wind us up in more trouble."

This brought howls of derision from the others who all knew Peaceful much better than did Joyce.

"Should head for the badlands and go 'round," he went on miserably. "That way we won't wind up in fuss with them gents who strung the wire."

"Get mum, all of you," Stone growled, bringing an end to the argument which was developing, even before it started. "We all know you'd be fit to be tied if I even thought of going round."

"Rusty tell you it all, Stone?" Dusty asked, while Joyce went to fetch coffee for her guests.

"What he knew about it. What's on that tricky Rio Hondo mind?"

"I figured that Double K might come back and that'd we'd give 'em a real Texas welcome, only I needed a few friends on hand to tote 'round the tea and biscuits for the guests."

Stone Hart smiled. He'd known Dusty for a few years now

and they'd sided each other in a couple of tight spots in that time. One thing he did know for sure. The situation up here must be very grave for Dusty to send for help during a drive. Dusty knew trail driving, knew it from the angle of hand and as trail boss, so he would not lightly send and ask for men.

"Stake 'em out the way you want," he said, setting the seal of approval on Dusty's actions and giving permission for orders to be passed to his men. Stone hired the men, it should be to him to make any arrangements for their employment, but he knew Dusty had a better idea of the situation and knew what would be needed in offence and defence.

"I'll have Johnny staked out on the range about a mile out towards the Double K, waiting for the first sound of their coming. When they get here I want some of the boys in the out-buildings, some here. I want that bunch boxed in and held tighter than a Yankee storekeeper's purse strings."

"Get to it, Johnny," drawled Stone. "Which's the way Double K'll most likely come ma'am?"

"That way," Joyce answered, a finger stabbing in the direction of the Double K house. "But they might not come that direction."

"It's likely they will," Dusty replied. "They don't know about Stone and the boys and'll likely think they've got nothing to worry about. So they'll come the easiest direction."

"Dusty could be right at that, ma'am," Stone put in.

Joyce noticed the trail boss never looked straight at her and tried to keep the unscarred side of his face to her all the time. She felt sorry for him, he must have been a really handsome young man before the Yankee sabre marred his face. Even now a woman would not find him revolting; the scar looked bad, but could have been far worse. Much as she wished to tell him her thoughts she knew any reference to his injury would offend Stone. He would not want a stranger to mention it.

The men stood around Joyce's table and drank their coffee, all except Johnny who knew what was expected of him and faded off into the dark astride his big iron grey night horse. Only Peaceful seemed to be worried by the forthcoming possible visit and Joyce got the feeling that he did not care as much as he pretended.

"What do you want from the rest of us, Dusty?" asked Rusty Willis.

"Stone, Doc and I'll stay at the house," Dusty answered with a grin. "And don't go saying we're pulling rank on you—because we are. Rest of you pick out your places and wait until you hear Johnny come back. Put your hosses in the barn, but keep them saddled. If Double K hit, I want them. Not one's got to get back to their spread."

"These Double K bunch, Cap'n Fog," put in one of the new Wedge hands, "How'd you want them, alive or dead?"

"Whichever way you have to take them."

Dusty's reply came in a flat, even voice, but every man present knew what he meant. Shoot if you must and if you must shoot, shoot to kill, that was Dusty's meaning. It was the way of a tough lawman, of the man who tamed Quiet Town. Such would be the orders he gave to his deputies when they went after a dangerous outlaw in the line of duty. In the same manner Dusty now spoke. He did not want killings or trouble, but if Double K forced them on him he would try and prevent his side from taking lead if he could.

"How about me, Dusty?" asked Joyce after the men went to their posts. She used his given name, having received no encouragement to carry on with his formal rank and title, and knowing far better than call a cowhand "mister" after being introduced.

"If they come, get in the bedroom with your man. Let Doc handle the fighting, he'll be in there. Stone, Johnny and I'll be out here."

"Don't you think it might be better to send that miserable looking man back to the herd?" she asked. "He looked terrified when he went out to the barn."

Two faces looked at her, trying to see if she was joking, then Dusty and Stone started grinning.

"You mean Peaceful, ma'am?" asked Stone.

"I don't know his name. Nobody got around to introducing me to any of you."

Taking the hint Dusty introduced her to Stone. She knew the Wedge boss by reputation but nothing more. He and Dusty seemed much alike in many ways. Polite, courteous, yet masterful. Men who gave orders and knew their strength without being over-aggressive or bullying. She could see how they extracted such loyalty from the men under their command.

"How many men do you have, Stone?" Dusty asked, forgetting the matter of sending Peaceful to the safety of the herd.

"My regular crew and nine more."

"Seventeen, huh? Double K have at least that many at the spread and more in town. You'll be needing half of your men to hold the herd back down there for a day or two while we sort this wire trouble out."

"There's folks relying on me taking their herds through, Dusty," Stone pointed out.

"I've thought about that too."

"What're you fixing to do then?"

"Wait hereabouts for Clay Allison to come closer, ride down tomorrow and meet him, ask for help."

Stone grunted. "I never knowed the Wedge to need Clay Allison to do our fighting for us."

"He's not fighting for you. He's fighting for himself, for every herd that comes up the trail, for every man who died making this trail and keeping it open in the early days," Dusty answered. "And I hope to keep it from busting into an open fight if I can."

"It'll come to fighting, happen Clay reaches here and the wire's still up," Stone answered.

"Not the way I want to play it. With him and your boys I reckon we have enough hard-country stock to make Double K think twice about locking horns."

"Would Clay Allison make all that much difference?" Joyce asked, looking from one man to the other.

"Enough, ma'am," Stone answered.

He knew Clay Allison, respected the man as a rancher and a trail boss of the first water, but there had never been any close ties between them. To Stone the end of a trail meant little more than selling his herd at the best possible price, paying off his hands, working out each ranch's share of the profits and taking his cut to be added to the bank balance with which he hoped one day soon to buy a ranch of his own.

To Clay Allison, already a rich rancher owner in his own right, the end of a drive meant fun, hoorawing the trail-end town, celebrations, wild and hectic parties with his hands and anyone who cared to join in the fun, before heading back home to Texas. Happen there should also be a chance to tie into some loud-mouth Kansas lawman who boasted he jailed Texans one handed, left-handed at that, then Clay Allison's trail-end was made complete.

So, beyond their mutual loyalty to the south in the War and their combined interest in keeping open a trail to the Kansas markets, Clay Allison and Stone Hart had little or nothing in common. Yet Stone knew Clay's name packed considerable weight as a fast-gun fighting man. With him along, backed by the Wedge's men, Dusty might be able to make the owner of the Double K open the trail without blood being shed.

"I'd like to leave three men here and send three across to the Jones spread, if that rides all right with you, Stone," Dusty drawled. "Just for a couple of days happen all goes well."

"Sure, I'll see to it," Stone replied. "We've made good time up to here and the beef could stand a couple of days' rest. I'll leave Rusty, Doc and Billy here."

Hearing the words Joyce could almost have sung with delight. She knew Rusty looked like he could take care of himself and any of the other hands, apart from the one called Peaceful, would also be a good man to have around. She decided Doc was being left to help care for her husband, although he did wear a fast man's gun-rig, she doubted if so studious a looking young man could make best use of it.

"Which spread's the further from Double K?" Dusty asked. "You or Jones?"

"We are."

"Be best to have Peaceful up there then. Should be far enough away from Double K to keep him happy," Dusty said.

"But we're farther from Double K—!" Joyce began, thinking Dusty misunderstood her words.

"Yes'm, that's just what we mean," grinned Stone.

Leaving Joyce to try and work logic out of the words, Dusty and Stone got down to discussing the events leading up to this night gathering. Joyce sighed, deciding she would never understand cowhands. She went into the bedroom to find her husband sleeping comfortably and Doc sitting by the window, cleaning his Army Colt.

Sitting his horse about a mile from the ranch house Johnny Raybold looked around him, studying the open range. Then he swung down and squat on his heels, letting his iron grey stallion stand with reins dangling. Tied or loose the big horse would not stray far from him, and never played up or tried to avoid him when he went to it. That was a quality Johnny often needed in his task as scout for the Wedge.

Johnny drew his Winchester from the saddleboot and then settled down for a long wait. He took out his makings, rolling a smoke and hanging it from the corner of his mouth, but did not offer to light it. The horse moved to one side and fell to cropping the grass.

"Fool chore this, ole hoss," he said quietly, after being on watch for an hour. "Bet Chow put Dusty up to it."

Snorting softly the horse moved closer to its master. Johnny grinned, realizing that Dusty could not have seen the Wedge's cook for a couple of years and could hardly have worked up this business with chow. It made him feel better to lay the blame on somebody for being sent on a chore that he, with the exception of the Ysabel Kid, could handle best.

Johnny knew little or nothing of the trouble in this section of the Panhandle country. He had been with the rest of the crew when Rusty Willis returned on the run with a message for Stone. Johnny found himself one of the group Stone selected to ride with him, leaving his segundo, Waggles Harrison, in charge of the herd. Why they came still remained something of a mystery to Johnny. He did not particularly care. A good friend needed help and Johnny needed to know no more.

Listening to the night noises Johnny stayed where he was, quiet, relaxed and without moving restlessly. Often he had done this kind of work and knew how to keep his mind alert and working without it interfering with his watching and listening. He thought of nights spent sitting by a fire, listening to the baying of coon-hound music as a redbone ran a line in the darkness. To Johnny no sound in the world came so sweetly as the trail song of a good hound dog. He thought of his return to Texas for the fall. He'd head down and see some kin who owned good hounds and—

Suddenly the thoughts ended. Johnny came to his feet in a lithe move. He stood with the rifle held before his body, face turned towards the sound which took his thoughts from hound music. For a moment he stood, listening to the night sounds and catching once more the faint crackle of shots in the distance.

Now Johnny had a problem on his hands. He did not know

if Dusty could hear the shots while in the house. So Johnny needed to decide if to stay here or head back with the word would be best. Then he decided. Dusty would want to know about the shooting, especially as there did not appear to be any sign of the Double K.

Johnny turned, he went afork his stallion in a bound, catching up the reins and starting his mount running towards the house.

In the house Joyce poured her coffee for her guests before making for the barn and serving the other men. She stifled a yawn and said, "They might not be coming tonight after all."

"Might not," agreed Dusty. "But—"

They all heard the thunder of a fast running horse's hooves and made for the door of the house. Outside they could just hear the crackle of shots. Joyce's face lost some of its colour.

"Lasalle's!" she gasped.

By now the other men were from the barn. A sudden bright flash showed down where the shots sounded, followed by a dull booming roar.

"Dynamite!" Dusty snapped. "Loan me a hoss, Stone. I've got to get down there."

Stone wasted no time. "Peaceful, loan Dusty your hoss. Stay here with Doc. The rest of you hit those kaks and let's ride."

For a man who professed to have no other aim in life but to avoid trouble, Peaceful showed some reluctance to being left out of the rescue party. He did not argue for he knew Mark Counter was out there some place, most likely where that explosion sounded. He led his big horse from the barn and jerked the Spencer rifle from the saddleboot.

Dusty went astride Peaceful's horse in a flying mount, grabbed the reins and put his pet-makers to work. The horse was no livery plug to accept a stranger on its back, but it sensed a master rider and did not try to make a fight. It set off across the darkened range at a gallop. The other men followed. They rode fast, pushing their horses. For all they knew, their help might be needed at Lasalle's place.

In the lead Dusty rode with fear in his heart. The dynamite had gone off at the Lasalle place and his *amigo*, a man as close as any brother, might even now be dead, blown to doll-rags by the Double K hired killers.

CHAPTER ELEVEN

The Hit At LaSalle's

"I'LL see that five thousand dollars and up another five," Freda Lasalle announced calmly, after studying the three kings in her hand once more.

The Lasalle's sitting-room looked bright and cheerful enough. Lasalle sat at the side table, reading a book and throwing his amused gaze at the high stake poked game at the dining table where his daughter backed feminine intuition against the skill and knowledge of the other two. Female intuition did not seem to be all it was cracked up to be for Freda owed Mark and Morg Summers about five hundred thousand dollars so far.

"I sure can't see how you always get the cards," she objected, after the betting as her three kings fell before Mark's low straight.

"Unlucky in love, lucky at cards," Mark answered.

An over-done snigger greeted his words, coming from Freda who reached for the cards. The game only started to stop her worrying about the fate of her friends and the non-arrival of Dusty, Rusty and Doc. On his ride to the herd Rusty had missed Lasalle's place and so none of the occupants knew what might have kept Dusty away. At last Mark insisted they played cards, needling Freda into the game to prevent her worrying.

To Morg Summers the night could go on for ever. He now held the position as official hand of the Lasalle spread and Freda seemed very friendly. Morg wondered how things stood between the girl and Mark Counter, felt just a little jealous and decided he did not have a chance against such a handsome and famous man's opposition. However he got the idea that Mark would be riding out as soon as the trouble came to an end and felt better about things.

The redbone hound sprawled before the empty fireplace for Mark would not allow a fire. Suddenly the dog raised his head, looking towards the front door and letting a low growl rumble deep in his throat.

"Douse the lights!" Mark snapped, thrusting back his chair. "Get to your places. Move it!"

His very urgency put life into their limbs. Morg blew out the lamp on the table and Lasalle doused the other. They could all hear the horses now, a fair sized bunch of them by all accounts. It looked like Tring had returned and meant to make up for his last visit and so brought plenty of help.

"Hit the back, Morg!" Mark ordered. "George, take that side and watch the barn. Freda, keep well down, gal. Don't none of you start throwing lead until I give the word."

For once Freda did not make any comment to Mark's orders. She knew when to have a joke and when to obey fast, without question. Mark had been in charge of the preparations for defending the house ever since they returned from town. He threw all his considerable knowledge into the matter. First he scouted around and found a secluded draw about two miles from them and on the side away from Double K. Into this went all the ranch's remuda along with Dusty and Mark's horses and their pack horse. Then, although he ached in every muscle and bone, Mark looked the house over and found but little needed attending to, beyond dousing the dining-room fire and making sure all the weapons were fully loaded.

Now the attack had come. The riders were on top of the slope and coming down towards the river. Suddenly shots thundered out, lead smashed into the house but its walls kept them out. The window panes shattered and bullets raked the room, but so far all the shooting came from the front.

Mark's matched guns were in his hands as he flattened on the wall by the window. He looked back across the room, eyes trying to pierce the darkness. From the look of things the opening volley hit nobody. He could see Lasalle's shape by the side window looking out towards the barn and outbuildings, holding his Le Mat carbine ready for use. Morg had already taken his place in the hands' bedroom and so would be clear. That only left Freda.

"Mark!" whispered a scared voice at his side, a voice trying to hide its fear. "I've brought your rifle. Papa and Morg are in place and ready. Why did those men start shooting?"

Before Mark could make a reply the Double K men came sweeping down the slope and into the water. He guessed that whoever had charge of the raid thought the occupants of the houses were all asleep and hoped to startle and confuse himself and his friends. The men knew of the hound's presence and that a chance of moving in silently was unlikely to succeed. So they hoped to startle, suddenly waken the people in the house and rush in on them before they recovered.

It was a real smart plan. Except that Mark and the others were fully awake and ready.

Suddenly Mark swung around towards the shattered window. He brought up his right-hand Colt, thumbing four rapid shots into the darkness, firing into the brown without taking sight. He heard a yell and guessed some of the lead took effect. The attackers yelled their surprise. He heard the frantic churning of hooves in water as they brought their horses to a halt or tried to change directions. Mark grinned and darted to the other window, beyond the door.

"Pour it into them, Dusty!" he yelled, firing three more shots, and trying to make out his two *amigos* were with him.

He heard the crash of his rifle from the window just vacated and twisted his head in time to see Freda flatten herself back against the wall. The girl once more showed she had courage and could think for herself. She guessed at what he tried to do and lent a hand.

The riders came ashore and fanned out, riding along the side of the house towards the barn. Lasalle cut loose with the old Le Mat, turning four of his nine bullets adrift towards the men. He did not think he had managed to hit anyone but his little effort caused a rapid swing about and dart to cover.

Not all the men had headed for the barn, a few went the other way but Mark already had thought of this and was by the other side window which stood open. He lined his right-hand Colt and used its last two loads on them. This time he saw a man crumple over, cling to his saddlehorn and turn his horse away.

"Freda!" Mark snapped. "Watch 'em, gal. I'll reload."

It took some time to strip foil from a combustile cartridge, nick the bottom to ensure the percussion cap's spark of flame struck powder, and place it in the chamber of the Colt, turn the chamber, work the loading rammer and force it home. Mark had done the drill so often he could manage it in daylight or dark, but he felt satisfied with himself that he remembered to have the spare loads laid out on the table, along with an open percussion cap box. He loaded both his guns and even as he did so fresh developments came.

The men from Double K, being met with a hot fire on three sides of the house, took stock of the situation. From the guns, and the yell they heard, it looked like Dusty Fog, Mark Counter and Lasalle were all in front and, unless Dune called it wrong, the Ysabel Kid had left for Bent's Ford. So it appeared the defenders had committed an error in tactics and left the rear unguarded. With this in mind a group of men moved in, swinging behind the barn, leaving their horses and running off across the range, meaning to come in at the rear.

"Hey, Freda!" Morg's voice came in an urgent whisper. "Bring me some shells for my rifle, please."

"I'll be right there," she answered.

"It's no use you-all trying to make me jealous, gal," drawled Mark. "I'm allus true to one gal—at a time."

"She doesn't show very good taste, whoever she is," replied Freda hotly, but in no louder voice than Mark used. "I wouldn't be your gal, Mark Counter, not even if you were the last man in the world."

"Gal," replied Mark, his teeth gleaming in a grin as he watched her back off from the table, keeping down. "Was I the last man in the world I'd be too busy to worry."

Freda gave a snort and thought of a suitable answer, although she doubted if her father would approve of it. She collected a box of bullets and headed for the bedroom to find Morg standing by an open window and looking out. He had his rifle in his hands, but her ten gauge lay on the bed by his side.

"Hi, there," he greeted. "Sure is quiet back here. Say, has that mean ole Mark been abusing you again?"

"He sure has. Whyn't you act like a knight in shining armour and go in there to demand satisfaction."

"Me?" grinned Morg. "I'm satisfied already. Who wouldn't be? Got me a starlit night, a real pretty gal to talk to and—hand me up the scatter, gal."

None of the speech had been in a loud tone, but the last few words came in an urgent whisper. Freda took up the shotgun, exchanging it for the rifle he offered her. Then she peered through the window and watched the dark shapes moving by the backhouse and coming towards them.

Gripping the shotgun Morg rested its barrels on the window ledge and drew back the hammers. The double click must have sounded loud in the still of the night, the group of men out back came to a halt for a moment. Then, apparently deciding the clicks to be imagination they moved forward, their weapons glinting dully in their hands.

Morg now had a problem. Never had he been in such a spot and he had never turned lead loose at another man. He did not want to shoot at the men, to kill without a warning. Then an idea came to him.

"She's loaded with nine buckshot, gents!" he called. "Hereby I lets her go! Yahoo! Hunt your holes, you gophers!"

His first words brought the men to an uneasy halt. The rest of his speech had the effect of making the men turn about and head for cover. He aimed low and cut loose with both barrels. A man yelled, staggered, but reeled on. Morg knew some of the lead had gone home but that the man he hit was not seriously hurt.

He passed the shotgun to Freda who whispered she would reload for him. At the shot, lead slashed from all sides at the house. A bullet smashed into the window frame, showering broken glass and splinters which caused Freda to cry out and twist around. Morg gave an angry growl, grabbing his rifle to throw shots at the spurts of flame around the building.

"Are you all right?" he asked.

The concern in his voice brought a thrill to Freda, a thrill she could hardly explain even to herself. Before she could answer the firing died down and Mark's voice came to her.

"How's it going back there? Is the roof still on?"

"Why shouldn't it be?" Freda replied, running a hand across her face and knowing the flying splinters missed her.

"I heard you fire that fool shotgun off!"

It took Freda a moment to catch Mark's meaning. She wished she could find a real smart answer. Then she remembered Morg's question and turned to him, seeing he watched her.

"I'm all right thanks, Morg. How about you?"

She laid a hand on his arm, he released the rifle with one hand to reach and trap the hand, holding it gently.

"Lord!" he said. "If they'd hurt you I'd—"

Freda bent forward, her lips lightly brushed his cheek. This was not the action of a well brought-up young lady. She and Morg met for the first time that afternoon, sure he had taken on to ride for her father but that did not mean he took on for any other reason than he needed work. All those thoughts buzzed through Freda's head after her impulsive action.

"There's nothing between Mark and me," she whispered.

"There's no gal any place waiting for me," Morg whispered.

Then they kissed, oblivious of everything. Two young people who suddenly found themselves in love. Then Morg gently moved her away from him and swung to the window. Any man who tried to harm Freda was going to get lead and would need to kill him first.

Unaware of romance blooming in the back of the house Mark Counter moved from front to the left side of the dining-room, watching through the windows, letting the Double K men do the shooting, saving his lead for when it would be needed to break an attack.

He flattened by the side of the window which looked out across the range. Men darted forward, coming towards the house. Then a shout from the other side reached his ears although he could not make out the words. The approaching party came to a halt and took cover rapidly.

Mark's fighting instincts warned him something was in the air. The men had been moving in undetected, or at least without warning that they had been detected. Yet they had taken cover in a hurry. This was not the actions he would expect of an attacking group coming in to their objective unsuspected. Anything unusual in an attack worried Mark and made him the more alert.

"Freda!" he called. "Freda!"

The second word brought her to his side. She realized that he no longer sounded easy-going and friendly.

"Go and warn both your pappy and Morg to be ready for something to start. That bunch out there have something tricky on their minds."

"What?" she asked.

"I wish I knew, gal."

The coldness of his voice made her feel as if a chilly hand laid itself on her. She knew Mark had guessed what the smart move might be—and that it was something terrible.

After delivering Mark's message to her father Freda returned to the bedroom and told Morg. He gripped her hand in his.

"Are you scared?" he asked.

"Not now I'm with you."

At the right side window Lasalle knelt watching the barn into which a fair part of the attacking force went. Due to Mark's prompt action on returning from Barlock they would find little to destroy and would not burn the building until after the attack. A lighted barn blazing merrily would make them much too easy targets for the defenders, so the barn and other buildings were safe during the attack.

Nursing the Le Mat, feeling the weight of the Army Colt in his waistband, he watched for the first sign of his attackers. He wished he could take time out to reload the fired chambers, but still had a fair few shots left and a load of grapeshot in the lower barrel, just waiting to be used.

Lasalle was no longer the defeated, tired man who rode to his ranch that morning, ready to call "calf-rope" and run. Now he stood firm, grimly determined to fight for his home, to defend it with his last breath.

A small group of men eased out of the barn, moving cautiously towards the house. Lasalle watched them, wondering if his best move would be to open fire now, or let them come in closer and make sure he hit at least one of them. He did not want to kill, but knew it might be necessary to get himself clear of this mess. He knew they did not suspect he watched them, or they would not be advancing so openly on him.

Just as he decided to throw a warning shot, the group halted. He saw a flicker of light, a glow as if a man had turned around and lit a match, shielding the flame with his body. Apparently one of the men had lit a cigarette or cigar, for something glowed redly in the darkness.

In a flash Lasalle knew something to be dead wrong. He knew that in the heat and madness of battle men often did strange things like singing, praying, crying or shouting. But they did not stop to light cigarettes. Nor did men sneaking up on a night attack a defended building.

Resting the barrel of the carbine on the window he took a careful aim. Drawing back the hammer he fired a shot and saw the man holding the red, glowing thing rock under the impact of lead, then go down, dropping whatever he held so that it spluttered on the ground by him.

Instantly consternation and pandemonium reigned amongst the party around the shot man. They yelled, shouted, and one bent, grabbing at the spluttering red glow on the ground. The others seemed to panic and not one of them thought to throw lead at the house. Lasalle aimed again, switching to the grapeshot barrel and touching off a shot, sending it into the body of the man bending to grab the thing from the ground.

Then the others turned, racing away, not merely running, but fleeing in terror, discarding their rifles as they went. They left a man sprawled on his back and another crawling on hands and knees, screaming after them.

"Dave! Stace!" he screamed in a voice none of the others who heard it would forget. "Come back he—!"

The rest ended in a thunderous roar and a sheet of flame which ripped the night apart, turning it for a brief instant, into day. The house shook, the remaining window glass shattered in the explosion's blast, but the walls held firm.

"Get to the windows!" Mark roared. "Pour it into them!"

His words came not a moment too soon. Hooves thundered, feet thudded and men shouted as they raced towards the house. Freda dashed into the front room with Morg's rifle in her hands. She reached the window and fired through it at the horsemen rushing up from the river. She heard the rapid crashing of Mark's rifle, saw a man drop from his horse and fired again. From the bedroom sounded the booming roar of the shotgun. Her father's Le Mat spat at the side and lead raked and ripped into the house.

"Mark!" Freda screamed, seeing a shape loom up at the window on the undefended side.

Mark turned, levering two shots, the first struck the wall close to the window, the second slammed into the man's face and threw him back from it.

A man sprang from his horse, landed before Freda's window and grabbed the rifle in her hands. She screamed, her finger closed on the trigger and flame lashed from the barrel. She saw the man reel back, smelled burning cloth and flesh, then screamed and fell to the floor in a faint.

His rifle empty, Mark let it fall to the floor and brought out the matched Colt guns. Now he was at his most deadly for he could handle the Colts like twin extensions of his own arms. Flame spurted from the left gun, causing a rapid withdrawal from the side window just as a man tried to throw down on him. A sound before the house brought him around, throwing a bullet into the shoulder of a mounted rider and causing him to turn his horse and head away.

Lasalle cut loose with his Le Mat, shooting fast and emptying the cylinder. Then he let the gun drop and drew the Army Colt to shoot again. He stopped one man with the Colt, which surprised him as he had never been much of a hand with a revolver.

At the back Morg's shotgun brought a hurried end to the attack and left one man moaning on the ground. The young cowhand felt sick, but the heat of the excitement kept it down. He had put lead into a man, maybe killed him. It was not a pleasant thought.

Then it was over. The defence had been too hot and accurate for hired guns to face. They broke off, dragging their dead and wounded with them, making for their horses. They split into two parties, one throwing lead at the house while the other mounted dead and wounded on horseback for they wished to leave as little proof as possible. Those were Mallick's orders when he organized the attack by almost the full Double K crew with the intention of wiping Lasalle's place from the face of the earth. Dusty Fog and Mark Counter had good friends who would come and investigate should they be killed. Nothing which might point to Double K must be found. The same applied now. Sure the men in the house knew who was responsible for the attack—but they couldn't prove it and Elben was the only law around.

"You can light the lamps now," Mark said as the men rode away, splashing through the water. "The mauling we gave them—My God! Freda!"

Almost before he reached her side Morg had arrived and Lasalle ran to where the girl lay on the floor.

She groaned and Mark struck a match, looking for some sign of a wound. He saw the fear and panic in her eyes. She stared wildly at him.

"What—where—!"

"Easy gal. They've gone," Mark replied. "Are you hit?"

"I killed one of them!" she gasped. "I shot—"

"Drop it, girl!" Mark's voice cracked like a whip. "It was him or you. Now lie easy until we find if he hit you."

Morg lit the lamp and stared at the girl in a distracted manner. Not until then did he feel the trickle of blood running down his face where one of the last shots threw splinters into him. Freda saw it and nothing could have shaken her out of the hysteria quicker.

"Morg!" she gasped, getting to her feet. "You're hurt!"

"Not him," Mark put in. "You can't hurt a feller from Montana by hitting him on the head."

The girl threw Mark a cold look and eased Morg into a chair. She saw the wound to be more messy than dangerous and prepared to care for it. Lasalle watched all this and a slightly puzzled look came to his face. Mark grinned and suggested they took a look outside.

Freda froze as she reached a hand to Morg's head. "That explosion!" she gasped. "What caused it?"

"Dynamite," Mark answered flatly. "Come on, George. Let's make sure they've left clean. Where's that old Bugle dog?"

Having shown commendable good sense and headed for the girl's bedroom when the shooting started, Bugle now came out, wagging his tail. He followed the two men to the door of the house. He stood outside and his head swung to one side, his back hair rose and he growled.

"Back in, *pronto*!" Mark snapped. "Freda, douse the lights."

Once more the room plunged into darkness and Bugle

headed for the safety of his mistress's bedroom.

"Get the guns loaded!" Mark growled. "We might need them."

The horses came nearer and Lasalle's house lay silent. Mark felt puzzled at the turn of events. He thought that after the mauling they took Double K would stay well clear. They might be sending a small group of determined men in, hoping the house suspected nothing, although Mark could not think how the group managed to get in the direction from which they came so soon after departing the other way.

"Yeeah!"

Loud in the night it rang. The old battle yell of the Confederate Cavalry. Mark realized that Dusty would send one of his friends to the Wedge to collect help and reinforcements. The explosion must have brought them on the run but they knew better than ride up unannounced to a house which had just been under attack.

"Hey Mark!" yelled Dusty's voice. "Answer up, *amigo*!"

"Come ahead and quit that fool yelling!" Mark called back. "What for you all waking folks up in the middle of the night?" He holstered his guns and threw a look across the room to where Freda and Morg were much closer than needed for first-aid or reloading weapons. "You can put the lamp on again. Unless you'd rather stay in the dark."

Freda and Morg gave startled and guilty exclamations, moving apart hurriedly and trying to look unconcerned as Lasalle lit the lamp.

"You're so sharp you'll cut yourself, Mark Counter," Freda gasped. "Why don't you go out and meet Dusty?"

"Why sure," agreed Mark. "Reckon you pair would like to be alone."

The nearest thing Freda could lay hands on that wouldn't be too dangerous was the discarded deck of cards. She grabbed them up and hurled them at Mark. He side stepped, grinned, winked at the blushing Morg, then stepped out to greet his friends.

CHAPTER TWELVE

The Map

"YOU all right, *amigo*?" Dusty asked, swinging down from the borrowed horse and walking towards Mark.

"Why sure. They didn't get any of us."

"What happened?" asked Johnny Raybold, showing his relief at finding Mark safe and unharmed.

"They hit us foot, hoss and artillery," Mark replied, hearing the others as they came from the house behind him.

"Get any of 'em, Mark?" Rusty Willis inquired.

"Not less'n these folks can shoot," scoffed Johnny. "He couldn't hit the side of a barn if he was in it."

Mark ignored the comments from his good friends. He stepped forward to greet Stone Hart and then introduced him to Lasalle, Freda and Morg. They were all invited in, but Johnny and Rusty turned their horses and headed across the stream to make a sweep across the range and make certain the Double K pack had headed home.

"I reckon there were getting on for twenty or more of them," Mark said, as the men gathered around the Lasalle's dining-room table and Freda, with Morg's help, went to the kitchen to make coffee. "They came down on us loaded for bear."

"That's a mean bear, needing dynamite to move it," Dusty answered quietly.

"That's the part of it I don't like," growled Stone. "Dusty, they've gone too far now. We'll have to paint for war."

"Likely. Comes daylight Mark and I'll head down trail and get Clay to come up here. Then we'll clear this whole section out. It'll be open season on anybody wearing a gun and riding for Double K."

Lasalle looked at the faces around the table. Tanned faces which showed little of their thoughts. Not one of them looked like the sort of man to back down once they set their mind to a thing.

"Why did they hit us tonight?" he asked.

"Way I see it, they had to make a grandstand play. They'd hit Gibbs and left him with his hide peeled by a blacksnake whip," Dusty answered. "Which same Pop Jones had called it quits. That left you. If you stayed on the other two might take heart and stand fast. You had to be brought down."

"But not with dynamite, Dusty," Stone Hart objected. "That's going a mite strong even for a bunch of hard-cases with the local law behind them."

"Maybe," Dusty drawled. "I'll feel happier when I've got Clay Allison here so we can make us some talk to the owner of the Double K."

"Something struck me about this Keller," Lasalle put in. "None of the Double K crowd even refer to him. When they say boss they always mean Mallick."

"Maybe haven't seen enough of Keller to call him boss," Mark answered.

"Or maybe he's not the real boss of this she-bang," Stone suggested. "It could be that Mallick's behind all this for his own benefit. Nobody's seen Keller from all accounts."

They were words of wisdom, although none of the others knew it. However before the subject could be followed further Rusty Willis returned with word that Johnny had taken off after the Double K men and would not be back for a couple of hours. Rusty had taken time out to circle the house on his return.

"Looks like you got at least four, maybe more," he said, then looked at Lasalle. "Was I you, I'd keep my gal inside comes morning."

"Why?"

"It's not a sight for her to see. Out where the dynamite went off," was the simple reply. "I'd say at least two of them were there, but it's kinda hard to tell for sure."

"Two's right," Lasalle said, his voice showing strain and a shudder running through his body. "One of them was wounded. I hit—"

"Drop it!" Mark snapped, gripping the man's shoulder in a

hold which made him wince and brought an end to his words. "You didn't ask them to come here in the night, or to try and dynamite your home. And it damned sure wasn't your fault they came to die."

"Mark's right at that, friend," agreed Stone Hart. "You stopped a man killing you, your daughter, Mark and that young feller in the kitchen. To do that you shot a man who was trying to throw dynamite at your place. It was his choosing, not you'rn."

Dusty thrust back his chair and came to his feet. He went to the kitchen door, opened it, closed it again, without Morg and Freda knowing for they were in each other's arms and kissing. Dusty knocked on the door, turning to wink at the others. Then he opened it and walked in. Now Freda busied herself at the stove and Morg seemed fully occupied with cutting bread for her.

"We'll be staying here for the night, Freda," he said. "Stone and the boys don't have their bedrolls along."

"I'll fix it," she replied, face just a trifle flushed.

An hour later Freda went to her room and climbed into bed. She heard the men settling down in the dining-room and wondered if she would sleep again, so great was the feeling surging inside her as she thought of Morg Summers. She doubted if sleep would ever come to her again.

Yells and whoops woke Freda. For a moment she lay on her bed, blinking in daylight which flooded her room. Then she gasped for she saw the sun hung higher in the sky than usually was the case when she rose. Rolling from her bed she sat on the edge, rubbing her eyes. Then she went to the window and peered out. She stared at the sight before her, wondering what had gone wrong for it seemed that Johnny Raybold and Rusty Willis were attacking Dusty Fog.

Freda had undressed and wore her night-gown now; she could not remember doing it the previous night, but appeared to have done so. Grabbing up her robe she quickly climbed into it. She saw Rusty grab Dusty from behind, locking hands around his waist from behind. Johnny had landed on the ground, but was getting up and charging into the attack.

The girl could not think what started the fight. She wondered why none of the others stopped it. With bare feet slapping on the floor, Freda darted from her room and through the kitchen. She tore open the door and went out. To her amazement her father and the other men sat around watching the fight and clearly enjoying it.

Even as the girl appeared Dusty bent forward, reached between his legs to grab one of Rusty's. Then he straightened and Rusty let out a yell and fell backwards with Dusty sitting down hard on him.

"Eeyow whooof!" Rusty bellowed, the air rammed from his lungs in the cry.

By this time Johnny was on his feet and charging forward. Dusty left the recumbent Rusty's body in a rolling dive forward. His hand clamped on Johnny's ankle in passing and heaved. Johnny gave a wail and lost his balance. He lit down on his hands, breaking his fall with the skill of a horseman taking a toss from a bad one.

Dusty retained his grip on the ankle and grabbed Johnny's free leg. He bent the legs upwards, crossing the ankles and sitting on them. Johnny's mouth opened and he let out a howl.

"Yowee!" he yelled. "Yipes, uncle, Dusty. Uncle!"

Never had Freda felt so completely baffled by a turn of events. She stared at her father, then at Mark and Stone who calmly smoked cigarettes, finally at Morg who seemed to be enjoying the scene.

"What happened?" she gasped, watching Dusty rise after receiving Johnny's surrender howl. "What happened?"

"That?" grinned Mark as the men got to their feet. "Why that's just Johnny 'n' Rusty showing Dusty how it's done."

"But—but—I thought—!" began a very irate Freda. *"Cowhands!"*

With that final yell, realizing that no young lady should be seen dressed, or rather undressed, in such a manner, she turned and fled to the house.

Johnny grinned wryly as he took up his hat. Ever since Dusty demonstrated the arts of ju jitsu and karate to them in Quiet Town, Rusty and he had tried to disprove its effectiveness. Whenever their paths crossed with Dusty's, the two Wedge hands banded together to show their friend they could lick him—only they never managed to do it.

"Say, Dusty," Johnny drawled. "You dropped this paper. Is it anything important?"

He held out a scrap of paper and Dusty frowned. Then the light dawned and Dusty thrust a hand into his levis pocket. He drew out the torn papers taken from Mallick's office on the previous day.

"It might be at that," he said. "Let's go inside and see if we can sort it out."

"I'll get the boys out to those two spreads first," Stone replied. "Then I'd best go down trail to the herd."

Dusty left Stone to attend to the matter and entered the house. He went to the table and sat down, spreading the pieces of paper out before him. Turning them so they all faced the same side upwards he started to fit them together. He found little difficulty in getting the scraps in order and forming a completed whole. A map lay before him, complete in design and outline, but without a single name to say what it might be a map of. It showed land contours, water-courses, woods even, yet not a single letter to identify the range it covered. An oblong outline ran around the inner edge of the map but it meant nothing to him.

"Where in hell is it a map of?" he said, more to himself than to Lasalle who stood by the window.

"Let me take a look, Captain."

For a long moment Lasalle studied the map, frowning and cocking his head on one side.

"I forgot about the pieces," Dusty drawled. "Picked them up in Mallick's office yesterday, but things happened a mite fast and I didn't get a chance to look at them earlier."

Then Dusty tensed slightly. He took a long look at the map, then reached into his pants pocket. He shook his head, rose and crossed the room to where a box of Winchester bullets lay. Taking one out he returned to the table and bent over the map. He drew a line from the lower edge about six inch from the right side to about an inch from the top, then still using the bullet's lead as a pencil, made a right angle turn and a line to the right edge.

"Does it look any more familiar now?" he asked.

Lasalle looked down at the map, he gave an explosive grunt of surprise as he saw the whole thing with the eye of a man who knew how to make a map.

"It sures does!" he breathed. "That's the Lindon Land

Grant. You didn't quite get the lines right, Captain Fog, but I recognize the physical features of the map now. But the way this is drawn it makes the Grant appear to cover all our range and right up to the badlands."

"Yeah," Dusty said quietly. "That's just how it looks."

Just at the moment Stone Hart entered from sending off his relief forces to the Gibbs' and Jones' places. He came forward and looked down at the map, seeing its significance.

"What do you make of it, Dusty?" he asked.

"I don't know for sure. But it'd take a trained man to make a map like this, wouldn't it?"

"Sure," Stone agreed. "This's been line-drawn from the original I'd say."

At last Lasalle found himself in a position to offer advice on something beyond the ken of the two Texans. He spent his service career in the Confederate Army Engineers and knew considerable about making maps.

"It was," he said. "The man who did it knew his work."

"A Government surveyor'd be able to do it I suppose?" Dusty asked.

"A well trained one would," Lasalle agreed.

"What're you thinking about, Dusty?" Stone asked, seeing the interest Dusty showed, although most people could have noticed no change in the small Texan's face or appearance.

"Just a hunch, Stone. I'll tell you more about it when I've met Clay."

He refused to say any more and Stone knew the futility of trying to get more out of him. After breakfast he still knew no more about Dusty's hunch but did not bother, he knew he would learn about it when Dusty had every detail worked out and not before.

"I'll head down to the herd and tell Waggles we're staying a spell," Stone said. "Johnny's gone ahead, should get them afore they head the cattle up."

They had finished breakfast and were preparing to start out. This time Mark would be riding with Dusty and they left warning that neither Lasalle nor Morg were to move far from the house and that they keep all weapons loaded.

"If they hit at you," Stone went on, after Dusty gave his grim warning, "get inside and fort up. Then make some

smoke, burn rags or something, get smoke coming up from
your chimney and we'll come a-running.''

"One thing, George," Dusty finished, turning his big paint
stallion's head from the ranch. "Try and stick that map
together for me."

"Sure, Captain Fog," Lasalle promised. "If you reckon it's
important."

"I reckon that map's the middle of all this fuss," Dusty
replied quietly. "Let's go, Mark. And don't worry if you hear
riders coming up from the south on towards dark, George.
It'll most likely be us."

After his guests left, Lasalle went around his buildings with
Morg at his side. They looked at the ragged hole left where the
dynamite went off and Lasalle could not restrain a shudder,
even though the other men had been up at the first hint of
dawn to clear away the ghastly horror.

"We'll do like Captain Fog said, Morg," Lasalle stated.
"Stay around the house and tidy things up today."

"Sure, boss. Say, can I have a talk to you—about Freda and
me?"

"I reckon you can," Lasalle replied. "Let's go to the barn.
I wonder how Pop Jones and Ralph Gibbs'll find things
today?"

At the Jones place a wagon stood before the door as
Peaceful Gunn and his party rode up. The old man and the
cowhand called Yance watched the trio of Wedge hands approach as they lifted chairs into the back of the canvas-topped
wagon. "Howdy folks," greeted the man called Shaun, his
tones showing his Irish birth. "Cap'n Fog sent us along to
help you."

"Knowed I shouldn't come here with this pair!" Peaceful
moaned, eyeing the Colt the cowhand held. "Nobody'd trust
me with villainous looking *hombres* like them at my back."

"Sure and here's me a descendant of kings of auld Ireland
being spoke ag'in by this evil-doer," replied Shaun, in his
breezy brogue. "Twas foolish to put all that gear into the
wagon when we'll only have to be moving it out again."

Then the Jones family and their hand started to smile. These
were the men promised to lend a hand with the defense of the
house. Pop looked right sprightly for a man who had been on

the verge of losing his home. He took out a worn old ten gauge and set percussion caps on the nipples ready for use.

"Let's us get this lot back into the house," he suggested.

With eager hands to help the work was soon done. At Peaceful's suggestion they left the wagon standing outside, then Shaun turned on his Irish charm and got a very worried looking Ma Jones to smile.

"You don't sound like any Texan I ever heard," she said at last.

"I'm the only Texas-Irishman in the world," Shaun replied. "Can't you tell from me voice, a Texas drawl on top of a good Irish accent. Say, ma'am, you wouldn't know how to make an Irish stew, would you?"

On being assured that Ma not only could, but would, make an Irish stew, Shaun gave his full attention to making plans for the defence of the house.

Five hard looking men rode towards the Jones place shortly after noon. In the lead came Preacher Tring, sitting his horse uneasily for the Kid's birdshot onslaught had caught him in a most embarrassing position. This did not tend to make Tring feel any better disposed to life in general and the small ranch owners in particular.

He growled a low curse as he saw the wagon standing before the Jones' house and without a team. Clearly Pop Jones thought the Double K were playing kid games when they said get out. Right soon Pop would get a lesson.

Then the men put spurs to their horses and rode fast, coming down on the ranch and halting the mounts in a churned up dust cloud before the house. Tring dropped his hand towards his hip, meaning to draw and pour a volley into the house.

"Don't pull it, mister!" said a plaintive voice from the barn. "You'll like to scare me off."

All eyes turned to look in the direction of the speaker and all movement towards hardware ended. This might have been due to a desire to keep the nervous sounding man unafraid—or because all they could see plainly of him was the barrel of a Spencer rifle, its .52 calibre mouth yawning like a cave entrance at them.

"Is it the visitors we have, Peaceful?" a second voice inquired.

The wagon's canopy had drawn back and a Winchester

slanted at the Double K men, lined from the source of the Irish voice. Then a third man sauntered into view from the end of the house, also carrying a rifle, while a shotgun and a fourth rifle showed on either side of the open house door.

"Who are you?" Tring asked.

"We work here," Shaun replied. "Who are *you*?"

"Tell that pair of ole—!"

A bullet fanned Tring's hat from his head. The lever of Shaun's rifle clicked and the Double K men tried to keep their horses under control without also giving the idea they could reach their weapons.

"Just be keeping the civil tongue in your head, *hombre*!" Shaun warned. "And if you've no further business here, let's be missing you."

Tring had brought only four men with him as he did not expect any trouble in handling the Jones family and because the ranch crew had taken a mauling on their abortive attack at the Lasalle place. He knew he and the others had no chance of doing anything better than get shot to doll rags at the moment. However a second party of men were at the Gibbs place, attending to Mallick's orders. Tring decided to gather them in and return to the Jones house. When he came he would not leave a living soul at the house.

It was a good idea. Except that the other party were having troubles of their own.

They came on the Gibbs place, six of them, almost all the unwounded fighting strength of the Double K out on the business of clearing the two weakened small outfits out of the Panhandle country.

One of the men jerked his thumb towards where a tall, slim, studious young man leaned his shoulder against a corral post, clearly having been working on repairing the fence.

"Hey you!" he barked.

Doc Leroy looked up almost mildly. "Me sir?"

"Yeah, you! what in hell are you doing?"

"Fixing the fence," Doc answered.

From the house window Joyce watched with a quaking heart. She wondered why Rusty and Billy were not on hand to help Doc.

"Then start to pull it down!" ordered the man, a man she recognized from the previous visit.

"Now that'd be plump foolish," said Doc.

The man's hand dropped towards his gun and froze immobile a good inch from its butt.

Doc's right hand made a sight defying flicker, the ivory handled Colt came into it, lining on the man, the hammer drawn back.

"Just sit easy, *hombre*," Doc said, but his entire voice had changed. "And pray I don't let this hammer fall."

A footstep behind her brought Joyce swinging around. She found Rusty had entered from the back and was making for the front door, his rifle in his hands.

"Ole Doc sure is surprising, ain't he?" grinned Rusty and stepped out to lend his friend moral and actual support just as Billy emerged from the barn, complete with Henry rifle.

"Mrs. Gibbs!" Rusty said over his shoulder. "Come out here, ma'am and bring your scattergun." Joyce complied and Rusty indicated the men with the barrel of his rifle. "Any of them here yesterday?"

She stabbed up the shotgun, lining it on the man who did all the talking. "He was the one who shot Sam."

"Drop your guns, all of you!"

The words cracked from Rusty's mouth and the men obeyed. Then they were told to move to one side. Rusty put down his rifle and removed his gunbelt. He walked forward, going to the man Joyce indicated. His hands shot out, grabbing this man and hauling him from the saddle.

Rusty slammed the man on to the ground. His right fist shot into the man's stomach and ripped up a left as he doubled his man over. The man stood taller than Rusty but he never had a chance. He tried to fight back, but against Rusty's savage two handed attack he never stood a chance.

After a brutal five minute beating the man lay in a moaning heap on the floor and Rusty, nose bleeding and chest heaving, looked at Joyce.

"Any more of 'em here?" he asked.

"You leave them, boy," Doc answered coldly. "These gents have just volunteered to mend the corral."

The men most certainly had not intention of volunteering, but they were given no real choice in the matter. Under the guns of the three Wedge hands the men went to work. They might have hoped that Tring and his bunch would come to their aid but Doc put a block to such hopes.

"Happen anybody should come up and start throwing lead at us," he told the men, "we'll throw some back and you bunch'll get it first."

So, while hating fence building, or any other kind of work, the men hoped that Tring and his bunch would not come and try to rescue them.

Luckily for them Tring did not come. He started thinking after he left the Jones place and decided that Gibbs most likely had backing. The odds in the game were coming to a point where Tring no longer fancied them. Along with the others of his party he headed back to Double K and waited to hear what the Gibbs raiding party found. They did not return until after dark and came in looking sorry for themselves after working harder than any of them had done for years.

At dawn the following morning every man pulled out, heading for Barlock where they aimed to have a showdown with their boss, get such money as they could and pull out.

The Double K lay silent and peaceful after the men left. All the dead had been disposed of and the wounded taken into town, so only Sir James Keller and his daughter remained on the premises.

CHAPTER THIRTEEN

His Only Name Is Waco

THREE thousand head of longhorn Texas cattle wended their way across the range country. They kept in a long line, feeding as they moved. To prevent them from breaking out of their line, rode the trail hands, the point men at the head of the column, then the flank and swing men and at the back came the drag riders. Behind them moved the remuda and bringing up the rear two wagons, one driven by the cook, the other controlled by his louse.

The scene was one Dusty Fog and Mark Counter had seen many times. Yet they never grew tired of looking at it. This was the scene which brought money to Texas, allowed it to become the great and wealthy State it now was.

For a moment the two men sat and watched the trail hands riding the herd, horses jumping into a sprint to turn some steer which tried to avoid its destiny by breaking from the line. The steer would be turned back and another try the same move a few yards further on.

"Look restless," Dusty drawled.

"Maybe Clay ran into fuss," Mark replied. "There he is, the old cuss, right out front with Smiler and a kid I've never seen before."

Dusty had also noticed this. He studied the three riders about half a mile ahead of the herd. They saw Mark and Dusty at the same time and Clay Allison's hat came off to wave a greeting. Then both parties rode at a better pace towards each other.

Although they had not met for four years, Clay Allison looked little different, tall, slim, well dressed, even though trail dirty. He managed to keep his black moustache and short beard trimmed and neat, the matched guns at his sides were also clean and hung just right for a real fast draw. Smiler, tall, gaunt and looking more Indian than the Ysabel Kid, lounged in his saddle at his boss's side.

The boy at Clay's right took Dusty's attention, held it like a magnet. Not more than sixteen years old, but he still wore a brace of Army Colts in low hanging fast draw holsters. He had blond hair, a handsome face but looked cold and sullen. His clothes were not new, but they were good and serviceable.

Dusty bit down an exclamation for the boy looked much as had his brother Danny. Except that this kid looked meaner, the sort who either built himself the name as a real fast man with a gun—or found an early grave.

"Howdy Dusty, Mark," greeted Clay Allison. "Didn't expect to see you on this trail. You got a herd ahead?"

"Nope, but Stone Hart has," Dusty replied. "There's some fuss up ahead, Clay. Bad trouble. Let's pull off to one side and talk it out."

Waving his hand to one side Clay Allison nodded his agreement. They rode well clear of the herd, then swung down from their saddles. The youngster did not follow immediately but sat his horse for a moment watching the approaching herd.

"Who's the boy, Clay?" Dusty asked, nodding towards the youngster.

"His only name is Waco," Allison replied. "Been with me for nigh on six months now. I met up with him down in Tascosa. He was in a bar and all set to take on half a dozen Yankee soldiers. So I cut in and helped him. Been with me ever since. That boy's fast, Dusty, real fast. And he knows it."

At that moment the boy whose only name was Waco rode to join the four men as they stood under the shade of a cottonwood tree's branches. The horses were allowed to stand and graze to one side and Allison nodded to the herd as they passed.

"They've been so spooked up for the past few days that you have to ride a mile from 'em to cough or spit."

Dusty grunted his sympathy. He knew how uncertain the behaviour of a bunch of longhorn cattle could be. They might go through a howling gale or a thunderstorm without turning a hair, or they might just as easily spook and take to running at their own shadows. It all depended on how they felt.

"What's ahead, Dusty?" asked Allison.

"Wire."

"WIRE!"

Three voices said the word in a single breath. Clay Allison, Smiler and Waco each spat the word out as if it burned their mouths.

"Who strung it?" asked Smiler.

"Now that's a problem," Dusty admitted. "It's across the narrows on the old Lindon Land Grant."

"Lindon never block the trail," Smiler went on, speaking more then he had spoken in months.

"Lindon sold out to an Englishman," Mark replied, watching the boy called Waco and paying particular attention to the way Waco studied himself and Dusty. "I reckon Dusty's not satisfied that the new owner's behind the wire-stringing though."

Dusty glanced at his big *amigo* and grinned. It looked like he couldn't fool Mark or keep his thoughts from the big cowhand after all these years. Before Dusty could make a reply to Mark's words, Waco put his say-so in.

"This Englishman got you scared, or something?" he asked.

"Or something, boy," Dusty answered, knowing youngsters of Waco's type.

Yet somehow Dusty got the idea there was better than the makings of a fast-gun killer in the boy. The face, while sullen, looked intelligent and did not carry lines of dissipation. Not that it would stay that way long. Clay Allison might be a rancher, but Dusty knew the kind of men he hired. Good hands with cattle, but a wild onion crew form the Pecos, men who handled their guns better than average and liked to show their skill. A boy growing and spending his formative years in such company had one foot on the slope and the devil dragging at his other leg.

"Boy!" Waco hissed.

"Choke off, Waco!" Clay snapped.

Waco relapsed into silence, watching Dusty now with cold eyes. He had been an orphan almost since birth, his name came from people calling him the Waco-orphaned baby on the wagon train where his parents died. In time it became shortened to but one name, Waco. He had been reared by settlers, but never took their name even though they treated him with such kindness and love as could be shared for they had nine children of their own. He grew in a raw land and carried a gun form the day he was old enough to tote one. Now he rode for Clay Allison's CA spread and he didn't let any man talk down to him, especially not a short growed runt like that cowhand talking to Clay. It surprised Waco considerable that Clay would waste time in talking with such a small and insignificant man.

"What're you down here for, Dusty?" Clay went on.

"I'd like you to bring your herd to a halt for a day or so and come up trail with me. Bring a few of the boys. I've got Stone Hart along. Between us we ought to be able to wind this up without starting a war."

"Wind hell!" Clay barked. "That wire's got to go and I say it ought to go around the feller who strung it's neck."

"He's got around twenty guns backing him," Dusty answered. "And there's a whole slew of folks up that way, small ranchers, who can't stand a war fighting over their land."

Whatever his faults, and they were many, Clay Allison respected the property and persons of people less fortunate in the matter of wealth than himself; as long as they did not encroach on his holdings or make trouble for him, which the small ranchers up here did not. He nodded his head, seeing what Dusty said to be the truth. He also knew Dusty would not be back here unless he had some definite plan. However he did not feel happy about being too far from his herd while they acted so spooked.

"Tell me about it as we ride," he suggested.

"You sure want some help," Waco suddenly put, in facing Dusty.

"How do you mean?" asked Dusty.

"Come high tailing it down here to ask Clay to fight your fight for you."

"That's enough, boy!" Dusty's voice took a warning note.

"Don't call me boy!" Waco snapped. "I'm a man grown with these guns on."

"Then try acting like one."

The words met with the wrong reaction on Waco's part. His right hand dropped towards his gun. He did not make it.

Dusty caught the warning flicker in the youngster's eyes, his left hand crossed his body, fetching out the Colt from the right holster, lining it with the hammer drawn back under his thumb. For a long moment he stood like that, the others not moving either. Waco stood still, not entirely scared but numb and unbelieving. He thought he was fast with a gun, but this small man did not just stop at being fast. Somehow it did not matter to Waco if lead smashed into him. He had made his play and failed, he knew the penalty for failure.

With his thumb trembling on the gun hammer Dusty waited and watched. Then suddenly he lowered the Colt's hammer, spun the weapon on his finger, holstered it and turned to walk to his paint horse.

Letting out his breath in a long sigh Clay Allison followed, then Smiler also turned and walked away. Only Mark and Waco stood where they had dismounted to hold their talk, under the shade of a cottonwood tree.

"He didn't have the guts to drop the hammer!" Waco sneered. "The d—"

Mark's big hand clamped on to the youngster's shirt, lifting him from his feet and slamming him back into a tree as if he weighed no more than a baby. Then Mark thrust his face up close to Waco's.

"Listen good to me, you hawg-stupid kid. Only one thing saved you from being killed or wounded bad. Dusty's brother was killed a few months back. You look a lot like him, except that he was a man, not just some trigger-fast-and-up-from-Texas kid."

With a contemptuous gesture Mark thrust Waco from him. Then he turned to go and collect his horse. Waco's face flushed with rage, his hand lifted over the butts of his guns.

"Turn around!" he snapped.

Mark turned, noting the stance. "What's on your mind, boy?"

"Nobody lays hands on me and lives to boast about it."

They faced each other, hands over the butts of their guns. The other three rode away, not knowing what went on behind them for their attention rested on the cattle.

Just what started the stampede they never discovered. It could have been any of a number of things, or none of them. It most likely stemmed from the ornery nature of the Texas

Longhorn steer, a breed of cattle never noted for the stability or gentleness of its behavior.

Whatever the cause, one moment the herd moved along in its normal manner. The next saw every steer bellowing and leaping forward, galloping into wild stampede which swept aside the hands, made them draw clear or be run down.

"Stampede!" roared Clay Allison. "All hands and the cook!"

The old range cry brought every man forward at a gallop. Now they must try to reach the point of the herd, turn it, make the leaders swing around until they joined on the rear of the column, then keep them running in a circle until they tired and came to a halt. Only it would not be as easy as all that. Those wild-eyed racing steers would not willingly turn.

Clay's shout and the noise of the stampede reached Mark and Waco's ears. To give him credit Waco dropped his aggressive pose even before Mark relaxed and the youngster made his horse's saddle before Mark reached the bloodbay. Their difference of opinion was forgotten. Only one thing mattered now. To ride and help turn the herd.

Racing his horse at a tangent Waco came boiling down on the herd's point ahead of the other men. He urged the horse on, cutting down so as to try and slam into the lead steer and make it swing. The horse he rode knew its business, had been trained for cattle work. It ran well, then put its foot in a gopher hole and went down. Waco heard the terrified scream of the horse as he flew over its head. His instincts as a horseman saved him, allowed him to land on his feet, running. Then he stopped and turned, the herd headed straight at him now, the leaders seeing a hated man-thing on his feet and at their mercy instead of on a horse where he was their master.

The youngster turned, he saw his horse struggling to rise, terror and pain in its rolling eyes for its leg had broken. His right hand dipped and brought out the Army Colt to throw a bullet into the horse's head and end its terror and misery. Then he turned and tried to run but high heeled cowhand boots were never meant for running on and a longhorn steer could keep a horse hard-pressed to catch it.

Nearer came the steers, their horns, which could go to a six foot spread, lowered and ready to rip into him. Waco knew it would be no use turning and trying to shoot his way clear. He found a situation where his skill with a gun stood for nothing and all he could do was run.

"Waco!"

A single shout reached his ears, ringing above the noise of the herd. He twisted his head and saw a paint stallion bearing down on him. He saw the small man who he dismissed as nobody, and nothing and who he tried to draw on, cutting in ahead of the cattle, coming across the widening front of horns. Waco knew that if Dusty slowed down the herd would be on them before they could make a move to escape the rush.

Dusty knew the danger also. He measured the distance between the running youngster and the onrushing herd. This would be tricky, one false move, a wrong step on the part of the seventeen hand paint and they would all be under the hooves of the stampeding herd.

Bending low in the saddle Dusty prepared to grab Waco's waist band. He gave quick, tense instructions.

"Get set, boy. When I grab you, make a jump. I'll sling you across the back of the saddle. Then hang on with all you've got."

Waco heard the words, felt the presence of the big paint at his side. Then a hand grabbed him by the pant's belt and he felt himself heaved up. He had not expected such strength, his feet left the ground and he felt himself dragged towards the paint's back. Then he grabbed the cantle of the saddle to help out, hauling himself to hang across the horse's rump. The double girths of the rig took the strain and stood it. Waco writhed, he felt a horn brush his leg, then the paint ran the gauntlet of the herd, cutting to one side of them. The leaders did not aim to be so easily cheated of their prey. They swung after the paint, with its near helpless bundle hanging over the rump and slowing it.

Racing his big bloodbay stallion ahead of any of the others, Mark brought it full at the lead steer. Seeing the huge horse tearing at him, the steer started to swing slightly. Mark gave it no chance to reverse towards Dusty but crowded in once more. Clay Allison came up, followed by his brothers Ben and Jack. Between them the four men started to swing the stampede around, away from where Dusty brought his horse to a halt and lowered Waco to the ground. He did not leave the youngster for there was still the danger of a stray longhorn coming up and the longhorn did not fear a man afoot.

"They've got 'em!" Dusty said with satisfaction. "Making 'em do a merry-go-round. That'll slow 'em down."

Waco did not reply. He looked at the small man, only he no longer saw Dusty as being small. He knew he owed the other man his life, not once, but twice. Dusty could have killed him back there when he tried to draw. Then at the risk of his own life Dusty came to rescue him. This was a kind of man Waco had never met before and did not know what to make of. Clearly Dusty gave no thought to the incident back under the cottonwood, his full attention being on the herd.

They watched the circle made, and the steers began to slow, being kept in a circle all the time. Slowly the movement came to an end but the hands continued to ride their circle.

Clay Allison and Mark swung from the herd, riding to where Dusty and Waco stood waiting.

"You came close to being the late Waco, boy," Mark said.

"Yeah," agreed Clay. "I never thought to see you alive when your hoss went down. Reckon you owe Dusty something."

Slowly Waco turned, his eyes on Dusty.

"I reckon I do. I'm sorry for what happened back there Dusty."

A smile flickered on Dusty's face. He knew what the apology meant to Waco. It had been torn from him for he had never felt he owed any man a thing, now he owed Dusty his life.

"That's all right, boy. You did the man's thing back there when you shot that hoss rather than leave it to be stampeded under by the herd. You might have got clear with no trouble if you hadn't."

"It was my hoss, never let me down. I couldn't let it down at the end."

Smiles came to faces of the watching men. Then Clay pointed back to the remuda which approached them.

"You've got your pick of any hoss in the bunch, boy. Go take it."

A grin came to Waco's face, softening the sullen expression. Until this moment Clay never referred to him as anything but his own name. It looked like Dusty had stuck him with a fresh title. Somehow he did not mind. The word "boy" was now spoken in a different manner. Now Dusty regarded him as a boy who would one day grow into a man.

"I'll lend you a hand to get your saddle out, boy," Mark drawled. "Come on."

There were good horses in Clay Allison's remuda. One of them caught Waco's eye. He took up the rope from the saddle he'd laid on the ground. With a quick whirl he sent a hooley-ann loop flipping out to settle on the neck of a big young paint stallion, a seventeen hand beauty as yet untrained in cattle work. This horse he led out. It had been three saddled, ridden the three times which a bronc-buster considered all that was necessary before handing the horse into the remuda and since then little ridden. Clay brought it along to test out anybody who wanted to ride it, only Waco aimed to be the only man who ever did.

"You've picked a mean one there, boy," drawled Mark, on whom the implication of the choice was not lost. "He's got a belly full of bed-springs that need taking out before he'll be any use."

"Then I'm going to have to take them out," Waco replied.

Dusty and Clay watched the herd settle down before they offered to do anything else. Clay sat his horse and cursed the fool steers which had run off a fair amount of beef in the stampede.

"Keep 'em here and range feed for a spell," Dusty suggested. "Two, three days on this buffalo grass'll put the meat on them again. And by that time, happen you go along with me, we'll have this wire trouble fixed and the narrows opened again."

"I'll go along."

"Leave the herd here, with Ben and Jack, get half a dozen or more men you can rely on not to start a shooting match unless they have to, ride to the Lasalle place, and we'll pick Stone up on the way. Then I'll tell all of you what I aim to do."

It said much for Clay Allison's faith in Dusty that he agreed to this without inquiring what Dusty's plans might be. He felt fully satisfied that Dusty not only had a plan but could also see that same plan through given a bit of aid.

Calling his brother Ben over, Clay told of Dusty's arrangements. Ben listened and gave his agreement. Then he jerked his thumb along to the remuda where Waco and Mark were saddling the big paint.

"Waco sure picked the beauty this time," he said. "Told me you said he could have hand-choice of the remuda and he wanted the paint, so I told him to go ahead. Why in hell did he pick that hoss out of the rest?"

A grin twisted Clay's lips and he glanced at Dusty's big horse which stood grazing to one side.

"I wonder why?" he said.

Three times the paint threw Waco, but each time he got up and mounted again. He showed he could really handle a horse and the fourth time on he stuck there until the horse gave in. Not until then did he join the other men at the fire and took the mug of coffee offered by the cook. His eyes were on Dusty all the time, his ears working to catch every word Dusty said. Not until then did he fully realize who Dusty was for nobody had introduced him.

After the meal Clay selected six men, including Waco, to ride with them and see about moving the wire.

"We're r'aring to go, Cap'n Fog," said one of the men.

"Then un-rear!" Dusty snapped. "There's a time to talk and a time to fight. We'll try talk first."

"Hell they ain't but a bunch of hired guns, way you told us, Dusty," Waco objected.

"You're just as dead no matter who puts the lead into you, boy," Dusty answered. "And a lot of innocent folks might get hurt at the same time."

Usually Waco would have scoffed at the idea of worrying about other people. This time he did not. He sat back and waited to hear what the others said on the subject.

"We'll do whatever you say, Dusty," Clay stated firmly. "Then if talk don't work we can always try making war."

The Lasalle house had a crowd in it after dark that evening, not counting the Allison hands who lounged around outside, letting their boss make the talk while they ate some good fixings.

In the dining-room Dusty, Mark, Clay Allison, Stone Hart and Waco sat with Lasalle and Morg. The girl came in and joined her father after serving a meal from the supplies the CA crew brought along. They had barely got down to business when Johnny Raybold arrived, bringing word that although visited by the Double K men the Jones' and Gibbs' houses were fine and without a worry in the world.

"Never seed ole Peaceful looking so miserable," he concluded, to show that all really was well.

"I thought I'd send him visiting to earn his pay," Stone remarked.

"I sure earned it," Johnny grinned. "Mrs. Gibbs done made a pie for the boys, had it all a-cooling on the window. Only it's not there any more." Here Johnny rolled his eyes in ecstasy and rubbed his stomach. "Man, that Mrs. Gibbs sure is one good cook. Not that you-all aint, Miss Freda."

This latter came as he caught an accusing gleam in Freda's eyes and remembered visiting the house and praising her cooking.

"I bet you say that to all the cooks," she replied.

"I do, I do. But I sure don't want to meet up with Rusty, Doc'n Billy for a spell, not 'til they get over losing their pie."

"Now that's a shame. That sure is a shame," Dusty drawled. "Because you're headed over there right now, then on to Jones'. I want them here with their wagons in the morning so we can take them into town for supplies."

"Sure," Johnny replied, secure in the knowledge that no reprisals could be taken on him while he rode on urgent business. "I'll tell them."

"Just one man with each wagon," Dusty went on. "The other two stay on and guard the house."

"Yo!" Johnny replied and left the room.

"What's your plan, Dusty?" Clay asked.

"Easy enough. We're going into town tomorrow in force. And we're serving notice on the Double K bunch that they get out of town. After that I'm getting some questions answered by Mr. Mallick, the Land Agent, whether he wants to answer or not."

"And after that?" Stone put in.

"I want to get this fence business ended one way or the other. I aim to run Elben out of Barlock so the Double K doesn't have the backing of the law. Then, if I have to I'm going to see Keller and show him the error of his ways."

CHAPTER FOURTEEN

The Freeing Of Barlock

THE town of Barlock lay sleepily under the early morning sun. Few people walked the streets. In the office of the Land Agent an emergency meeting had been called. Mallick sat at his desk, sullen and scowling. Jackieboy Disraeli sat in a chair with a pout like a petulant schoolgirl on his face. To one side, by the door, stood Knuckles, leaning against the wall and looking about as intelligent as the wooden planks behind him. Before the desk stood Elben, and a man from the Double K, a hired gun who had slipped away early in order to have a chance at making some money at the expense of his friends.

"So you came here with a warning?" asked Mallick, in a mocking tone as he watched the man's face.

"Yeah."

"Why?"

"I reckoned it'd be worth something for you to know what Tring's fixing to do," replied the gunman.

Mallick looked at the man, and his voice still stayed mocking. "I see. So Tring and the rest are coming here to make us pay them for work they botched and couldn't complete."

"Yeah."

"And you thought you would warn us out of the goodness of your heart?" piped Disraeli, also watching the man.

"I reckoned it'd be worth at least a hundred dollars for you to know," answered the man, throwing a contemptuous look at the fancy dressed man.

The sudden anger which came to Disraeli's face should have warned the man of his danger, but he was more interested in talking himself into money, then getting away from town before the others arrived. Disraeli snapped his fingers and pointed at the man.

With a slow, almost beast-like snarl Knuckles left his place. He moved faster than one might have thought possible for so bulky a man. The gunman heard Knuckles and started to turn, his hand dropping towards the butt of his gun. Knuckles drove out a big fist, throwing it with all his power. Like the arrival of a thunderbolt it smashed into the side of the man's head as he turned. He flew across the room, his head snapped over and hanging at an unnatural angle. The others watched him hurl into the wall, hit it and slide down.

Crossing the room, Elben bent over and looked down at the man. Then he lifted scared eyes to Disraeli and Mallick. The Land Agent stood staring, but Disraeli remained in his seat, sadistic pleasure etched on his face.

"He's dead!" Elben said. "His neck's broke."

"So?"

There was challenge in Disraeli's one-word reply, mockery too, for Disraeli liked nothing better than to see stronger men who might have treated him with derision and mockery but cowered before the awful might of Knuckles. He watched Elben, seeing the marshal's eyes flicker to Knuckles who ignored the man he had struck down and killed and was now leaning against the wall again.

"I only told you," Elben answered. "What do you want us to do with him?"

"That's for you to decide," Mallick answered. "It was self defence on Knuckles' part. Now get down to your office and come back in a couple of hours with some of your men and clear that carrion out of here."

After the door closed on Elben's departing back, Mallick and Disraeli exchanged glances.

"I think we're finished here, don't you?" Disraeli asked.

Mallick nodded. "I think we are. What next?"

"We run. I have a friend in New York who can get us on a boat for Europe and we can disappear into some big city if we find that the law is after us. That is one advantage to being of my race, Mallick, the brotherhood of my people will shield us from the Gentiles."

"And what about me?" asked Mallick.

"You too, old friend. A little more money might help us though."

They exchanged glances. Both had money from their

scheme, although not as much as at first expected. The hiring of gunmen took much of the cream from their profits but the same men had been a necessity.

"Keller has the money to complete the purchase," Mallick remarked. "And for his running costs as he calls them. And he had a collection of jewelry, as you told me when you first put this idea to me. He'll be at the ranch, alone except for his daughter and with that bad ankle won't be any a problem. He'll never suspect anything until too late."

An evil gleam came to Disraeli's eyes. "Yes that's the idea!" he said, slapping his hands together like an excited girl. "I'll have revenge for my brother and see that accursed Sir James Keller suffer."

"Let's destroy all the papers on the Lindon Land Grant, and do a thorough job this time!" Mallick said. "Then we'll get the wagon, the money, and go to the Double K."

Half an hour later only the ashes of burned paper lay in the waste-paper basket, the body of the gunman sprawled by the wall. The doors were locked, that at the front bolted also for Mallick's party left by the rear.

They called at the saloon where Disraeli emptied his office safe, took all the money and the deeds to the business from it. Then, after making sure that no incriminating papers remained the two men went to where Knuckles had a fast two horse carriage awaiting them. They left town and took cover in a wood while Tring and his men rode by, then they headed across the range in the direction of the Double K.

When he found the birds had flown Tring cursed savagely. A look over the painted lower half of the Land Agent's office windows showed him the room held only the body of a man who would have sold them out. The safe door hung open and clearly Mallick was gone. So had his partner Jackieboy Disraeli, when they came to the saloon. A boot sent his office door flying open but once more the Double K had arrived too late.

"We'll take it out of here boys," Tring said waving a hand towards the saloon. "And anything more we need this stinking lil town's going to give us."

His plan only partially succeeded. The men headed for the bar where scared bartenders poured drinks and emptied the till for Tring and the hired gunmen. They drank and then one of the men standing by a window and watching the street, gave a warning shout.

Silence fell on the room. They heard the sound of hooves, many hooves and gathered to see who came to town. Mutters of surprise and fear rose from amongst the men as they recognized the men who led the well armed party into town.

"There's Dusty Fog and Mark Counter!" one man said. "We never touched either of them when we hit Lasalle's."

"Naw. They weren't staying in the house 'cause they was scared neither," another went on, putting forth the reason one faction of the raiding party offered for Dusty and Mark not coming after them in revenge for the attack on Lasalle's. They was waiting for help."

"And they got it!" a third put in. "That's Clay Allison and Stone Hart up front and some of their boys along."

"They coming in here?" asked a fourth man, casting an eye on the rear door.

"Nope, going through."

They formed quite a party, coming down the main street. The four men in the lead each famous in his own right. Behind them came the Gibbs and Jones' wagons, driven by the women and flanked by men. Stone had called a further four men from his herd, bringing the fighting force to fourteen, but they were fourteen who might have made a troop of cavalry think twice about attacking.

"There's the stores, Clay," Dusty said. "Get to it."

In his store Matt Roylan looked at the two gunhung deputies who now lounged at the counter and decimated his profits by their constant dipping into cracker barrel or candy jar.

"How the hell does your boss expect me to make a living with you scaring trade off?" he asked.

"Whyn't you go and ask him?" answered one of the men, then looked towards the door.

Horses and a wagon had halted outside. Then boots thudded on to the sidewalk and up to the door. It opened and two tall men stepped inside, two men with low hanging guns, although one of them did not look more than sixteen years old.

"The name's Clay Allison," said the bearded man and jerked a thumb to where Ma Jones stood by her wagon. "The lady aims to buy supplies and I'm here to see she gets them. Understand?"

The two deputies understood. So did Roylan. He removed his apron, walked around the end of the counter and shot out a hand to grip each collar of the gunmen. With spirit and delight he hustled the two men across his business premises, doing what his heart craved to do ever since they first came here. He heaved the two astonished deputies through the door, ran them to the edge of the sidewalk and hurled them off. With a delighted grin Roylan looked down at them.

"That was gentle!" he said. "The next of you shows his face in here gets it damaged!"

One of the deputies sat up, mouthing curses. His hand went to his side, to grip the butt of his gun, eyes glowing hate at Roylan's back as the storekeeper turned to Ma Jones.

Waco lunged through the door, his right hand Colt coming clear and lining on the man.

"Loose it!" he snapped. "Then on your feet and find a hoss. The next time I see you I'll shoot."

Watching this Clay Allison felt puzzled and then smiled. Waco would have shot the man without a chance had this happened yesterday. Waco also felt surprised at the change in his outlook. His first instinct had been to shoot, to send lead into the gunman. Then, at the last instant, he held his hand. He knew Dusty Fog had said no killing unless it became necessary. He could not see Dusty, or Mark, wanting truck with a fool trigger-fast-and-up-from-Texas kid who cut down a man in cold blood.

So Waco watched the man get to his feet, then kept the two deputies under observation as they walked away. He stood aside and let Roylan and Ma Jones enter the store.

"I had to do it, Ma," Roylan said. "So did Banker O'Neil. They threatened his wife and family unless he went along with them. It's over now."

She nodded. "It looks that way."

Mrs. Gibbs traded with the other store. She found that her escort would consist of Stone Hart, Rusty Willis and Peaceful Gunn. They made for the store where Peaceful and Rusty insisted on entering first, to sort of watch things and kind of make sure the deputies didn't get too festive when Mrs. Gibbs entered. This was Rusty's idea. Peaceful moaned about it being safer inside than on the streets where already Dusty's men were letting out their wild cowhand yells, firing guns into the air and doing all they could to produce the local law.

In the store Jake Billings leaned his old frame on the counter and glowered at the pair of deputies, one of whom lit his third free cigar from Jake's private stock.

"You pair's supposed to be deputies," he said. "Whyn't you get out there afore those cowhands ropes the town and hauls it back to the Old Trail with them."

"Not us. We're special deputies," replied one of the men, his face bearing marks of Mark Counter's big fists.

They looked at the door as Rusty Willis and Peaceful Gunn entered. The two cowhands separated, crossing the store to halt one by each deputy. Peaceful removed his hat and held it in his right hand, mopping his brow with a large red handkerchief and letting his moustache droop in an abject manner.

"Them rowdies out there," he said in his usual mournful and whining tone for such an occasion. "They're causing so much fuss that I'll just get me some t'baccy and light out afore the marshal comes and jails everybody in sight."

If anything could have lulled the suspicions of the two deputies, Peaceful words were most likely to succeed. Neither of the hard-cases gave him another glance. The second deputy looked at Rusty who stood by him and took up a heavy skillet.

"Chow asked me to get him one of these," he drawled, looking at the deputy. "You reckon this'n'd be all right?"

"How the hell would I know?" snapped the deputy, then looked to where Stone and Mrs. Gibbs came through the door. "What do you want?"

"The lady's here for her supplies," Stone answered.

"Then she can get the hell out of—!" began the deputy by Peaceful.

His speech did not end. Peaceful moved at a speed which amazed Joyce, when she thought of his usual lethargic movements. His hat lashed back, full into the man's face. Two pounds of prime J. B. Stetson could hurt when lashed around with the full power of a brawny arm. The gunman's hand, almost on his gun butt, missed and he gave forth a startled, pain-filled yell.

The second man sent his hand flying towards his gun and almost made it. At his side Rusty gripped the heavy skillet by the handle and swung it sideways, using the edge like an axe blade against the man's stomach. With a croaking cry of pain the gunman doubled over, holding his middle. Up lifted the pan to come down with a resounding and very satisfying clang, on to the temptingly offered head. Billings let out a whoop of delight, but the gunman gave only a moan to show his disapproval of Rusty's actions.

With tears in his eyes, the deputy Peaceful assailed with his hat dropped a hand towards the butt of his gun. Steel glinted in Peaceful's hand, the bowie knife which mostly rode at the peace lover's left side, now lay in his hand, its clipped point driving at the man's stomach, Joyce let out a gasp of fear for she expected to see the deputy drop writhing in agony and spurting blood on the floor.

At the last instant Peaceful changed his aim slightly, the knife rose and then cut down, the razor sharp lower edge ripping through the leather of the man's gunbelt causing it to drop. The deputy's hand clawed air for his holster now hung mouth down by the pigging thong and his gun lay at his feet.

"I'm a man of peace, I am!" warned Peaceful and cut again, this time through the gunman's waist band causing him to grab hurriedly at his pants. "And if I sees you again after you go through that door I'll prove it!"

Taking the hint, and holding his pants up at the same time, the deputy headed past Joyce and out through the door. She watched him go and smiled a little. It appeared that the hardcase Double K were not as hard as she at first imagined.

She knew why her friends acted in the way they did. Stone Hart might be accepted as a master trail boss, but his name did not carry the same weight as Clay Allison's in gun fighting circles. So Stone and his men arranged to take care of the deputies before announcing their presence, or at least to make sure that the two deputies could be rendered harmless by having Rusty and Peaceful on hand before Stone brought Joyce intot he building.

"About these supplies, friend?" Stone asked.

Billings grinned. "You can have them, Joyce. I didn't dare go again Mallick until I had some backing. But I got it now. What do you want?"

"It telled you we ought to've gone round!" Peaceful wailed. "I—"

Joyce spun to face him and stabbed an accusing finger at his face. "You're a fake!" she yelled. "And if you ever mention peace and quiet to me again I'll drag you east by the ear and make sure you get some."

The threat brought a heart-rending sigh from Peaceful. "There," he told Rusty miserably. "For this here lady I forget me true and beautiful nature, and that's all the thanks I get."

Since the arrival of the Texans there had been a steady departure from the Jackieboy Saloon. Men who took pay for their fighting ability drifted out, mounted their horses and rode out of town. The word had passed around that Barlock would be unhealthy for any hired gun who took pay from Double K and they aimed to stay healthy as long as they could.

One of the men who went was Preacher Tring. Unlike the others he did not have his horse before the saloon, but left it saddled and ready down by the civic pound. He left the saloon by its rear entrance, having an idea that his prominence in matters of the Double K, including the attack of the Lasalle house and attempted dynamiting, would put him high on the list of those most wanted by Mark Counter and Dusty Fog.

Tring went to the civic pound, a walled corral in which stood the horses of Elben and his deputies. His own horse waited at the rear and he passed around to the rear of the corral. Just as he was about to mount and shake the dust of Barlock for ever from his feet, he saw a man come around the side of the town marshal's office and halt standing facing the rear door of the building.

A hiss of satisfaction left Tring's llps. The man was Dusty Fog. More he clearly did not suspect Tring's presence or he would never have been foolish enough to present his back in such a tempting manner.

Never again would Tring have such a chance of killing Dusty Fog. The small Texan's back was to him, his attention fixed on the rear door of the marshal's office. Tring's horse stood saddled and only needed mounting for a rapid departure to safer pastures once he sent lead between Dusty's shoulders. Ever since Dusty drove him from the Double K, Tring had nursed hatred and swore he would be revenged. Now it seemed he would be given his chance.

Not suspecting the danger behind him, Dusty Fog stood watching the rear door of the town marshal's office. He took no part in the general freeing of Barlock and clearance of the Double K hired guns. For himself, Dusty reserved the duty, if not the pleasure, of handling the matter of Mallick's tame lawman.

Dusty never made any move without good reason. His reasons for removing Elben were simple. The man wore a law badge. He might not have been elected by true democratic principles but he held the badge and while he wore it he had certain rights and privileges. So Dusty aimed to see Elben and use moral persuasion, of his own style, to make Elben resign from office. In other words Elben was to be offered the chance of resigning, or being resigned forcibly. Dusty did not intend allowing Mallick the protection of a law badge when they met and discussed the matter of the Lindon Land Grant.

The office door opened and Elben emerged carrying a saddle and looking back across the room. Dusty knew at what Elben looked. On the front porch Mark Counter stood waiting and Elben wondered when the blond giant would come after him to take reprisals for the attack upon his person on Mark's last visit to town.

Whatever his other faults, and they were many, Elben counted himself as being smart enough to know when to yell "calf rope" and get clear of danger. He had seen the eviction of his deputies from the stores and the departure of Double K men so knew his term of office was due for a sudden termination at the hands of the enraged citizenry of Barlock.

With that thought in mind Elben took his saddle which he kept in his room. He emptied the office safe of various little trinkets and keepsakes presented by people around town, including the donations made by various sources to his election campaign funds. These he stuffed into a saddlebag, took up the saddle and headed for the back door, aiming to collect a horse and ride out.

"Going someplace?"

The words brought Elben around in a startled turn. He stood with the saddle in his right hand, his left hovering over the butt of his gun. Then he stiffened and his hovering hand froze for he recognized the small man standing before him.

"Yeah, Cap'n," he said. "I'm going someplace."

He thought of the money in his saddlebags. Money extorted from various people around town. To be caught with it was

likely to wind him up in jail for a fair time and he didn't want
such a thing to happen. Yet he did not see how he could avoid
it.

At that moment Elben saw Tring sneaking along the side of
the corral behind Dusty. This would be his chance for Tring
held a gun and clearly aimed to use it. Elben watched the man
raising the gun, licked his lips with the flickering tip of his
tongue and prepared to take a hand. He could get off a shot
into Dusty Fog even as Tring fired, showing his heart to be in
the right place. Then he and Tring would be free to make good
their escape. For a share of the loot Tring would carry his
saddle while he rode bareback until they had time to halt and
get the saddle on Elben's mount.

Elben tensed slightly as Tring aimed the gun. At the same
moment he heard a voice yell one word.

"Dusty!"

A tall, blond youngster burst into view around the corner of
the office, his hands fanning down towards the butts of his
guns. Instantly everything burst into wild and sudden action.

Hearing the yell and seeing the danger, Tring turned his gun
and fired at the newcomer, his bullet fanning by Waco's
cheek. Even as he did so. Dusty flung himself backwards and
to one side, hands crossing and fetching out his matched guns.
At the same instant Elben let his saddle fall and clawed out his
right hand gun to take a hand in the game.

Dusty's matched guns roared, slightly less than three-
quarters of a second after his first move. He threw his lead at
Tring, shooting to prevent the man correcting his aim and cutting Waco down. In doing so Dusty put his own life in peril for
he had his back to Elben and the ex-town marshal's gun was
already sliding clear.

A warning flicker caught the corner of Waco's eye, brought
his attention to Dusty's danger. He ignored Tring, ignored the
fact that the next bullet from the gunman might hit him. He
aimed to save Dusty Fog's life even if he died doing it.

Even as Dusty's lead smashed into Tring, rocking him over
into the corral fence and sending him down, Waco shot Elben,
shot him in the head, aiming for an instant kill to prevent him
being able to trigger off even one shot.

"You fool kid," Dusty said quietly, but there was admiration in his voice. "Why in hell didn't you put lead into
Tring?"

"Figured you could handle him, and that *hombre* behind you sure didn't aim to play spit-balls," Waco replied.

One look at Elben told Dusty the marshal offered no danger to him now. He heard running feet as men came to investigate the shooting. then he holstered his guns and walked towards Waco.

"You risked Tring killing you to save me," he said, speaking quietly.

"And you hauled me out from under that stampede," Waco replied. "Figured to get even, but," he looked at where Tring lay sprawled by the corral, "you're still one up on me."

Mark reached the scene first, coming with guns in his hands. He holstered the weapons, looked at the scene before him and read its implications. He had seen Waco leave the store and pass between the two buildings, disobeying Dusty's orders, but could also see that likely Waco's disobedience saved Dusty's life.

"Why'd you come here?" he asked.

"Me'n Clay'd done our lil piece down at the store and I figured to see how this here moral persuasion worked," Waco replied with a grin.

"You did the right thing, boy," drawled Mark and slapped Waco on the shoulder. "For once."

A grin came to Waco's face. He doubted if he could have been given greater praise than that.

"Let's get to the Land Agent's office, Mark," Dusty said. "These gents here can attend to the bodies."

After unlocking the rear door with a powerful kick from Mark's right leg, Dusty led the way into the office. Mark and Waco followed on his heels and they stood behind Dusty, looking at the body by the wall, then at the charred remains of many papers lying in the waste-paper basket.

"Looks like we got here too late," Dusty said.

Mark did not reply. He went to the body and looked down at it, seeing the bruise left by a fist and the way the neck hung. It had taken a man with exceptional strength to deliver such a blow and one man sprang to Mark's mind.

One thought led to another, Mark's nostrils quivered as he sniffed at the sickly scent which still hung in the office.

"Remember that first time we came to see Mallick, Dusty?" he asked. "We smelled this same scent in here then. Thought it might be some calico cat Mallick had been entertaining. Only I

know it wasn't. That fat little swish* who owns the Jackieboy
Saloon uses it. And the trained ape he had with him was strong
enough to have bust this feller's neck with a punch."

"Best go along to the saloon then," Dusty replied.

As Dusty expected, the saloon's owner had departed with
Mallick and nobody appeared to know where they had gone.
However, on going outside to see that everything in the streets
was peaceful and the Double K men cleared out of town,
Dusty met Matt Roylan. After the storekeeper thanked him
for freeing Barlock from the clutches of the gunmen, Roylan
remarked that he had seen Mallick, Disraeli and Knuckles
making a hurried departure in the direction of the Double K.

Before any more could be said an interruption, in the shape
of a fast riding man, stopped the conversation. They all recognized George Lasalle and wondered what brought him into
town at such a speed.

"Captain Fog!" Lasalle gasped, even before his horse slid
to a halt. "Miss Keller came to visit us this morning. Her
father thinks he bought all our land. She asked Freda and
Morg to go back with her to the Double K house to see and explain things to her father."

"Dusty's face looked suddenly grim. He turned to the
listening men and they saw that he considered the situation to
be very grave.

"Mark, Waco!" he snapped. "Get your horses. Mallick's
headed for the Double K and happen he finds Freda and Morg
there all hell's due to pop!"

* Swish: HOMOSEXUAL

CHAPTER FIFTEEN

Mallick's Plan

THE redbone hound raised his head and gave a low growl which caused Morg Summers to drop the hammer, come to his feet and reach for his gun. It made Freda Lasalle lay aside the bowl of peas she had been shelling, while sitting on the front porch, so she could talk with Morg as he repaired a section of the flooring damaged in the fight. Freda threw a look to where her shotgun leaned by the door for she caught the sound of horse's hooves.

"One horse, gal, coming easy," Morg said, but did not relax. He raised his voice: "Boss! We got callers!"

This brought Lasalle to the door of the barn. He stepped from the door and crossed the open to the house, a hand resting on the butt of the Colt in his waistband. On the porch he looked at the other two, then at the dog which, having done his duty in giving a warning, now lay on the porch with an eye on the open house door in case a sudden departure to the safety of his mistresses's bedroom be called for.

"A gal," said Morg, as the approaching rider came into view on the river bank, then turned her horse and rode to where the bank sloped down towards the ford, her eyes on the house.

"And a pretty one," Freda answered.

"Sure. Rides good too," said Morg, his hand going out to gently squeeze her arm. "I bet she can't cook as well as you do. And I never saw a riding outfit like that afore."

Woman-like, Freda's first look had been at the newcomer's clothes. Even at that distance she could tell the clothes were good quality and well-tailored. She had never seen a woman wearing a top hat or an outfit like that worn by the newcomer but grudgingly admitted the clothes looked good and the girl had a figure to show them off.

Sitting her horse with easy grace, Norma Keller rode along the river bank, studying the small house and the three people before it. She reached the top of the slope and rode down towards the water. Then she remembered something the army captain who commanded their escort from Dodge City told her one night. Halting the horse at the edge of the water she raised a hand in greeting.

"May I ride across?" she called.

"Come ahead," Freda answered, watching Norma and seeing the easy way the other girl rode through the water and towards the house.

"Good morning," Norma greeted, halting the horse. "I appear to have lost my way. I saw smoke from your chimney and rode this way. It puzzled me somewhat. Mr. Mallick did not mention that there were any tenants farming on our property."

"Tenants—farming!" snorted Freda, more annoyed because the other girl drew praise from Morg than for any other reason.

"I'm afraid this isn't your land, Miss Keller," Lasalle put in, guessing who the girl must be for he had heard upper-class British accents before.

A slight frown came on Norma's face. "That's strange. I pride myself on being a good judge of distance and I thought I had at least another two miles before I came to the end of our property."

Lasalle saw the light immediately. He also had to admit the girl was a good judge of distance for there would be another two miles or so more—if the Lindon Land Grant covered the area shown on the map he fixed together for Dusty Fog and which still lay in the side-piece drawer.

"I think there's something you should know, ma'am," he said, stepping forward. "Would you come inside please."

"Thank you," replied Norma. "I would like directions to the house though."

"You must have a cup of coffee first," Freda put in, her hospitable nature coming to the fore. "We haven't had a chance to meet you so far."

"Thank you again," smiled Norma. "I think I will stay. I

haven't met any of the neighbors yet. Papa managed to crock his ankle up and we haven't managed to get around much as yet."

She slid down from her saddle without needing any help and, a point in her favor, attended to the horse before she came on to the porch. She looked down at Bugle for a moment and he beat his tail on the porch floor.

"I say," she said. "He's a redbone, isn't he?"

"Sure is, ma'am," agreed Morg. "Real good one, too."

"Papa hopes to bring some foxhound and staghounds from England if the hunting is worthwhile," she replied. "Are there any foxes about?"

"A few," Lasalle replied. "But more chance of cougar, or bear."

"I never thought of hunting such dangerous beasts with hounds," Norma remarked. "It sounds interesting."

The girl's attitude surprised Lasalle and puzzled him. She did not appear to have any idea of the trouble the Double K men caused throughout the Panhandle country. In fact, from the way she acted, she did not appear to know there were other people in the country. Lasalle decided to show the girl the map and tell her how Mallick and his men acted in her father's name. It would be interesting to see her reactions.

With that in mind Lasalle escorted Norma into the dining-room and seated her at the table. Then he crossed to the side-piece and took out a map and a deed box. Norma glanced at the kitchen where Freda had gone to make the coffee and slam things about. A smile crept to Norma's face for she had not failed to notice the other girl's hostile looks and read them for what they were, the jealousy of a young girl very much in love.

"Have you seen anything like this before, ma'am?" Lasalle asked, spreading the map before her on the table.

She looked down at it, then raised her eyes to his face.

"It appears to be a map of our est—ranch," she answered. "But what is this piece marked off for?"

"I can show you better on this map," Lasalle replied, opening the metal deed box to take out and open another map of the area. "This is the correct shape of the Lindon Land Grant. This part down here is not a part of the Grant. There are, or were, four small ranches on here."

Norma frowned. "I'm afraid I don't understand," she said.

"The map Papa received from Mr. Mallick showed that we own all the block of land. I forget how many thousand acres it came to. What does this mean?"

"I think I'd better start at the beginning and tell you everything," Lasalle replied, taking a seat and facing the girl.

Starting at the beginning and hiding nothing, neither making things worse nor better, Lasalle told Norma of the happenings since Mallick offered to buy them out. The girl watched him, her face showing horror as he spoke of one family driven from their home and the other three attacked, brow-beaten, having pressure brought to bear on them to sell and clear out.

Looking at the shattered windows, the bullet holes in the walls and sidepiece, Norma's lips drew tight and grim.

"You mean that my father's employees did this?" she asked. "Attacked your home, whipped that poor chap and wrecked his home?"

"They did."

Strangely it never occurred to Norma to doubt Lasalle's word. She thought of the sullen men at the ranch, of little incidents, like that party which returned late one night cursing and making a lot of noise. Norma fancied her judgment of character and liked this family even though they had not introduced themselves nor she to them.

"Papa and I have only been here a few days," she said. "And with Papa having crocked his ankle he hasn't been able to look over his property. He loathes riding in a carriage of any kind. But he must be told. Would you come with me to the ranch and help me explain?"'

"We will," agreed Lasalle.

"And of course Papa will discharge all the men and make restitution for the damage caused in his name," said Norma. "I promise you that not one of the men will remain here when they return from their work today."

"What work's that, ma'am?" Morg asked.

"I don't really know. They all rode out early this morning and I haven't seen anything of them."

Three faces looked at each other, Lasalle, Freda and Morg exchanged glances which were pregnant with expression.

"Morg, take Miss Keller and Freda to the Double K. I'll head for town to warn Captain Fog!"

"Be best!" Morg agreed.

All thought that the hired guns might be gathering to make one last final onslaught on the small ranchers. In that case a fighting force such as Dusty gathered would be of vital importance.

Freda dashed into her bedroom to change for the trip while Morg left to catch and saddle two horses. Lasalle and Norma talked on and the more they talked the more sure of Sir James Keller's innocence Lasalle became.

The door to Freda's bedroom opened and Norma looked towards it, a smile came to her lips.

"I say, that is a fetching outfit," she said, studying the shirtwaist, jeans and high heeled cowhand boots Freda now wore. "I must get something like it. I'm afraid these togs are more suited for a Hunt meet in Leicestershire than for out on the range."

In a few seconds Freda had lost her jealous suspicions and was talking clothes with Norma like they had been friends for years. The girls took their horses and with Morg riding on one side, Norma on the other, Freda headed them in the direction of the Double K house.

Talk passed amongst them as they rode across the range. Norma wanted to know so much that the sullen hard-cases who formed the ranch crew could not, or would not explain. She managed to preserve a nice balance of keeping Morg answering her questions without giving Freda anything to complain about. In fact Freda could tell of conditions in this section of the range far better than Morg. Norma told the other two of her adventure with the cougar and Freda recognized the Kid's description.

When the Ysabel Kid did not return from Bent's Ford, Freda had worried but Dusty and Mark told her not to. They stated flatly that Double K didn't hire a man capable of catching up to, or downing, their *amigo*. Sure the Kid hadn't returned, but most likely he had good reason for it. Red Blaze might need help with the herd, some word from Ole Devil Hardin might have been received, or the Kid might be around, staked out on the plains somewhere, watching every move the Double K made. Their very confidence reassured Freda. From what Norma, they knew each other's names by now, said the Kid had been busy on his way north.

They came to the big old Double K house, a fine, stoutly

built, two story wooden structure strong enough to act as a fort in time of trouble. Right now it looked silent and deserted, a few horses in the corral moving about, but not a sign of life. The bunkhouse and cookshack looked empty, devoid of life, the chimney of the latter showing no smoke to give evidence that a cook prepared food for all hands.

"They're not back yet," Freda said and Norma nodded.

Morg loosened his gun in its holster as they rode towards the house. He felt worried about the emptiness, it did not seem right. He wondered if Norma might be leading them into a trap.

The front door of the house opened and a tall, burly man stepped out, leaning on a cane. He wore a round topped hat—known as a fez or smoking cap in more refined circles—a dark green smoking jacket, well pressed trousers. On one foot was a shining black shoe, the other had bandages around it. His face looked tanned, healthy, but not vicious. It looked very much a man's face and one Morg felt could be trusted and who would make a real good boss.

"Papa!" Norma said, dropping from her horse and going to the man. "I'd like you to meet two good friends, and neighbors, Freda, Morg, this is my father."

"Pleased to meet you," Sir James Keller said. "Come in and I'll see if I can scare up a drink. The blasted cook took off this morning with the others. Don't know what they're playing at."

"They're not playing, Papa," Norma replied seriously. "Come inside. Freda's father told me some distressing news."

The inside of the house still looked much the same as when Lindon owned the place for it had been sold furnished. Freda remembered the library into which they were taken, it looked out on the north range. The window was open and the room cool after the ride. Keller proved an excellent host, he produced chairs for his guests and seated them at the desk.

"Like to offer you something," but I'm not much at cooking," he said. "Do you have trouble with your help, Miss Lasalle?"

Freda smiled at Morg. "If I don't watch him. Morg's our only hand. We don't have a large spread like this, and I'm the cook. If you like I'll throw up a meal for you. I'd like to."

"Then Norma can help you," Keller replied with a grin.

"Time she learned how to cook."

"I can cook," smiled Norma. "It's just that I don't like eating what I've cooked." Then her face lost its smile. "You had better hear what I discovered first, Papa."

Keller threw a look at his daughter's face, then took his seat behind the desk. Norma told what she learned at the Lasalle's house. He did not speak until she finished. Then he slapped his hand on the table top, a hand which looked as hard as any working rancher's.

"I see," he said.

"Wish I did, sir," Morg drawled.

"It's easy young feller, very easy. I was thinking of making a change of scenery. Decided to come out here. I'd been out west three years ago, hunting, and liked the look of it. So Norma and I held a conference and decided we'd buy a place out here. Arranged it through the British Embassy, they contacted various chappies and got wind of the Double K. Felt it might be an omen, two K's and all that, so we said we'd take it. Got it at so much an acre, deuced great oblong of land."

"Only it isn't oblong, papa," Norma put in. "Mallick sold us land which was owned by other people."

"And then he tried to drive us out, make us sell for a fraction of the value of our places," Freda put in hotly, seeing the light for the first time. "So that he could show you the full area you have bought."

"By gad!" boomed Keller. "So that's the bounder's game. I left it in his hands to keep things going for me, after I put down the deposit. It appears he ran it all right."

"But why'd he wire off the Old Trail?" asked Morg. "He must have known that'd make trouble when the herds came up."

"I don't know!" snapped Keller. "All I know is I aim to horsewhip the bounder when I lay hands on him."

At that moment the door opened and Keller started to rise, his face showing anger. Freda's nostrils caught a whiff of a sickly sweet scent she seemed to recognize, one she did not attribute to Norma for the English girl had better taste than use such vile stuff. Along with the others Freda started to turn and a gasp of horror came to her lips.

Mallick stood in the doorway, a revolver in his hand, lining on the men. Behind, holding the fancy Remington Double

Derringer, stood Disraeli and looming over them, empty handed but no less deadly, Knuckles.

"I'm here, Keller," Mallick said.

The men moved into the room, Knuckles leaning a shoulder against the door while the other two stepped inside. Morg stood half risen from his seat, his hand clear of his gun. He was no gun-fighter and his reactions did not have the ability to make split-second moves. Under the guns of the two men he could not take a chance at drawing his weapon and fighting back.

"Drop the gunbelt, cowhand," Mallick ordered. "Kick it this way."

Morg did as ordered. He knew he had no chance but to obey. He felt Disraeli watching him all the time. Felt also that the fancy dressed little man had not forgotten what happened in the saloon. Slowly Morg unbuckled the belt and lowered it to the ground, kicking it to one side.

"Stay where you are, Sir James Keller!" hissed Disraeli. "No heroics or we shoot down the two girls then this man. Ah! I thought that would stop you. You English gentlemen, with your high and mighty code of morals. You would attack us and risk being killed if only your life was at stake. But not to endanger the lives of these others."

"It sounds as if you know English gentlemen," Keller replied quietly.

His words brought a snarl of hatred from Disraeli. "I know you. I know you well. So did my brother. So did my brother Emmanuel. You remember him, Sir James Keller?"

"I can't say I've had that pleasure," replied Keller calmly. "Now may I ask what you want here?"

"We want money," replied Mallick. "The money to complete the sale of this ranch."

"With or without the part you don't own?"

Mallick growled out something in his anger. "So, I thought Miss Lasalle was here for something. It makes no difference. We want every cent you have in the house. And all your collection of jewelry."

"Really?" answered Keller, still as calm as ever.

"Don't fool with us, Keller," warned Mallick. "We've too much at stake to play games."

"We could always let Knuckles have fun with the girls," purred Disraeli.

"One thing's for sure," Morg put in. "You wouldn't have any use for fun with a gal."

Smiling, a vicious smile which did not reach his eyes, Jackieboy Disraeli minced across the room. His hand lashed out, the Remington's foresight raking Morg's cheek and rocking his head back. Morg started to rise and with an almost beast-like snarl Knuckles bounded forward. With speed and agility which was surprising in such a man, Disraeli stepped aside. Knuckle's huge hands shot out, closing on Morg's throat and squeezing.

"Stop him!" Mallick barked out the order. "You hear me, Disraeli, stop him."

At the same moment Mallick jumped forward and caught Freda's arm, holding her as she tried to throw herself at Knuckles. Disraeli looked at Mallick, a slobbering sneer on his lips. Then he gave the order and Knuckles opened his fingers, letting Morg flop back into his chair. The young cowhand sucked in breath and looked ready to throw himself into the attack again.

"Tell him to sit still, Miss Lasalle!" Mallick ordered. "I might not be able to stop Knuckles again."

"Morg!" Freda gasped. "Don't move."

"Look here, Mallick!" barked Keller, standing up and ignoring the gun Mallick swung towards him. "Get this lot over and let's have you out of my house so I can start making up for what you've done to people around here."

"It's just like we told you," Mallick replied. "I want the money you've bought along to complete the purchase of this place and any more you have, as well as that collection of jewelry you own."

"And who told you about that?" Keller asked.

"I did!" Disraeli spat out the words. "I did. To avenge my brother, Emmanuel."

"You seem to think I know this brother of yours," Keller replied, speaking to gain time, in the hope that something might happen to get them clear of the danger they found themselves in.

"You knew him. You and your accursed kind knew him.

You ruined him. You brought him to be hanged. Have you
forgotten Emmanuel Silverman. My brother!"

"Silverman," said Keller softly. "Silverman is it. I remember him. Money-lender, owner of crooked gambling hells,
sweat-shop owner. I remember him and it is true I helped lay
the trap which brought proof of his guilt. And he killed two
women trying to escape, shot them in blind panic—"

"Stop!" Disraeli screamed.

"Keep Knuckles back!" Mallick snarled the words out.
"Do it, Disraeli, or by God I'll kill him. We want something
from Keller and he can't give it to us if he'd dead or unconscious."

For a moment Disraeli stood with his mouth hanging open.
Then slowly, with an almost visible effort, he got control of
himself.

"You helped hang my brother and I swore I would have my
revenge," he said. I learned of your plans to come out here,
Sir James Keller. I came ahead. I met Mallick and we managed
to get ourselves in, he as Land Agent and I in a saloon. Then
we offered this Lindon Land Grant for sale and you took it.
Mallick thought only of the profit, his percentage of the sale
and the extra for the small ranch properties. I thought of
revenge. We sold you several thousand acres of land which did
not belong to the Lindon Grant, and hoped to drive its owners
out, to sell to you at a profit. I thought of stringing the wire
across the trail. Soon the trail herds would be coming north.
When they saw the wire they would attack the man who
ordered it to be there. And they would blame you for that. I
would have avenged my brother."

"In a most courageous manner," Keller replied.

"Cut the talk!" Mallick snarled. "How about that money,
or do I turn Knuckles loose on your gal?"

"You're welcome to what money I have," Keller replied.
"A matter of a thousand dollars."

"Don't fool with me, Keller!" snarled Mallick.

Keller shrugged and sat at his desk. "I've never felt less like
fooling. My good chap, do you expect me to carry the amount
this place costs in a valise? I intended to pay for my place,
when I was satisfied with it, by a certified order on the First
Union Bank in Dodge City. I brought a thousand along as
running expenses and no more.."

For a long moment Mallick stared at Sir James Keller who met his stare and then looked away. Mallick turned towards Disraeli and snarled:

"He's telling the truth, damn it to hell!"

"And as for my collection of jewelry, as you call it," Keller went on. "I left it in the bank at Dodge City, in my strongbox. So it would appear that you can't have that either."

Disraeli gave a scream of rage and frustration. The hand holding the Remington quivered. For a moment Keller expected a bullet to slam into him for the man stood facing him and lining the gun. Norma, face pale, tensed, her hands opened and curved into talons as she prepared to try and defend her father. Morg watched this, he knew that the girl would jump Disraeli at any moment. He knew the little fat man would shoot her out of hand, then cut down Keller. There was only one way to stop, or delay it.

"Hey, swish!" he said. "You watch yourself, or I'll let Freda hand you alicking and sh—"

With a howl of fury Disraeli swung around. He seemed ready to burst into tears and screamed. "Get him, Knuckles! Gouge his eyes out!"

Gamely Morg flung himself at the huge man, straight into the huge hands which clamped on to his throat. Morg felt himself lifted and shook like a dog in the big man's hands. Desperately he lashed out a kick at Knuckles, felt his boot connect with the man's shin but Knuckles gave not a sign of knowing it landed. Only his grip on Morg's throat tightened.

Shooting out a hand, Mallick grabbed Norma Keller's wrist and dragged her to him, thrusting his revolver barrel into her side. His move ended Sir James' attempt at opening the top desk of the drawer wherein lay a magnificent ivory butted 1860 Army Colt.

"Freeze, Keller!" Mallick snarled.

His warning went unheeded by Freda. With the ferocity of a bobcat defending its young she threw herself straight at Knuckles. She screamed, although it was doubtful that she knew the screams left her lips. Full on the huge man's back she hurled herself, one arm locked around his throat, the other trying to rip hair out and failing changed to scratching at his face.

Letting out a howl like a fattened shoat that had felt the butcher's knife. Disraeli jumped forward. His left hand caught Freda by the neck of her blouse and dragged at it, trying to get Knuckles free. The buttons on the blouse popped but the girl clung on. Then Disraeli raised his other hand to bring the gun down on to Freda's head. He struck hard but the girl's hair prevented the worst of the blow, even so it knocked Freda down.

Snarling like a wild animal Disraeli raised his hand again. Sir James Keller started to open his desk drawer. His daughter's life lay in the hands of Mallick but he could not see either the girl or cowhand killed in cold blood.

Faintly, as from a long way off, Freda heard words, Mallick snarling a warning, Disraeli cursing her in his high-pitched voice. Even more faintly she heard the thunder of approaching hooves. Then everything went black.

CHAPTER SIXTEEN

Waco's Decision

THE Ysabel Kid felt puzzled as he rode by the side of the leading wagon. By now they were so far into the Double K range that he could make out the empty, deserted look of the buildings, and still no sign of the hired guns who had roamed the range on his way north.

He looked up at Weems and the housekeeper as they shared the wagon's box with the taciturn driver.

"That there's the house, Bill," he drawled. "Looks a mite too quiet for me."

"I'm afraid you have the advantage over me there, Kid," Weems answered as he squinted his eyes and tried to make out more than a few tiny buildings.

Since leaving Bent's Ford on the day after the Kid's rather hectic arrival Weems had changed. With the Kid he acted in a friendly manner and even thawed out to some small extent with the menials, the two grooms, as he called them, who drove the wagons and the 'tween-maid who was the lowest of the low amongst female employees. He still made them keep their places, but he relaxed slightly under the Kid's influence.

Much to his surprise, Weems had found the Kid to be anything but an uncouth savage. True he lacked some schooling, but he made up for it in matters practical and there was little he did not know about how to live most comfortably while travelling in Texas.

For his part the Kid found Weems to be far from helpless and a man with some knowledge, even if shy on other vital subjects. He enjoyed the trip down from Bent's Ford and would be sorry to part from his new friends at the end of it.

After another mile Weems could study the buildings. He

grunted as he looked the main house over.

"Not exactly like our country house in Yorkshire," he said. "A sturdy enough structure though."

"Reckon," replied the Kid.

His eyes took in the general deserted aspect of the ranch buildings and he did not like what he saw. Three saddled horses before the front of the main house, a two-horse riding wagon behind the big barn, like somebody didn't want it seen. To the Kid it spelled out but one thing, trouble.

The wagons rolled nearer, coming down from the north towards the buildings. His right hand near the butt of the old Dragoon Colt, the Kid sat relaxed but watchful and alert for trouble.

A scream shattered the air, coming from the big house, followed by more.

"What's that?" Weems gasped.

He spoke to the Kid's back for on the first scream a touch of the spurs sent Blackie racing for the house. As well as he could tell the screams came from the room towards which he now made.

Through the window he saw Knuckles choking Morg. Mallick holding a gun on Norma while Sir James stood at his desk, hand still on the drawer of the desk. He also saw Disraeli drag Freda from the huge man and raise the Remington Double Derringer to strike down at her. Of all the people in the room, the Kid knew only Freda. How she came to be at the Double K he could not guess, who the rest might be he also did not know. He could tell who sided with Freda from how they behaved.

The big white stallion raced towards the house but at the last moment, when it seemed certain to collide with the wall, Blackie turned. The Kid, ready for the turn, left his saddle. He held his Dragoon Colt in his right hand as he flung himself through the air. Hands covering his head, the Kid went through the window carrying its glass and framework in a shattered wreck before him.

He lit down on the floor, rolling like he'd come off a bad one. Disraeli released Freda and allowed her to slump to the ground. Flame spurted from the small Double Derringer and splinters kicked to one side of the Kid's rolling body. He lined the Dragoon and touched off a shot. The bullet ripped into

Disraeli's chest and tossed him backwards across the room. At the same moment violent action broke out amongst the others.

Snarling like an animal Knuckles hurled Morg to one corner and turned to face the Kid who lay on his back, the smoking Dragoon still in his hands. Seeing the huge man bearing down on him the Kid knew his danger. Knuckles might not carry a gun but was no less dangerous for it. His huge hands and great strength along with his beast-like rage, were fully as dangerous as any gun once he got close enough to lay hands on a man.

Only he did not get close enough. The Kid's big old Dragoon boomed out again and Knuckles at last met a force his strength could not withstand. One third of an ounce of soft round lead ball, .44 in calibre, powered by forty grains of prime du Pont powder, drove up, entered his mouth and shattered its way out through the top of his head. the force of the blow knocked Knuckles back so he crashed into the wall and slid down never to rise again.

The Kid's sudden and unexpected arrival took Mallick, Keller and Norma by surprise. Keller thrust back his chair and came to his feet. Mallick turned his gun away from Norma, thinking to line it on the blackdressed shape. Then Norma took a hand, reacting with cool courage even as the Kid's gun cut down Disraeli. She drew back her boot and lashed out a kick, the riding boot catching Mallick on the front of his shin. The man let out a howl of pain, released her arm and staggered back. Norma's face lost all its color as she saw Knuckles take lead. With a gasp she slid to the floor in a faint.

Gun in hand, Mallick still did not make a fight of it. He saw Sir James open the desk drawer and saw the Kid starting to turn. Then he flung himself back through the library door slamming it behind him. He raced along the hall to the main door and spun around to fire a shot. He backed through the main doors, firing again and sprang to the ground outside.

Behind him, from the house, he heard running feet and sent another bullet through the door. From the house sounded a piercing whistle then a voice yelled one word:

"Blackie!"

Hooves thundered behind Mallick. He started to turn and saw a huge white stallion charging at him. Saw its laid back ears, the bared teeth, heard its wild fighting scream. Desperately he tried to turn his gun, he fired one shot which missed.

He never had the chance to fire another. Blackie came at him, rearing high on its hind legs, the fore hooves lashing out. One ripped into the top of Mallick's head, crunching home with wicked force. Mallick screamed once, then he went down under the savage and awful fighting fury of the enraged white stallion.

The Ysabel Kid and Sir James Keller came from the library side by side although as yet neither knew who the other might be. They were not at the front door when they heard the screams.

"God!" gasped Sir James. "What's that?"

"Stay here, friend," replied the Kid who knew all too well what "that" was. "And keep those gals inside."

With that the Kid plunged out to get control of his horse. He hoped that Weems would show enough good sense to either stay well back, or keep the womenfolk to the rear of the building. That bloody wreck on the ground was no sight for female eyes, or male eyes either, happen the man had a weak stomach.

Quickly the Kid quieted his big white stallion, getting the fighting fury out of it. Then he led Blackie around the house and saw the wagons rolling up at a good speed. He went into the saddle in a lithe bound and rode to meet them.

"Take them around back, Bill," he said. "And keep the women out here, don't let them go around front. There's been a mite of trouble."

After entering and seeing the master's library and passing through to the front of the house, Weems decided the Kid had, as he often did, made quite an understatement when he spoke of a "mite of trouble".

Even before the men could do more than take Freda and Norma to another room, they heard hooves. The Kid, gun in hand, went to the front door, followed by Sir James and a shaken, but armed, Morg. They saw three men riding fast towards the ranch house.

"Don't shoot!" Morg croaked, speaking through a throat which seemed to burn red hot. "They're friends."

"I'd never have knowed," drawled the Kid, holstering his Dragoon Colt as he went to meet Dusty Fog and Mark Counter and a tall, blond-haired boy he had never seen before.

In a few moments Morg managed to introduce Dusty and
the others to Sir James Keller and Weems explained the Kid's
presence. Then they went inside to start the work of cleaning
up.

It was two days after the death of Mallick and his partner.
The spacious dining-room at the Double K held a large bunch
of men. Dusty, Mark, and Kid were on hand, Waco, who had
been like a shadow to Dusty for the past two days of wire
removal and starting to clean up after the departed gunmen,
sat to one side of the OD Connected men. Stone Hart and
Clay Allison represented the trail driving interests. Lasalle,
Ralph Gibbs, sitting awkwardly in his chair, and Pop Jones
had been asked to come, along with Matt Roylans and the
Barlock banker. Weems, back to his official capacity, glided
around and served drinks from the stock brought in the
wagons along with much of Sir James' belongings.

"From what Mallick told me," Sir James said. "He
planned to sell me several thousand acres beyond the true
boundary of the Double K and showed on the map I received
from him. I paid by deposit and was to complete the deal when
I'd seen the property. Then he set out to try and buy the small
ranchers out as cheaply as possible or run them out. He did
not expect me for another month, but our ship made better
time than we expected and I brought my daughter ahead with
an escort supplied by an army friend. However I'd managed to
crock my ankle and so could not ride around and that gave
Mallick a chance to force the last three spreads out."

"How about the wire?" Clay Allison asked.

"Bought in my name by Disraeli and put up to try and make
trouble between the trail herds and myself. He hated me for
something that happened in England and helped Mallick
arrange this entire thing. He hoped I would either be ruined or
killed by the enraged trail crews."

"He near on had his way," drawled Stone Hart. "Happen
Dusty hadn't been on hand and seen what was coming off;
well I reckon I might not have stopped to think. You was on to
Mallick from the start, weren't you Dusty?"

"Not right at the start. I guessed most of it when I pieced
together the map I found in Mallick's office, and tied it in with
the hit at the Lasalle house when they tried to dynamite us out.

That meant we'd hit on to something vital and Mallick wanted us dead before we could use it. Didn't know what part Disraeli had in it though. We'd sniffed that scent he used in the office and tied him in with Mallick. So I figured they were trying to sell land they didn't own.''

''Well,'' said Sir James. ''It's over now. Norma and Freda have both recovered from the shock of what happened in my study. It was just a bluff on the part of Mallick saying I intended to take over the bank notes. So he could put pressure on the small ranchers. Of course I insist on paying for all damages caused by my men.''

''There's no call for that,'' objected Ralph Gibbs. ''They weren't your—''

''They rode for my brand and ignorance of their actions is no excuse. I ought to have known what they were doing. By the by, Ralph, did you and your lady talk over my offer?''

''Yeah. We'll take you up on it. And we both thank you for making it.''

Only Dusty of the others knew of the offer. Full compensation for his injuries and the damages for his property. Then if he wished, to sell his land to Keller, and take over as foreman of the Double K, with a house built on the property. Joyce and Gibbs discussed the matter at length and decided to give up trying to run a one-horse spread one step ahead of bankruptcy and take the security of a good post as foreman of the Double K.

''The only thanks I'll need, old son,'' Sir James said with a grin. ''Is that you get this spread working. How about getting hands?''

Sir James suddenly grinned again and remembered his position as host. He changed the subject and for a few minutes the men talked over past happenings and future plans. Then the party broke up for the trail bosses wished to get back to their herds and the others to their various tasks.

On the porch Sir James Keller shooks hands with Captain Dusty Fog. Of all the others Dusty had got on best with the Englishman for they were much alike and, had Dusty been born in the same circumstances as Sir James he would most likely have carried the same three letters before his name.

''I owe you a lot, Dusty,'' Sir James said. ''You can rely on me to keep the Old Trail open. Give me time and I might even make a Texan.''

"Yeah," Dusty agreed, shaking hands with the other man while Mark and the Kid waited with the horses ready to ride north once more after the OD Connected herd. "You might at that. We'll come down this way and see how you're settling in. And don't worry, you'll have hands coming looking for work, maybe even some of the old crew when word gets out. Ralph Gibbs'll pick you good men."

He turned and went to his horse where Freda Lasalle stood.

"You remember to come in and visit any time you're out this way," she said.

"We'll do that, gal," Mark promised. "See you sometime."

Waco stood by Clay Allison and watched the three men riding away. He felt empty, lost and sick. Some instinct told him that his destiny stood before him. The chance to change from a trigger-fast-and-up-from-Texas kid to a respected man. But he took on with Clay Allison to finish the drive and a *man* did not walk out on his responsibilities just because it suited him to do so. He must finish his drive and hope to meet the man who he now regarded as his idol again.

"Dusty was telling me as how he needed another hand to help him with the OD Connected herd," Clay remarked. "Asked if I could spare one. So I said I'd more hands than I need. Could let one go all right."

Now it lay before Waco. The chance he wanted. He knew his life would change, his very outlook must change if he rode after Dusty Fog. He knew he would most likely work harder than ever he did with Clay Allison. Against that he knew that he must get clear of Clay Allison, or forever be marked with the CA brand. Sure he might become a tophand, but always folks would say, "He rode for Clay Allison" and think twice before hiring him just for cattle work.

For the first time in his life Waco faced up to what he was becoming. Five men died before his guns since he left his adopted home. Five men failed to beat him to the shot in arguments which might have been passed over. Each time the other man asked for death. But there came a time when a man with intelligence asked himself where it all would end.

Waco had the answer. It could end here—or with him riding the same trail as many another fast Texas boy.

He held out his hand to Clay Allison, reading Clay's hope that he would follow Dusty Fog, reading the thought behind it, that Clay did not want Waco to become like him.

"Thanks, Clay," Waco said.

He mounted the big paint stallion and rode after Dusty Fog.